The images that make up the letters of *The Re-Use Atlas* on the cover are all sustainable, waste or reused materials. You can find a key to them below:

T – Coppiced sweet chestnut, used at Streat Hill, East Sussex, UK

H – Ash dieback, in Glyndebourne, East Sussex, UK

E – Straw bales

R – Close-up of mycelium insulation by BIOHM

E – Over-fired waste bricks, at Ibstock Brick Chailey, East Sussex, UK

U – Reused brick, Lendager Group

S – Pretty Plastics tiles, made from waste plastic

E – Waste fibre to felt, a:gain

A – CLT at 6 Orsman Road, London, Waugh Thistleton

T – Waste carpet tiles, from The Waste House, Brighton, UK

L – Waste chalk, used at Streat Hill, East Sussex, UK

A – Surplus second-hand steel, Cleveland Steel

S – Recovered roses, from Sala Beckett, Flores & Prats Arquitectes

© Duncan Baker-Brown, 2024

Published by RIBA Publishing, 66 Portland Place, London, W1B 1AD

ISBN 9781914124129

The right of Duncan Baker-Brown to be identified as the Author of this Work has been asserted in accordance with the Copyright, Designs and Patents Act 1988 sections 77 and 78.

All rights reserved. No part of this publication may be reproduced, stored in a retrieval system, or transmitted, in any form or by any means, electronic, mechanical, photocopying, recording or otherwise, without prior permission of the copyright owner.

British Library Cataloguing-in-Publication Data
A catalogue record for this book is available from the British Library.

Commissioning Editor: Liz Webster
Production: Marie Doinne
Designed and typeset by Mercer Design, London
Printed and bound by Short Run Press, Exeter
Cover design: CHK Design

Cover printed on Wibalin® Recycled, a high quality, uncoated, dyed-through paper made from 100% recycled paper fibres derived from both post-consumer waste (PCW) and industrial waste (PIW).

While every effort has been made to check the accuracy and quality of the information given in this publication, neither the Author nor the Publisher accept any responsibility for the subsequent use of this information, for any errors or omissions that it may contain, or for any misunderstandings arising from it.

www.ribapublishing.com

THE RE-USE ATLAS

SECOND EDITION

DUNCAN BAKER-BROWN

A DESIGNER'S GUIDE TOWARDS A CIRCULAR ECONOMY

RIBA Publishing

CONTENTS

Acknowledgements VI

About the Author VI

Foreword VII
Prof Graeme Brooker

Preface X
Prof Walter R Stahel

Introduction 1
Duncan Baker-Brown

PART 1
Setting the Waste Scene 3

CHAPTER 1
Resource Matters 4
Duncan Baker-Brown

CHAPTER 2
What a Waste! 11
Cat Fletcher

CHAPTER 3
The Political Narrative 14
Dr David Greenfield

PART 2
Circular Inspirations 25

Introduction 26

STEP 1
Recycling – Reprocessing Waste 27

STEP 2
Reusing Waste 45

STEP 3
Reducing Waste 93

STEP 4
The Circular Economy 131

PART 3
**The Ongoing
Waste House Story 179**

(A STEP 2 PROJECT)
Duncan Baker-Brown

PART 4
Looking Forward 193

CHAPTER 4
**Product Moments,
Material Eternities 194**
Prof Jonathan Chapman

CHAPTER 5
The Wiki Waste Workshop 198
Nick Gant and Ryan Woodard

CHAPTER 6
It's All Change Now... Isn't It? 206
Duncan Baker-Brown

Endnotes 213

Index 219

Image credits 223

ACKNOWLEDGEMENTS

The second edition of this book has been a long time coming. So, first of all I would like to thank my Editor at RIBA, Liz Webster, for having the patience of someone with limitless patience. I would also like to thank Kathryn Glendenning and Marie Doinne for their expert proof reading, as well as for everybody (there are over 60 of you) I interviewed over the last two years. Your knowledge and energy have helped transform this second edition of the book into a mostly new book.

The first edition was enabled by me getting a sabbatical from teaching. Unfortunately, there was no sabbatical time for this second edition. Therefore, even more than with the first edition, I completely relied on colleagues at my practice BakerBrown Studio to keep the business running smoothly while I ran around looking for fantastic new case studies. So, thank you to Rebecca Kinneavy, Tiziana de Ronco, Emma Petrykow, Lee Fox, Johana Krejci, Josh Burton, James Gladman, Tony Graham, Stephen Belcher, and Tom Cuthbert for your continued support and encouragement.

As before, there are many people who give me advice and informal mentoring that allow me time to think, ask questions and reflect. I would therefore like to thank Dr. Ben Sweeting, Professor Graeme Brooker, Mina Hasman, Smith Mordak, Nick Gant, Alan Davies, Siobhan O'Dowd, Keir Black, Ian McKay and Anthony Roberts for their continued support.

Finally, I would like to thank brother Byron for his constant encouragement, and of course, my gorgeous wife Kate and my lovely daughter Molly-Rose who have been a constant inspiration and support.

Duncan Baker-Brown
28 June 2024

ABOUT THE AUTHOR

Duncan Baker-Brown BSc. DipArch FRSA ARB RIBA

Open Researcher and Contributor ID:
0000-0003-2777-5503

Duncan is a practicing architect, academic and environmental activist. He has practised, researched, and taught around issues of sustainable development and closed-looped systems for more than 25 years. He recently founded BakerBrown, a research-led architectural practice and consultancy created to address the huge demands presented by the climate and ecological emergency as well as the challenges of designing in a post-COVID world. Over the years Duncan's practices (and academic 'live' projects) have won numerous accolades including RIBA National Awards and a special award from The Stephen Lawrence Prize for the Brighton Waste House – the prize money has since been used to set up a student prize for circular, closed loop design at the University of Brighton.

Duncan is the University of Brighton's Principal Investigator for the NW Europe INTERREG FCRBE project. He was responsible for curating the pedagogic outputs for the FCRBE team. Said outputs are the subject of a book The Pedagogies of Re-Use (Routledge, June 2024), co-edited with Professor Graeme Brooker. Duncan co-Chairs RIBA's Climate Action Expert Advisory Group, sits on the Governance Board of the UK Net Zero Carbon Buildings Standard and until recently at on the Steering Group of UK Architects Declare. He is Climate Literacy Champion (Principal Lecturer) at the School of Architecture Technology & Engineering University of Brighton.

FOREWORD

Prof Graeme Brooker, academic, author and interior designer;
Head of Programme, Interior Design at the Royal College of Art

Anything but Retrofit…

The first edition of this book was published in 2017 and Duncan asked me to add a foreword to it. I was very happy to contribute and was even happier to see that the author had used the word *reuse* in the title. I called that foreword *Tabula Plena*. In it, I alluded to the fact that the book was coherently articulating a world where everything that was already with us was available for subsequent reuse.

Tabula Plena was a direct riposte to the 20th century's *Tabula Rasa* (blank slate), the erasure of all to make a cleared site and to start again. I wanted to make readers aware that so many people have been working creatively for a long time with the ambition that one day society will understand and accept that we should stop making our world from scratch.

Reuse describes the resistance to all forms of 'extractivist' environmental degradation, unsustainable resource depletion and the excessive and wasteful processes of the built environment. *Reuse* foregrounds utilising what is already here, contingencies, maintenance and the prioritisation of repairing, preserving, adapting and redistributing the existing. It advocates for the care of space and its occupants. *Reuse* is the language of the 21st century.

To establish the correct terms and language for the work that we do is incredibly important. In the UK, the word *retrofit* is regularly applied to describe *reuse*. However, *retrofit* refers to the environmental performance of a building so it is misguided to use the term to describe the creative complexities of working with the existing. Language disputes may appear trifling compared to the issues that we face, but the phrase *moving away* in the final text of COP28's report in reference to the world's dependence on fossil fuels speaks volumes. The refusal to explicitly state the undeniable and fundamental issue – that fossil fuels must be left in the ground where they belong – was *weak language*, which will impact millions if not billions of lives. Language is power: it must be explicit, articulate and coherent in these times. *Reuse* moves the existing forward; it projects cities, buildings and materials into new spheres of operation that words like *retrofit* and *moving away from* do not.

When writing the *Tabula Plena* foreword, I hoped that the words *single-use* and *provenance* would come to refer not only to plastic bags and the origins of a good meal in a nice restaurant but also to buildings. How easy it would really be to legislate for the non-demolition or the careful extraction and redistribution of all in-use building material. It would be relatively straightforward to legislate to ensure materials remain within a harvest-mapped zone of provenance to the build site. Yet regulatory frameworks for this type of work remain elusive and still appear distant as fundamental ambitions for buildings and cities. Tax relief for reuse, in the UK at least, also remains a frustratingly distant ambition.

More positively in my sphere of practice (education), all manner of reuse pedagogies and processes have been absorbed and integrated into so many aspects of what is taught. Since my first book on reuse two decades ago,[1] interiors has always been the discipline and the primary creative field where reusing existing buildings has been its speciality, its strength, its *forte*. It was where these creative processes were highly valued and explicitly taught. It is great to see that schools of architecture have finally caught up with this. The blank slate/newbuild approach is of the last century, along with what we hope is the last gasp of petroleum-fuelled 'starchitecture' and its associative blank-slating parametricism. It is inspiring to see so many students foregrounding the understanding of how to reprocess matter and obsolete material into something that is put back into the cycles of use. My superREUSE platform at the Royal College of Art has been reworking obsolete buildings and matter for almost ten years now.[2] New programmes focused solely on reuse are springing up at Manchester School of Architecture and Hasselt University, Belgium. Reusing materials leads to new research, thinking and knowledge that is different to the usual design processes, where starting from scratch is prevalent.

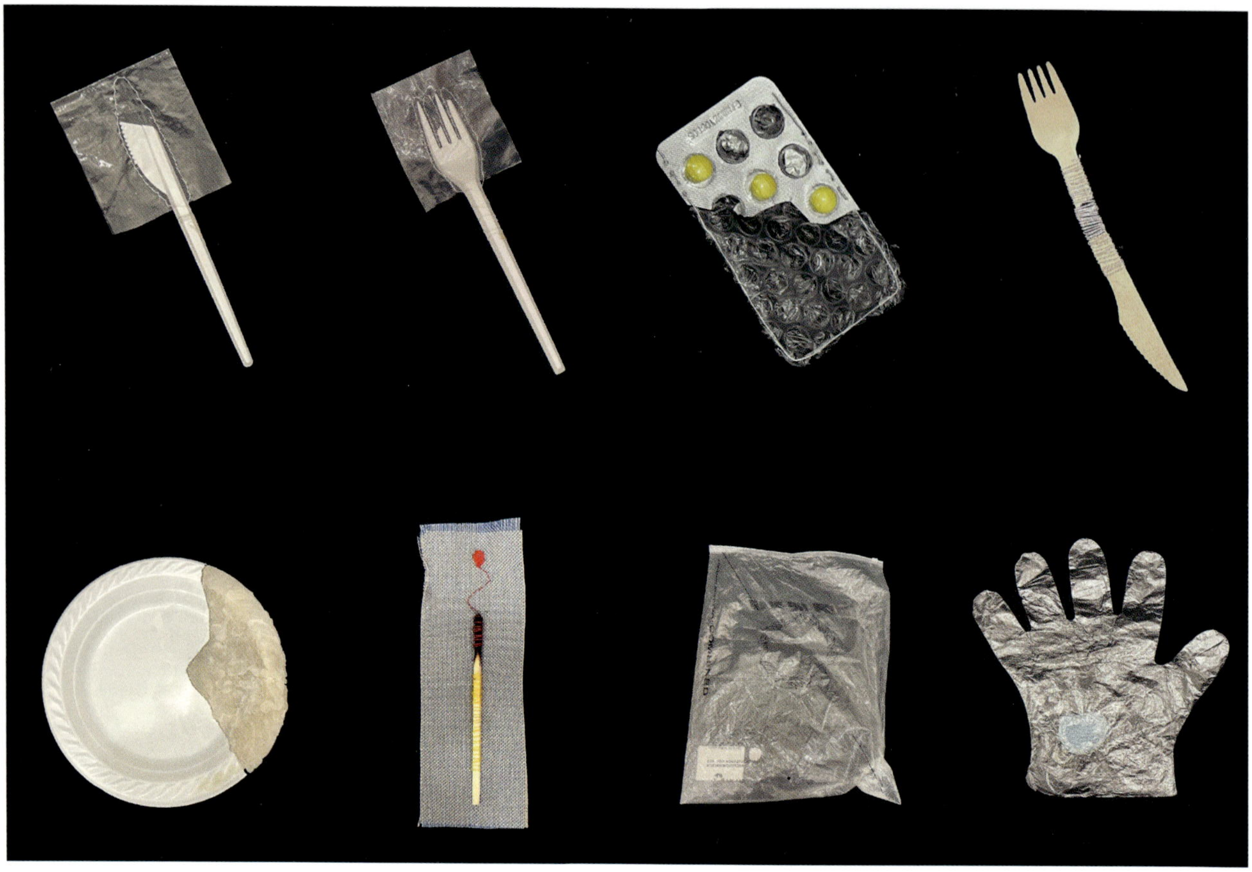

Clockwise from top:

Figure 0.1
The (A)mend project. An experiment in exploring the pedagogies of repair.

Figure 0.2
A Compression Artefact (the name is taken from a term used to describe Chat GPT) – this model is about learning how to interpret new and old.

Figure 0.3
Working with everyday objects to release their potential.

FOREWORD

Contingent strategies require a very specific sensibility: one that is prepared to rely on what is either already in situ, or what is about to be found or exposed during the processes of change. This sensibility is apparent in all aspects of this book. It denotes the inclination to understand and accept the qualities of extant materials, in order to transform them. It is an approach that is significantly distinguished from the idea of design as unfettered origination, or of innovating ideas out of the ether. *The Reuse Atlas* brings this sensibility into sharp focus through the outline of how linear systems can be made circular through closed-loop processes and thinking. Materials, objects and spaces are found, repurposed, transformed and adapted in an applied manner. Each idea in this atlas, each case study, each agent and participant in the processes of 'closed-looping', is turning the linear to circular in a hands-on manner. By doing this, their work epitomises significant behavioural change. It is an approach that values existing entities, extant matter, objects that are already in circulation and which have become the site for mediation and transformation into something they were often never intended to be.

In the previous and also this atlas, I have been struck by how artists, architects, designers, educators, writers, policymakers and all kinds of people have transcended normative boundaries of creative work through collapsing distinctions between objects and environments as they all get reconfigured into new spheres of production and use. The processes of reuse collapse agendas, redistribute values and render traditional built-environment processes and languages obsolete. This is an enduring part of the processes of reuse, as use and value are changed, scales of matter are diminished or enhanced, stuff is redundant, revalued and subsequently reconfigured and disciplinary-specific approaches melt away into the background. When architecture is rendered into furniture, or waste products become a building, the originators and makers also shift across boundaries as their roles in the thinking and fabrication processes are *undisciplined*.

The first edition of *The Reuse Atlas* was a timely and comprehensive book, filled with projects and ideas, work that was suffused with the compelling enthusiasm of its author and the extensive knowledge and work of so many excellent contributors. The tenacity of the ideas and work in the book made for a densely packed, accessible and highly enjoyable read. The book has now been refreshed and this second edition gives a chance to reflect on how those provocations, challenges and the work being done in this field have evolved and been responded to.

This book is thoughtful, compelling and infused with the knowledge of a person working at the forefront of these challenges. All I ask is that we call this work reuse, or at least anything but *retrofit*…

PREFACE

Prof Walter R Stahel, architect and industrial analyst

Reuse and the Circular Economy

I am fortunate to live in a house that was built in 1756 – at least that is the age of the purlins, small trees that were cut and immediately put on the roof in those days. So the reuse and repair of building stock, with periodic remanufacturing and technological upgrading of key components, is something I have been familiar with for 40 years. As with any old building, the house has a 'soul', a unique character, which first had to be discovered and then protected in any refurbishment – a continued challenge as the legal environment changes.

The term 'use', and the optimisation of the use or utilisation of manufactured objects, is at the core of the circular economy, not the term 'cycle' as one might have expected. This distinguishes the circular economy from the linear industrial economy, which optimises the production of the same objects up to the point of sale.

The term 'reuse' implies a change in utilisation, ownership or location; armed forces are among the reuse champions as they heavily depend on mobility in using most of their equipment. The Bailey bridges[1] and inflatable pontoon bridges are typical examples of military reuse inventions. Reusable inflatable structures are common today for such temporary applications as funfairs, sports events and temporary bridges on remote construction sites, but also as seasonal structures such as tennis halls or to store cars during wintertime.

Reuse associated with fixed permanent structures offers multiple opportunities: the structure itself, its components or its materials. It involves the 'factor time' and defines a new type of sustainable quality, combining technology, risk and sustainability management.

For designers, the factor time implies adaptability, flexibility, even humbleness – we do not know the future, but we can prepare for it. Durability is not created by an object's solidity (witness the German bunkers on the French Atlantic coast, or the oldest Swiss timber houses dating from around 1250 AD) but by its desirability (Europe's Gothic cathedrals).

The circular economy has been part of human development since the beginning as a strategy to overcome poverty and scarcity: 'Use it up, wear it out, make it do or do without.' The building waste of the past included timber beams, dimension stone and bricks, components which could be reused to build new structures: castles were destroyed and their material reused; German *Trümmerfrauen* (debris women) cleaned the bricks on World War II bombsites for reuse to build new houses.

But the modern circular economy is based on overcoming saturated markets and abundance, not scarcity. The linear Industrial Revolution, focused on increasingly efficient manufacturing processes, has enabled humankind to overcome scarcities of food, goods and shelter, but its success increasingly creates situations of saturated markets, unmanageable waste (such as space waste and plastic objects accumulating in the oceans) and overconsumption of natural resources, which are incompatible with the limited carrying capacity of Planet Earth. Paris has started to study the refurbishment of buildings as a new policy mainly because it has run out of landfill sites for building waste.

Shelter and clothing are among the most basic requirements for the survival of humans, according to Abraham Maslow, followed by safety, belongingness and love, esteem and self-fulfilment.[2] To put it crudely, architecture has followed Maslow's evolution from adopting caves for shelter to building ego – monuments of cultural identity.

With regards to resource consumption, the building and construction industry is the industrial economy's biggest consumer of material resources, and the biggest producer of waste. As most of this waste comes in the form of inert materials, the problem is one of mass and volume rather than toxicology. Timber that had been treated chemically is 'waste'.

Figure 0.4
The Hy-Fi Tower by The Living, New York, 2014, constructed using organic bricks grown from mycelium.

The actors of the linear industrial economy manage the resource consumption up to the point of sale, where ownership and liability are passed on to the buyer. The use and operation of buildings, another major consumer of resources, principally energy for heating and cooling, are managed by the owner-occupier, not the builder. Solving the problem of waste is left to local authorities.

The actors of the circular economy are managing manufactured capital (stock) in time, by (re)using goods, components and materials with the objective of preserving the stock's economic value, based on a philosophy of caring and stewardship and considering the whole life cycle of goods, with a focus on the (re)use phase.

An example of component reuse is the deep retrofit of New York's Empire State Building in 2010. It included the on-site remanufacturing of its 6,514 windows into triple-glazed super-windows.

> Cutting winter heat loss by two-thirds and summer heat gain by half, the advanced glazing, along with improved lighting and office equipment, will cut the building's peak cooling load by one-third. This load reduction allowed the renovation of the old chiller plant, slated for replacement and expansion, saving more the US$17 million in budgeted capital expenditure.[3]

When Nestlé renovated its headquarter building in Vevey, Switzerland, in the late 1990s, it developed a reuse strategy for the same problem. The existing windows were donated to Bosnia, where many school buildings had been heavily affected during the Bosnian War, and where the windows from Vevey – in perfect working condition – could be directly reused.

Reusing materials for the same application is becoming the norm in some European countries in road resurfacing and demolition-rebuilding projects. 'Ceramic waste' can be reused as aggregate in new concrete structures, but needs the establishment of new material standards and testing methods. The stock of buildings is a strategic resource base for future use, if we learn to sustainably deconstruct buildings at the highest level of value preservation. 'Urban mining' is one of the new terms for the recovery of waste materials for reuse.

Yet the reuse of materials to prevent waste is also a management option in new infrastructure projects. In Switzerland, construction of the Gotthard Base Tunnel – the world's longest rail tunnel, completed in 2016 – produced the equivalent of five Giza pyramids of mining waste,[4] which was used as raw material to build the new (infra)structure of the project, including spray-concrete for the tunnel itself. Of the 28 million tonnes of rock excavated, 15kg was delivered to the Swiss post office, ground into fine powder and, using a special paint, integrated into a special issue of postage stamps named 'Gottardo 2016'.

Figure 0.5
Performance economy: introducing time in the economy.

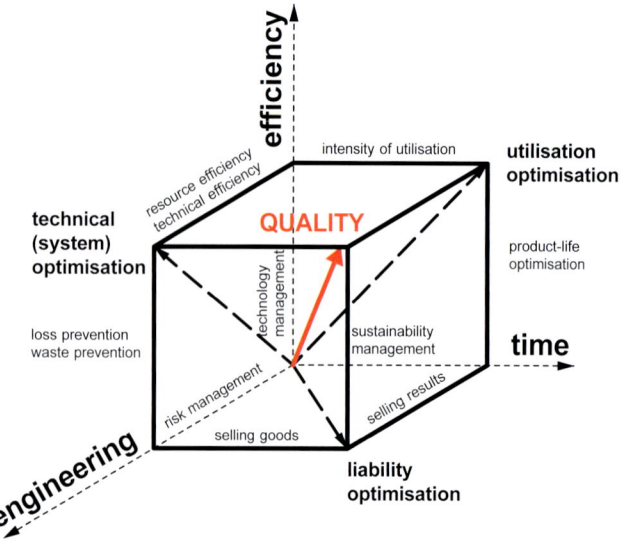

For society, the circular challenge of the existing built environment is twofold: how to finance the operation, maintenance and replacement of our ageing infrastructure, and how to best adapt building stocks to changes in demand and technological progress. Changes in demand come both from markets (churches are transformed into residential or commercial property, for instance) and society (energy needs have to be decoupled from CO_2 emissions through energy savings or substitution; and urban planning may set priorities for the future that differ from the past). And some buildings become part of the national heritage, our cultural capital, and need to be preserved accordingly.

Why is the circular economy more sustainable than the linear industrial one? The activities of the circular economy are ecological because they are regional and low carbon, use few resources and preserve the water, energy and material embodied in the goods. And these activities are labour intensive, on a micro- and a macro-economic level. A 2015 Club of Rome study of seven EU countries found that a shift to a circular economy would reduce a nation's greenhouse gas emissions by up to 70% and grow its workforce by about 4% – the ultimate low-carbon economy.[5] The solutions with the highest preservation of monetary value are normally also the most environmentally friendly and most labour-intensive ones: reuse, repair, remanufacture. Despite the higher labour input, these activities are economically viable because material resource inputs are greatly reduced, compared to the industrial economy. But they are disruptive, using essential labour, not productive labour.

A circular economy manages and reuses manufactured capital – infrastructure, equipment, goods, components and materials – in loops, taking into account that time is a key factor: doubling the service life of goods halves the resource consumption in manufacturing and halves end-of-life waste volumes. But while building waste in the past consisted of components such as dimension stone, bricks and timber that could be reused as such, modern constructions use composite materials such as steel-reinforced concrete, welded structures and plastics which cannot be 'undone'.

Today's building industry thus faces a triple challenge of:

- developing efficient and waste-free construction methods, enabling a later reuse of components and materials
- designing buildings for minimum resource consumption during operation and maintenance, which includes flexibility and adaptability to changes in use
- developing methods enabling the deconstruction of buildings and infrastructure while preserving the highest value.

These challenges have long been met with Japanese temples, which are periodically dismantled and rebuilt. In the Netherlands, architect Thomas Rau has built branch offices of banks using slightly oversized timber beams to facilitate shaving before a later reuse.

Emergent nearly waste-free reusable construction methods include modular system buildings: for instance, temporary multistorey structures for office and residential space using purpose-fitted ISO shipping containers now exist in a number of countries. Modular construction systems using standardised steel beams and panels of corrugated steel sheet have been used for a long time, especially for industrial and agricultural halls in the US. Prefabricated elements made of timber panels have started to be developed for multistorey hotels and schools since fire legislations have been changed in countries such as Switzerland. And changes in fire regulations now allow the construction of high-rise buildings with load-bearing timber structures in many countries, including Canada (Vancouver), Switzerland and Japan.

Designing buildings for minimum resource consumption during use is becoming mandatory in a number of European countries with regard to energy use. However, efficiency may be reduced in residential buildings because inhabitants may not comply with the necessary restrictions (sleeping with closed windows; cooler room temperatures than inhabitants prefer). Plus-energy buildings – which produce more energy than they use and thus are autonomous – were a favourite with former New York City mayor Michael Bloomberg because of their social contributions: they provide lighting to their surroundings and prevent people getting blocked in lifts during power cuts (blackouts), which have become more common in recent years for a number of reasons. Buildings thus will increasingly have to be designed as urban systems solutions.

With the current focus on climate change, designing buildings for zero CO_2 emissions during use has opened up new options, such as heating systems based on hydrogen fuel cells – which have been in use in Japan for 20 years. For heritage buildings, this enables a reduction in CO_2 emissions while preserving the building's exterior (e.g. without adding insulation panels).

The development of methods to deconstruct high-rise buildings has recently started in Japan. The ANA Intercontinental Hotel was probably the first attempt to deconstruct a high-rise structure using an eco-friendly and resource-saving process. The building was demolished top down in 2014 beneath a turban that was lowered hydraulically floor by floor to minimise noise and dust emissions; a vertical shaft with a goods lift in the middle of the building allowed the deconstructors to recover components and sorted materials, while generating energy from the downward lift transports. A future task could be the deconstruction of nuclear power stations in Germany, the last of which were decommissioned in 2023, long before the end of their technical life, as part of the *Energiewende*, the political decision to rely entirely on wind and photovoltaic energy for the future electricity supply. In 2021, Switzerland started deconstructing its first nuclear power station in Mühleberg as a learning-by-doing project.

Can appropriate design, such as eco-design, at least partly solve this problem? Let us look at the 12 Principles of Design for Environment (Eco-Design), defined by IDSA, the Industrial Designer Society of America, in 1992.

The 12 IDSA Principles of Design for Environment

- Make it durable.
- Make it easy to repair.
- Design it so it can be remanufactured.
- Design it so it can be reused.
- Use recycled materials.
- Use commonly recyclable materials.
- Make it simple to separate the recyclable components of a product from the non-recyclable components.
- Eliminate the toxic/problematic components of a product or make them easy to replace or remove before disposal.
- Make products more energy/resource efficient.
- Use product design to educate on the environment.
- Work towards designing source reduction-inducing products (i.e. products that eliminate the need for subsequent waste)
- Adjust product design to reduce packaging.[6]

Many products of modern technology – IT, photovoltaic panels, windmills – violate the fifth and sixth of these principles: their production cannot use recycled materials, and some of the materials, such as silicon joints, components using nanotechnology or carbon fibre laminates, cannot be recycled. The Internet of Things (IoT) will probably increase the number of components of modern technology in future buildings, multiplying the problems posed by construction waste.

A danger is that the construction industry will be regarded as an elegant way to 'eliminate' the bulk of this waste, namely components made of fibre laminates, the volume of which is rapidly increasing. Carbon laminates today are extensively used in mass-produced goods such as aircraft, cars and windmills. Some French researchers have studied ways to cut carbon laminates into small cubes and use them as 'eco-friendly' aggregate in reinforced concrete – 'eco-friendly' because they replace natural sand and gravel and thus reduce the environmental impairment of concrete production.

But – and this is a huge but – what goes in will come out when the buildings are demolished or deconstructed, many decades later. We would simply displace the waste problem in time, leaving an undesired heritage to our children – certainly not a sustainable solution.

Reuse poses new challenges, both risks and opportunities, to designers, architects and engineers. Architecture is thinking in systems to create systems solutions. And architecture is about time. A lighthouse on such a forlorn rock as Fastnet Rock is timeless functionality: form follows function. But it is not only about architecture, it is primarily about shipping safety, improving our quality of life.

Built structures are moments of history frozen in stone, the durability of which depends on their desirability over time more than the materials chosen. So architecture is about culture. Besides reuse, there are other strategies to achieve higher resource efficiency, such as dematerialisation through technological progress – witness pneumatic structures in construction and transport infrastructure – which can offer solutions, as well as sufficiency.

In the late 1960s, I worked as a young architect for John R Bicknell and Paul A Hamilton, two chartered architects in London, on the Paddington Maintenance Depot (PMD), near Little Venice. Built to maintain the lorries of British Rail, it fits into a triangle between Grand Union Canal, Harrow Road and West Way, and consists of a low-level oval building and an office block, separated by a road, making optimal use of a then urban wasteland – a singular building, which received a Concrete Award distinction. When British Rail later abandoned its lorry fleet, the building became redundant and was saved from demolition only after having been awarded a Grade II* listing. After a long period of neglect, this landmark has finally been reused, with some interior transformation, as headquarters of the Monsoon fashion label. It is now, a long time after the death of Messrs Bicknell and Hamilton, a jewel in the new fashionable pedestrian zone between Paddington and Little Venice, along the Grand Union Canal.

Reuse is nature's principle: waste is food in a cascading chain to bacteria. All waste is therefore made by 'industrial man', be it in space, water or on land. Extending the use phase of built structures through reuse is not only a strategy to achieve higher resource efficiency, it is a conscious decision by people – planners, owners, politicians and architects – on how we shape our future.

A circular industrial economy is not a 'nice to have' but probably the only strategy that will answer the three societal needs of our time. A transfer to a circular industrial economy will enable the creation of:

- **a low-waste society**, through intelligent resource and risk management (together with cultural changes in individual behaviour – from consumer to caring user)
- **a low-carbon society**, by using green electricity and preserving the embodied water, electricity and CO_2 in our current buildings and goods
- **a low-anthropogenic-mass society**, by preserving the existing stocks of infrastructure, buildings, equipment and vehicles.

Reuse, repair and remanufacturing with technological updating in the circular economy are the most sustainable business models available today for industrialised regions, and even for less industrialised ones once these have built the necessary infrastructure for health, shelter, water, food, education and mobility which guarantee their populations a decent quality of life.

Figure 0.6
Rusting drum on a beach in Sicily.

INTRODUCTION

Duncan Baker-Brown

How to Read this Book...
And Why, Perhaps, You Should

How can designers and architects respond to the huge challenges that the 'circular economy' demands? There are many books that have been published over the last ten years or so that have attempted to define the concepts of the circular economy and to speculate upon the benefits, whether they be financial, environmental or social. There are even a couple of books that look at the challenges facing the people who design the stuff that will need to become a material resource for the future.

This book considers many of the issues that present themselves as we take steps to turn our throwaway, linear culture into a circular system similar to the ecosystems found in the natural world. We demonstrate, via exemplar projects from around the world, various strategies that, crucially, take one on a transformative route *towards* a circular economy: a route that acknowledges that there are other issues to consider, not least that of clearing up the mess humankind has created over the last 1,000 years or so. So, we will also look at projects that encourage the first phase of this process and will include the cleaning up of our oceans and landfill sites, working with existing buildings and neighbourhoods, etc. We have included upcyclers and hackers, retrofitters and super-users, as well as the emergent closed-loopers.

While I want this book to be able to be read at length, I suspect that more often it will be dipped into as a reference. In addition to the 'prequel' and 'sequel' essays in Parts 1, 3 and 4, I have focused my energies on writing a series of short case studies on a particular design or, in some cases, a design approach (Part 2). All are based on interviews I conducted with the main protagonists. I have also written a short opinion piece at the end of each case study, by way of a summary, but also with the aim of encouraging further debate – you might, after all, disagree with me!

The case studies are divided into four main chapters, or 'steps', each one taking you nearer the concept of the circular economy. This gives you an idea of the challenges and opportunities involved as you navigate a route towards circularity.

It was important to have the word 'atlas' in the title of my book, as I want it to act as a guide for designers, architects, clients and students, to help them negotiate the often-confusing language and rhetoric surrounding this latest response to the challenges humankind faces while feeding off Planet Earth's limited resources. I have had the opportunity to interview many people at length, from all over the world: people who are dealing with various aspects of living more in harmony with the natural environment. All interviewees were asked *why* they were pursuing their particular interests, and most particularly *how* they were going about their circular work within the linear economy the prevails today.

My idea is that this book also acts as a litmus test of what is actually happening in the third decade of the 21st century in the worlds of sustainable design and architecture. Originally, I considered writing a book that just focused on emerging attempts to design in a completely closed-loop, circular way. Prof Dr Michael Braungart, co-author of the seminal text *Cradle to Cradle: Remaking the Way We Make Things*,[1] is often quoted as saying that sustainable development promotes the idea of being 'less bad'. He has stated, 'Recycling and reusing stuff is not worth the effort. It is merely slowing down the inevitable.'[2] *Cradle to Cradle* promotes the wholesale behaviour change required to live in harmony with Planet Earth as a circular economy. This is, in my opinion, correct. However, we are not starting with a clean, fresh and vibrant planet. Humankind has literally wrapped the surface of Planet Earth with the detritus associated with our day-to-day lives. This has been happening at an ever-increasing rate since we abandoned the idea of being hunter-gatherers and started cutting down forests to plant crops for food. It has now occurred to such an extent that many scientists consider that we have entered (since the end of World War II) a brand-new, humanmade geological era, 'The Anthropocene'.

Why am I mentioning this? Well, it is because, although I sympathise with Prof Dr Braungart's position, I cannot ignore the need for dealing with what could be called 'the great clean-up', that is the cleaning-up of ocean plastic, the mining of landfill

Figure 0.7
Calf on a rubbish dump in Melkhoutfontein, South Africa.

sites, the reuse of existing materials and structures residing in our cities, towns and villages. I have included inspiring projects that aim to turn traditionally linear systems, resulting in the pollution of our oceans and landscapes, into mini circular systems that begin to clean up our environment while producing new products, employment and, in some cases, social empowerment out of discarded waste material. This work is hugely important as humankind makes the difficult transformation from a dumb, linear metabolism, using unintelligent, toxic materials for ridiculously short periods of time, towards something more circular. During this extremely difficult and challenging process, the simple, rather basic, techniques of 'recycling', 'reusing' and 'using less' material will be elevated in status because of the benefits to the natural world of clearing up material flows that are normally ignored and putting them back into circulation.

This may sound like 'being less good' and, even, naive or hopelessly optimistic. However, we cannot simply clear up the difficult waste material that wraps the surface of our planet and bury or burn it. We need to put it back into the emergent circular economy via cleverly designed products and buildings that allow for easy disassembly, facilitating reuse until we can find a way of safely disposing of the synthetic, toxic materials mainly invented by humans in the 20th century.

I have had a particular experience as an architect in practice in the UK. Like many, I also teach in a school of architecture. Combining academia with everyday building sites has led me towards the idea of testing concepts through a series of 'live' construction projects that have also been a pedagogic vehicle involving students. Testing ideas in 'real' environments fascinates me. With this preoccupation in mind, the choice of case studies for this atlas has been informed for the most part by a requirement that products and buildings must perform to current performance regulations. For me, it is the answers to my questions 'Why?' and 'How?' that make the case studies most useful for everybody trying to assess the potential for introducing concepts around circular metabolisms, and particularly the circular economy.

The Reuse Atlas is divided into four distinct parts, all of which have been updated and/or added to for this second edition. For example, this edition contains 39 case studies instead of 22, with 28 of them brand new. Part 1 of the book, 'Setting the Waste Scene', includes an updated chapter written by a co-founder of Freegle UK, Cat Fletcher, who takes a careful look at the real challenges of reducing the waste associated with our lifestyle choices. Dr David Greenfield then re-examines the bureaucracy and legislation that hinders the flourishing of a circular economy, as well as considering what legislation is needed to help things along. Part 2 of the atlas is dedicated to 'Circular Inspirations': the aforementioned 39 case studies. Part 3 focuses on 'The Ongoing Waste House Story', which was the project that got me completely immersed in this subject area, and one that continues to attract new research projects as well as thousands of visitors every year. Finally, Part 4 includes essays from experts considering issues that will enable a successful circular economy. Nick Gant and Ryan Woodard explore the idea of waste as an agent for social empowerment. Prof Jonathan Chapman discusses the concept of 'emotional longevity' in relation to the design of products. What is it that makes us not want to throw something away? The final chapter, 'It's All Change Now… Isn't It?', reflects on the big positive changes that have happened since 2016, when the first edition of this book was written. It also considers some of the challenges that continue to hinder the mass uptake of circular systems in large commercial developments, and ultimately poses the very pertinent (not rhetorical) question, 'We know what to do, so what's stopping you?'

I hope you enjoy my new and improved atlas.

Duncan Baker-Brown

January 2024

PART 1
Setting the Waste Scene

CHAPTER 1
Resource Matters 4
Duncan Baker-Brown

CHAPTER 2
What a Waste! 11
Cat Fletcher

CHAPTER 3
The Political Narrative 14
Dr David Greenfield

CHAPTER 1

Resource Matters

Duncan Baker-Brown

It's all about managing resources, and humankind has never been good at that

Ever since our hunter-gatherer ancestors began to try alternative lifestyles around 10,000 years ago, humans have had ever-increasing problems finding resources. Although exhausting and dangerous, the hunter-gatherer technique followed the route of accessible resources. Settling down and relying on one place to provide everything required to satisfy the ever-changing human needs has always proved to be a big challenge. On occasion, it has resulted in hunger and localised extinction of whole societies.

There are, however, many examples of long-established communities that have lived in harmony with their natural environments. Some of these still exist. It is perhaps less well known that there are recent examples of larger contemporary societies that did the same. Herbert Girardet, in his book *The Gaia Atlas of Cities*,[1] states that as late as the 1980s, 13 of China's major cities functioned as what many would define as sustainable cities, i.e. the city fed the hinterland, and the hinterland fed the city. That all changed when China embraced elements of the 'Western' free-market economy and broke away from its established, closed-loop systems in search of linear consumerism.

It is, of course, a lot easier to find examples of humankind's rampant consumption of resources. Our appetite for stuff is insatiable.

There is a famous photograph by LA Hoffman, published in 1913 but labelled '1880 Northern Montana'. When the photograph was taken historians estimate that there were only 300 wild buffalo left in the whole of America. Hunters then proceeded to kill nearly all these buffalo, leaving only 23 alive. All pure North American buffalo alive today, and there are about 15,000 of these (with many more cross-bred with domestic cattle), are descended from those last 23 survivors. Humans do not know when to stop consuming resources. Acting in a measured, balanced and sustainable way does not come easy to human societies. That is why we are in the middle of a mass extinction of species and some resources are scarce, while even plentiful resources are difficult to access.

Many people just don't believe there is a different way of existing. However, my colleague at the University of Brighton, Dr Ryan Woodard, can cite the precise year when the UK 'invented the concept of waste'. It was 1861 and that was the year when the wealth and plundered resources from the massive British Empire made the country so resource wealthy that it could afford to make bricks only out of new material. Up until that point rubbish was reused whenever possible. Dustmen literally were mainly collecting dust, and that could be used in the manufacture of bricks. Perhaps one could conclude that the idea of a linear economy has only been prevalent for around 150 years.

In the meantime, while the devastating consequences of accelerating global heating present themselves daily across our whole planet, underwritten by ever more terrifying statements issuing from either the Intergovernmental Panel on Climate Change or United Nations Secretary-General António Guterres, governments across all continents are legislating for opening up new oil and gas fields in the name of sensible energy strategies that will enable energy independence, new jobs and wealth, with the stability that this brings us all. In other words, drill for gas and oil to create wealth so that we are rich enough to defend ourselves against the more frequent storms, floods, fires and droughts that global heating presents us with. At the

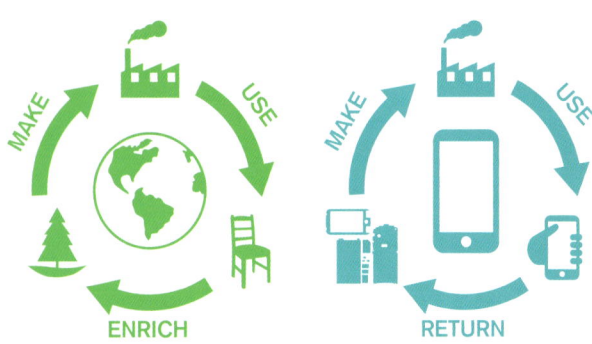

BIO-SPHERE   **TECH-SPHERE**

same time, there have been recent positive steps. Outcomes from COP27 in 2022 were generally noted for so-called Global North governments trying to wriggle out of commitments made at previous COPs. However, there was agreement at COP27 that 'loss and damage' payments would be made by Global North countries (such as the UK and US, who have benefited the most from burning huge amounts of fossil fuels over the last 250 years or so) to countries from the Global South that have suffered the most from the consequences of fossil-fuel-accelerated global warming. In addition, the inauguration of Luiz Inácio Lula da Silva as President of Brazil in December 2022 has seen deforestation rates reduce by nearly 34% in just six months, with the new president unveiling a plan to end deforestation by 2030.[2] Although this news is extremely welcome, I could just as easily have mentioned the latest right-wing US governor pledging to put an end to 'green' energy schemes in order to reinstate 'pro-American' fossil-fuel burning for a betterment of all true 'patriots'. It really does feel like the future of a planet inhabited by humans relies completely on the whim of popularist politicians.

Despite this I am convinced that we are at the beginning of another Industrial Revolution: one that can take best advantage of 'big data', hyper-fast communication networks and, critically, a greater understanding of our host planet, to enable humankind to make well-informed decisions when considering which resource streams to tap into. It is well understood that many large corporations, academic institutions, NGOs and even national governments are considering ways of functioning in a much more intelligent way that works with the natural circular systems Planet Earth supports when it is healthy. The stupidity of digging down for carbon in the ground while the sun burns your back is not lost on many people today. *Cradle to Cradle*[3] threw down the gauntlet to humankind: to stop beating itself up about the environment; to stop being 'less bad'; to design circular systems instead of linear ones, and be positive while doing it,

because it has the potential to improve the lives of many more people than our current linear system does – and it will do, while allowing Planet Earth to recover and heal. Humankind needs to ease off its dependency on dumb materials, while creating intelligent new ones that work like their natural counterparts. However, the most exciting bit of the *Cradle to Cradle* challenge for me is that it can only happen if we *design* new systems, materials, products and places that allow circular systems to flourish. That is why I was compelled to write this book. I also believe, as Cat Fletcher (see Chapter 2) and many others do, that design *will* save the world, or at least be the catalyst that allows huge populations of humans to live in harmony with it. Sophie Thomas, former Director of Circular Economy at the RSA,[4] underlined this point. During her time at the RSA, Thomas oversaw the 'Great Recovery' programme. In one of the numerous papers produced, *Rearranging the Furniture*, Thomas states:

Research has shown that over 80% of the environmental impact of products we use every day is built in at the concept design stage, and that very little account is currently taken of the end-of-life implications of these designs. Moreover, if the system has not been designed to take account of the actual products, materials and behaviours that flow through it, there is very little point in merely changing the design of a single product. A keyboard designed for disassembly will still end up being shredded and put into the e-waste furnace unless a logistical system has been designed to divert it out of the existing infrastructure.[5]

So, what is a circular economy?

Things are changing. More people – individuals as well as multinational corporations – are concerned about where the ingredients that go towards manufacturing their products come from. Whether it is the environmental or social consequences

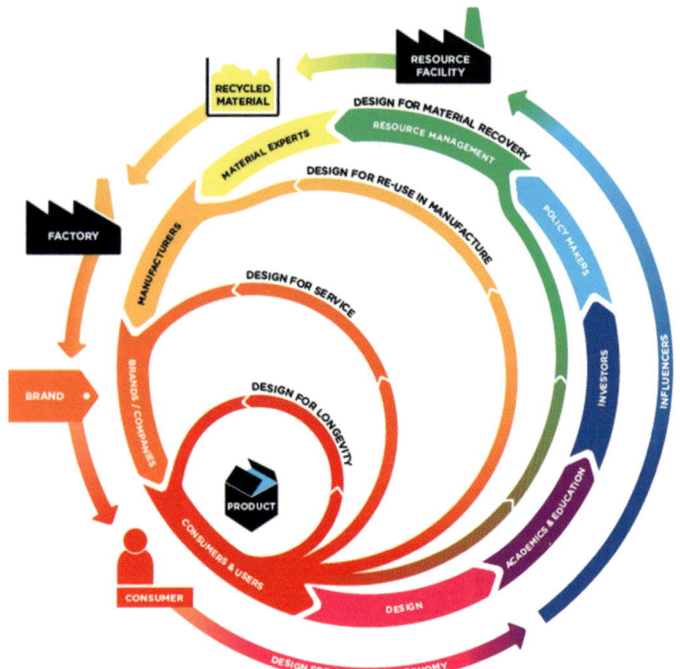

Figure 1.1
Four design models developed by the RSA as part of its 'Great Recovery' programme, June 2013.

associated with their projects, more and more companies, large and small, are not prepared to put up with the negative PR associated with illegally mining the raw materials for their products, or the displacement of indigenous communities. Some of the largest companies supplying the construction industry are actively doing positive things to clean up the environment and promote equitable trade. The issue of ethics is now being taken seriously, and that huge topic is the subject of numerous books, exhibitions, conferences and symposiums. At the same time, dropping the well-intentioned but thoroughly misunderstood and much-maligned word 'sustainable' from the environmental debate could be helping matters. I believe that the concept of the circular economy, or circular metabolisms (more people get 'economy', obviously), is more easily comprehended as a positive, smarter way of living that emulates natural systems and will give increased benefits to everyone.

As stated earlier, many human cultures have worked in harmony with their immediate environment. However, since the beginning of the Industrial Revolution in the mid-18th century, the consumption of natural resources has grown exponentially, and unsustainably. Today, you can expect nearly 90% of the raw materials used in manufacturing to become waste before the product leaves the factory, while 80% of products get thrown away within the first six months of their life.[6] However, material flow analysis conducted in 2010 by UK government-funded

WRAP (Waste and Resources Action Programme) concluded that nearly 20% of the UK economy is already operating in a circular fashion.[7] It went on to predict that this could rise to nearly 30% by 2020. So many economies could be hitting the ground running as they attempt to adopt this new practice. The European Union recognises the huge potential the circular economy presents society. It published its EU Circular Economy Package in December 2015 that outlined an Action Plan and an annex with a detailed timetable for implementation. The document dwells upon the number of new jobs and wealth generated by a circular economy. This was followed by the Circular Economy Action Plan in March 2020.[8] In 2015, WRAP published data predicting that an expansion of the circular economy could generate as many as 3 million new jobs and reduce unemployment by 520,000 across the EU by 2030.[9]

That is quite a lot of statistics for one paragraph. For a moment I want to pause and consider where the concept of the circular economy, or 'economy in loops' as it was initially explained, came from. In 1976, Prof Walter Stahel, architect and industrial analyst, presented preliminary ideas considering this concept to the European Commission. Entitled *The Potential for Substituting Manpower for Energy*, it was co-authored by Genevieve Reday and described a future of an economy in loops with its positive impact on job creation, economic competitiveness, reduced dependence on natural resources and the prevention of waste. It was later published under the same title.[10] Many people credit Prof Stahel with coining the expression 'Cradle to Cradle' in the late 1970s. By 1981, he had synthesised his ideas in his award-winning paper 'Product-Life Factor',[11] which identified a number of concepts that practitioners featured in this atlas are putting to the test. For example, Prof Stahel identified that the ultimate sustainable business model in a closed-loop economy would be the idea of 'selling utilisation' instead of products.

During the 1980s, Prof Stahel and Prof Michael Braungart met on numerous occasions at conferences. Prof Braungart was promoting the idea of 'cradle back to cradle'. Today there are a

Figure 1.2
BBM's RIBA House of the Future, Milton Keynes, 1994.

Figure 1.3
Sketch of Romney Marsh Visitor Centre, Romney Warren, Kent, by BBM, explaining how it is designed for remanufacture.

number of independent think-tanks and academic institutes around the world doing fine work developing ideas, providing training schemes and even certifying products. The first of these, Product-Life Institute in Geneva,[12] was formed in 1982 by Prof Stahel. By 1987, Prof Braungart had formed his own Environmental Protection Encouragement Agency[13] (EPEA), calling it 'the cradle of Cradle to Cradle', and offering courses, workshop and training, as well as Cradle to Cradle certification for products. In 2010, the famous solo long-distance yachtswoman Dame Ellen MacArthur formed the Ellen MacArthur Foundation[14] with the specific aim of accelerating the transition to a regenerative circular economy. Combining thought leadership and education with big business, this foundation has quickly become an influential think-tank, a catalyst for discussion and publisher of papers and books. In the summer of 2016, the University of Bradford awarded the world's first Circular Economy MBA to Gin Tidridge.[15] Tidridge completed the course while still working as a sustainability specialist at massive hardware, furniture, garden and lifestyle product supplier B&Q. Interestingly, Tidridge focused on exploring whether a supply chain can be described as a 'closed loop' within the B&Q business model. The University of Bradford, together with Cranfield and TU Delft, are all members of the Ellen MacArthur Foundation's 'Pioneer University network'. TU Delft has seen more than 16,000 students enrol in its free online circular economy course since its launch in 2015.[16] There is momentum behind this concept.

My personal journey towards a circular economy

Since building my first project, the RIBA House of the Future, in 1994, I have been interested in the numerous ingredients that go towards making truly sustainable developments. Over the years I have become more and more interested in unpacking the supply chain associated with construction projects, and trying out different material sources with the aim of CO_2 reduction, the preservation of ecosystems, the creation of work, etc. Many architects and designers clearly understand the principles of designing buildings that require little or no traditional energy sources to perform properly. The greater challenge, it seemed to both my partner (Ian McKay) and I, was the reduction of the carbon and 'ecological footprints' associated with the actual design, construction and occupation of said low-energy buildings: whole-life costing, in other words. So, naturally, re-examining material sources and construction systems, in addition to issues of programme (what goes on in the buildings we design and what type of lifestyles they encourage) were two of our main pursuits over the three decades (and counting) of practice and teaching that we enjoyed immediately after finishing the RIBA House of the Future.

During the first decade of the 21st century, my practice, BBM, was one of a number considering the potentials of designing buildings using locally sourced, nontoxic, organic and replenishable materials. This countered a rush to burn timber due to UK government 'green' incentives encouraging the burning of biomass. We wanted to prove that most timber and other biobased materials could be used in high-performance building: to literally 'lock' CO_2 rather than release it back into the atmosphere.

Figure 1.4
'The House that Kevin Built', completed in only six days, in 2008.

In 2001, we constructed the first public building utilising straw bales: the Romney Marsh Visitor Centre. It was also 'built for demolition', using mainly local materials that could easily be pulled apart; the building is a simple material store for the future. We followed this in 2005 with the first residential building in the UK using locally sourced sweet chestnut cladding. Chestnut is very interesting as it is extremely durable (the Romans imported it and used it in their roads), but also because of the ancient 'working' forests that still survive in Sussex and would support even greater levels of biodiversity if worked again. The potential for our landscape to supply and inform the aesthetic of contemporary building became apparent again.

By 2007, we felt able to curate an exhibition that toured the Southeast of England, entitled 'Built Ecologies: Translating Landscape into Architecture',[17] which considered ideas around how our landscapes could inform buildings if they supplied them with material. The exhibition also looked at the potential for genuinely low-carbon developments, employment and perhaps a renewed 'sense of place' and a local identity, once commonplace in the UK.

In 2008, BBM were contacted by Talkback Thames, the production company behind the popular (ubiquitous?) 'Grand Designs' TV programme. The team were keen to do a live version of the programme. We were asked to test our ideas and prove that a prefabricated dwelling made from over 90% organic, replenishable material could be constructed live on television in only six days. This we did, and our team also created the UK's first dwelling with an A+ Energy Performance Certificate. The building was constructed with zero waste on site, and it was disassembled, with the ground floor forming part of a research project at the University of the West of England (UWE). The rest of the building parts were sent back to suppliers. Perhaps what was most interesting about this project was the fact that it could be built in the first place. When I was first approached, I said to the producer that if they had contacted me a year earlier, I wouldn't have been able to meet the challenge. However, I had noticed that a number of UK practices (Architype, Feilden Clegg and White Design among them) were developing a suite of materials, and even inventing construction systems, that could meet this challenge. It reminded me of another point in architectural history (the 1970s), when emergent 'High Tech' architects developed, and even invested in, the companies supplying the prefabricated construction systems to deliver their futuristic visions. Was there an embryonic architectural movement developing here?

Although 'Grand Designs Live' attracted more than 5 million viewers a night, 'The House that Kevin Built' (THTKB)[18] was up, down and gone in a week. Quite a strange project to work on when you consider how slow architecture normally is. The speed of the project also meant that the knowledge gained by our team was not exchanged at all. So, I was keen to repeat the process of rebuilding THTKB, but to slow it down to about six months, in order to offer it as a pedagogic tool involving design and construction students, and to properly capture and share the knowledge gained in the process.

The rebuilding of THTKB didn't happen. However, the idea captured many people's imaginations, including Prof Anne Boddington, the Dean of the College of Arts and Humanities at the University of Brighton, who was able to persuade her colleagues in the estates department to provide land for the project. However, by 2011, I began to realise there were new emergent themes that our THTKB rebuild project could, or even should, address.

In April 2011, I met with Diana Lock from the government-funded organisation 'Remade Southeast'.[19] Lock was insistent that many large corporations only had one big theme on their

Figure 1.5
A new country house in East Sussex made from materials found on the surrounding private rural estate.

minds, and that was how to continue to make their products and deal with the very real challenges of 'resource security'. Whether due to war, unreliable governments or environmental despoliation due to mining and forest clearing, manufacturers were looking at alternatives to relying almost completely on raw materials to create their products. The other pressing issue was the emerging tough legislation on the safe and proper management of waste generated in manufacturing, as well as other legislation on the need to reduce the amount of waste generated. Corporate responsibility throughout the whole process was another big issue. Lock stated that old-fashioned 'linear systems' would be gradually replaced by 'circular systems': sensible companies were looking at strategies to reduce their dependence on raw materials, as well as their capacity to create waste. In other words, to look at how to redesign their products, systems and contracts so that they were kept in the middle part of the linear process and thus were turned into a circular, closed-loop process, giving greater security to the businesses, and therefore providing a more profitable strategy.

I soon found out that many companies were indeed looking at unpacking the way they produced their products. Apple Inc, for example, was keener to lease its products as it had invested in the physical and virtual infrastructure required to accept products back from its customers, clean them up and literally re-lease them. Armed with this information, it was obvious that if the construction and manufacturing industries could alter the way they practise, they could have a hugely beneficial effect on the environment. The construction sector is responsible for 37.5% of Europe's total waste generation (the total waste is 2,135 million tonnes, or 4,815kg per capita), which equates to about 800 million tonnes of material going to landfill or incineration every year. This is slightly down on the 2015 figures quoted in the first edition of this book. The construction sector is followed by mining and quarrying at 23.4%, which equates to 499.6 million tonnes and is over 230 million tonnes below 2015 levels, which can be seen as good news.[20] In the UK, over 60% of all waste generated comes from the construction industry.[21]

Housing and infrastructure, eating, drinking and travelling are responsible for just over 60% of European resource consumption.[22] Looking at the whole of Planet Earth, the construction and habitation of buildings consumes over 50% of annual raw materials.[23] It should be noted that since the first edition of this book was published in 2017, humans have increased the annual amount of raw materials harvested and mined from about 60 billion tonnes in 2012 to over 120 billion tonnes in 2022.[24] In short, going by the figure of 50% mentioned earlier in this paragraph, the construction and habitation of buildings currently consumes 60 billion tonnes of stuff every year!

The UK construction industry throws away 15 to 20% of all material arriving on site.[25] In other words, for every five to six dwellings built in the UK, one dwelling's worth of stuff (including demolition waste) goes to landfill or even incineration. Since the 1960s, it has been cheaper to throw materials at a construction site rather than let the labour force run out of things to do. That situation is changing as the cost of raw materials and the stuff it is processed into goes up, as well as the cost of sending material to landfill or incineration – or energy from waste, as some people call that particular disposal process.

Part 3 of this atlas discusses the project that became the Waste House.[26] Initially, I had the aim of constructing a building mainly using surplus and waste construction material heading for landfill and incineration. However, it quickly became more of a polemic – a project raising awareness of many of the issues discussed within this book. Ten years after it was first constructed in 2014, I am very proud to say that the Waste House still raises awareness of the potential value of so-called 'waste'. It has continued to fulfil one of its original ambitions –to be an ongoing 'live' research project while also serving as a learning space – and has attracted many research projects. Two of the EU-funded Interreg research projects that utilise the external fabric of the Waste House are discussed in some detail Part 3. As I write this chapter (in October 2023), I am very happy to report that the Waste House is still accepting visitors on Wednesday afternoons, with recent guests including local schools, technical colleges, many overseas visitors and even the Chair of the Environment and Climate Change Committee from the UK's House of Lords.

There has been a fair amount of unexpectedly good news since the publication of the first edition of this book in 2017. For example, more than 1 billion people now live in regions that have declared a 'climate and ecological emergency'. The UK government has committed to making the country net zero carbon by 2050, with over 90% of UK local authorities pledging to do the same by 2030. There has also been a huge increase in awareness of the massive problems created by our need to consume stuff at an ever-increasing rate. For example, in the UK Sir David Attenborough's 'Blue Planet II' was broadcast in October 2017, and consequently it felt like most people suddenly knew about the huge 'gyres' of rubbish collecting in all our oceans and, crucially, why that is a problem. Some greater awareness came as a result of the COVID-19 pandemic – the built environment community had time to think, network and write as workloads significantly reduced, especially during the first lockdown. In the UK, numerous construction sector guides were published (from LETI, RIBA, UKGBC, RICS, IStructE, ICE, etc.), providing what reads like a consensus across our industry of what an authentic whole-life-carbon descent plan from now until 2050 might look like. As I write this, it feels like we are only a few years away from whole-life-carbon benchmarks being part of our building regulations.

Because of the greater understanding of why the reduction in consumption of stuff is a very big deal, the second edition of *The Reuse Atlas* has taken quite some time to write. Simply put, since the last time I wrote the book in 2016, there have been many more outstanding examples of construction projects doing exactly what we need them to do – to REDUCE, to REUSE and, as a last resort, to RECYCLE before consuming new resources. I am told by people who know better than me that second editions of books normally contain 25 to 30% new content. Well, I can state here that over 90% of the Part 2 case studies in this book are brand new, proving that businesses at all scales, together with their design teams, lawyers, financiers, (crucially) insurers and the associated supply chains are taking advantage of the many opportunities presented by reusing the previously manufactured, or, as I've put it many times before, to 'mine the Anthropocene'.[27]

I believe, as I did last time I was finishing up this chapter, that there are many new and different ways of developing the built environment while creating new business opportunities and models that don't rely on destroying our natural resources to achieve these aims. Perhaps it will be these new 'hunter-gatherers' who will make the most of the Anthroposphere?

CHAPTER 2

What a Waste!

Cat Fletcher, Co-founder of Freegle UK

It is seven or more years since I first wrote this chapter. I have left it intact, as so much said back then remains the same (or worse!) and the message still very much needs repeating and reinforcing. If you read no further than this sentence, please know that whatever imperative there was when this book was first published in 2017, it has intensified. The time for preventative measures is mostly long gone. We need fast and purposeful change across the citizenship, business, government and media if we are to live within our earthly means and not waste our very existence.

In summary, WE DON'T HAVE TIME TO NOT TAKE ACTION.

But, nevertheless, a lot has happened since 2017 – and not all of it was on the horizon or on anyone's bingo card! We have experienced a range of micro and global events (many shocking, whatever your perspective or location) – we are still navigating an exhausting existential roller-coaster ride. Some of these momentous happenings have unintentionally reduced waste and carbon emissions and nudged better behaviours; others have reversed years of valuable progress to a cleaner and greener future; some have been good and bad at the same time.

Global lockdowns reduced transport pollution and evoked citizen appreciation of nature and clean air, but at the same time increased online purchases. And just when we were making great leaps with reducing single-use plastics, we flooded the globe with billions of pieces of single-use PPE. Oil and gas price hikes inspired energy-saving activity for those not previously motivated to consume less (which is good), but also caused a cost-of-living crisis. We've seen anti-environmentalist actions from Donald Trump, including revoking the USA's signature on the Paris Agreement; former Brazilian president Jair Bolsonaro wanting to chop down the Amazon; and the decimation of fauna and flora from wildfires, floods, heatwaves and droughts.

The salient point here is that no matter the perspective on these recent events, they have created a global mess, showing very little 'joined-up thinking'. There's the problem. We're not going to get out of here alive without co-ordinated policy, business models and action across all nations to reduce consumption, to prevent waste rather than mismanage it and to implement adaptations in every way so we can all live well with less carbon being emitted along the way.

The upside of this conundrum is that it can embolden those of us who care to speak up to take action ourselves. Politicians and corporations cannot be trusted to lead the way and implement the best policies and changes.

The volume and range of voices who want to make the world fairer and truly sustainable has exploded across generations and borders. Much of this has been possible because of advances in technology. A good thing, right?

There have never been more ways to engage in positive change, to carry out real-life actions wherever you live, to contribute to relevant campaigns and to talk and debate about it along the way. There is good progress and lots of good work is being done. Importantly, technological advances have provided the means for *anyone* to action positive change.

But, at the same time, the other guys have access to all those technological advances, too. All those self-serving think-tanks, unethical businesses, fossil fuel companies, all those celebrities with their overconsumption – their power has been emboldened, too. Not because they are right, but because they have so many channels to influence other people's voting choices, consumer habits and social attitudes. And they generally play dirty or play the ignorant card. The over-consumers and science-deniers who wish to blindly carry on wasting precious resources and making equality an impossible dream have also taken advantage of social media and multiple digital outlets, and have responded to our collective emergencies. They cause disruption and fear through divisiveness, bullying and mis-information.

We are ALL drowning in information, apps, networks, carbon calculators, streams, websites, causes, campaigns, podcasts, zooms, advertisements, books, blogs, political dogma, evidence,

Figure 1.6
Think before you buy.

analysis, research and choices, so many, many choices. If you're reading this book then arguably you may not need a nudge to change your behaviour, attitude or professional direction to be part of the solution to the continuation of life on Earth. But it's very possible that you are feeling overwhelmed or confused, depressed or unmotivated, tired and exhausted (spinning too many plates, trying to navigate hundreds of channels of constantly updated streams of communication) and very possibly exhibiting symptoms of eco-anxiety. With that in mind, near the end of the chapter I offer some links to resources that indicate what's changed since 2017 for good and bad, but please avoid feeling guilty.

Global economic and political systems enable and allocate stupendous amounts of energy, materials, labour and land to produce an over-supply of products that are ultimately incinerated – or landfilled, or stockpiled, or hoarded: pick your own outcome – whether or not those products are ever used. This generates endless financial rewards for those in such supply chains, while abusing our finite planetary limitations and people. Large international corporations are rewarded handsomely for wasting resources, time, energy and the human spirit. This is 'our' totally legitimate, endorsed, successful business model in which we are mostly not complicit, nor rewarded. It's institutional irrationality. That's what needs to change. You don't need to personally feel responsible for it being so. Just make sure you vote and spend your money in ways that challenge and hopefully change that ludicrous status quo.

If something new is cheap to buy, then someone or something has been exploited somewhere. Don't be cheap.

Please take inspiration from all the case studies, projects and people elaborated on in this book. We actually do have many solutions to big problems: there is no silver bullet, so every little action really does matter (it all adds up!). We are all trapped in a broken system, many of us furiously swimming against the tide – don't go under! We need each other to transform all the existing but crazy humanmade wasteful systems for those who will follow us and live in the built environment that we leave behind.

Good-news stories

On that note, absorb these good-news stories from the business sector: many organisations are genuinely moving in the right direction and some corporations are actually adopting grassroots-trialled-and-tested solutions on an industrial scale (and it's not all greenwashing) and there's a growing plethora of enterprises, community initiatives and charities tackling waste in a myriad of streams. Think: repair, reuse, mend, rent, share, upcycle, retrofit, refill, swap, make, take back, refurb, salvage…

Selfridges: repair, reuse, refill

Butler S, 'Selfridges wants half of transactions to be resale, repair, rental or refills by 2030', *The Guardian*, 2 September 2022, https://www.theguardian.com/business/2022/sep/02/selfridges-wants-half-of-transactions-to-be-resale-repair-rental-or-refills-by-2030 (accessed 20 February 2024).

Ikea: buy-back scheme

BBC, 'Ikea starts buy-back scheme offering vouchers for old furniture', 5 May 2021, https://www.bbc.co.uk/news/business-56981636 (accessed 20 February 2024).

https://www.ikea.com/gb/en/customer-service/services/buy-back-quote (accessed 20 February 2024).

John Lewis: producer responsibility

John Lewis's Circularity and Waste Strategy, launched in October 2020, includes the following commitments:

- All John Lewis product categories will have a 'buy back' or 'take back' solution by 2025.
- John Lewis will continue to develop sustainable rental and resale options for customers.
- We aim to help halve our customers' household food waste by 2030.
- In October 2022, a further commitment was added: All new John Lewis own-brand products will meet circularity criteria by 2028.

https://www.johnlewispartnership.co.uk/csr/our-strategy/circularity-and-waste.html (accessed 20 February 2024).

Loop: reusable packaging

Loop is a global reuse platform enabled by a multistakeholder coalition of manufacturers, retailers and consumers that aims to Eliminate the Idea of Waste®.

https://exploreloop.com (accessed 20 February 2024).

The Renew Hub, Manchester: biggest reuse depot in the UK

https://www.suez.co.uk/en-gb/our-offering/success-stories/our-references/the-renew-hub-delivering-re-use-on-an-industrial-scale (accessed 20 February 2024).

https://www.suez.co.uk/en-gb/news/press-releases/220929-the-stuff-of-life-new-suez-report-sets-out-asks-of-government-to-reduce-consumption-and-help-households-reduce-expenditure (accessed 20 February 2024).

Trialling refill in supermarkets

BBC, 'Asda trials refills at "sustainability store"', 16 January 2020, https://www.bbc.co.uk/news/business-51132164 (accessed 20 February 2024).

Lidl, 'Lidl GB becomes first UK supermarket to trial on-shelf smart refills', 13 October 2022, https://corporate.lidl.co.uk/media-centre/pressreleases/2022/on-shelf-refill-trial (accessed 20 February 2024).

Horton H, 'Refillable groceries to be made available to every UK shopper', *The Guardian*, 2 March 2022, https://www.theguardian.com/environment/2022/mar/02/refillable-groceries-uk-shopper-waitrose-morrisons-refill-stations-plastic-waste (accessed 20 February 2024).

The UK is producing less waste

The UK has improved its ranking in the Global Waste Index, moving from 20th place in 2019 to 18th place in 2022 (with the best-rated nation being given first place, and the worst-rated nation 36th place). https://sensoneo.com/global-waste-index (accessed 20 February 2024).

Use your head and your heart

An unlikely but deep ending to this updated chapter on waste is a quote from the actor William Shatner (Captain Kirk from 'Star Trek'), after his journey into space in 2021:

Every day, we are confronted with the knowledge of further destruction of Earth at our hands: the extinction of animal species, of flora and fauna… things that took 5 billion years to evolve, and suddenly we will never see them again because of the interference of mankind. It filled me with dread.[1]

So, with all of the above in mind, no matter what your role in the built environment (clients and policymakers especially take note!), please use your head and your heart to prevent waste and to conserve our planetary ecosystems.

As Sir David Attenborough would say, 'Live the way you want to live but just don't waste.'[2]

Be resourceful. In every way. Stop destroying things. Reuse what we already have.

Do more with less. Dream better.

And do your bit to help make the best built environment on Earth, everywhere, for all people. Because there is no Planet B.

CHAPTER 3

The Political Narrative

Dr David Greenfield, FCIWM FRSA CEnv, RAEng Visiting Professor

What do our governments and politicians need to do to facilitate a circular economy? How far off are we when you consider recent so-called supportive UK legislation, and is there possible salvation with the EC Circular Economy Package II?[1] Dr Greenfield will speculate.

Introduction

This chapter looks to explore how circular economy policies will impact on the construction, demolition and excavation (CDE) sector. The sector is among the biggest sources of waste in terms of volume and weight across Europe and has the perception of placing innovation, political pressure and profit over environment.

The stagnation of circular economy policy in the 20th and 21st centuries

One of the great politicians of the early 20th century, Theodore Roosevelt, had views that would today be lauded as forward-thinking and circular in their context. In his seventh State of the Union address on 3 December 1907, he opened with, 'The conservation of our natural resources and their proper use constitute the fundamental problem which underlies almost every other problem of our national life.' He went on to state, 'To waste, to destroy our natural resources, to skin and exhaust the land instead of using it so as to increase its usefulness, will result in undermining, in the days of our children, the very prosperity which we ought by right to hand down to them amplified and developed.'[2] Profound words that today would be applauded as progressive at any of the too numerous conferences, exhibitions and debates on the circular economy that rarely result in actions.

Fast-forward over a century and on 2 December 2015, Frans Timmermans, the European Commission's First Vice-President, in launching the new EU Circular Economy Package, echoed Roosevelt's views:

We need to retain precious resources and fully exploit all the economic value within them. The circular economy is about reducing waste and protecting the environment, but it is also about a profound transformation of the way our entire economy works. By rethinking the way we produce, work and buy we can generate new opportunities and create new jobs.[3]

The European Commission adopted the new Circular Economy Package to forward plan to 2030 with an ambition of boosting 'the EU's competitiveness by protecting businesses against scarcity of resources and volatile prices, helping to create new business opportunities and innovative, more efficient ways of producing and consuming'.[4] Many observers would suggest that we have lost a century in trying to regain the momentum of the early 20th century. However, while historical retrospect is quite interesting, we are where we are and now have to look forward, learning the lessons over the last century.

Exploration of the reason the circular economy is required

The concept of the circular economy (CE) is not new; it has just gained a momentum that hitherto has not been seen. It mainly concerns structuring the economy in a sustainable way, with the priority being to use materials efficiently and reduce and ultimately eliminate waste flows. The materials cycle is the central issue. Figure 1.7, from Rabobank, highlights the concept.

The concept of the circular economy is to maximise the circularity of materials within an industrial society, by designing products and buildings that can be dismantled and refurbished and reused. This reuse concept is at the top of the traditional hierarchy but has been seen by many as 'too difficult'. The circular economy suggests that extending the life span of products can be achieved in various ways – repair, upgrading,

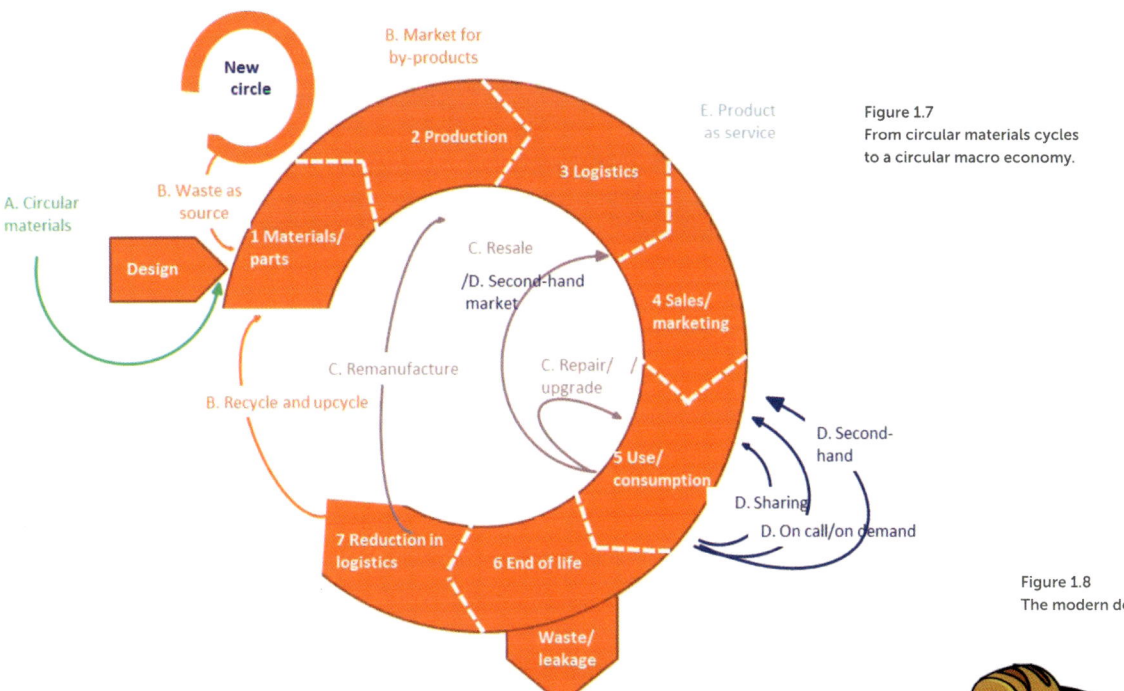

Figure 1.7
From circular materials cycles to a circular macro economy.

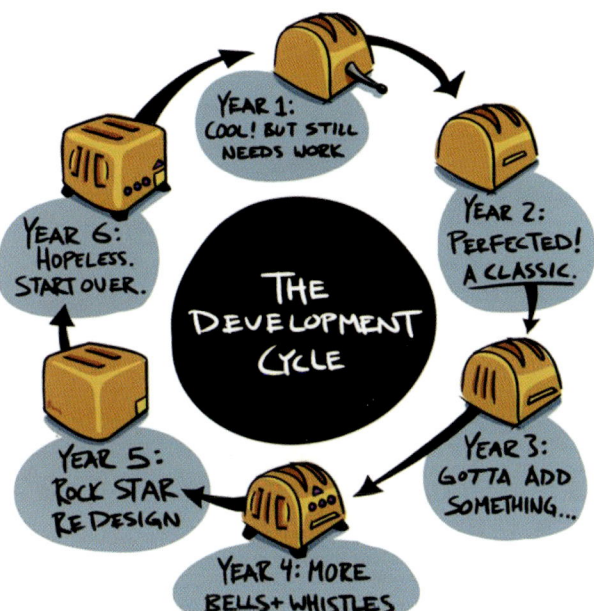

Figure 1.8
The modern development cycle?

remanufacture or remarketing of the same product – and that the more the design is focused on this and the more valuable the product is, the faster this happens.

Weight-based material flow analysis conducted in 2010 by the Waste and Resources Action Programme (WRAP) estimated that one-fifth of the UK economy was already operating in a circular fashion.[5] So are we doing well enough to not need a policy lever?

Where did it all go wrong?

So why should we worry? Can't we just continue the way we already are? Perhaps one of the biggest names in the music industry and 'eco-trepreneur' Will.i.am in an interview for the launch in 2015 of his collaboration between Coca-Cola and Harrods, EkoCycle, shows us: 'The reason why you have waste is because companies purposefully made things to break. It's called "planned obsolescence", and it started in the 1950s when governments gave incentives to companies to make shit to break to boost our economy.'[6] The rationale behind the strategy is to generate long-term sales volume by reducing the time between repeat purchases (referred to as 'shortening the replacement cycle').[7]

Arthur Dellea writes in Hubpages, 'In the computer industry, there are examples of forced obsolescence, because of fewer competitors.'[8] For example, Microsoft can get away with redesigning the visual side of the Windows operating systems and applications more frequently because they have established global computing standards with a 'comply or die' mentality.[9]

The concept of built-in obsolescence is not just confined to consumer goods, it's also entirely applicable to new buildings and the fittings that are contained within them. One of the principal questions is how can policy affect this perceived industrial mentality and change the way designers approach

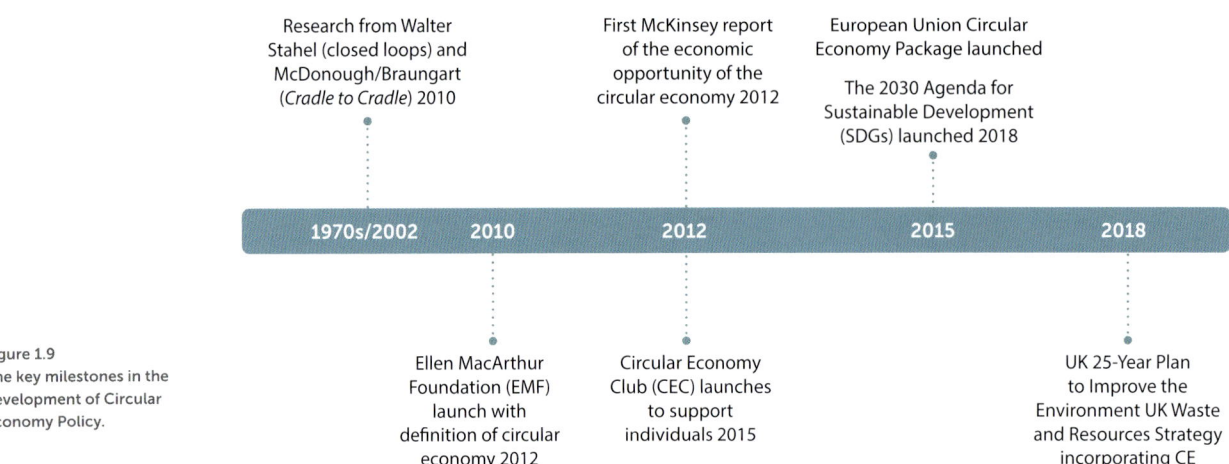

Figure 1.9
The key milestones in the development of Circular Economy Policy.

the use of materials and products to avoid obsolescence, and to design so that maintenance is easy and feasible? Sophie Thomas, former Director of Circular Economy at the RSA, sums up the new thinking well: 'Gone are the days of sustainable design, now we have to learn to think about life cycles, and designers have a key role to play.'[10]

Origins of the circular economy policies

The Guardian suggests that the circular economy is touted as a practical solution to the planet's emerging resource crunch. It highlights that reserves of key resources, such as rare earth metals and minerals, are diminishing, while exploration and material extraction costs are rising.[11] Many schools of thought have been subsumed into the worldwide phenomenon that is the circular economy; while the name is new, the influences aren't, indeed the Ellen MacArthur Foundation (EMF) suggests the following influences:[12]

- Cradle to Cradle
- Performance Economy
- Biomimicry
- Industrial Ecology
- Blue Economy
- Regenerative Design.

Its practical applications to modern economic systems and industrial processes, however, have gained momentum since the late 1970s, led by a small number of academics, thought-leaders and businesses. One of the fundamental claims of the circular economy momentum is recognised by the House of Commons Environmental Audit Committee (EAC):

'A "circular" approach of reusing resources, maximising their value over time, makes environmental and economic sense.'[13] This recognition by the EAC gives proponents of the circular economy the reassurance that the government understands the merits of moving to a circular approach but doesn't guarantee that it will succeed.

Using policy to dictate change

The circular economy instigates a robustness to reuse that considers the practicalities of material management, rather than waste management. One of the bastions of the resource and waste management policies is the waste hierarchy that was introduced in 1975, as part of the European Union's Waste Framework Directive (1975/442/EEC). The waste hierarchy emphasised the importance of waste minimisation, and the protection of the environment and human health. As a policy mechanism, it is one of the best known in Europe and demonstrates that the right policies can be highly influential.

Over time, the hierarchy has been adopted by member states as a central plank of policy. In trying to invigorate the concept within the existing policy framework, a revised resource management hierarchy was created in 2013 to include the concepts of circularity.

In the new resource management hierarchy, the aim is to maximise and clarify the solutions available through the circular economy. In essence, this has meant the hierarchy has grown up, with new layers added at the top for dismantling and refurbishment, reuse for alternative uses, closed-loop material recycling and material recycling.

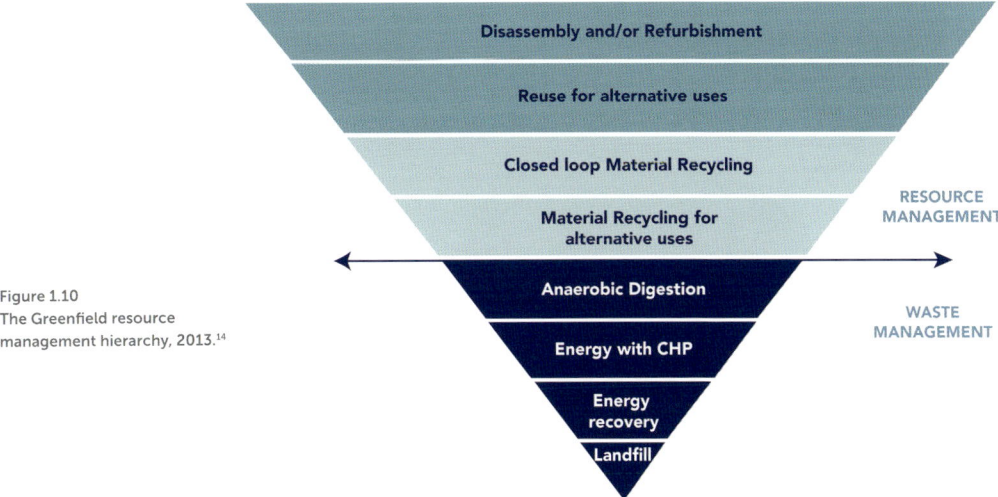

Figure 1.10
The Greenfield resource management hierarchy, 2013.[14]

While this new hierarchy may give much guidance to many people, unless it is adopted as a policy it seldom has the reach to impact on a national scale. One of the key challenges is how do advisors influence civil servants to push the boundaries of policy?

Existing UK policy and approach

Depending on your political leaning, photographer and environmentalist Ansel Adams' view on politics – 'It is horrifying that we have to fight our own government to save the environment'[15] – is either far-fetched or accurate. He is right in visible short-term cases, such as the way the UK government's change in the Feed in Tariffs (FITs) occurred in 2015, but in many ways inaccurate in the long term, such as the UK's Environmental Protection Act 1990.

The UK government describes a circular economy as 'moving away from our current linear economy (make–use–dispose) towards one where our products, and the materials they contain, are valued differently; creating a more robust economy in the process.'[16] In itself, this is a very accurate portrayal of the concept as identified by the Ellen MacArthur Foundation (EMF), but it does not go into the detail identified by the EMF: 'A circular economy is one that is restorative and regenerative by design, and which aims to keep products, components and materials at their highest utility and value at all times, distinguishing between technical and biological cycles.'[17] Should we be worried by this mismatch? Probably not: having a definition that recognises the concept is a far-reaching step, but it needs to be backed up by actions.

According to Julie Hill, author of *The Secret Life of Stuff* (2011), what started as a theoretical construct is gradually becoming an idea accepted by businesses and some policymakers as conveying an important aspiration for the future, namely, to keep resources in economic use for as long as possible.[18] If this acceptance continues, then perhaps policy will make the change; however, adoption by the construction sector is still the challenge. A selection of important EU and national policies is shown below to demonstrate progress in the last 10 years.

2015: The EU's Innovation Deals for a circular economy

In the 2015 EU Action Plan for the Circular Economy, Innovation Deals were identified as a mechanism to stimulate innovation and support the transition towards a circular economy.

2018: The UK 25-Year Plan to Improve the Environment

This outlines ways to reduce plastic pollution, while encouraging recycling and resource management. It focuses on maximising resource efficiency and minimising environment impacts at end of life, including:

- working towards our ambition of zero avoidable waste by 2050
- working to a target of eliminating avoidable plastic waste by the end of 2042
- maximising the value we get from our resources during their lifetime; looking at the whole life cycle (production, to usage, to end of life).[19]

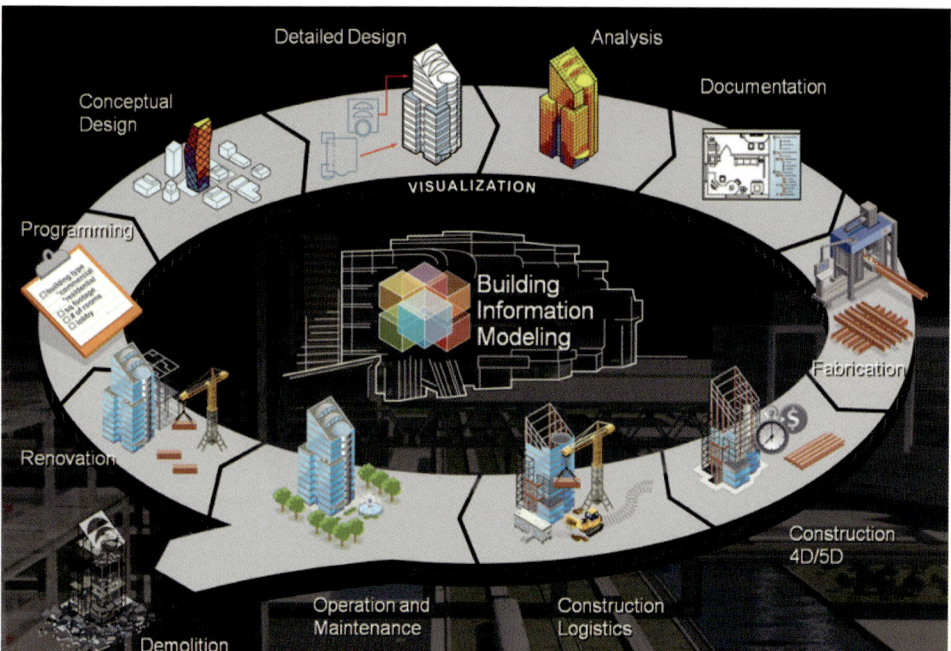

Figure 1.11
The BIM design model.[20]

2018: Resources and Waste Strategy for England

The first major waste policy intervention for England since 2011, this strategy highlights the importance of minimising waste, promoting resource efficiency and moving towards a circular economy.[21] It combines actions to be taken now, with firm commitments for the coming years, to meet a clear longer-term policy direction. It includes major reforms to the way resources and waste are managed, such as extended producer responsibility (EPR), consistent recycling collections and deposit return systems (DRS) for drinks container. While it addresses construction, demolition and excavation (CDE), it doesn't go far enough.

2020: EU Circular Economy Action Plan[22]

This is one of the main building blocks of the European Green Deal. It targets how products are designed, promotes circular economy processes, encourages sustainable consumption and aims to ensure that waste is prevented, and the resources used are kept in the economy for as long as possible.

2021: Waste Prevention Programme for England

This programme was set out in the policy paper 'Prevention is Better than Cure: The Role of Waste Prevention in Moving to a More Resource Efficient Economy'.[23] The objective was to improve the environment, while protecting human health, by supporting a resource-efficient economy, reducing the quantity and impact of waste produced.

Opportunities

The first three decades of the 21st century will continue to see a huge amount of major new construction and redevelopment. The rising skyline in London, which seems to be getting a few new skyscrapers every year, highlights this.

In July 2014, the Mayor of London published the 'London Infrastructure Plan 2050'.[24] This articulates the mayor's ambition that London becomes a world leader in the development of the circular economy so that it is best placed to reap the rewards of this transition. The plan projects that by 2036 there will be an additional one million households living within the Greater London area.[25]

So how do we build one million new homes in within a circular economy?

Circular economy policy and BIM

The requirement for a well-designed waste management system should form a fundamental part of the design and planning process because 80% of all environmental costs are predetermined during the conception and design phase of a project.[26]

In 2015, the UK government put in place policy that gave the potential to deliver this: 'Digital Built Britain, Level 3 Building Information Modelling – Strategic Plan'.[27]

Figure 1.12
Extract from the Brighton and Hove City Council Circular Economy Action Plan.

Building Information Modelling (BIM) is a process involving the generation and management of digital representations of physical and functional characteristics of places.[28]

The starting point of the BIM model is very similar to that of the circular economy: they are both of a circular nature and see demolition and waste as the least desirable option. However, they vary in how much effort is put into design and testing. This is crucial as it gives the opportunity for all stakeholders to consider the operation and maintenance stage of the building.

Using the concepts of BIM and all of the rhetoric around waste management, the definition of circular economic development might be understanding the supply chain for that project: the architects, material purchasers, developers, facility managers, operators, financiers, electrical, mechanical and civil engineers and potential users need to be involved in the final design of the programme. This may mean longer lead-in times to begin with but will allow for consideration of circular concepts such as leasing of materials rather than purchase, fittings that allow for dismantling and reuse, flexible spaces that will extend the lifetime of the development and design that will allow for maintenance.

Examples of policy failures and solutions

Policy needs to influence best practice. For example, it's all well and good everyone considering the operation phase and meeting current standards, but do those standards allow for circular design at that stage? Since the last edition of this book, there have been a number of new regional and city policies and Circular Economy Routemaps in the UK that incorporate targets for the construction, demolition and excavation (CDE) sector.

Brighton and Hove City Council Circular Economy Action Plan

In 2022, Brighton and Hove City Council launched its Circular Economy Action Plan, focusing on how the council can influence change through both internal and external impact.

Circular construction and maintenance

As a constructor of buildings and roads, the public sector can specify circular materials, designs and methods of construction and maintenance for new and existing developments

Buildings
The following actions will be introduced to deliver a circular city:

2022
24. Pilot reclamation audits and deconstruction of existing buildings for new build housing projects, using reclaimed materials on site wherever possible.
25. Separate construction waste streams from housing maintenance projects at the council's Housing Centre.
26. From 2022 undertake a Circular Economy opportunities assessment and evaluation of all new build housing construction projects.
27. Set outcomes for all new build housing projects using the RIBA Climate Challenge 2030 Targets and Checklist (subject to Housing Committee agreement in September 2022).
28. From 2022 undertake a whole life carbon assessment process on all new build housing projects.

2023
29. Undertake research and feasibility for implementing materials passports on new building housing construction projects and develop a strategy for implementation.

2025
30. By 2025 specify in project briefs at least 50% of all materials used in a new development are recoverable at the end of life of the building on all new build housing projects.

2030
31. By 2030 specify in project briefs at least 60% of all materials used in a new development are recoverable at the end of life of the building on all new build housing projects.

The action plan is focused on the two topics that give the city the most challenge: food and construction. There is a comprehensive set of construction-sector actions, shown in Figure 1.12; while many of these are pilots, there are two that stand out as setting a precedent for others to follow:

- From 2022 undertake a whole-life carbon assessment process on all new build housing projects.
- By 2025 specify in project briefs at least 50% of all materials used in a new development are recoverable at the end of life of the building on all newbuild housing projects.

It is especially good to see a target for 'recoverable materials'. The challenge for the council will be to demonstrate success.

The action plan is very short, concise and shows how the council will work with partners to make circular happen, after much collaborative internal and external engagement. This size and type of action plan is something that should be adopted by all policymakers in the future to enable actions to be delivered.

Figure 1.13
Material mapping of structural systems in the Helsinki metropolitan area.

Figure 1.14
Helsinki CIRCuIT development tracker.

Circular Construction in Regenerative Cities (CIRCuIT)

Circular Construction in Regenerative Cities (CIRCuIT) is a collaborative project that ran from 2019 to 2023 and involved 31 ambitious partners across the built environment chain in Copenhagen, Hamburg, the Helsinki region and Greater London. The objective of the programme was to bridge the gap between theory, practice and policy and showcase how circular construction approaches can be scaled and replicated across Europe to enable cities to build more sustainably and transition to a circular built environment.

Two of the most interesting aspects for future circular solution implementation will be the building material mapping, shown in Figure 1.13. This GIS map highlights building materials for each individual building, by colour coding, supported by detailed information as a pop-up. While this could be seen as just an interesting piece of research, it is vital in providing evidence of how and where refurbishment can occur and where material banks are.

The second element of the project that links to material mapping is the development tracker, as shown in Figure 1.14. This tracker

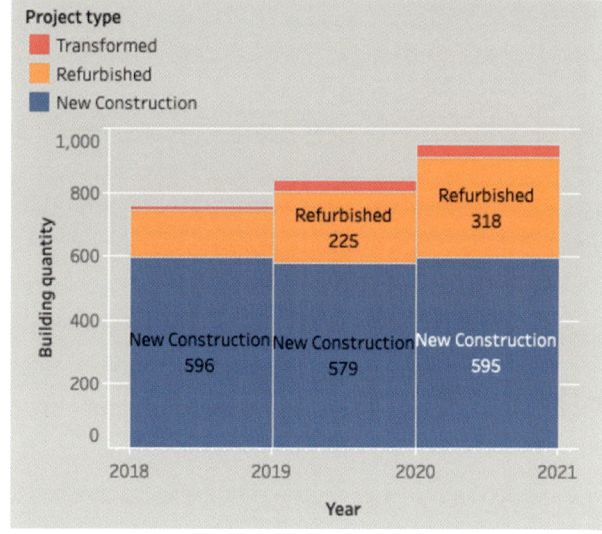

shows the emergence of refurbishment as an accepted procedure. By presenting this data in the simple graphical form it reinforces the notion that refurb is not just acceptable but is increasing. This type of information sharing is important in shifting the behaviour of the private sector in the city.

Design for a Circular Economy Primer

In 2020, the Greater London Authority launched the Design for a Circular Economy Primer[29] that focuses on shifting to circularity by planning and design interventions. It was written to support

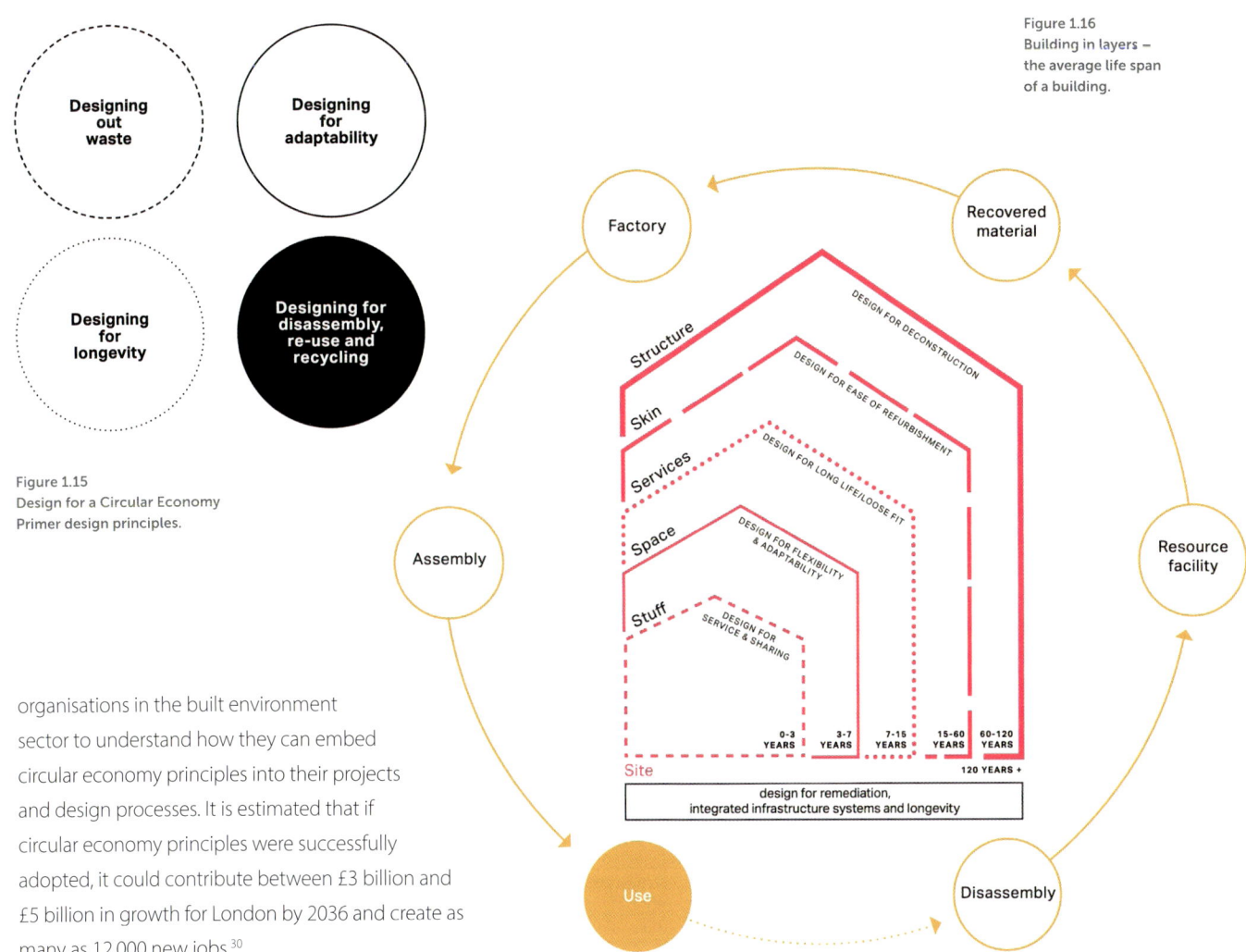

Figure 1.15
Design for a Circular Economy Primer design principles.

Figure 1.16
Building in layers – the average life span of a building.

organisations in the built environment sector to understand how they can embed circular economy principles into their projects and design processes. It is estimated that if circular economy principles were successfully adopted, it could contribute between £3 billion and £5 billion in growth for London by 2036 and create as many as 12,000 new jobs.[30]

The Design for a Circular Economy Primer is an exemplar of a collaborative approach across different disciplines, with championing by the Mayor of London, which brings unprecedented credence. The Primer states, 'The circular economy requires new approaches to development by everyone involved in making, managing, maintaining, using and renewing our buildings and infrastructure.'[31] This life-cycle thinking and cross-disciplinary approach is a beacon for other cities and regions to follow.

While the Primer does not specifically set targets, unlike the Brighton and Hove City Council Circular Economy Action Plan, it does show the way for developers to follow, through the creation of a template for developers to complete, highlighting all of the reasons for pursuing circularity. One of the strategically important messages is the diagram shown in Figure 1.15. This sets out the narrative for new development.

The major shift in development is the requirement that any developer who has a development referred to the mayor (according to multiple criteria, including developments above 150 units) must include 'a Circular Economy Statement prepared in accordance with [the] guidance document'.[32] This statement is an important shift in enabling developers and planners to incorporate circular design into new developments.

Tower Hamlets Reuse, Recycling and Waste Supplementary Planning Document

In 2021, the London Borough of Tower Hamlets published a Reuse, Recycling and Waste (RRW) Supplementary Planning Document (SPD).[33] This SPD was written to incorporate circular thinking into the design of new developments for waste management during the operational life of new developments. The principles of the Mayor of London's Primer of a template for developers and a decision tree were expanded upon in this publication.

There are two elements that are potentially a game-changer for circular development.

1. DECISION TREES

The decision tree (shown in Figure 1.17) centres around the users' needs during the operational lifetime of the building in terms of how to maximise occupier reuse (high-level circularity) and recycling (medium-level circularity).

The decision tree indicates the 'expected RRW system', with large developments above 50 units expected to have an Automated Waste Collection System (AWCS), followed by an Underground Recycling System (URS), instead of the traditional basement bin store. This is an important shift to show that the design of the building is centred around reuse and recycling of materials.

2. 'THE 10 STEPS TO OCCUPATION'

The 10 steps set out how to engage with the planning and waste management teams in preparing for planning applications. These 10 steps are shown in Figure 1.18 and include links to multiple template documents, including a template RRW Plan and a detailed RRW checklist that indicates the developers' choices of system, including types of containers, waste stream and recycling rates.

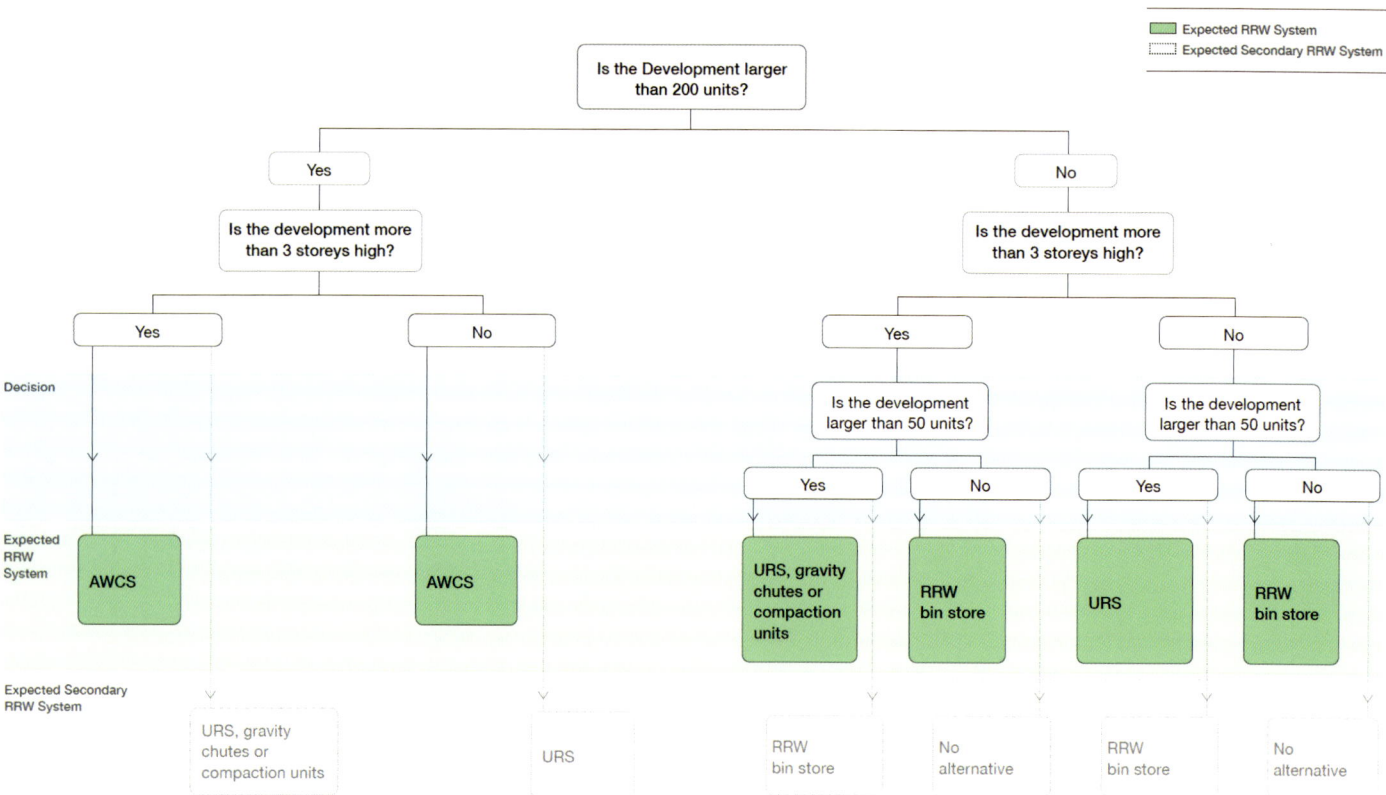

Figure 1.17
Tower Hamlets Reuse, Recycling and Waste Supplementary Planning Document decision tree.

Figure 1.18
Tower Hamlets Reuse, Recycling and Waste Supplementary Planning Document, '10 steps to occupation'.

	Pre- application		
1	**Step 1:** Identify the appropriate RRW system		See Section B.01 and RRW Decision Tree
2	**Step 2:** Prepare the Expected RRW Checklist		See **Appendix 2**
3	**Step 3:** First meeting with Planning, Waste and Recycling Team and Highways officers.[2] Method for achieving RRW objectives during use of the development		See **Appendices 2** and **4**
4	**Step 4:** Further liaison with Planning, Waste and Recycling Team and Highways officers		See **Appendix 2**
	Preparing and submitting a planning application		
5	**Step 5:** Prepare an RRW Plan: Completed RRW Checklist; RRW Overview and Objectives document objectives; and, full draft RRW Plan.		See Part B See Appendices **2** and **3**
6	**Step 6:** Submit planning application with RRW Plan		See Part B
	Construction and Pre-occupation		
7	**Step 7:** Compile the final RRW Plan		See Part B See **Appendix 3**
8	**Step 8:** Pre-occupation site visit		See Part B
9	**Step 9:** Waste/Highways approval		See Part B See Appendices **5**, **6**, **7** and **8**
	Occupation of the development		
10	**Step 10:** Monitoring: Developments greater than 200 units – submission of annual data relating to performance against RRW objectives		See Part B See **Appendix 10**

West Midlands Combined Authority Circular Economy Routemap

In September 2021, the West Midlands Combined Authority (WMCA), a partnership of 17 local councils and three local enterprise partnerships (LEPs), launched its Circular Economy Routemap.[34] The Routemap was designed to kickstart the 'region's journey to a green industrial revolution'. The Routemap has taken elements of the Mayor of London's Circular Economy Primer and the Brighton and Hove Circular Economy Action Plan, such as focusing on sectors (circular manufacturing, construction and food) and giving clear template documents. The main departure from these two documents is the baselining exercise, which resulted in a material flow analysis of the construction, demolition and excavation sector, as shown in Figure 1.19.

The Routemap is 90 pages long and has a huge amount of detail in it, such as the construction, demolition and excavation material flow analysis, which shows a reliance on virgin raw materials; and there are too many initiatives to highlight individually. However, there is one standout output from the Routemap: an action plan (shown in Figure 1.20), which includes enabling actions and was written by very well-engaged stakeholders, who retain responsibility for delivery.

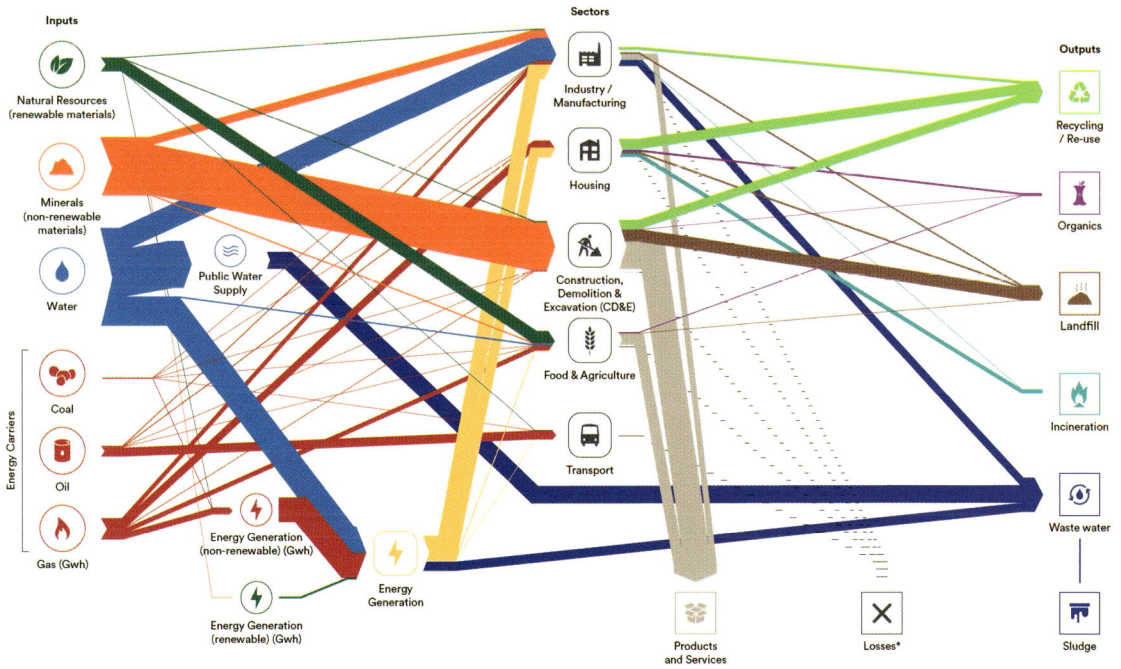

Figure 1.19
The West Midlands Combined Authority's construction, demolition and excavation (CDE) material flow analysis (MFA).

Brownfield Land Reclamation

What? Set up a facility and associated advisory services to unlock the development potential of brownfield sites of all sizes.

Why? To reduce resource consumption, wasted materials on brownfield sites, and the amount of soils and virgin materials imported.

Role of WMCA? Enable and Influence. Lead on own sites.

Partners: See Appendix 8 for complete partners list.

Next Steps:
- Explore option for the National Brownfield Institute to become leading facility.
- Convene partners to develop incentives including for smaller sites.
- Create a register of brownfield sites and develop a data-sharing platform.

Circular Repurposing Programme

What? Develop and implement circular approaches for refurbishing and repurposing commercial and residential properties, as well as public buildings and spaces.

Why? To minimise construction waste, to reduce virgin material extraction and to revitalise unused space.

Role of WMCA? Enable and Influence. Lead on own sites.

Partners: See Appendix 8 for complete partners list.

Next Steps:
- Audit public spaces, high streets and unused/vacant commercial spaces to create a region-wide revitalisation investment prospectus.
- Support R&D in circular products, services and approaches that support repurposing and refurbishing.
- Publish guidance on alternative financing and delivery models.

West Midlands' Circular Economy Routemap

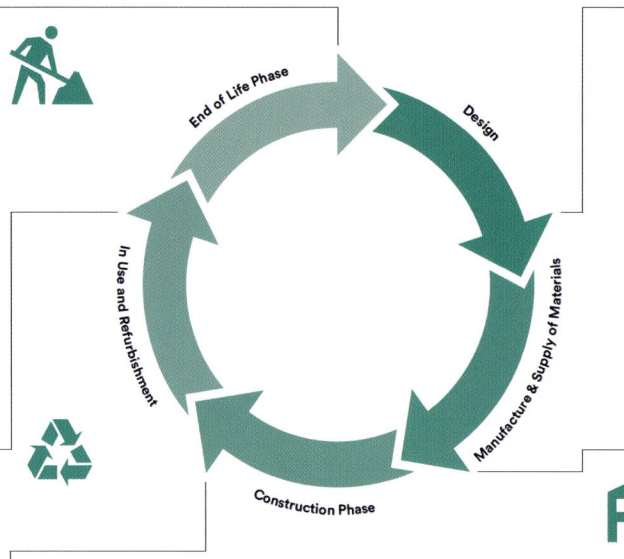

Zero Waste Construction Hub

What? Launch a physical and virtual hub to recover and exchange materials, as well as share and incentivise circular design and processes.

Why? To use fewer materials and reduce waste on construction sites, to encourage material exchange within the built environment.

Role of WMCA? Enable and Influence. Potential delivery partner.

Partners: See Appendix 8 for complete partners list.

Next Steps:
- Determine best location for material recovery and exchange hub(s), developing feasibility and funding proposal.
- Mobilise and convene regional supply chains around circular construction methods (including MMC and AMC).
- Launch virtual hub and share best practice guidance and incentives for circular construction processes.

Circular Strategies for Infrastructure

What? Develop circular strategies and action plans for major infrastructure projects and utility providers.

Why? To mobilise and scale up circular supply chains, to encourage innovation, and to support circular, sustainable utility provision.

Role of WMCA? Enable and Influence. Lead on own sites.

Partners: See Appendix 8 for complete partners list.

Next Steps:
- Identify and convene major infrastructure and utility companies and their supply chains to develop projects and incentives.
- Create a forum for infrastructure and utility companies to share best practice.
- Publish best practice guidance for circular strategies for infrastructure and utility companies.

Circular Building Product Initiative

What? Support the development of leading, regional circular buildings' systems, products and service offers.

Why? To create a suite of regional circular building products, to increase the number of circular products and services, to support regional job creation.

Role of WMCA? Enable and Influence. Lead on own sites.

Partners: See Appendix 8 for complete partners list.

Next Steps:
- Work with the Zero Carbon Homes Task Force and other key partners to select ten regional building product manufacturers/suppliers.
- Convene partners and experts to explore creation of a consortium of regional organisations to act as a one-stop shop for circular buildings' products, services and systems.

Figure 1.20
West Midlands' Circular Economy Routemap, circular construction strategic interventions.

Figure 1.20 lists five interventions, and for each intervention shows:
- what the intervention is
- why it has been chosen
- the role the WMCA should take
- the role of partners
- next steps.

These five elements are currently each being undertaken in a collaborative fashion, based on local priorities. This Routemap is perhaps one of the most detailed created, and it gives the most granular level of detail of how to take the next steps.

Conclusion

This chapter has explored the history of circular economy politics, emerging planning and government policies and some of the challenges associated with construction in the 21st century.

In reality, most of the challenges of getting the construction, demolition and excavation sector to change aren't now about how to get policymakers to introduce policies, as this is starting to happen across the globe. It's about getting architects, material purchasers, developers, facility managers, operators, financiers, electrical, mechanical and civil engineers and potential users to buy into the circular economy and understand the benefits. Since the first edition of *The Reuse Atlas*, there has been a significant increase in policy adoption, strategy writing and action planning; however, this has occurred in all too few major cities so far. It is important that the sector refocuses and moves towards new methods of designing, planning, constructing and dismantling, with an understanding of circularity at the heart of all decisions.

This chapter has demonstrated that there is a significant level of high-quality policies in existence. What we need now are action plans tailored to local circumstances, rather than a raft of rehashed Routemaps and polices that explain the reason why change is needed, without stating the route to that change. Let us all adopt the circular economy business model of sharing, and share the need for change and get on with making the change.

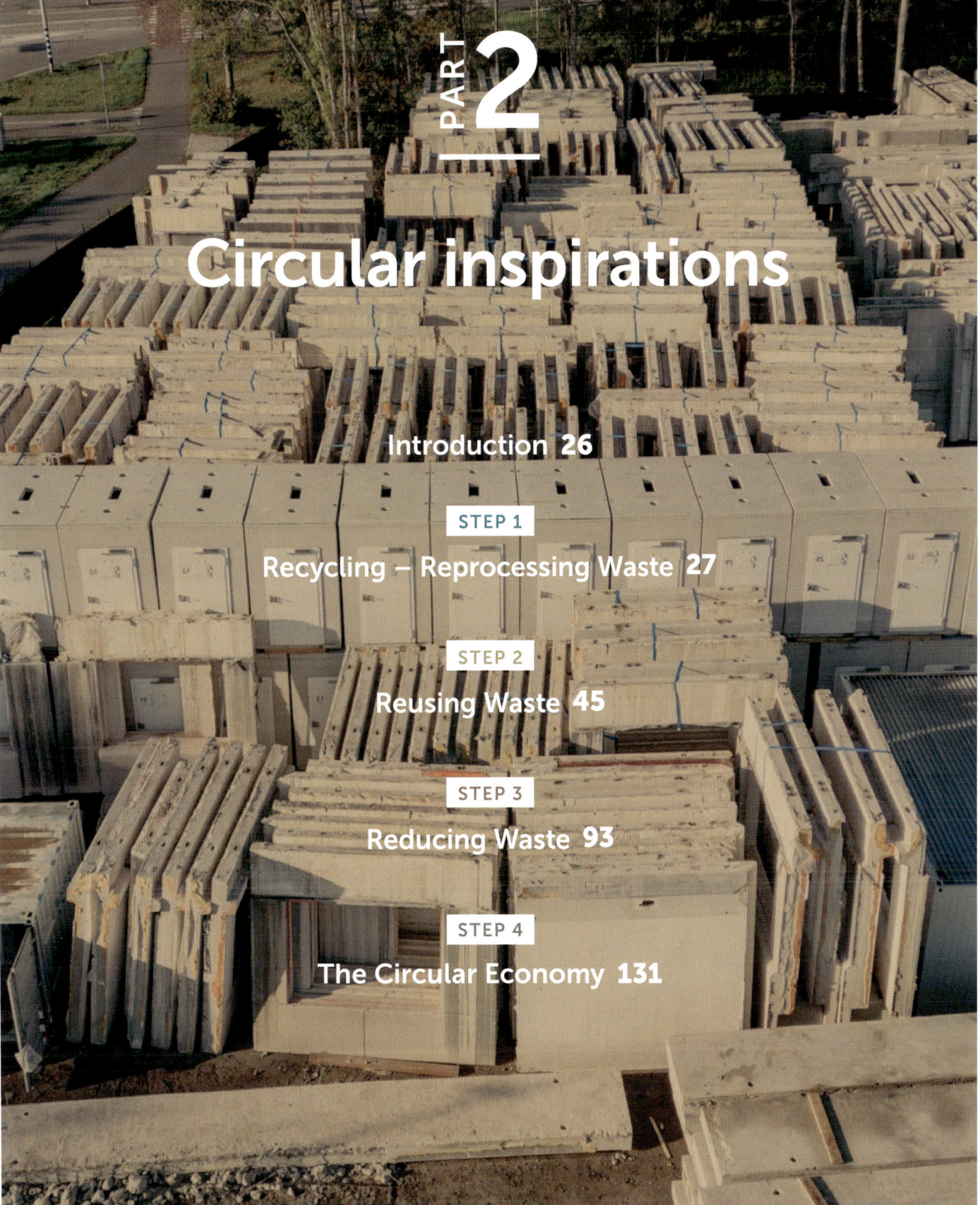

PART 2
Circular inspirations

Introduction 26

STEP 1
Recycling – Reprocessing Waste **27**

STEP 2
Reusing Waste **45**

STEP 3
Reducing Waste **93**

STEP 4
The Circular Economy **131**

INTRODUCTION

This part of *The Reuse Atlas* is to be read as a series of 'steps' towards the reality of a circular economy. Many people are busy envisioning what this will look like. However, it is a long way from how most people currently exist on the planet, i.e. as a linear metabolism: finding stuff, processing it, utilising it and casting it aside. The idea of designing things in such a way as to ensure they are always a useful resource for either the natural or synthetic worlds is quite alien to most people.

In the meantime, many ideas and concepts that consider living in harmony within natural ecosystems, as opposed to outside of them, have certainly gained popularity over the last 30 years or so. Green/eco/low-energy/Passivhaus/hacking/reuse cafés/upcycling/designing for demolition, etc. are all words and ideas that more and more people are getting to grips with.

While considering the idea of this book back in 2016, I was concerned that there were many different interpretations of what it means to be a 'green' designer or one who is sensitive to environmental issues. I am also aware that many reuse and 'being less harmful to the environment' ideas are dismissed within Cradle to Cradle philosophy as simply slowing down the inevitable – for example, recycling plastic cups into fleeces to wear simply prevents that plastic from ending up in our oceans for a couple of years. The plastic ends up as toxic waste eventually. I feel that this oversimplifies some initiatives that are positively influencing behavioural change.

I am keen to spend some time dwelling upon the positive and negative points associated with recycling, reuse, upcycling, hacking, retrofit and so on. The ideal of a circular economy is clear, but I am concerned that it appears to be such a big leap from where we currently stand that there is a need for some clearly defined stepping stones to help us along our way to a more circular existence.

One of the biggest challenges that faces humankind is how to exist without damaging so much of our planet's natural resources. This is done as we mine for resources, as we refine them, utilise them and then when we throw them away. In one way or another, humankind has managed to practically wrap the landscape with our cities, roads, flight paths and landfill sites, while our oceans are filling up with plastic waste: a pretty gloomy state of affairs.

However, most of that development has only happened over the last 150 years or so, and it should be noted that we have only been manufacturing plastic for a little over 100 years. Until biodegradable options are commonly available, there needs to be an emphasis on cleaning up the vast areas of oceans and landscape that are currently undermined by our dangerous waste. This 'big clean-up' will create a huge amount of material that in theory could be put to good use, or reuse.

So here we go with a collection of inspiring case studies that I have assembled.

Figure 2.1
Material experiments involving the author and colleagues and students at the University of Brighton.

STEP 1

Recyling – Reprocessing Waste

DEFINITION

STEP 1 PROJECTS recycle waste into a new product or material. The case studies and initiatives presented here should be seen as the first basic step towards reducing humankind's negative impact on Earth. Reprocessing waste is not a particularly sophisticated approach as waste material is recycled by either being ground down, melted, pulped, etc., often into a less useful and second-rate 'new' material. The processes can also involve waste and mixing materials together that will make future disposal even more difficult. Recycling processes also consume valuable energy and water. However, recycling does identify 'waste' as a valuable 'resource' and reduces (or at least delays) the amount of material being burnt or going to landfill. This is a basic first step towards 'circularity' and one that many organisations are taking very seriously, especially since Sir David Attenborough was so successful in raising awareness of the amount of plastic in our oceans. As a result, many companies are looking into ways to clean up our oceans and shorelines to save marine wildlife and to take plastic out of the food chain. Their approaches may vary, and obviously it is a mind-blowingly massive task. The challenge is articulated rather well by the global environmental organisation Parley for the Oceans, who explain the processes required via their 'AIR' initiative (Avoid/Intercept/Redesign). A quote from Parley's website pretty much sums up why recycling forms an integral part of our route *towards* circularity.

❝

Awareness campaigns, clean-up operations and recycling initiatives allow us to help alleviate immediate threats to marine wildlife and reduce the use of virgin plastics in product design, manufacturing and distribution. In close collaboration with major brands, we also work to reduce overall plastic use. But we can only end ocean plastic pollution in the long run if we invent smarter materials and synchronise the economic system of mankind with the ecosystem of nature. Therefore, Parley with its global expert network is operating an extensive research and development programme to invent alternatives and to establish new industry standards.[1]

Introduction – emerging construction materials made entirely from waste flows

Since I wrote the first edition of this book, there has been a huge growth in understanding how to find legitimate ways to reduce the waste we all make daily. In addition, the established waste procurement industry has had a bright light shone on it. In the UK, Sir David Attenborough's 'Blue Planet II' series, first broadcast in 2017, was hugely impactful, capturing the attention of a nation who had never really considered where all that plastic waste we consciously and unconsciously use actually ended up. Nowadays, there are regular newspaper articles on reducing waste, separating and recycling it at home, and innovative ways of recycling it into new stuff. Other articles highlighting how the UK regularly exports its waste to other countries, to be burnt or left to hang around in open rubbish dumps, are also commonplace now. Waste is a hot topic.

The objective of this part of the book is to champion certain approaches and identify some of the many sources of waste flows that are worth highlighting – bearing in mind the often-quoted notion that if we encourage the collection and recycling of waste flows, we could be encouraging the continued wasteful, linear and environmentally detrimental malpractice of whatever industry creates the waste in the first place. I am a huge advocate of imposing legislation on manufacturers that will insist they take back their products at the end of their 'first lives'. Asking end users to deal with the most difficult part of a product's traditional cradle-to-grave life cycle is just dumb and irresponsible. Sending worn-out products back to manufacturers will force them to think of ways of making this profitable, which I believe will include designing products to be a useful resource; to be updated and reused, on many occasions, before being recycled into still-valuable source material again.

It is the above argument that means that recycling can sometimes be considered part of a future circular metabolism. Outlined below are examples of products and materials that satisfy this point, that are beyond first-phase prototyping, and are, on the whole, readily available as part of the construction sector supply chain.

It is in the sphere of substituting conventional insulation products for sustainable, low-carbon, nontoxic options where sustainable innovations have often taken hold. For example, let us consider insulation made from sheep's wool. When it was first marketed in the UK in the early 2000s, this product was made from surplus and waste processed wool from the carpet and textile industries, with the very first iteration being imported from New Zealand. The issue of the large embodied carbon footprint associated with using this product in the UK has gradually been addressed to a point where UK-based designers can now specify insulation made of waste wool from UK sheep. There are now numerous variations of this product, and it is a great alternative to 'traditional' high (embodied) energy insulation products. It performs as well, but because of the inherent oils naturally occurring in the wool, the product is water resistant, which is a great benefit when the woollen insulation batts are hanging around a wet building site. Many readers will have witnessed rain hitting mineral insulation batts fixed to the external face of a building, getting absolutely saturated while waiting for the external cladding to be fixed sometime in the future. When mineral wool gets wet it contracts, but it doesn't expand when it dries and therefore it loses its ability to insulate. Sheep's wool insulation batts are rain resistant.

However, there has been a recent development in the product where recycled polyester has been added to the sheep's wool to make it easier to install on site, and to prevent 'sagging' of the material over the years as it sits between timber studs. This is an unfortunate development. I am uncomfortable with mixing synthetic with organic waste, as this renders the product redundant at the end of its life. Sheep's wool would naturally compost at the end of its life. If one adds polyester into the mix, composting is not an option. Worst still, in the future people may think that they are dealing with 100% wool insulation and compost it anyway. This will leave a nasty residue of polyester fibre in the ground. Best not to mix the bio and tech spheres.

In addition to waste wool, you can get insulation made from waste cotton, hemp, flax, denim and, of course, recycled newspaper cellulose. However, today there is a new generation of construction products utilising waste materials, both organic and synthetic. These materials are beginning to emerge from the laboratories and help our buildings turn waste into a valuable resource.

You will see with the case studies in this section that there are many products out there that are made from the huge and constant flows of waste plastic. There are many inventive projects for collecting waste on land and even in our oceans, as well as an increased understanding that plastic and microplastics are everywhere – on all landscapes, in all waterways, in the atmosphere, in the food chain, in our blood. Therefore, we cannot avoid considering ways to recycle it into useful products, where the suppliers are committed to receiving their old products at the end of their first lives and repurposing them – turning destructive, linear processes into mini circular systems, while not adding to the destruction and pollution of the natural world.

At one level, the biggest issue we have is communicating the benefits of turning linear systems into circular ones. As we are dealing with the idea of locating and recycling waste streams, I think we should acknowledge one of the most high-profile promotors of this practice: Dave Hakkens, an industrial designer currently based in Eindhoven. When Hakkens graduated from the Eindhoven Design Academy in 2013 he had developed two projects: firstly, Phoneblocks, an open-source modular smartphone designed to reduce the huge problem of electronic waste. Interestingly, it was produced the same year as Fairphone launched its first model for sale. However, it was Hakkens' other graduation project that caught my attention and has led to his YouTube channel attracting over 50 million views. This is Precious Plastic, an ongoing movement that facilitates the collection and processing of waste plastic into new products – and it does it by providing anybody who is interested with a series of machines and tools that can grind and melt waste plastic, and even injection-mould it into new products. Precious Plastic is an open hardware/digital common type of project aimed at small-scale designers and makers. In effect, it allows DIY designers an opportunity to recycle plastic and produce their own products on a small scale. All parts of the process of building your own plastic recycling machine, through to the production of recycled plastic artefacts, are described on easy-to-use videos, and perhaps the most interesting aspect of this movement is the fact that it is free to join, and that it is a thriving community with over 500 recycling workspaces in more than 100 countries. Hakkens suggests that 380 tonnes of plastic have been recycled since 2019, while there have been 100,000 downloads of the Precious Plastic toolkits.

Sharing new ways of doing for free (i.e. by open sourcing it) to effect systems change is a big deal. My colleague Nick Gant writes very eloquently about the positive social, economic and environmental impacts of recycling and reuse on formerly disenfranchised communities in Part 4, Chapter 5.

In 2019, Prof Michael Braungart, speaking at 'The Waste Zone' event in London, declared to the audience that people often feel overwhelmed when thinking of how best to solve the environmental problems associated with waste. He went on to suggest that the first thing to do was to focus on one small thing only and to do that one thing well. He particularly recommended that the problem of single-use nappies would be an excellent area to focus on.[2] WRAP (Waste and Resources Action Programme) has stated that by the time they are potty trained, a baby could have used between 4,000 and 6,000 single-use nappies, which equates to 2 to 3% of all UK waste sent to landfill annually, with a depressingly large and growing percentage of this waste flow being nappies for adults. That's more than 3 billion nappies annually![3] Obviously, this product has its reusable option, but not many people feel able to work with this – a typical challenge with systems change. So, the short-term option has to be to find solutions to reuse this material.

There are now roof tiles on the market that are made of salvaged nappies and other sanitary products; products that divert these from landfill are to be applauded. Lightweight Tiles has developed a roof tile for the residential home market that is made from nappies which have had their numerous polymers separated in specialist recycling plants. It is early days for this product, and interesting that the company is quite coy about the material source of their products, despite big green credentials. Maybe it is currently a bit too challenging to expect people to specify this roof tile for the foreseeable future. However, there are numerous other start-ups taking up the challenge, including Nappicycle in Wales, which is reprocessing used nappies into fibres and pellets that are then a source material for a huge array of products, ranging from insulation quilts through to rigid sheet materials. Again, these products are not commonplace. So, my question is, 'What is needed to effect systems change; to turn linear, environmentally damaging processes into closed loops?' And, if you can find a solution to the huge single-use nappy problem, please get in touch with me, and Prof Braungart.

In 2017, my colleagues Nick Gant and Ryan Woodard joined me in working on an EU-funded Interreg project called SB&WRC, standing for Sustainable Bio and Waste Resources for Construction. We were charged with finding waste streams near to our base, the Waste House in Brighton. In particular, we were asked to find an awkward textile waste flow and reprocess it into insulation for the construction sector. We partnered with Veolia, our local waste management company. We asked them what was their most troublesome waste textile material. Without much hesitation, they suggested duvets and other bedding products. In Brighton and Hove, it's currently cheaper to buy a new single duvet than it is to get one washed! So, when Veolia collected duvets for us for a week, we easily had over 100 to experiment on – and this is documented in Part 3 in this book. However, what is interesting for this part of the book is that our prototype insulation batt was simply old duvets washed and then carefully placed in one of the 400 x 900 x 2400mm ply cassettes that form the external walls of the Waste House. By the time we had replaced the internal and external wall finishes, the duvet insulation batts were properly fire resistant while providing a U-value of about 0.10 W/m^2.K. Crucially, these duvets were simply reused, not recycled.

Another growth area in this sector is the recycling of demolition and 'spoil', which includes soil, clay, etc., from construction sites. This material constitutes over one-third of the 120 million tonnes of UK construction waste sent annually to landfill and incineration, so it's good news that there is a growing interest within the construction sector in reusing and recycling this former waste product. An early exponent of this approach is a company called StoneCycling. As with Dave Hakkens, this company was started at the Design Academy in Eindhoven, with an ambition to create new building materials from waste building materials. The founder of the company, Tom van Soest, 'started to grind, blend and process them in different ways'.[4] Among the numerous products van Soest produces is a series of attractive building bricks made from construction rubble (i.e. bricks and mortar). As with many of these companies, there is a secret ingredient or two.

However, there are now many actors in this sector, with Local Works Studio (more of whom later in this chapter) one of the most interesting companies applying traditional pre-proliferation-of-oil construction techniques, combined with a truly contemporary climate-emergency-focused sensibility, to produce beautiful 'new' products from what many would describe as construction waste. Interestingly, Local Works Studio is collaborating with larger established companies such as BC Materials in Belgium to roll out large numbers of bricks (more than 90,000) made from site spoil. Even developers are getting in on the act. Ben Spencer of GS8 in the UK has just completed a development of 12 homes in east London. Instead of removing the 100m^3 of spoil (created by digging down for foundations) from his site, Spencer collected the material and

Figure 2.2
Biohm mycelium insulation panels.

Figure 2.3
Biohm 'Orb' samples made with waste streams including grass, coffee and cork.

created 10,000 air-dried non-load-bearing earth bricks, some of which he used to form internal walls in the new homes. He has the others in storage for his next development.

Another group of waste flows worth highlighting is that of organic, compostable waste, which includes food waste and agro-waste. Since I wrote the first edition of this book, this sector has grown exponentially. Another part of the SB&WRC Interreg project I worked on asked us and our partners – the University of Bath, UniLaSalle in Rouen and ESITC Caen – to consider the potential for waste straw and sunflower stems to create insulation products. Straw panels of various types in the construction sector are relatively well known. However, insulation made from pith gathered from the huge amount of sunflower stems disposed of annually in France was news to me. In addition, my colleagues from UniLaSalle were prototyping sunflower pith for car dashboards, with the skin of the sunflower stem being reused as the surface finish, allowing the pith to create the firm but compressible car dashboard – incredible.

There is also an interesting cluster of organic materials being developed into products such as bricks, insulation and packing materials. These materials are literally grown in factory conditions. For example, one of the leading companies developing biomaterials, Ecovative, has a portfolio of organic materials that are marketed as 'safe, healthy and certified sustainable'. Myco Board is like a timber particleboard, but instead of using glues to bind the fibres, mycelium (the vegetative part of a fungus) is used. The same company produces the revolutionary Myco Foam that could replace much of the ubiquitous plastic packaging, as well as thermal and acoustic insulation. It is grown to order, while mixed with other waste organic matter such as corn husks, waste timber, etc. Bricks have also been grown by mixing corn husks (waste agricultural by-product) with silica (abundant) and mycelium (see the Hy-Fi case study, in Step 4). The resultant brick is solid and lightweight and durable to a point, though not a durable as a clay brick – yet.

As well as growing new organic materials, there is a lot of research into the reuse of agro-fibres, sourced as a residue of plant fibres (from the vast agricultural industries) that are often burnt, allowed to biodegrade or, worse, sent to landfill. However, for over 20 years a number of institutions have been looking into the potential of this waste material to benefit the automotive, aircraft, textile and construction industries. One of the leading centres for research is the Institute of Building Structures and Structural Design at the University of Stuttgart. Junior Professor Dr-Ing Hanaa Dahy, leading the BioMat Department there, specialises in biobased materials and material cycles in architecture. Dahy and her colleagues are busy identifying sources of agro-fibres and testing their

Figure 2.4
Biohm 'Orb' lights made with coffee chaff and earth mix.

application in architecture. Prototypes are in the form of green bio-composites and agro-plastic, where the natural fibres are bonded with biopolymers – all nontoxic and biodegradable. One of these developments is the Bio-flexi product, where elastic binders compound agricultural fibres to be applicable in various free-form applications and furniture. The materials have the potential to replace toxic, non-degradable, off-gassing plastics and participate in preserving forests, as wood fibres are being replaced by agro-fibres in this case. Current product experiments include prefabricated external cladding modules for buildings, including products like TRAshell, STRAWave and others, composed of green agro-fibre thermoset composites, free-orientated short natural fibres and plant-based thermoset bioresin. Agro-based particles are sourced from plant residue streams, including coconut shells, cereal straw and black coal ash, then used as an agro-filler. It's all very interesting for the near future: perhaps, truly organic architecture.

At the point of writing, though, perhaps the most high-profile of the start-ups looking at providing organic products for the construction sector is London-based Biohm.

Biohm is currently in the process of obtaining BBA (British Board of Agreement) Certification for its rigid insulation products made of mycelium (which consumes organic waste to grow), together with other products made from an organic component they call Orb that binds food-waste fibres and even soil. It has even developed a mycelium strain that can consume waste plastic to grow, so that one day a mycelium insulation production line could be 'fed' by waste petroleum-based insulation. Mycelium products are discussed in more detail in the Hy-Fi case study, in Step 4. However, while compiling *The Reuse Atlas*, it was interesting for me to consider in which section of the book mycelium products should reside: Recycling, Reusing, Reducing or Circular Economy.

> ## OPINION
>
> What we can see is that there are two strategies for these emerging materials. The first strategy locates a troublesome waste material (i.e. something that is quickly filling up landfill sites and is difficult to reuse, a material such as disposable nappies or building rubble). It then reprocesses this material into a useful, perhaps reusable product. The second strategy is to grow organic materials that could potentially replace materials that don't currently have an end-of-life strategy, such as plastics. The second strategy is perhaps the most exciting and forward thinking, while the first begins to deal with the environmental problems associated with materials that, while they have only been around in a big way for 100 years or so, and while they have been very useful, have had a massive negative impact on the planet.

CASE STUDY No.1

Adam Fairweather and Smile Plastics

THE STORY

Adam Fairweather set up Re-worked in 2005 as a project that became incorporated in 2010. It was a nonprofit business investing in green and social enterprises. This approach originated from Fairweather's research at the University of Brighton in 2003–4, where his lead project considered waste streams from within the coffee industry that could be recycled conspicuously within a circular economic model. In 2003, café culture was growing rapidly, along with the 'grab and go' fast-food culture that requires large amounts of packaging. Fairweather saw a huge opportunity to recycle coffee grounds into high-value products that could engage communities to challenge perceptions around waste and hopefully encourage reuse and recycling.

By 2004, Fairweather had developed a biodegradable polymer material that, incredibly, was made from waste coffee grounds. This material can be moulded into a robust and, crucially, reusable coffee cup to replace the ubiquitous paper/plastic throwaway cup. Re-worked received several grants to develop this work, initially through developing the material and subsequently through creating a working supply chain model. Although the coffee cup was never commercialised, it led to a spate of interesting new products and collaborations.

Re-worked soon began a collaboration with recycling pioneers Smile Plastics, a producer of decorative recycled plastic panels. Founded in 1994, its products have been used around the world in spaces such as the V&A, Design Museum, Wellcome Collection, The Body Shop, Selfridges and Paul Smith. Fairweather developed a working relationship with Jane Enfield and Colin Williamson, the founders of Smile Plastics. From 2004, they allowed Fairweather to do production work on his experimental materials in their factories. So, Fairweather was allowed to experiment while learning how to use the Smile Plastics machinery. Unfortunately, Smile Plastics may well

Figure 2.5
Shredding waste plastic at Smile Plastics.

Figure 2.6
Blending waste plastic at Smile Plastics.

Figure 2.7
Full sheet of recycled plastic coming off the production line.

Figures 2.8 and 2.9
Smile Plastics in a kitchen designed by CAN Architects.

have been a bit ahead of its time and it folded in 2008, just as Fairweather was creating a business circuit with it. However, in 2014, Fairweather contacted Enfield and Williamson and asked for their blessing to allow him to relaunch the Smile Plastics brand again, as he was convinced it still had the potential to be impactful and successful. As Fairweather said to me, 'The product had lost its voice and sadly designers had lost the opportunity to use this amazing, recycled material.'

Re-worked no longer exists. As Fairweather says, 'Since 2003, it has been a vessel for work looking at sustainable materials and future material languages. It has now taken over the Smile Plastics brand and growing this brand is our main focus at the moment.'

Now Fairweather and his life and business partner Rosalie McMillan are focusing on building the company, with ideas of creating a network of low-carbon businesses across the country

> **OPINION**
>
> I first interviewed Adam Fairweather for this book in 2016. Looking back on my summary then, I am struck by how the case study works just as well for this latest edition, although so much has happened to Fairweather and Rosalie McMillan. So, I am leaving it as it was, except to say that their time has come. Thanks to their skill, tenacity and business vision, Smile Plastics is their current main focus, and as a result is now a successful and expanding company, sticking to its mission to prove that so-called waste is a valuable resource that can be recycled into beautiful products.
>
> This case study proves just how vibrant and creative the UK design industry is. It also shows how determined individuals need to be to make a success of their ideas. Fairweather has had to reassess the whole supply chain, as well as the production methodologies within it, to enable his designs to be realised. He has also been 'light on his feet', never allowing a brilliant design idea that was perhaps ahead of its time and not destined for mass production to become a vanity project. He learnt from that experience and then moved on to other circular-economy-focused projects. It is perhaps the challenges presented by the closed-loop concept that interest Fairweather most, not a particular solution.

Figure 2.10
Detail of Smile Plastics in a kitchen designed by CAN Architects.

Figure 2.11
'One day, these Smile Plastics kitchen work surfaces could be recycled back into kitchen chopping boards!'

(they are based in Wales) that develop their own products but have the opportunity of learning from their (almost) 20 years of experience. Fairweather thinks that one of the reasons Smile Plastics is successful today and expanding (it currently employs more than 50 people) is because of the huge popularity of Dave Hakkens' open hardware/digital commons plastic recycling project Precious Plastic, which created an opportunity for anyone interested to set up their own miniature recycling company. Precious Plastic currently has an international network (Hakkens is based in the Netherlands) of over 40,000 people in over 500 companies. Smile Plastics has also found itself at the right time with the right people. Fairweather still has time to be creative, while McMillan (also a creative) is able to ensure that the business plan is sound. Today the company can sell you 100% recycled and recyclable plastic products made from 100% waste material from their Classic Collection, which will be familiar to most designers and architects who loved the original products. They can also develop 'custom materials' with clients. This process allows clients to 'blend a custom material' with Fairweather and his team, much like Hakkens' Precious Plastic project. Finally, the company offers a design and making service for products made with Smile Plastics materials, supplying the wonderfully creative architect Mat Barnes of CAN Architects with beautiful kitchen cabinets made from waste plastic chopping boards. As Barnes says, 'One day these kitchen cupboard doors could be recycled back into kitchen chopping boards!'

CASE STUDY No.2

Gum-tech

THE STORY

It is a little-known fact that UK councils spend over £150 million a year removing chewing gum from pavements and other surfaces. Chewing gum is humankind's most common habit, with over 3.74 trillion sticks of the stuff made every year. This equates to over 100,000 tonnes of gum manufactured annually. There is one very well-known negative outcome from all this chewing and that is where most of the gum ends up: on our pavements. It is estimated that 90% of all paving slabs have

Figure 2.14
The original Gumdrop Bin.

Figure 2.12
A mini bin for chewing gum.

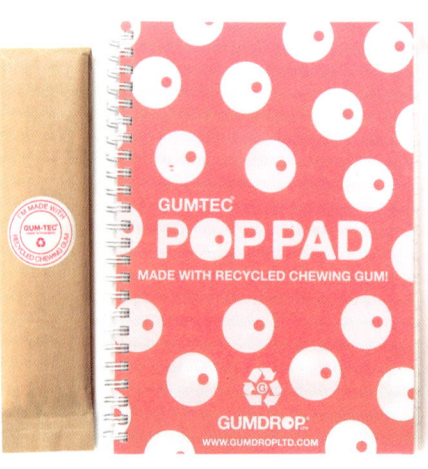

Figure 2.13
Stationery made from waste chewing gum.

Figure 2.15
Gumdrop soles on Adidas Stan Smith shoes.

discarded chewing gum on them, with Oxford Street in London playing host to over 250,000 blobs.[5] The removal of this waste is an expense most local authorities would rather not have, and many cannot afford.

In 2009, Anna Bullus was studying design when she had an idea to create bins specifically designed to deal with the problem of collecting chewing gum. What was even more interesting is that Bullus discovered that waste gum could be reprocessed into a range of plastic-type compounds that could then be used as a resource in the rubber and plastics industry. It took Bullus only eight months in college to prove the concept. However, it took another five years to commercialise and scale up the process to recycle chewing gum into marketable Gum-tec compounds that can be infinitely reprocessed without losing any of their first-generation qualities. Recycling often renders a material less effective than the first time it is processed, but not in this case.

What Bullus proposed was hugely ambitious. She wanted to create a genuinely closed-loop recycling process that added value to an environmentally destructive material. By designing a chewing gum bin that was actually made of waste chewing gum, Bullus has simultaneously reduced the environmental burden of this plastic while creating a clever product that requires this material to enable further production of Gumdrop Bins. By collecting bins when they are full and reprocessing them again into more gum bins, Bullus has created her own closed-loop system. Bullus has plans to utilise these compounds as a material source for other products, such as Gum Boots and pretty much anything else that can be effectively extruded, injection- and blow-moulded using these recycled plastic compounds.

OPINION

Anna Bullus has had a brilliant idea that digs down deep and completely understands the problems associated with the waste product we know as chewing gum. The Gumdrop Bin relies on being an eye-catching object, if only for a couple of seconds. If it succeeds in enticing you to throw away your old chewing gum (and apparently over 46% of gum normally thrown on the ground ends up in these bins, if installed) then it has also allowed you, the end user, to participate in a genuinely circular, closed-loop production process.

As with all Step 1 case studies in this book, the Gumdrop Bin can be criticised by Cradle to Cradle experts as perpetuating the production of one of an expanding family of unintelligent plastic materials: unintelligent because it is toxic to the natural environment, cannot or is hardly ever reused (although in this particular case it can be recycled), and it doesn't biodegrade. It therefore creates huge environmental problems if left to be simply thrown away. Bullus has skilfully turned this linear metabolism that is the normal life cycle of chewing gum (made, chewed, stuck on a pavement) into a circular metabolism involving the potential for perpetual reprocessing, which in turn reduces the environmental burden.

Recent increases in the cost of shipping materials across the planet, together with an increased awareness of the environmental issues, has, according to Bullus, resulted in a massive increase in enquiries into Gum-tec materials, mainly from the automotive and fashion sectors. However, Bullus is also developing products for the construction sector, with window seals and damp-proof courses being some of the ideas currently being considered. Gum-tec has recently developed its own yarn made from old chewing gum. This has opened up possibilities for creating own-branded shoes and fashion items, which, as Bullus is keen to point out, is an opportunity to ensure that products sent out into the world can come back to Gum-tec for recycling at the end of their 'first' useful lives.

Being in control of product development allows Bullus the opportunity to impose closed-loop systems. This is not always possible. Gum-tec recently collaborated with Adidas to produce a series of special Stan Smith training shoes with recycled chewing gum soles. The range was very popular and sold out very quickly (Bullus thinks that about 350,000 were made). However, Adidas will not be taking back these shoes when they are worn out. So, they will most likely be thrown away.

Getting involved in the synthetic plastics business is complex, and environmentalists will often state that by recycling you are justifying the manufacture of more virgin plastic. Bullus is quite rightly critical of the current acceleration of 'greenwashing', especially in the fashion sector. She is more encouraged by the automotive industry, which she says appears to be more committed to sustainability than most. However, if Bullus can develop products that people want, products that can be returned to Gum-tec at the end of their useful lives, then she will have created a genuinely closed-loop system that will go some way towards raising the profile of responsible resource management.

CASE STUDY No.3

Overtreders W and Pretty Plastic

THE STORY

Hester van Dijk and Reinder Bakker have known each other since secondary school. They both studied what van Dijk describes as 'the arty side of product design' at the Design Academy Eindhoven. With the help and encouragement of the Academy, they formed Overtreders W straight after graduating. Pledging to 'never have a boring day', the pair were determined to practise in an unconventional way.

With the opinion that 'there is no need for a new chair design', the partnership focused on three-dimensional environments instead. They were determined to go for projects outside their comfort zone; to get 'acquainted with territories that were previously unknown to us'.

Pretty quickly, they were designing installations for festivals, trade fairs and exhibitions, which, of course, put them in clear sight of the huge amount of waste generated by temporary and short-lived products and structures. Van Dijk describes how they were trying to reuse some beautiful timber from a trade show that was being taken down. When they arrived 30 minutes later than planned to pick up the material, it had already been smashed up and thrown away into massive skips, along with everything else that had been standing for only a few days.

This situation did not sit well with van Dijk and Bakker, who were determined to reduce the amount of waste created by their own projects.

They currently inhabit a rarefied place in the world of architecture: that of maverick designers and thinkers determined to shake up the system by looking at it in a fresh way. As they state on their website, 'The best ideas may occur when strolling through unknown terrain.'[6] They now have an enviable track record of designing award-winning temporary pavilions that can be assembled and reused again and again. And with this approach, they are perhaps best known for their People's Pavilion, a 300m^2 building that existed for just nine days, built entirely out of borrowed materials. Thinking through the design of the People's Pavilion, van Dijk and Bakker realised that in fact all materials and resources are 'borrowed from the finite resource stock of our planet', and that the big problem is simply that humans are usually 'bad borrowers' with no concern as to how we acquire resources, use them or dispose of them.

This case study also discusses the offshoot company Pretty Plastic set up by van Dijk and Bakker, together with Peter van Assche of SLA Architects. At the beginning of 2015, the three directors were able to look at a shipping container's worth of waste plastic. It immediately occurred to them that this material was not only beautiful, but potentially reusable/recyclable into future products. So, they set up their company Pretty Plastic and started experimenting and prototyping what would become an external wall tile for buildings. Their tiles varied in colour, and to a certain extent texture, depending on the colour of the source material. These were the qualities that van Dijk, Bakker and van Assche enjoyed; qualities that gave their tiles an authentic narrative and hinted at the provenance of the source material. In short, their tiles have character and an identity. However, after

Figure 2.16
Shredded waste PVC processed by Pretty Plastic.

Clockwise from top left:

Figure 2.17
Pretty Plastic black tiles made from recycled plastic, installed on a music pavilion for the St Oelbert Gymnasium in Oosterhout, the Netherlands, designed by Grosfeld Bekkers van der Velde Architecten.

Figure 2.18
Close-up of the black tiles on the music pavilion.

Figure 2.19
Multicoloured versions of Pretty Plastic's recycled tiles.

Figure 2.20
Close-up of one of Pretty Plastic's coloured tiles.

visiting many of the leading plastic product manufacturers in the Netherlands, there was little enthusiasm for their slightly unpredictable tiles. Traditional suppliers of plastic products were used to producing them quickly, cheaply and definitely with a consistent colour and texture.

The Pretty Plastic team still believed there was a commercial future in recycled plastic products, so they set up their own production facilities (the Pretty Plastic Plant) and for a number of months they produced more than a thousand tiles for interior design projects. They then secured the commission of the People's Pavilion for Dutch Design Week in 2017 that required more than 9,000 unique plastic upcycled tiles. It was at this point that the Belgium recycling company Govaplast offered to take over the engineering and production of the Pretty Plastic tiles. In 2019, their tiles gained Class B Fire certification (NEN-EN 13501-1), which allows their tiles to be applied to any building, and in 2020 the first new permanent building with Pretty Plastic tiles was completed, a music pavilion for the St Oelbert Gymnasium in Oosterhout, the Netherlands.

OPINION

The fact that recycled material might look different to the material in its first life is a characteristic that can be embraced. If the performance of the recycled product is what it needs to be, then its heritage can be expressed and even celebrated. Van Dijk and Bakker, like many pathfinder designers and architects before them, have had to create products for their projects that live up to their design ethos and expectations. As product designers that have drifted into architecture or, as they state, 'become acquainted with territories that were previously unknown to us', Overtreders W are shaking up our industry, proffering new ideas and questioning the way we normally do things. They haven't been trained to design conventional buildings, they have been trained to question the norm, to consistently ask questions and, crucially, to collaborate. As they say, 'We make our best work when clients give us trust.'

CASE STUDY No.4

Local Works Studio

THE STORY

This is the story of a couple of people who have known each other for over 25 years. They have a shared sensibility and clarity about the way they want to effect system change, and they readily describe themselves as 'stubborn, optimistic and collaborative'.

Local Works Studio was formed in 2017 with a clear mission to create an alternative way of doing; to effect positive system change in a world where the normal response to the climate and ecological emergency didn't feel urgent enough. It was set up as a partnership between landscape architect Loretta Bosence, who is a tutor at the Bartlett School of Architecture, and her life/business partner Ben Bosence, who graduated from the Royal College of Art. Ben studied ceramics, only to become an expert in vernacular construction techniques after working for a large workshop in Brighton making traditional moulded terracotta and bricks. He then set up a successful building conservation company and spent a number of years restoring historic buildings and learning about the traditional materials and construction techniques. Loretta has a background in sculpture and photography and obtained her master's at the Slade School of Fine Art, later jumping careers to landscape architecture, via studying advanced practical horticulture and running a garden design-and-build business specialising in experimental learning environments.

Local Works Studio's work is big on narrative: on place, on people, on process and system change, and they are passionate about turning linear systems into circular ones. They rigorously (remember they describe themselves as stubborn!) apply these interests to a wide variety of work, ranging in scale from a single artefact, via installations, whole buildings, landscapes and design strategies for neighbourhoods… and they do this in collaboration with community groups, academic institutions, designers, architects, engineers and artists.

I have placed Local Works Studio in the Recycle section of this book because, although Loretta and Ben do much of their work in the world of reuse and closed-loop systems, they are well aware that if one actually takes part in a very well-managed deconstruction project, there will always be a certain percentage of material that is only fit for reprocessing, i.e. recycling. So, it's their recycling work, often associated with their reuse projects, that is focused on here.

Ben once said to me that what he liked about vernacular construction materials (based on lime and clay) is that as they age and erode, they fall to the ground, and if you were so inclined, you could scrape this material up, add a bit of water and reuse it. Within a couple of months of this statement, my University of Brighton colleague Nick Gant had suggested that we work with Ben and Loretta on an Interreg project called 'SB&WRC' (Sustainable Bio and Waste Resources for Construction). As part of this project, Ben and Nick designed and prototyped insulation batts made from synthetic duvet filling, as well as from duck and goose feathers from posh duvets. Ben and Loretta also created tiles made from waste oyster shells. (For more on this project, see Part 3 of this book.) This technique represents a significant saving in resources. Ben states, 'We're working with 50kg of oyster shells per m^2 of hung tile. Traditional clay tiles would require 78kg/m^2. So, less material than normal and, of course, this was waste material on its way to landfill.'

Local Works Studio has always combined rigorous research with teaching and a deliberate approach to practice. This is probably how Ben and Loretta have been able to apply their research to 'real projects' so quickly. They are currently working on building projects where they help us (Nick Gant and myself) apply a 'research mapping exercise', looking for material sources at the Waste House site (see Part 3), near to site, in the locale; anything rather than import new. This technique has allowed Ben and Loretta to come up with concrete-type copings, clay and lime plaster, renders and tiles made from waste glass and other materials such as rubble, chalk and clay found on site, or created as part of the construction process. And they are doing this type of work with numerous other practices.

Figure 2.21
Local Works Studio were the material specialists for a building project in East Sussex. Pictured are chalk and clay plaster samples made with materials found on site.

Figure 2.22
New windowsills made from waste bricks and chalk found on the East Sussex site.

OPINION

Ben and Loretta have a relatively small company, and it will be interesting to see how they continue to develop. Ben is at pains to point out that Local Works Studio is a prototyping workshop. So, for example, they are currently working with UK architects Carmody Groarke on a large extension to the Ghent Design Museum. The museum's director was keen to ensure that this project had a low embodied carbon footprint. Working with a grant from Circular Flanders, the museum has been able to invest in developing innovative low-carbon construction systems and material sources. Local Works Studio was commissioned to come up with ideas for low-carbon material options for the building. Ben and Loretta travelled to the site of the museum extension and tested the soil that would be displaced by the project to see if it was possible to use it as source material for new bricks. It was. What is rather unusual is that the material they tested was suitable to make mechanically compressed hydraulic bricks that are not fired, just compressed. And even more interestingly, these completely unfired bricks could be used as the external finish of the extension to the Ghent Design Museum. Ben claims that the embodied CO_2 saving alone is profound: they have approximately one-third of the embodied energy of a typical clay-fired brick. In addition, these hydraulic bricks are made with material lying around on the actual building site. Now they know the material in Ghent is up to reuse, they have partnered with a local brick manufacturing company – in this case BC Materials in Belgium – who themselves specialise in using excavated earth of construction sites to make building materials, to scale up the process. This will save on the road and sea miles that would have been created if Local Works Studio had manufactured the bricks. In addition, Loretta points out that as the bricks are not fired, they can be made in urban environments – on site even – as no firing of bricks means no air pollution. They are also interested in raising awareness of this way of working, so the bricks will also include other waste streams found near to the Design Museum, in this case ceramic WC pans and wash-hand basins destined for landfill.

Like many companies providing an authentic low-carbon alternative to normal practice, Ben and Loretta are busy sticking to their principles, navigating a world that is beginning to realise that the only way to exist in harmony with our host planet is to apply wholesale system change, not to greenwash 'business as usual'.

Clockwise from top left:

Figure 2.23
Burnt masonry waste sorted for reuse as window cills on site in East Sussex.

Figure 2.24
A hydraulically compressed silt-and-spoil brick prototype.

Figure 2.25
Reprocessing waste chalk for new plaster on site in East Sussex.

Figure 2.26
Lime mortar and brick prototype using materials from burnt-out house on site in East Sussex.

CASE STUDY No.5

a:gain

THE STORY

While interviewing architect Anders Lendager about his famous Resource Rows housing scheme (see Resource Rows case study in Step 2), he mentioned a number of different offshoot projects he has been responsible for since establishing his own eponymous practice. This is typical of thought leaders, pathfinders and early adopters. For example, in the early days of High Tech, a few of the UK pathfinder architects had to create their own modular steel sandwich panel companies to supply the appropriate product for their innovative buildings. Similarly, Lendager Group and other consultants need authentic second-hand products and materials for their expanding portfolio of projects with the circular economy at their core.

a:gain is just such an operation. Initially set up in 2021, it already offers a collection of different products that are either second-hand taken from deconstructed buildings, or items reprocessed from waste streams created by the deconstruction industry. In addition, a:gain spends just as much effort finding waste flows from other sectors to repurpose for the construction sector.

However, as Mathias Ruø Rasmussen, Head of Product Development at a:gain, states, initially when he was at Lendager they developed products for specific pilot projects in the studio with the ambition of showing off new ways of reusing waste material. This often led to many of the 'cool ideas being left behind', because although realised, these ideas were never expanded. Once the project was completed, the practice would move on to the next project, often leaving early 'proof-of-concept ideas' unrealised.

a:gain is an independent company formed by taking out some of the development team from Lendager with the mandate to develop products made from waste and surplus material, not architectural projects. Crucially, this allows the team to consider if their ideas are scalable and attractive to the construction sector, and then hopefully many practices who are interested in reuse will want to specify their products.

a:gain currently operates with a core team of six or seven people. Like many busy start-ups, the skill sets of the founding team are broad and diverse, ensuring they can develop quickly

Figure 2.27
Textile waste for soundproofing – gathered and processed by a:gain.

Figure 2.28
Fibre for soundproofing felt – gathered and processed by a:gain.

and successfully. So, in addition to Ruø Rasmussen, who is an architect with experience of reuse, there are engineers, product designers, material specialists, architectural technicians, investors and, crucially, a capable salesperson. But perhaps most important of all at this early stage of development, a:gain has a link with Anders Lendager, who provides a captive audience interested in its products. When I interviewed Ruø Rasmussen, a:gain had just done a pitch to Bjarke Ingels Group (BIG), which suggests that it will do well.

a:gain relies on its numerous partners because it has no in-house testing or production capabilities. However, a:gain is definitely the product lead; its team are instrumental in deciding what ideas to follow, in organising the testing and prototyping, as well as agreeing what the product looks like and which company to partner for the production. To ensure that a:gain's Intellectual Property is not lost, it has contracts with the companies that create the source material for these 'new' products made from waste.

One of its latest partnerships is with the established Danish parquet flooring company Junckers, which has large marketing, sales and technology departments. a:gain took a look at the waste flows and surplus material generated by the production of massive amounts of hardwood flooring and worked with Junckers to come up with innovative ideas for the collection and manufacture of an alternative floor finish. The first of these, Funderø, is a combination of either oak and ash or beech and maple offcuts, and is currently for sale on a:gain's own website. Alternatively, you can buy another timber floor finish called Hjælmø, made from second-hand pine glulam boards and window frames.

Nærø acoustic felt is produced from worn-out workwear. The source material is sorted and cleaned before being ground into short fibres suitable to be felted. In addition, a fire retardant is added. Once the felting process is complete, the result is a non-woven, dense, textile material suitable for commercial acoustic

Figure 2.29
Reused flooring waiting for distribution.

From top:

Figure 2.30
Soundproofing textile colour options.

Figure 2.31
Reprocessed Junckers flooring by a:gain.

Figure 2.32
Junckers 'Classic Danish' timber flooring made from different Junckers offcuts.

panels. Although currently for sale on a:gain's website, Ruø Rasmussen points out that the product is still being developed for improved fire and flame resistance.

One final product to highlight is Flarø. Ruø Rasmussen describes how a:gain collects beech packers used between large steel beams when they are loaded up, stacked and transported. These packers are actually high-grade solid lumps of timber that are used on numerous occasions, and so they get a proper battering. a:gain collects, planes and cuts them into beautiful beech planks, adds oil or lacquer and reuses the material as an interior finish. Ruø Rasmussen states, 'What is particularly lovely is that the mould, water penetration and marks made by many impacts only help create a beautiful finish for this "new" product made from a material destined for incineration.' a:gain combines this timber with its own Nærø acoustic felt to create a modular acoustic wall batt.

OPINION

Mathias Ruø Rasmussen is clear that the first task when they set up a:gain was to try to focus on the most impactful and commercially viable products. Now the a:gain team has the time to develop products fully, they can spend time looking into ways to meet the exacting needs of our industry, while also meeting the high-level objectives of dramatically reducing the consumption of natural raw materials. They try to make their products as similar to existing products as possible, so that designers and constructors don't have to relearn their respective ways of doing in order to be impactful. I guess it's like saying, 'You can be circular and we (a:gain) will take the systems change required on the chin for you!'

a:gain is turning waste that has its origins in the factories and the construction sites of our industry into products supplying these very same sites; turning a linear system into a closed-loop circular one. Good work.

STEP 2

Reusing Waste

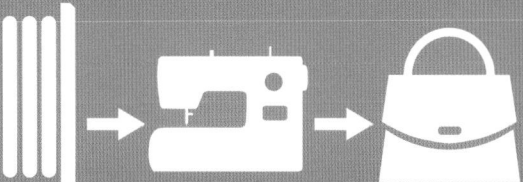

DEFINITION

MAKING PRODUCTS by reusing either synthetic or organic material adds value to materials that would normally be thrown away. These products require inventive designers that see potential in stuff others discard. Crucially, the following reuse projects do not reprocess waste material and therefore they do not have the large carbon footprints associated with Step 1 recycling projects. This is a big leap forward from recycling as the value of the waste resource can stay the same or, on occasion, it can increase.

AN INTRODUCTION TO URBAN MINING

For the record, I believe it will be competing city states and regions that give us hope for systems change, not national governments preoccupied with numerous other 'big issues' before they can think of addressing the climate and ecological emergency in an authentic way. With over 50% of the world's population now residing in cities,[1] and 84% of the UK's population living in urban areas,[2] cities are now the main driver for economic and system change and have the potential to power a successful circular economy. Most resources flow in and out of cities: they are the main facilitators of mass linear 'take, make and throw away' consumerism. Unlike natural ecosystems, where waste from one part is a resource for another, cities in the Global North tend to keep resource flows separate, thus facilitating the speedy flow of vast amounts of stuff in and out of our metropolitan environments.

This essay highlights the pathfinders and early adopters who are endeavouring to break down silos and turn linear flows into circular opportunities and, in the case of the built environment, to become 'urban miners', reusing the previously manufactured to create our new low-carbon, healthy, inclusive and climate-resilient cities.

There is no getting away with it. We humans consume a huge amount of stuff, and you will read many different statistics in this book that try to make this more tangible. How can we comprehend what 50% of 120 billion tonnes looks like? This is the amount of raw materials humans mine and harvest from the Earth each year, and 50% is the share that the construction and habitation of buildings takes.[3] Perhaps it is better to put it like this. Nearly 90% of all raw materials harvested and mined

Figure 2.33
Cities are material stores.

annually are destined to become waste, and a massive 80% of products bought today are thrown away within six months.[4] It is obvious that humans need to apply a brand-new sensibility to the way we exist, one that mirrors the way healthy, natural ecosystems function, where the act of throwing 'away' is demonised and adequately penalised, and where the act of keeping, adapting and reusing is encouraged and subsidised.

Reuse is the big deal

As stated previously, the art of reusing adapting/bodging/not throwing much, if anything, away was once the preferred way of functioning for most of humankind until we simply forgot how to reuse. The 20th century established mass consumerism as a way of life for the Global North and installed the myth of endless growth on a finite planet. So how can we change these relatively recent bad habits and relearn what we used to know: that there *really* is no such thing as waste, just stuff in the wrong place?

The main point of the Step 2 – Reusing Waste section of this book is to shine a light on construction projects employing reuse strategies that benefit all parties, and that create beautiful built environments delivered on time and on budget, while reusing as much existing built fabric and material as possible. However, it should be noted that reuse is the most challenging of the practices. As Step 4 – The Circular Economy will highlight, designing new buildings as closed-loop circular systems waiting to become resources for future buildings is relatively straightforward to do; it's simply that there isn't the will or knowledge to make this practice more commonplace. Step 3 considers ways in which we can reduce our consumption of resources to achieve our needs within the built environment sector. Like Step 4, it is challenging and involves systems change, but in many ways, it is quite straightforward when compared to reuse. Step 2 – Reusing Waste only works well if we can work with the previously manufactured: to quote myself, we must 'mine the Anthropocene' or the Anthroposphere, but unfortunately most of this stuff has not been designed with deconstruction and reuse in mind.

Reuse is difficult to do

Attempting to deconstruct buildings that date from the early 20th century up until the present day is a huge challenge. They represent the greater part of the built environment in Europe and North America and tend to be constructed as monoliths fused together using 'wet trades' such as poured concrete (often reinforced with steel) or bricks and blocks stuck together with cement-based mortars stronger than the masonry they bind together. More up-to-date building systems, such as modular steel and aluminium composite panels, are often glued together. Even more recently, and all in the name of airtightness and low operational carbon emissions, the external fabric of buildings is sealed using expanding plastic foam that renders future reuse almost impossible.

Despite all the above, the good news is that there is an increasing number of consultants, contractors and clients learning how to deconstruct buildings or elements of buildings that for decades have been thought too difficult to reuse. In addition, times are rapidly changing. Due to the current cost-of-living crisis, most humans living in the high-consuming Global North understand that resource security is a thing of the past. Construction projects are struggling to get built due to a lack of new materials and available labour that inevitably leads to prohibitive construction costs. And so, I would argue that *now* is the time to work with, rework and keep what we have already constructed; to think of the existing built environment as valuable 'infrastructure' for a new built environment, one that sees the many values of the existing, and adapts it to a low-carbon, climate-resilient version of its previous self without tearing the former down and throwing it away. And please remember what Kevin Lynch wrote in 1990 in his book *Wasting Away*: 'We cannot throw anything away, since there no longer is an "away".'[5]

Before we dive into the inspirational case studies that make up the greater part of this book, I wanted to give credit to the people and networks, both physical and digital, that make reuse, or what is increasingly being known as 'urban mining', a viable option. And to do that I wanted to go back about 50 years in time, back to the mid-1970s when former architecture student Thornton Kay was given the opportunity to clear 1.25 acres of derelict land in the centre of Bath in southwest England. The idea was that Kay would set up a salvage yard which would take advantage of the many 18th- and 19th-century buildings being torn down in favour of 'modern' developments. Kay soon became one of a growing number of people concerned about the loss of valuable built heritage and spent the next decade helping to raise awareness of its cultural and architectural value. By the middle of the 1980s, he was employing more than 100 people and was partially responsible for getting large areas of Bath protected from demolition and listed by English Heritage. Along the way, he got to campaign directly to central government, encouraging the reuse of architectural components.

In 1990, Kay set up Salvo, the first printed directory of salvage companies across the UK. By 1995, Salvo had launched its first online directory and rapidly expanded, providing national reclamation directories for Ireland, France, Spain, the Netherlands, Belgium, Germany and even the USA. Kay points out that between 1970 and 1990, when Salvo started, the UK was easily the world leader in the reclamation and reuse of building materials. Unfortunately, since 1990, the amount of reclaimed and reused material as a percentage of the total construction materials has been gradually falling. By 2018, it represented only about 1% of all construction materials.[6] One of the reasons for this has been the steady rise of recycling instead of reuse, perhaps partly driven by a misunderstanding in the 1990s on the part of the UK government, who failed to appreciate the difference between reuse and recycling.

In 2016, Salvo claimed to have demolition statistics from nine countries representing 50% of the world's population. With this information, it was able to estimate that the mass of buildings demolished every year worldwide was about 8 gigatonnes. Of this, around 800 million tonnes, or 10% of the total materials and products from demolished buildings, would be easily reusable if the buildings were carefully deconstructed. All it needed was a greater awareness across the construction sector of the huge potential that reuse presents. Salvo also pointed out, 'A quarter of the world's annual energy is used to make 15Gt of new building products each year. The energy used emits $10GtCO_2e$, which is a quarter of the world's emissions.'[7]

In 2018, Salvo was invited by the team at Rotor in Brussels to be part of the international Interreg project known as FCRBE (Facilitating the Circulation of Reclaimed Building Elements in Northwestern Europe), which 'aimed to increase by 50% the

Figure 2.34
Salvo reuse platform.

amount of reclaimed building elements being circulated on its territory [six Northern European countries] by 2032.'8 This project is discussed at length in other parts of this book; however, it should be noted here that it has produced numerous open-source guides to deconstruction and, crucially, to the reuse of said deconstructed elements in new construction projects. FCRBE will also provide a directory of 1,500 'suppliers' working in this emerging deconstruction sector. In addition, my colleagues and I at the University of Brighton were responsible for curating and hosting the pedagogic output of the FCRBE project: a summer school we named the School of Re-Construction, for students of architecture, design and engineering that worked with FCRBE themes.

I also want to acknowledge that there are many challenges that appear to prevent us all introducing principles of the circular economy into a vast construction industry designed to make short-term profits from a predominately linear take-make-and-demolish system. If we have half a chance of changing this apparent status quo, there are many questions that need answering. I have listed a few below:

- Where can I find a deconstruction company?
- Who does pre-deconstruction audits?
- Who knows how to deconstruct a building?
- How do you know what an old building is made of?
- How can I get a performance warranty on second-hand material?
- What system is best to invest in to help deconstruction and reuse – a digital exchange platform or a massive warehouse/re-manufactory?
- Do I have the time or the money to invest in reuse?
- Will my bank provide me with a loan for a reuse project?

And this one, particularly pertinent to the UK: 'If I retrofit my house, the government charges 20% VAT on all labour and materials. If I demolish my house and start again, there is no VAT, so isn't it cheaper to demolish?'

I am hoping that most, if not all, the above questions will be answered by this book as it describes the exciting and vital ground-breaking work being done by a rapidly increasing collection of individuals and groups across Europe and beyond.

I want also to briefly consider the pioneers who kicked off the contemporary debate around how best to procure second-hand material from the existing built environment. I will start with Superuse Studios, who are based in Rotterdam and have quite correctly earned an international reputation for delivering buildings and landscapes made from previously used materials. This work is discussed later in this chapter (Case Study No. 2). However, and perhaps even more impactful than this, Superuse invented an early GIS- (geographic information system) informed web-based digital platform highlighting the availability of second-hand materials and components in real time. Launched in 2012, oogstkaart.nl was one of the first live digital marketplaces for reusable materials that worked at a national level. To prove that this system could work, Superuse created buildings and playgrounds from materials harvested from the oogskaart.nl site, although it should be pointed out that the platform is open to everybody to use.

Superuse doesn't own warehouses that sort, clean and store deconstructed stuff until a project requires all or part of it; it works with digital platforms. However, it is worth considering the physical and digital infrastructure required to support the circular economy. Rotor Deconstruction, for example, is a cooperative based in Brussels for the sole reason of organising the reuse of construction materials. Its services include an active Acquisition Team dedicated to finding materials and establishing partnerships. Rotor Deconstruction also prepares and processes materials suitable for selling in its own shop and digital platform. Rotor Deconstruction is predominately analogue when compared to Superuse's digital approach. The question is, which way will predominate? This is a question that probably needs to be answered quickly, as we see the

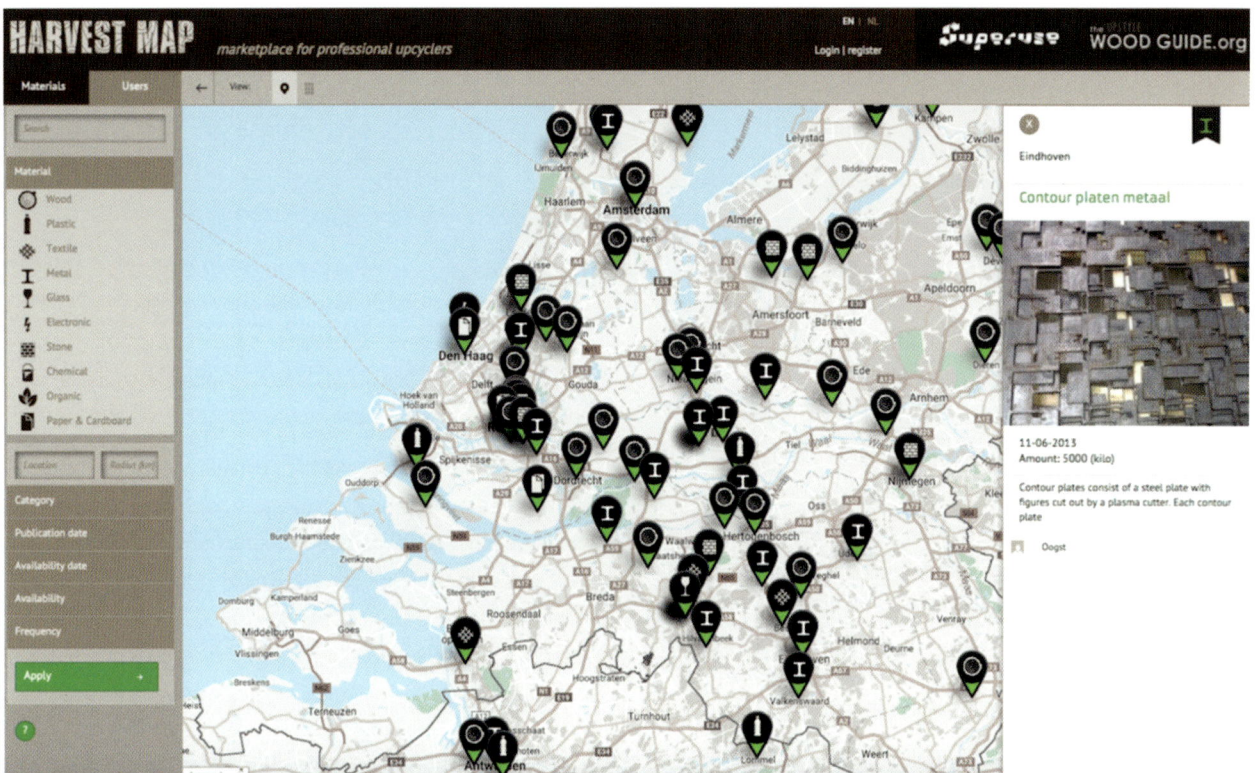

Figure 2.35
The original Harvest Map by Superuse. The map uses geographic representations to help identify and prioritise waste materials near to a specific project site.

number of metropolitan authorities across the UK and Europe which have published ambitious Circular Economy Routemaps, declared themselves 'doughnut cities'[9] or net zero carbon by 2030 (!). They are quickly realising that the digital and physical systems are not in place to make it viable.

It is likely that the digital and physical will work in partnership. Circular economy construction hubs, re-manufactories, or whatever they end up getting called, will be required to act as a buffer between the 'famine and feast' scenarios that the second-hand supply chain really presents. Deconstructed materials also need to be checked, cleaned, tested for appropriate levels of performance, given new warranties, etc., before they can be sent off into the supply chain. In addition, deconstruction and reuse creates its own waste streams, and they need to be reprocessed into useful materials as well. We will require 're-manufactories'. In addition, while we are still developing an understanding of the potential of reuse, these re-manufactories will also need to be centres of research and learning.

The other big question being asked at the moment relates to establishing the best methods for identifying the types and amount of reusable (rather than recyclable or disposable) materials in an existing building. One of the pioneers of these deep digital survey techniques is Dr Elma Durmisevic. Founding Director of 4D Architects and creator of the Laboratory for Green Transformable Buildings, Durmisevic is the curator of Sarajevo's brilliant Green Design Biennale. She was also the Principal Investigator for the impactful research realised by the Horizon 2020 EU-funded 'Buildings as Material Banks' (BAMB) Project. In addition, over the last 20 years Durmisevic has pioneered digital tools that can survey existing buildings and not only quantify what the buildings are constructed of, but also ascertain the quality of individual elements. The 3D models (often 'exploded' for visual clarity) created by Durmisevic's digital tools are also colour-coded in order that one might quantify not only the type and quantity of material and component, but also its state of repair and therefore its ability to be reused

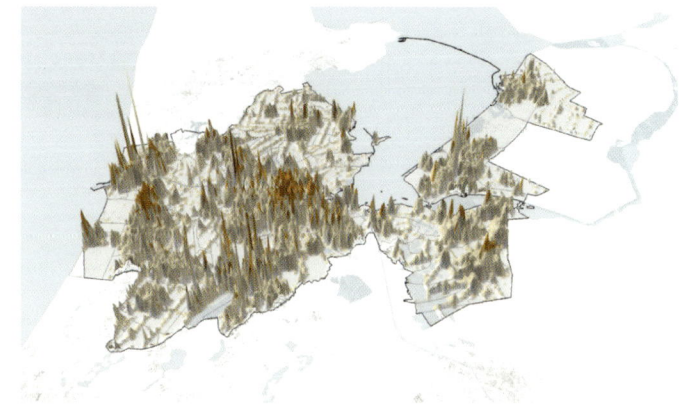

Figure 2.36
Amsterdam construction material resource map by Metabolic.

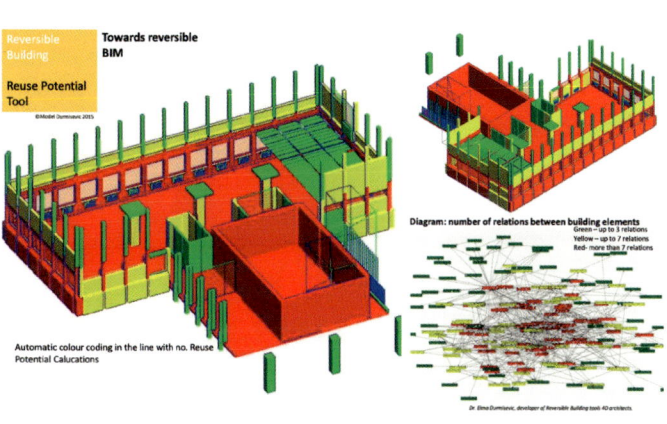

Figure 2.37
Reuse metabolic tool by Dr Elma Durmisevic.

or at least to be recycled. When I interviewed Durmisevic in 2022, she mentioned a project for a hospital complex in the Netherlands which was due for demolition. Durmisevic had completed one of her deep digital surveys, as a consequence of which the modular steel frame was currently available for sale online, although it was still installed within the building fabric of the hospital. If the frame was sold, it would transform the demolition project into a much more financially lucrative deconstruction project.

Durmisevic's granular surveys are complemented by vast amounts of high-level data assembled by consultants such as Metabolic of Amsterdam. What is particularly interesting about Metabolic's work is the ability to map the flow of pretty much anything, including energy, water, clothes and food consumption, in and out of cities. In all cases, Metabolic will map the 'outwards' waste flows generated as a consequence of 'inward' flows of resources. This is the stuff of 'big data', and it is particularly exciting to see how the groundwork of Superuse, Rotor Deconstruction and Dr Elma Durmisevic can be complemented by, and indeed complement, the work of Metabolic. Metabolic's maps also include mapping what cities are made of. Metabolic has the construction data on whole cities and regions in the Netherlands, and it is this data that can help us all understand the potential of a single existing building, neighbourhood or region, to provide materials for future developments. Metabolic has been commissioned by the City of Rotterdam to map the 'resource potential' of future demolition sites across the region. In addition, it has been made aware of the design of future development sites. The idea is that when the development sites are ready, the demolition sites will be activated and turn into donor deconstruction sites providing second-hand resources for new buildings. It is incredibly exciting to see examples of strategic circular thinking at the scale of cities and regions because when it is implemented at this scale, the circular economy makes complete sense to most people.

Demolition companies have always been aware of the potential for reuse instead of throwing away: it's just that they haven't always had the financial incentives to do so. However, no one can get deconstruction done without the help, expertise and knowledge of demolition companies. In short, architects and engineers know how buildings are put together and demolition companies know how they come apart. What is now extremely exciting is the fact that an ever increasing number of demolition companies are rebranding themselves as 'deconstruction companies': this isn't superficial 'green branding'. The wonderful work of architectural office cepezed, in Delft, would not be possible without one of these ex-demolition companies, namely Lagemaat, which applies a forensic approach to surveying existing buildings, using the types of software pioneered by Durmisevic and her colleagues. When I interviewed Arend van de Beek, the Circularity Programme Manager for Lagemaat, he was able to show me examples of large (10,000m^2+) buildings from the 1970s that had been digitally surveyed to such an extent that the pre-demolition audit had quantified nearly every element of the building. This was quantified as a 3D model, colour-coded to represent material type and quality, which could be plugged

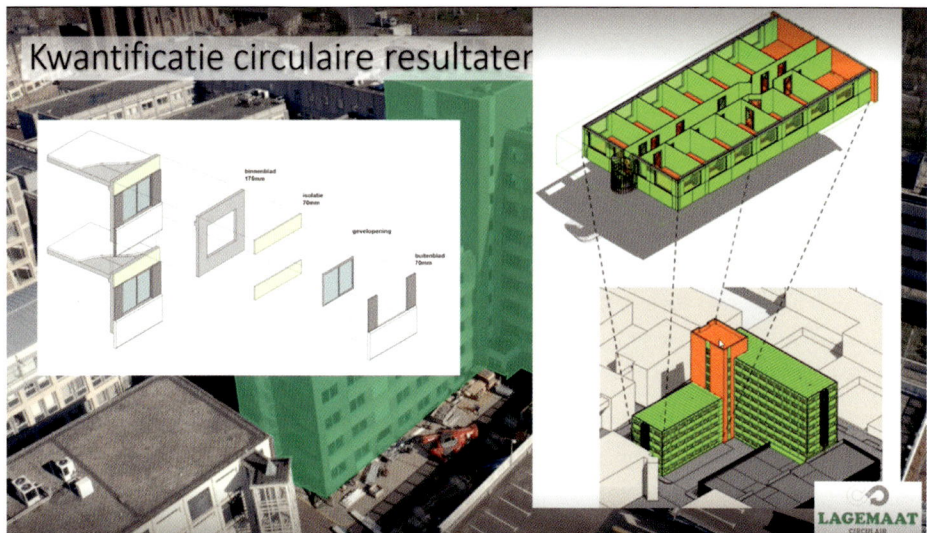

Figure 2.38
Reuse Revit BIM model by Lagemaat.

into a BIM model, together with the most comprehensive of spreadsheets itemising the building as a kit-of-parts for disassembly and reuse by others.

In 2018, a group of 12 demolition companies, including Lagemaat, formed Insert, which is a national network, digital platform and marketplace for reusable building materials and raw materials. Insert supports circularity across the Netherlands by creating an active marketplace for reused construction materials. In addition to creating material inventories, it provides vital storage for deconstructed materials, with six large warehouses across the country. This is an important service, as anybody who has tried building with second-hand materials will tell you, it's either 'famine or feast' and extremely difficult to know what is available when you need it on site. Networks like Insert create the kind of certainty that makes the transition to circular systems viable for us all. Insert will assist customers searching for particular products. As well as managing materials and components from the built environment, it salvages and redistributes trees and shrubs being removed from public spaces that are being 'regenerated'.

Although addressed in some detail in several case studies in this book, before I complete this chapter introduction, I would like to briefly discuss ways in which the reuse industries are dealing with the ubiquitous issues of performance and warranty.

Michael Baars spent many years in the property industry before forming New Horizon in 2015. New Horizon finds buildings destined for demolition and, if appropriate, deconstructs them and sells as many parts as possible back to the original suppliers. This approach relies on the buildings being relatively new (20 to 25 years maximum), as the older they are, the less likely that the original suppliers are still trading. It is also an ingenious way of ensuring that these second-hand materials keep, or have re-established, their particular performance warranties, and obviously it will be the original suppliers, who know their products better than any, who take responsibility. Unfortunately, it also highlights the scandal that is the perceived short life span of mainly office buildings that are demolished for 'commercial' reasons although they are still viable.

New Horizon's approach, as with other urban miners, requires deep intrusive surveys to ascertain the type, quality and quantity of materials for harvesting. The company then approaches the original material suppliers and works out a deal to sell back. If it works as a financial proposition, New Horizon will deconstruct said building. One aspect that is particularly interesting is that New Horizon can deconstruct a building in the time others take to demolish. This sounds extraordinary, unbelievable even. However, Baars noticed that, over the last 30 years or so, the construction process for commercial projects had been streamlined over and over, resulting in construction contracts taking less time on site. What he also noticed was that the time set aside in a construction programme for demolition generally stayed the same. Consequently, Baars spent time refining his own demolition programmes so it took less time to complete than the norm, resulting in keener pricing than his competitors.

Figure 2.39
Insert deconstruction platform.

One of the other ways to assure the performance of a second-hand product is to find companies that have been salvaging and reusing for decades. Unfortunately, as Thornton Kay noted when I interviewed him, these companies are getting fewer every year. One example is Cleveland Steel, which has spent 30 years 'downcycling' steel pipework designed for the oil industry to the construction industry. Managing Director Roy Fishwick uses the term 'downcycling' because performance standards for the oil industry are higher than for the construction sector, and therefore it is relatively straightforward for Cleveland Steel to know what is required to ensure the proper performance for second-hand steel. Now many people are asking them to procure second-hand steel frames from deconstructed buildings. It's a different type of steel section to the norm for Cleveland, but due to their experience with steel tubes, they are happy to offer the appropriate performance warranties that other suppliers are finding more challenging. Knowledge, experience and data are key to a successful reuse industry.

I want to end this section on a positive note. Over the last couple of years there has been a keen interest in reuse from structural and civil engineers based in the UK. The Institution of Structural Engineers (IStructE) has been shining a light on the potential of the circular economy for several years, and this has been echoed by the number of practices offering structural designs with different embodied carbon figures, running from highest down to lowest. In addition, many engineers are providing the deep-dive surveying services required to ascertain, say, the exact specification and amount of reusable steel frame in an existing building that was originally due for demolition. This approach highlights what we might call the 'embodied value' in an existing building, which can turn a run-of-the-mill demolition contract into a much more valuable deconstruction project. As I write, I have been made aware of new buildings being designed in the UK where the structural engineers have specified second-hand steel frames currently standing in buildings waiting for deconstruction.

I believe we are on the threshold of a brilliant age of reuse. However, despite the efforts of change-makers – like Steve Gilchrist of Circular Steel, the Excess Materials Exchange (now in the UK), as well as material passport innovators such as the Madaster Foundation and Rachel Hoolahan at Orms – it will be legislators who can make the biggest impact on enabling the business case for reuse. In 2022 and 2023, the UK Parliament refused to sanction a Carbon Emissions (Buildings) Bill on three occasions. If adopted, the bill would lead to a new law that would make sure that the building regulations in England and Wales insisted that building owners submit whole-life carbon calculations for newbuild and retrofit projects. The implications of this are profound because as soon as embodied carbon is quantified, and levels are benchmarked for our industry (the UK Net Zero Carbon Buildings Standard is due in 2024), it won't make any sort of financial, let alone environmental, sense to demolish a building and throw it away.

CASE STUDY No.1

Rural Studio

THE STORY

Rural Studio (USA) have a worldwide reputation, with over 30 years of inspired undergraduates and hundreds of beautiful buildings made for the sort of money more affluent people would spend on a new kitchen. For many architects and designers, they are the epitome of the well-informed, well-meaning architecture practice, for they are a practice as well as a school of architecture with a strong ethical position. They also pretty much single-handedly made live projects the *de rigueur* pedagogic tool for modern schools of architecture.

They came to the attention of many in 1994 when they completed the first of their Client Houses in Masons Bend, a community of only 100 people in Alabama. The Bryant (Hay Bale) House was quickly followed by a number of distinctive looking houses employing unusual material sources, such as car tyres, straw or carpet tiles. Rural Studio cofounder Samuel Mockbee wanted to expose students to 'the classroom of the community'. However, students were also exposed to the idea of inventing new construction techniques and finding alternative material resources as the budgets for these projects were so small: US$15,000 per house. Their early works were distinctive: they were visually striking and often beautiful, particularly the Glass Chapel in Masons Bend from 2000, famously reusing 80 car windscreens scavenged from a nearby breaker's yards, and the elegant Antioch Baptist Church from 2002.

Those early projects were inspiring, but they were creative one-offs, and some were less successful than others. In 2010, the Rural Studio Strategic Plan asked for all their buildings to be renovated so that they would consume less energy or even generate it. Rural Studio started to concentrate more on improving their own facilities: looking at ways of growing food by setting up their own farm on their own land, creating a 'solar greenhouse', a 'food forest' and a commercial kitchen. Water collection and irrigation is also integral to the Strategic Plan.

The second decade of Rural Studio's practice was marked by an increased emphasis on considering ways in which their architecture could fit into the local vernacular and local needs. Projects such as the Fire Station (2004) and Town Hall (2011) in Newbern, Alabama, were developed after local officials approached Rural Studio, not the other way around. Some of their early projects had satisfied an individual's needs while leaving many in the community feeling confused or even angry. As Andrew Freear, Director of Rural Studio since 2002, told me, 'In my initial years at Studio, the design/build process was pretty hit or miss, quite undisciplined. Students would just start building and assume it would be okay. Frequently their decisions were a response to earlier mistakes in the building process – artful camouflage.'

Learning from their earlier mistakes (and successes), and being open and transparent about them, is perhaps one of the most inspirational aspects of Rural Studio's approach to learning and practice. They now have put their one-off Client House programme on hold in favour of their 20K House Product Line, which aims to provide well-designed, cheap housing to a wider audience. At first glance, these homes look a lot less interesting as they adopt the much-loved features of the local vernacular. However, upon closer inspection they are just as inventive, but less visually flamboyant, and they work with local resources that can include waste or low-grade materials. The 20K House programme also aims to provide dwellings that are easy and cheap to maintain and, crucially, that are straightforward to raise a mortgage on.

Clockwise from top left:

Figure 2.40
Two of Rural Studio's 20K Houses.

Figure 2.41
Construction of Newbern Town Hall, Alabama, completed in 2011.

Figure 2.42
Newbern Town Hall, corner detail.

Figure 2.43
The opening of Newbern Fire Station in 2004.

Figure 2.44
The opening of Newbern Town Hall in 2011.

REUSING WASTE | STEP 2 | 55

OPINION

After perhaps unintentionally making a big impact in the mid to late 1990s, Rural Studio have steadily evolved. Creating student accommodation finished with car number plates or a chapel using car windscreens as curtain walling was inspiring at the turn of the 21st century. To create buildings in collaboration with some of the most disenfranchised communities in the USA, and to make these buildings look so self-assured and beautiful, was awe-inspiring. However, these early buildings were perhaps too experimental, and the Rural Studio team were sometimes too quick to solve a problem with a new building. They successfully identified material resources previously overlooked, but as projects were always built on a meagre budget, as with all 'prototypes', sometimes bits of them failed. The problem with the Client House projects is that people were living their everyday lives in these experiments. The larger-scale community and infrastructure projects – the bridges, birding towers, baseball grounds, chapels and playgrounds – were better places to be experimental.

Figure 2.45
Lions Park playground.

After over 30 years of teaching and practice, it is perhaps the larger-scale projects where Rural Studio's combination of design inventiveness, community collaboration and cost-effectiveness has been most successful. Their 2010 'playscape' in Lions Park, Greensboro, Alabama, is a perfect mix of a carefully considered brief and a typically inventive Rural Studio design focusing on demonstrating the adaptability of a valuable product destined for recycling – in this case, an unlimited supply of 55 high-grade galvanised steel barrels. The project budget could not afford concrete, so when Damon Smith of IP Callison turned up at one of Rural Studio's Soup Roast Reviews offering to donate an unlimited supply of these barrels, Andrew Freear and his students began thinking of ways they could work with this valuable resource. The barrels are manufactured in India and then sent over to the USA, where they are filled with mint oil used in the manufacture of chewing gum and toothpaste. By giving them to Rural Studio, IP Callison avoided the cost of crushing and recycling these barrels, as dictated to them by industry standards. As usual, Freear is candid about the successes and challenges this project presented the team. The design solution used free material resources in an efficient manner: 'One detail, a welder, a calibrating level and a crane,' as Freear states. However, as is often the case with the realities of reusing materials, there is a lot of repetitive manual labour, often with boring tasks such as de-nailing second-hand timber. In this case, it was what Freear describes as 'a monotonous, soul-destroying building process', although that actually sounds like many construction processes. However, it does point out that reusing materials destined to be thrown away does not save money, it saves natural resources. It is a conscious decision made by clients, designers and makers to be material efficient, but it often comes with a higher labour input.

CASE STUDY No.2

Superuse Studios

THE STORY

Rotterdam-based Superuse's original name, 2012 Architects, came about because some of the founder members of the studio were living in a street where 18 houses were planned to be demolished. Jan Jongert and his colleagues proposed an alternative vision that preserved all the houses, but audaciously asked the municipality to lend them the houses for 15 years until 2012. The community renovated the houses and when 15 years had passed, they were able to buy them from the municipality at affordable rates: a positive tale of social sustainability.

The name 'Superuse' comes from the idea of improving the value and usefulness of a product or material from its original intended use. Connecting different systems that are normally kept separate does this. So, for example, if a glass bottle is reused as a brick that forms part of a building, its life and usefulness are hugely extended from that originally intended. Jongert refers to this as 'the creative "click"… Understanding that the function can change.' For him, the difference between everyday reuse and Superuse is the ambition of the creative challenge involved. Superuse requires people (often designers) to propose future scenarios for discarded material that extend its life and add value, and this always requires a new perception and understanding of the potential of these materials to be substantially more useful than previously thought.

Similar in many ways to Rotor in Brussels, Superuse are taking on the challenges of resource efficiency and closed-loop systems in a systematic manner. They produce academic papers on subjects pertaining to resource management and flows, they teach (Jongert is a professor at the Royal Academy of Art in The Hague), design buildings and advise their regional and national governments.

From top:

Figure 2.46
The existing Kamphuis school building on the island of Brienenoord.

Figure 2.47
A resource map for the new Kamphuis school building.

Figure 2.48
Deconstruction, reconstruction storyboard.

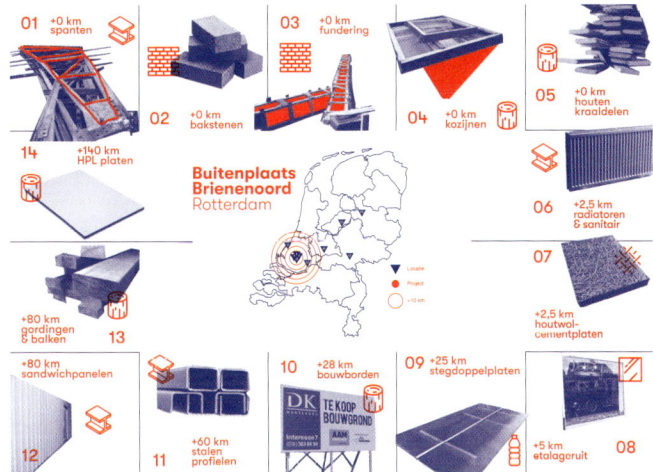

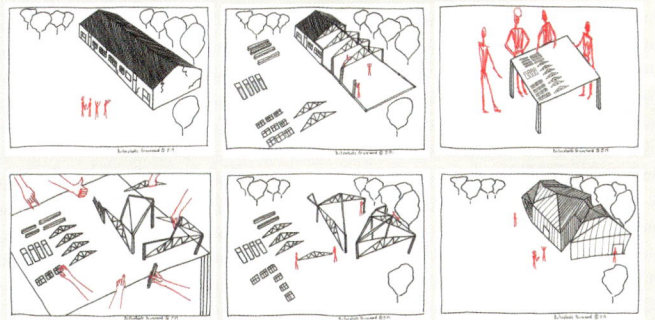

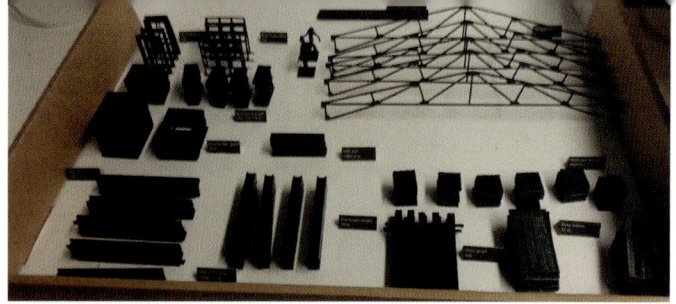
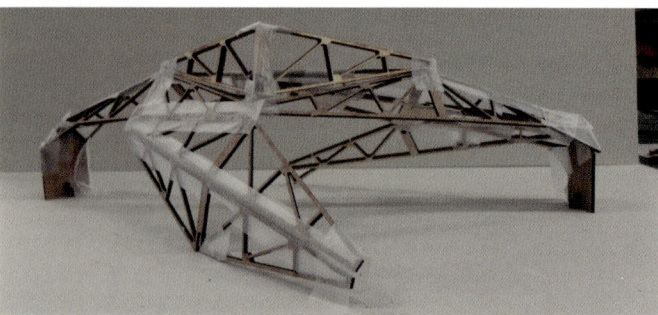

From top:

Figure 2.49
Architectural 3D printed model in a box.

Figure 2.50 Model experiments with sticky tape.

Figure 2.51
The steel frame is reassembled on site.

Figure 2.52
The timber frame is reassembled.

Figure 2.53
External image of the 'new' school.

In 2005, they completed what for many is Europe's (if not the world's) first contemporary house made from a selection of waste material. Superuse procured this using their Harvest Mapping methodology. The house is interesting enough and has been extensively published. It famously reused steel profiles from a redundant textile machine for the main structure, as well as for one of the façades. Timber from massive cable reels was also salvaged for other façades. Many other sources of waste material (including house 'for sale' signs for the linings of kitchen cupboards) were used to deliver this project. The project is of particular note as it highlights very clearly some of the real challenges facing a client and their design team. For example, the design team cannot show their client exactly what the final building will look like until the material has been sourced. How does one design a building without understanding what all the finishing materials will be before starting on site? Designers working with so-called waste sources must continue to be creative throughout the duration of a project, not just at its inception.

As the result of pursuing a 'material-experimental design approach', Superuse have assembled a multidisciplinary team dedicated to 'turning cities into a living web of connected material processes and flows'. This is an unconventional way of perceiving a city, albeit one that more people appreciate. In order to make this preoccupation relevant, and financially viable, Superuse have developed a series of tools, such as the Relevance Indicator and the Environmental Impact Calculator, that help them ground their design strategies in rigorous scientific practice. Their Harvest Map uses geographic representations to help identify and prioritise waste materials near to a specific project site. As well as highlighting surplus and waste materials currently available via a 'live' interactive map, this platform also provides useful information to facilitate the repurposing of materials, elements and components that would otherwise be discarded. It also encourages people to become 'scouts' looking out for neglected material flows.

Figure 2.54
Internal image of the 'new' school.

Since this case study was published in the first edition, Superuse have continued to lead the way with thought-provoking projects and initiatives, such as 'Blade-Made' (blade-made.com), which raises awareness of the huge amounts of waste wind turbine blades that are buried in landfill every year, while simultaneously providing community-led projects reusing this brand-new mega waste stream. Superuse do not duck from reusing what at first glance look like unattractive waste flows and rendering them useful and aesthetically pleasing. I'm thinking of the massive flow of unwanted uPVC windows that every Northern Hemisphere country sends to landfill or incineration every year. Superuse 'harvested' uPVC frames being removed from a housing development. They also found a company in Rotterdam prepared to refurbish these old uPVC windows so that they would be cleaned up and even cut to the new sizes required. This enabled them to reclad a former aircraft hangar with these refurbished windows, while transforming it into new workspace for high-tech companies.

In 2020, Superuse produced one of my favourite reuse projects, the new Kamphuis school building on the island of Brienenoord in the Netherlands, which supports social, cultural, culinary, artistic and educational activities. The project presented several challenges, not least that there was a limited budget and access from the mainland to the island was restricted. Superuse rose to these challenges by developing designs for a new building that reused 90% of the old building, including the foundations. This approach dramatically reduced the need for new material to be transported onto the island. However, what is most striking about the new building is that it looks nothing like the original. Superuse employed a radically different design process focused on the creative reuse of the original building broken down into different elements. First, they carefully measured the existing building and then had the components (roof trusses, load-bearing walls, etc.) 3D-printed at a scale of 1:50. In partnership with the client group, Superuse then experimented with what had become a kit-of-parts. The result is rather incredible: a new building constructed from the old, but the shape, interior spaces and even the architectural language is completely different.

OPINION

In many ways, Superuse Studios look like a conventional design studio, perhaps because their completed projects are extensively published in the design press. However, this practice is really a multidisciplinary group with a clear research agenda that includes scientists, academics and material specialists supported by designers, who are all focused on interrogating the challenges a circular economy presents. I believe what sets them apart is the ability of their designers to identify these challenges within different industries (construction, food, etc.) and then, in partnership with the rest of the practice, to create a collection of devices and working methodologies that help enable a change from the current 'linear' systems to something resembling a closed-loop system. Whether it is the Harvest Map technique/platform for identifying resource flows, the Cyclifier platform introducing disconnected flows to each other, or Recyclicity, which connects different individuals and organisations in the process of demolishing buildings to encourage reuse, Superuse are dedicated to providing inventive mechanisms that facilitate these processes. It is their combination of inquisitiveness, rigorous research, knowledge and creativity that makes this practice highly significant. They are inventing some of the tools we will all need to practise within a more circular economy.

CASE STUDY No.3

Hub67 by LYN Atelier

THE STORY

Andrew Lock founded LYN Atelier in 2009 after winning a design competition. Fairly soon they were getting commissions for temporary buildings such as The Festival Village below the Queen Elizabeth Hall on London's South Bank. This project gave them the opportunity to explore collaborative design processes (in this case involving up to 200 artists).

In 2011, after raising their profile, LYN Atelier were invited to bid for what became the 'Hub67' project: a temporary community centre made from material collected in shipping containers after the Olympics closed in 2012. The Olympic Delivery Authority (ODA) had a huge site in the Lea Valley where there were deconstructed buildings such as temporary food kiosks, banks, etc., as well as running track, seating, concrete barriers and lots of other valuable material. The ODA was keen to prove that it could create something meaningful for one of the communities near to the Olympic site. Initially, Lock told me, it was really difficult to assess the potential of the resources, as they were only allowed an hour or so on site. Instead of providing a detailed design proposal for their competition-winning bid, they produced more of what Lock called a 'statement of intent: a working methodology'.

Even when they got the commission, Lock says that access to the site was limited: the contractors were busy doing other tasks for the ODA. Also, and this is a theme repeated many times in this case study, the ODA's bureaucracy was huge and cumbersome, set in place for multimillion-pound massive stadiums and infrastructure projects. Even though Hub67 was only a £350,000 temporary community building, the ODA procurement route started off being the same as for these different kinds of projects. Whenever Lock and his colleagues needed to visit the material site, they had to complete a risk assessment on each occasion, and then they would only have about an hour on site. As a consequence, Lock soon developed a keen eye to spot potential building material. He soon noticed that there were a lot of steel

Figure 2.55
Hub67, Hackney, completed in 2014.

Clockwise from top left:

Figure 2.56
Members of the local community assembling cladding made from second-hand material, for Hub67.

Figure 2.57
Second-hand building components from the 2012 London Olympics, waiting to be taken to the Hub67 site.

Figure 2.58
Second-hand building components being assembled on their new site.

Figure 2.59
The façade of Hub67.

Figure 2.60
Reused materials on the Hub67 façade.

Figure 2.61
The Hub67 interior, fitted out with second-hand material.

> ## OPINION
>
> This case study proves that if a design team and building contractors work closely together, extraordinary things can happen. LYN Atelier had to overcome an almost complete lack of information on the type of material they had to use, as well as limited information on the performance (thermal and other) of this material once it arrived on site. The construction contract made little, if any, allowance for the fact that this building was made out of second-hand materials. As a consequence, the main contractors had to assume the normal responsibilities regarding the structural integrity of the building. This included, in effect, stating that second-hand materials and construction systems were 'fit for purpose', when there were no written performance specifications, certificates, guarantees or evidence of any sort. It required the experience and expertise of the design and construction teams to overcome this unusual constraint.
>
> If there is a clear objective and desire to deliver an innovative product, designers and makers can overcome huge obstacles to work things out. However, in this case it has been done at risk to the designer's professional indemnity insurance and the contractor's building insurance. I guess the main thing to observe is that this project was designed and delivered without any legislation or any systems, networks, whatever, in place to assist in their vision to prove that a perfectly functioning new building could be constructed out of the second-hand remains of other buildings.

frames with glazed and insulated composite metal panels, the remains of the banks and food vending machines. He secured nine of these to create Hub67. Cladding came in the form of the external finishing for the Olympic Training Centre. Once installed, they only had to get one of the roof elements rebuilt from new, as there wasn't a correctly falling existing roof element to reuse.

It should be noted that the original suppliers of this material were supportive of Lock reusing their product, as they were keen to demonstrate how their product was indeed designed for remanufacture. Nevertheless, on reflection, the acquisition of this second-hand material that was appropriate for reuse was very time-consuming and stressful. This situation was brought about by accident, simply because the clients had not had the time to think through the implications of constructing a building out of second-hand material.

The contractual setup was also not appropriate for a small construction project made of second-hand material. The main contractor for the project was a small building company not used to working with 500-page contracts such as the type the ODA normally issued. They successfully negotiated the contract size down to a mere 75 pages. However, the Construction Contract was still a 'standard' NEC with its normal onerous obligations for the building contractor to guarantee the proper performance of the resultant construction. This immediately raised the question, how does one guarantee the performance of a building made from second-hand materials without the data that proves the quality or standards of these materials? This issue reinforces the need for material passports discussed later on in this book. The contractor took an informed risk. They assumed that as the building would be used for only three years, they would probably not test this issue of building fabric performance.

The main challenge that Lock and his colleagues had to overcome was that the definition of a 'temporary building' as far as the building regulations is concerned is a building occupied for up to two years. The Hub67 building needed to be occupied for over three years. The consequences of this were profound. The external fabric of Hub67 had to meet the airtightness and insulation levels described in Part L2, which was brand new legislation at that time. Despite this, they were able to meet this additional challenge. The project was built on budget and on time (constructed in a little over 12 weeks), which, considering the unusual constraints and challenges faced for the design and construction team, and indeed the client, is a real achievement.

CASE STUDY No.4

The Rubber House and Recyclinghaus by CITYFÖRSTER

THE STORY

CITYFÖRSTER were founded by 11 students graduating from the Hanoverian School of Architecture in 2005. Young and radical, with ideas to 'make architecture totally different to "the old ones"' who preceded them, for many this was a practice doomed to failure – surely with 11 founders it could not function properly? Nearly 20 years later, and with seven of the original founders still part of the practice, CITYFÖRSTER are going strong, and are still trying to do things differently from the norm. With sustainability at the core of what they do, the practice has always combined architecture with urban design. As founder Nils Nolting told me, 'Working at an urban scale has always allowed us to be more impactful (from the point of view of sustainability) than if we were designing just a single building. At an urban scale we can influence lifestyle decisions that can reduce carbon emissions.'

Their name translates to 'City Forester', which picks up on the German word for sustainability, *Nachhaltigkeit*, which refers to the sustainable practice of planting trees for future generations. Nolting acknowledges that over the years the practice has had to apply a fair bit of 'visionary pragmatism' to their projects to get things built. However, this hasn't stopped them delivering several highly innovative projects.

The first is the Rubber House, completed in 2011. This modest (in scale) but delightful house was Nolting and his colleagues' winning entry for the Dutch Eenvoud/Simplicity design competition. Inspired by vernacular Dutch agricultural barn structures, it focused on a strategy of material reuse, with new materials being organic and carbon locking. Hence the structure is a prefabricated, cross-laminated timber (CLT) system bolted together. The original design proposed to clad the building with second-hand rubber conveyor belts. Unfortunately, this element was not realised, due to the team's naivety in Dutch building regulations. With the benefit of hindsight, the practice has now developed a way of 'designing by availability': to propose materials, second-hand or otherwise, that are readily, rather than hopefully, available. In the case of the Rubber House, a system of prefabricated concrete foundations was installed rather than the normal in situ cast system more commonly used in Germany and the UK. This approach allows for future reuse. One interesting design feature of this early prototype is the way that Nolting overcame the challenge of specifying exact structural openings in the CLT before he knew the size of the second-hand windows he would salvage. The solution was simple: they don't need to fit! The windows are cleverly planted over the pre-cut structural openings as part of the external insulation 'wrap', so that window frames oversail structural openings, revealing CLT

Figure 2.62
Second-hand windows being taken from a local office building, to be installed in the Recyclinghaus.

Figure 2.63
Glass cladding for the Recyclinghaus was sourced from a local office building.

Figure 2.64
A farm building was the source for bricks and tiles for the Recyclinghaus.

Clockwise from top left:

Figure 2.65
Waste bottle tops were used for bathroom walls.

Figure 2.66
Stone setts came from a local reclamation yard.

Figure 2.67
The new CLT structure of the Recyclinghaus.

Figure 2.68
Second-hand paving slabs were used for the floor.

Figure 2.69
External view of the completed Recyclinghaus.

Figure 2.70
Rammed earth and bottle tops inside the Recyclinghaus.

through the glazing at window head. It's a delightful way to communicate a completely different way of procuring materials.

The Recyclinghaus, completed in 2019, is a one-off experimental house commission also won in a design competition in Hanover. The commissioner, a large housing and construction company called Gundlach, was getting increasingly concerned about the amount of waste generated by the construction sector, as well as its vast embodied carbon footprint. The brief was simple: 'Design a 100% recycling house.' It also asked the winning team to study the material/waste flows associated with their own construction projects, with an ambition of diverting some of this material to create the new house.

CITYFÖRSTER's approach was similar to that applied to the Rubber House – this time using NUR-HOLZ elements, a glue- and metal-free solid wood construction method developed by a company based in the Black Forest (sequestering over 100 tonnes of CO_2), with second-hand and recycled material applied to the external skin and internal finishes. This time they knew the site, the city, its particular building regulations and, crucially, the emergent second-hand supply chain, or what we will call 'resource flows', which were located early on in a Resource Map. Materials for external cladding were located and specified early on, while internal fixtures and fittings were sourced while the construction project was live. This reduced the need to store materials on or near to site. Second-hand materials were gleaned from other commercial projects their clients were working on. The retrofitting of a large 1980s public building supplied the Recyclinghaus with aluminium windows, together with corrugated iron sheets and fibrous cement panels that were cut to size and decorated black. Profiled glass cladding panels were gained from another demolition project. Upon inspection, the windows required new triple glazing; however, the old windowpanes were reused on a local community pavilion project. Similar to the design principle already applied in the Rubber House, Window frame sizes this time were not suitable for the façade cladding, so part of the façade above the windows sails across the openings. Foundations were made from recycled concrete aggregates, with the ground oversite formed from an insulating layer of crushed 'foamglas' finished in compacted gravel. Internal bathroom fittings were second-hand, with internal finishes made from waste bottle tops. Second-hand stone setts create external hard standing, with some internal floors finished with either reclaimed paving slabs or a form of terrazzo made from lime and broken bricks. Other salvaged bricks form internal walls. Wall insulation was made from recycled cocoa bean sacks.

OPINION

These two projects demonstrate how an impressive collection of materials that are normally discarded can be reused if the whole design team, including the client, work closely together. Project architect Nils Nolting acknowledges candidly that working with second-hand material, and especially that normally designated as waste, is 'a constant play between having too much or too little of something'. While this is a common reality for anybody dealing with the reuse of materials, it should be noted that at the time of writing, many cities and municipalities are looking into the physical and digital infrastructure required to temper and mitigate this situation of 'famine or feast'. And, of course, companies such as Rotor in Brussels and Insert, with its national network across the Netherlands, are already providing what might be called the 're-manufactory' facilities, receiving this material and redistributing it into the construction supply chain.

There will always be a need for one-off case study houses testing innovative design. However, when it comes to issues relating to reducing resource consumption and its direct link to the climate and ecological emergency, our industry needs to embrace these ideas immediately and roll them out at an industrial scale. CITYFÖRSTER are particularly impactful because they are working on innovative reuse projects with larger commercial construction companies, which are becoming increasingly aware of the potential benefits (financial, social and otherwise) of dramatically reducing the amount of product used in a project by designing out waste. Finally, I am really enjoying the emergence of a reuse/adaptation aesthetic clearly identifiable in the work of Nolting and his colleagues at CITYFÖRSTER, one that is borne out of an architecture sensibility focused on designing out waste.

CASE STUDY No.5

Superlocal by Maurer United Architects

THE STORY

Nicole and Mark Maurer formed Maurer United Architects in 1998, basing the collective in Maastricht, the Netherlands. Combining interests in architecture, fashion (Nicole) and hip-hop (Mark), this practice was always going to approach architecture from a different perspective.

Starting with a commitment to 'being original, better and different', Maurer United sought out projects that allowed them to look at things in a new way; to find original design and technical solutions. They also insisted on working closely with the end users of the projects they designed. And with this in mind, it wasn't long before they were working with the kind of people who inspired them in the first place. Early projects saw them working with skating communities and graffiti artists, and soon Mark was referring to his graduation working methods that took inspiration from DJs using samples, loops and scratching existing music to make something new. At first this way of working sometimes confused clients, who often had an understandably preconceived idea of what to expect from an architect.

Fast-forward to the present and there is an ever-more receptive audience for the type of projects that Maurer United produce. As Mark told me, 'Now with times changing so fast, with new environmental global goals, huge technological developments, and an urgent need to change our ways, somehow it feels like our approach fits better with people. We need to think differently, and that's what we do.'

One such client was social housing provider Heem Wonen. The district of Kerkrade, on the border with Germany, just east of Maastricht, was suffering from depopulation: young people were leaving in high numbers, with the population predicted to reduce by 27% over the next 30 years. The dense, high-rise 1960s slab blocks were apparently not fit for purpose. A first response had been to demolish one of the slab blocks, but this had in fact forced people away from a place and community that they loved. A new approach was required, and for a time Maurer United were employed as sort of 'art directors' for the site, considering new ideas and approaches to make sense of this situation. They quickly drew from their experiences of working closely with communities and set about interviewing the residents of Kerkrade, who made it clear that they wanted to stay, and definitely didn't want to live next to a demolition site.

Reinterpreting the existing built infrastructure for a new situation by reusing only material that is already on site resulted in an approach Maurer United named 'Superlocal'. In 2018, the Superlocal Pavilion was created – entirely out of material from one apartment literally cut out of one of the empty residential slab blocks. By sticking to only using material from the demolition process, Maurer United created a thought-provoking icon for the district of Kerkrade, not a habitable building to live in. In fact, the local council declared that the pavilion should be made a local monument.

So, what was the point of the Superlocal Pavilion? As well as being a rebuilt architectural artefact, it also tackled head-on issues of cultural, technical and social heritage, raising awareness of concerns overlooked with the first phase of demolition, and, as Nicole notes, 'a combination of the material and immaterial'. While developing the idea for the pavilion, Maurer United also undertook extensive consultation with the local community living in the existing housing, much of which was still intact. The resultant booklet, known as *The Neighbour Book*, was handed out at the opening of the pavilion.

Heem Wonen, Maurer United Architects and their partners then put together a successful bid for substantial EU Urban Innovative Actions (UIA) funding to support their concept for a Super Circular Estate that expanded on the ideas explored in the Superlocal Pavilion, but at the scale of a whole residential estate. As such, the transformation of the Kerkrade high-rise estate into a mixed-use residential community with an increase in the quality of the landscape between buildings, including increased biodiversity and the opportunity for growing vegetables in communal gardens, had to be undertaken with the highest rates

Figure 2.71
Existing apartment block salvaged and retrofitted into duplex apartments and terraced homes.

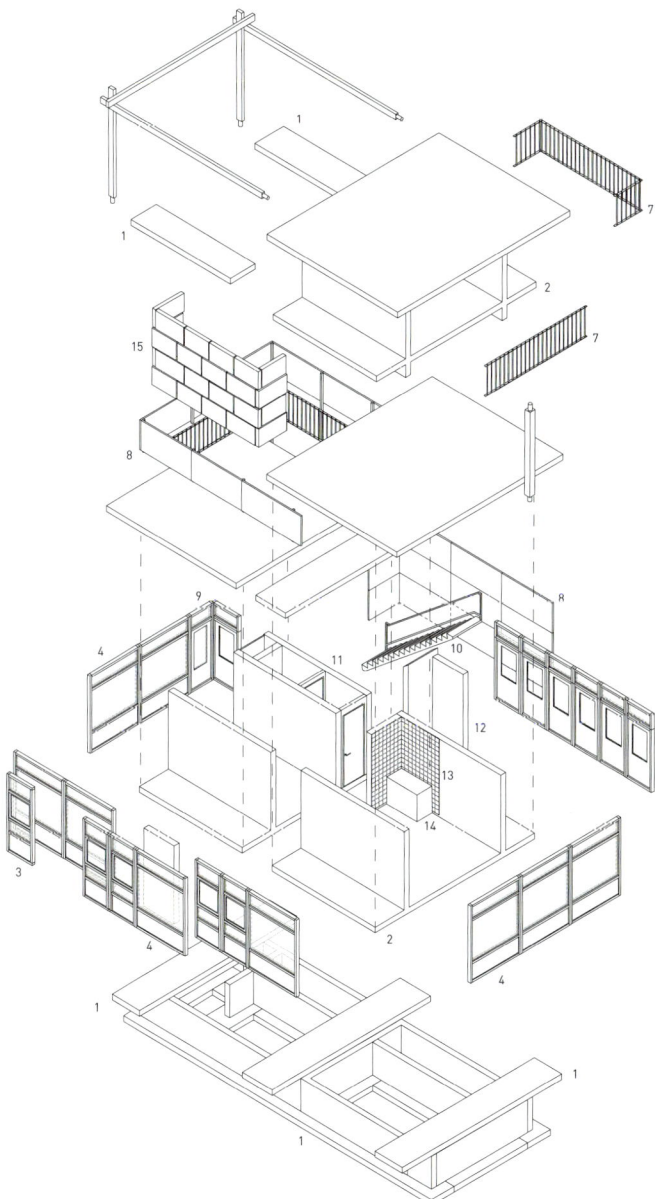

Figure 2.72
An exploded axonometric of the Superlocal Pavilion, describing material sources.

Figure 2.73
The old slab block was used to construct the Superlocal Pavilion.

REUSING WASTE   STEP 2   67

Clockwise from top left:

Figure 2.74
Assembling the Superlocal Pavilion from old slab block.

Figure 2.75
The completed Superlocal Pavilion, made of waste.

Figure 2.76
The existing frame and decks were reused for the Superlocal Pavilion.

Figure 2.77
The retrofitted flats, with the
Superlocal Pavilion in the foreground.

of materials and component reuse, creating the smallest amount of waste possible. In addition, the existing sense of community, together with the cultural and architectural histories of the estate, needed to be cherished for future tenants. Reuse was not just for materials. A further three prototype homes – made from waste from buildings deconstructed on site – were developed by other architecture teams to further test other material flows from deconstruction projects. Maurer United were also commissioned to retrofit one of the slab blocks into 125 new apartments, thus avoiding the deconstruction of the building. Close consultation with current and former residents had been running for almost five years. Maurer United knew what the community liked about the old housing, as well as what they thought needed improving. Interestingly, the retrofitted apartments stayed as deck access, as this is where people met up with their friends and neighbours. However, the ground and first floors were either converted into communal facilities or into a row of terraced homes, giving the neighbourhood a diversity of tenure not available before.

OPINION

Maurer United Architects' radical approach to the practice of architecture may have confused clients initially, but with a climate and ecological emergency presenting huge challenges, accompanied by seismic changes in the way we go about our everyday lives, their thoughtful reappraisal of what constitutes an authentic contemporary architectural practice has gained many admirers. The provocative, 'punkish' Superlocal Pavilion engaged the community within which it was created, creating an iconic, polemical statement of intent that has caught the attention of clients and municipalities across Europe, who are desperately looking for authentic, low-carbon solutions to today's most pressing issues. And then the 'uninhabitable' Superlocal Pavilion spawned the forward-thinking, community-engaging, heritage and culturally sensitive Super Circular Estate low-carbon-retrofit scheme that is currently ongoing. Maurer United Architects are that rarest of things: a mature practice who have stuck with the authentic radical approach to design that they started out with over 25 years ago. They have finally found a receptive, climate-literate audience willing to trust in their collaborative methods. At long last their time has come.

CASE STUDY No.6

Entopia Building for Cambridge Institute for Sustainability Leadership

by Architype, Feilden + Mawson, ISG, Max Fordham, BDP, Cambridge Architectural Research, 3PM, Gardiner and Theobald, Eve Waldron Design

THE STORY

The story of how the Entopia Building came about is worth including for numerous reasons – it's a 'deep retrofit' of a 1920s former telephone exchange building in Cambridge, situated in a conservation area, with an enlightened client, and a design and delivery team with an enviable track record of delivering authentic, low-carbon architecture projects. However, what is of particular interest is the dedication of the whole team in sourcing an array of low-carbon materials and components for a project that could have legitimately declared itself as low-carbon simply by reusing the old telephone exchange building alone. This team goes one or two steps further.

A common adage I often hear is that 'you are only a good as your client and brief'. I can turn this statement on its head by suggesting that the Entopia project is successful because of the extremely well-informed client group, who employed an equally able concept design team to create and test a brilliant brief. Integral to this team was Prof John French, working for the clients and end users, the Cambridge Institute for Sustainability Leadership (CISL). French has a long-established track record delivering low-carbon buildings – he was the client representative for The Enterprise Centre at the University of East Anglia (see Step 4).

The client-side architect, Architype's Wendy Bishop, described how she and her design team colleagues worked hard establishing the whole-life-carbon performance benchmarks for this project. Targets involved working to EnerPHit Classic retrofit standards, BREEAM Outstanding (still pending in-use sign-off), as well as employing the WELL Building Standard to ensure that the internal working environment was as healthy as possible.

Low embodied carbon, together with the specification of nontoxic biobased materials, was also a big deal with the whole delivery team. However, one of the earliest challenges that the project faced was that of increasing the levels of natural light in the building. As a former telephone exchange, it had not been designed for human occupation. Consequently, Architype and BDP spent some time building a case (via digital data modelling of five different window scenarios, from the existing to the preferred) for replacing the existing multi-paned single-glazed timber sliding sash windows with high-performing triple-glazed tilt-and-turn windows with frames tucked behind the solid wall, with a new, highly light-reflective window reveal. The local planning authority was against the proposed change and the project was in danger of being refused at planning unless the team reverted to the original 'faux' Georgian/Victorian windows. Undeterred, Architype and BDP presented their argument as follows. Replacing these windows with the contemporary windows would increase levels of natural light by 77% and reduce heat loss by 35%. Combined with the energy and carbon case, the Planning Committee felt compelled to vote in favour of this innovative approach to transforming this piece of 1920s infrastructure, set within Cambridge's conservation area.

Once the scheme had planning approval, Architype and BDP were asked to stay on as client advisers, allowing Feilden + Mawson to develop the scheme for RIBA Stages 4, 5, 6 and 7, together with Max Fordham and CAR, with contractors ISG delivering the actual retrofit project and interior designers Eve Waldron Design working directly with CISL to design and procure the FF&E (furniture, fixtures and equipment). Taking embodied carbon very seriously is, of course, commendable. Wendy Bishop notes that the team were looking at an overall life cycle of up to 100 years. Although upfront embodied carbon figures are relatively easy to achieve, it is almost impossible to predict future maintenance cycles. So, these targets are completely dependent on the behaviour of future building owners.

Figure 2.78
The low-carbon retrofit strategy for the Entopia Building.

The other major retrofit strategy for this predominately solid-brick building was to wrap the external solid masonry walls internally with 40mm of cork and clay 'Diathonite' insulating plaster, applied directly to the inside of the solid-brick external walls, plus another 40mm of wood fibre board. This achieved a U-value of 0.316 W/m².K. Existing floors are made of concrete, so the often-tricky detail of timber joists bearing into external brick walls is avoided. Interior ceilings were coated in a layer of Sonaspray acoustic insulation made of waste newspaper, which is often left exposed or combined with a layer of slatted timber. Conventional PIR insulation was applied to the basement floors as biobased materials would not be able to last very long in these damp conditions. In addition to these relatively modest insulating interventions (achieving

Figure 2.79
Window design development studies for the Entopia Building.

Figure 2.80
Timber-fibre internal insulation was applied to the existing wall.

Figure 2.81
The completed Entopia building, window detail.

Figure 2.82
The Entopia Building, completed in 2022.

Figure 2.83
Reused steel frame on the roof of the Entopia Building.

equally modest and therefore achievable U-value targets – the overall area-weighted U-value is 0.25 W/m^2.K), the improved airtightness, a mechanical ventilation with heat recovery (MVHR) system and air-source heat pump (ASHP) all combine to improve the operational energy usage from 373 kWh/m^{2}a to a predicted 48 kWh/m^{2}a.

Of particular interest is the variety of second-hand materials that contractors ISG were able to incorporate into this project. For example, the reception desk designed by Piercy & Company was originally installed back in 2017 in the Copyright Building in Central London, where ISG were doing a refit for Netflix. The desk was due to be skipped because of an upgrade to reception security, but instead ISG had it adapted so it could be reused at Entopia, with a crack in the stone surface visibly repaired, inspired by the Japanese Kintsugi method. In addition, Cleveland Steel sourced 4 tonnes of second-hand steel for the frame for the rooftop PV array. The frame members had formerly been used by Pinewood Studios to support cameras on a film set.

Perhaps the most interesting, challenging and potentially most impactful reuse of a waste stream were the 350 second-hand LED lights salvaged from another ISG refurbishment project. The lights were part of a temporary 'Cat A' fit-out for a commercial office building that ISG were refurbishing. It is currently common practice for landlords to invest in a temporary 'Cat A' fit-out to attract potential tenants. Once lease agreements are signed, most tenants will then rip out the 'Cat A' fixtures and fittings, replacing them with the branded interiors they require. This practise creates a huge and very pointless waste stream. In December 2022, the British Council for Offices (BCO) recommended that 'Cat A' is eliminated from office fit-out unless specified by the incoming occupiers. It also speculated that virtual reality could be used as a zero-resource alternative to a wasteful 'Cat A' fit-out, showcasing the potential of office space. ISG, in partnership with Collecteco, were able to locate and convince the original LED suppliers to inspect their previously sold fittings and honour the remaining portion of the original warranty. The lights were originally set within a ceiling system but were reused sitting proud under a soffit with additional luminaires providing uplighting. This move gained the project a BREEAM innovation credit.

OPINION

The success of this project is clear for us all to see. It has been possible because all the essential components that make a successful project are in place. The client, their brief, the design team and the contractors delivering the project are all on the same page, demonstrating a deep understanding of how to design and deliver an authentic, (whole-life) low-carbon retrofit project that is a delightful and healthy place to inhabit.

CASE STUDY No.7

Cleveland Steel

THE STORY

Forward-thinking design teams cannot affect systems change on their own. We need parties to work together to change linear metabolisms into circular ones. One part of the construction sector that has reappraised the way it functions is the supply chain, and with an increased understanding of what embodied carbon is, and the importance of dramatically reducing the whole-life carbon footprint of the built environment, companies that can provide high-performing second-hand products, preferably near to site, are becoming essential for any project wanting to classify itself as 'circular'.

One such company is Cleveland Steel, which seems to be constantly grabbing the headlines, supplying thousands of tonnes of second-hand steel products to an ever-greater number of high-profile developments. This might sound like hyperbole, but Cleveland Steel has quietly been doing this since 1973, and it's only now that many people are seeing the value in what it does.

Cleveland Steel has been supplying high-grade tubular steel to infrastructure projects across the UK, whether bridges or quays requiring deep piling or the primary structure of some of the Premiership's best-known football stadiums, as well as the moving roof structure for Centre Court at Wimbledon.

When Cleveland Steel started out, its business plan was simple. It acted as the contact between the oil industry that had lots of surplus steel pipe, and the construction industry that needed high-performing steel structures. The oil industry consumes a lot of steel, and when a consultant designs, for example, a 150-mile-long steel pipeline they will order 151 miles and the manufacturer will then make 152 miles of steel pipeline to allow for defects, wastage etc. – just like the rest of the construction sector. So, there is often a huge amount of surplus steel tube around, and this has been the case for 50 to 60 years. Apart from Cleveland Steel, there are only another three stockists of this material in Europe, and Managing Director Roy Fishwick estimates that between them they hold between 350,000 and 500,000 tonnes of steel tube.

Cleveland Steel is based in North Yorkshire, where it has a 100-acre site holding over 65,000 tonnes of stock, while employing 840 people, and most years selling over 20,000 tonnes of steel. When it started, it was literally just loading up steel tubes from the oil industry and transporting them to construction sites. Now it has expanded its services to include the cutting, welding, coating, shot blasting and testing of steel tubing destined for construction sites across the UK. Fishwick told me, 'We have the provenance of confidence. It's one of the big advantages of our business model; the ability to trace where the material came from and to what standards it was designed to perform'. Fishwick notes that many people trying to employ reused material in their developments are 'absolutely terrified about trusting the performance of a second-hand product'. However, Cleveland Steel has been doing this for over 50 years, so feels confident it can make value judgements on the performance of a piece of steel tubing, whereas people new to this way of doing are, quite understandably, cautious.

I first heard of Cleveland Steel when Fishwick told me about how he had saved about 20% of the cost of supplying and installing a new factory building for the Cleveland Steel site, by deconstructing a steel-framed building in Ireland, shipping it over to the UK, and reassembling it. Reuse was quicker and cheaper. Saving over £900,000 on a £5 million project was impressive enough, and when you consider the saving on natural resources, it is obviously a win-win. So now Cleveland Steel is dealing with the procurement of second-hand steel members, as well as complete frames. When I pressed Fishwick again about design liability and, in particular, whether his insurers were demanding higher premiums now that Cleveland Steel was diversifying, his point was that they were selling a 'product that had previously performed'. He also pointed out that Cleveland Steel's main industry had been supplying steel tubes to support massive infrastructure projects, so its insurers were not concerned with the expansion into the world of one-off buildings.

Cleveland Street has recently supplied surplus steel tubes and second-hand steel frames to many construction projects, including a massive new wharf for the Port of Dundee

From top:

Figure 2.84
Second-hand steel from Cleveland Steel installed on the roof of the Entopia Building for CISL (see the previous case study).

Figure 2.85
Reusing a second-hand steel mega-shed from Dublin saved Cleveland Steel over £900,000.

Figure 2.86
A second-hand steel tube in Cleveland Steel's yard.

Figure 2.87
A second-hand steel tube and 'I' beams.

(1,070 tonnes of surplus steel tubing), the retrofit of the Entopia Building for the Cambridge Institute for Sustainability Leadership (4 tonnes of second-hand steel frame; see see previous case study), as well as two projects with Fabix, namely the extension and retrofit of 55 Great Suffolk Street in London (21 tonnes of second-hand steel) and Roots in the Sky, which is the former Blackfriars Crown Court (approximately 130 tonnes of second-hand steel).

OPINION

For many of us, the challenges associated with turning linear systems back on themselves into closed loops appears daunting, if not impossible. However, it is often noted by organisations such as WRAP (Waste and Resources Action Programme) that about 20% of the construction industry is already 'circular'.[10] In other words, some parts of our industry are already having a go at changing well-established linear 'take, make and throw away' practices. Cleveland Steel is part of this positive statistic.

When biologists describe how a healthy natural ecosystem functions, they often point out that 'waste' from one part of the system is 'food' for another. Cleveland Steel has successfully found an unwanted waste stream from one system (the oil industry), and then located another system (the construction industry) that can use it. The fact that it has been doing this for over 50 years means that, now that this way of working is highly valued, Cleveland Steel is in an excellent position to expand into other areas of the circular economy, such as procuring second-hand steel frames for new developments. Cleveland Steel's vast experience underwriting the performance of second-hand products is also invaluable, as an industry with far less experience mulls over the very real challenges of how to distribute second-hand stuff safely to the construction sector. Cleveland Steel has even worked out how to deal with the big problem of either too much or too little second-hand material – it can store steel tubes in its huge 100-acre compound for years, if not decades. This enables it to create a relatively stable flow of resources for its ever-expanding collection of clients.

CASE STUDY No.8

Cycle Station by ProRail and de Architekten Cie

THE STORY

ProRail runs and maintains all the Netherlands' railway infrastructure: track, stations and other support buildings, as well as providing 'traffic control' to make sure that trains run safely and on time. It is responsible for planning more than 1,200 maintenance and construction projects every year. With more than 4,500 employees, ProRail is a crucial part of the infrastructure of the Netherlands, and as such it is no surprise that it is trying to engage with contemporary issues that are important to the nation: issues such as designing out waste and introducing closed-loop systems.

ProRail has an Innovation Department and for this book I interviewed Eva Dijkema, the sustainability policy adviser as well a part-time academic at TU Delft. Unlike many ProRail employees, preoccupied with making things run smoothly day-to-day, Dijkema and her innovation team think about what innovations need to be considered further into the future, and for the most part that means looking at ways to make the railway system more efficient, smarter, quicker and better. Dijkema says that she focuses on 'the edge between innovation and sustainability'. Much of her time is spent convincing people that there will be benefits by adopting new sustainable practices. However, she also admits that her role gives her time to explore innovative ideas.

ProRail is not a commercial entity and as such it has what Dijkema describes as 'an independence of function, and a responsibility to make sure that the modal shift is going to happen'. This means a shift away from a high-carbon-dependant lifestyle to one that ensures people will take the train instead of the car and the plane. ProRail works closely

Figure 2.88
External view of the Cycle Station, architect's render.

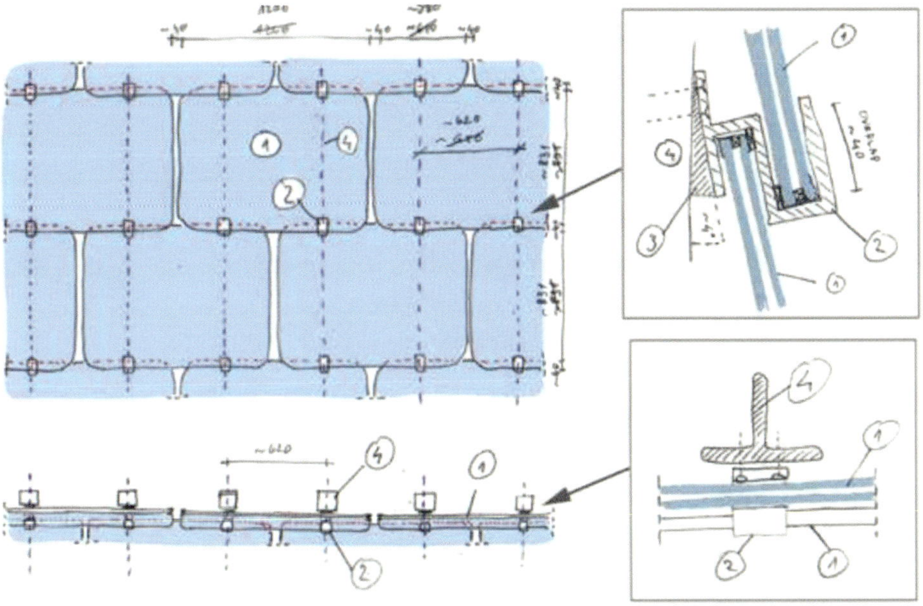

Figure 2.89
Detail drawing describing the reuse of old train windows for the Cycle Station.

Figure 2.90
Salvaged railway track for the new building's structural frame.

Figure 2.91
Salvaged train windows for the Cycle Station's external rain screen.

with the government and the EU to ensure that commitments to massive greenhouse gas reductions made in the Paris Agreement are adhered to. This means that on a day-to-day basis ProRail must make sure that tracks and buildings are constructed and maintained in a sustainable way.

One of the best ways for an infrastructure company to reduce its carbon footprint is to reduce the amount of resources it consumes.

Like many large infrastructure companies in the Netherlands, ProRail has its own internal roadmap to net-zero carbon, called 'Going Growing Green', which was developed in partnership with central government. Launched over six years ago, this initiative led to the appointment of a Sustainability Director four years ago, which in turn has led to a number of innovative, low-carbon, sustainable capital projects. One such project has been the development of new signal boxes that are modular, factory formed, zero waste and constructed with nearly 100% biobased material. And because they are lightweight, they are easily repairable, adaptable, extendable, removable, demountable and, crucially, low carbon and part of the organic biosphere. These structures will gradually replace the current concrete signal boxes.

Larger low-carbon projects are envisaged at ProRail. One that is in an advanced stage of design is a new bicycle parking facility in Eindhoven by Hans Hammink of de Architekten Cie. ProRail is investing in the expansion of parking facilities across the

Figure 2.92
The Cycle Station's rain-screen cladding, architect's render.

Figure 2.93
Interior image of the Cycle Station, with its salvaged rail track steel frame, architect's render.

Netherlands. This Cycle Station has, of course, been designed to circular principles, for numerous reasons, not least because the site in Eindhoven is expected to be redeveloped in the next 15 to 20 years to make way for a large residential development.

So, working in partnership with ProRail, Hammink was able to identify vast second-hand material harvesting opportunities. This has enabled the structural columns to be constructed from reclaimed steel railway track, with second-hand 'I' beams forming the roof structure. Double-glazed windows will be supplied from redundant 'Sprinter' trains, providing the external cladding for the building. The building will provide temporary parking for 5,000 bicycles, as well as a rooftop public space next to Eindhoven's main station.

OPINION

When a major infrastructure company is state owned it has additional duties to its end user, the general public, in excess of providing profit and dividends for its shareholders. ProRail is just such a company with a sense of responsibility to change the status quo and make that modal shift towards a steep carbon decent plan in line with the Paris Agreement. To do this it has to invest in innovation, with a highly impactful but dedicated small team of 25 brilliant people. ProRail is also enabled by a progressive national government providing the legislation and incentives to transition towards a circular economy.

CASE STUDY No.9

Cork House and Phoenix House by CSK Architects and The Bartlett, UCL

THE STORY

Matthew Barnett Howland and Oliver Wilton are Associate Professors of Environmental Design at The Bartlett School of Architecture. However, where Wilton is 100% focused on academic pursuits informed by innovative practice, Howland is also Director of Research and Development at CSK Architects. Wilton and Howland collaborate on research-based practice and are perhaps best known as the designers behind the multi-award-winning Cork House (with Dido Milne, also at CSK Architects). Cork House's high profile is partly due to the beauty of the building itself, as well as the clarity of the challenge: how to prove that an organic waste material from a vastly diminished industry can create a low-carbon home in the UK. As Wilton stated when I interviewed them, 'Cork House is like a plant-based Lego kit; it strips out complexity, like a dry-stone wall.' The project was not so much about cork as a way to progress research into what they call 'form follows life cycle'. Wilton continued, 'Life cycle is often used when people are really talking about life span, which is a lot more linear and therefore not so interesting. Life cycle comes from biology, where you are talking about an organism that reproduces, but most buildings don't reproduce.'

Cork House focuses on a particular life cycle and reuse approach that relates to the provenance of the material while maintaining the sanctity of the biological matter itself. The source material for the project started as a waste product from the cork industry. It is then reprocessed by heating it to about 250°C and pressure-cooking it into solid cork blocks or 'plant-based masonry', bound together with suberin which is actually 50% of cork matter. This process means that no synthetic binders are required, and therefore one day cork blocks can join the biosphere – hopefully only after numerous deconstruction/reconstruction cycles, as Cork House is designed to be a material store for future projects.

When I asked them why they hadn't rolled out lots of Cork Houses, Wilton and Howland reminded me that they are primarily researchers and architects, not entrepreneurs. As such, they are currently pursuing their original research question via a collection of practice-based projects focusing on reusing second-hand stone, which, as Howland points out, isn't such a big leap from the Cork House: 'Tectonically speaking, it is a stone form of construction – just warm, squidgy stone!'

Phoenix House is another project informed by their research into repurposing stone *spolia*. It is inspired by a similar approach to design that inspired Cork House, i.e. 'simple parts, simple ways of assembly and a focus on simplicity'. As Howland explained, 'A simple form of construction would typically be a fundamental part of enabling reuse, and compressive structures are nicely set up to be glue free and easy to disassemble, whereas tensile structures often require gluing elements together.'

Phoenix House sits on St Leonard's Hill in Windsor, which has been the site for a number of large houses for over 300 years – until about 100 years ago, when the largest incarnation of the country house was unceremoniously blown up by the new lord of the manor after unsuccessful attempts to find a new owner. This drastic action rendered the house – or 'Gateaux Chateaux', as Wilton called it (I couldn't leave that out!) – uninhabitable. The extensive plot was bought at auction in the late 1940s by the grandfather of the current owner, who has commissioned CSK Architects to design a new family home. And so, this project, which achieved planning approval via the National Planning Policy Framework (NPPF) paragraph 79 'truly outstanding' clause, will be constructed from stone (main floor) and brick (forming the lower-ground accommodation) that still lies around the site adjacent to the existing ruins that will form the entrance portico for the new home.

The process of developing a tailored method of reuse was undertaken as a standalone feasibility exercise by CSK Architects and The Bartlett, which comprised the construction of one prototype portal for the trabeated stone frame structure proposed for the upper-ground floor of the new house. Some 64 pieces of stone were extracted from the site and cleaned

Clockwise from top left:

Figure 2.94
Existing foundations at the Phoenix House site.

Figure 2.95
Stone found at the Phoenix House site was stacked.

Figure 2.96
Numbering the stone found on site.

Figure 2.97
3D scanning of stone on site.

Figure 2.98
A 3D scan of salvaged stone.

Figure 2.99
A 3D scan plus speculation of remodelling potentials.

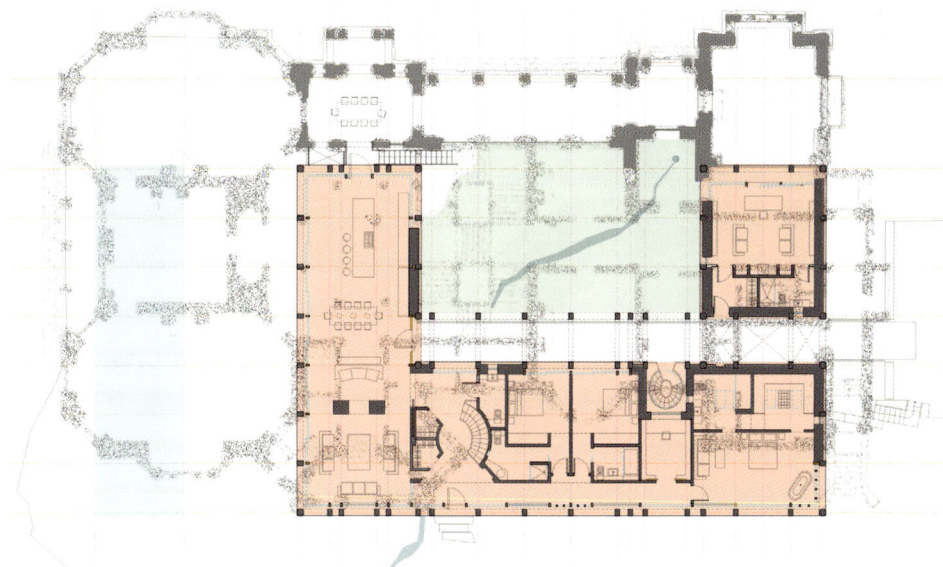

Figure 2.100
A plan of the 'new' Phoenix House.

Figure 2.101
A plan of the original house and scattered stone remnants.

Figure 2.102
An axonometric of existing structures, reused elements and new elements.

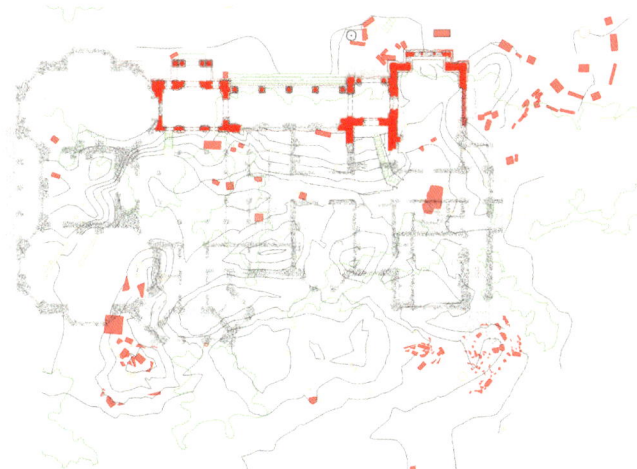

and numbered; these were scanned by Thomas Parker from The Bartlett to create an inventory of parts, or a 'digital quarry'. From this inventory, 'best-fit' components were selected to construct a digital model of the portal; and detailed fabrication drawings were supplied to the Stonemasonry Company in Lincolnshire, who cut and assembled the prototype portal at their workshop.

As well as looking at different ways to tie together second-hand stone into a single lintel or column, the team were interested in the potential architectural language and hierarchies this *spolia* approach presented them. For example, much of the stone was heavily carved and ornate. Should that stay 'as found' or to a greater or lesser degree should they smarten it up by cutting off the fancy bits? This consideration also creates an opportunity for architectural hierarchy, where more important elements are left untouched. Ironically, because of this approach, the plainer/secondary stone elements will have a bigger carbon footprint than the fancier stones, and, as Wilton states, one achieves a 'cut less get more' approach, which is the opposite to what one gets with new stone.

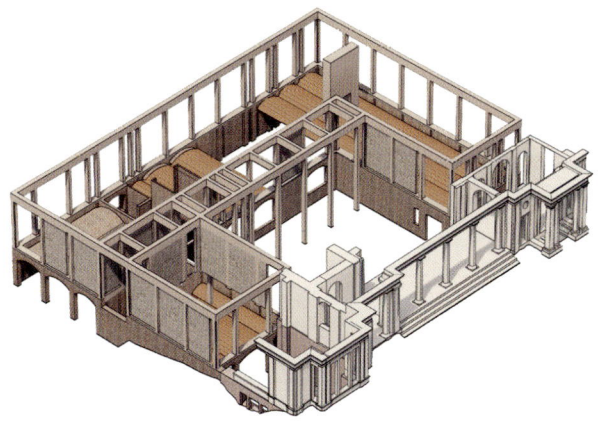

Howland points out that although the material is free, the process of gathering, cleaning, cutting and assembling second-hand stone costs slightly more than delivering new dressed stone to site. However, there is a greater level of delight in reusing stone with a previous constructed life and history, especially when it relates to the site itself. Wilton also points out that by applying this 'form follows life cycle' method to deliver tailored architectures, the result is unlike that which you

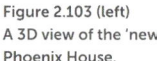

Figure 2.103 (left)
A 3D view of the 'new' Phoenix House.

Figure 2.105 (below)
A 3D view of salvaged stone forming the 'new' portico.

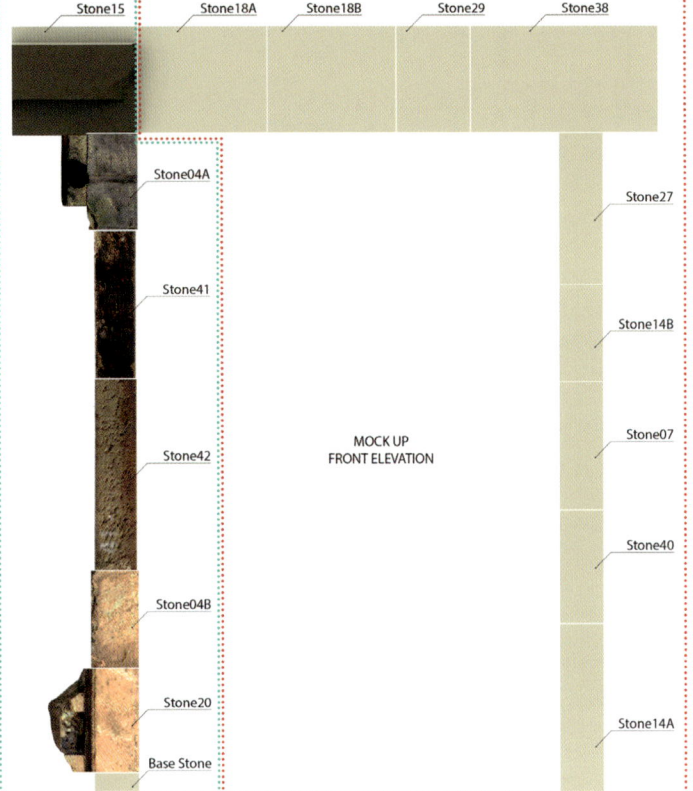

Figure 2.104 (above)
A sketch of the stone portico, using cut and uncut salvaged stone.

Figure 2.106 (above)
A stonemason setting out the prototype stone portico.

Figure 2.107 (below)
Assembling the salvaged stone portico.

Figure 2.108 (below)
Detail of the stone portico demonstrating the difference between freshly cut stone and stone left as found.

would achieve by simply working with new brick and stone. It should be noted that the project will be upcycling bits of stone into reusable building components, so that when the house is deconstructed it will be taken down as a group of useful components: columns, beams, etc., not just lumps of stone.

When I ask if this is simply an academic exercise, Wilton and Howland are quick to point out that the main live project has gone through a value-engineering exercise as part of a two-stage tender process. The result, I am assured, is a project that is less 'temple like and more domestic' than before. I can confirm that at the point of writing, archaeological excavations have been completed and the groundworks are due to start imminently, which is excellent news.

The whole building will be a material bank for the future, and due to the skill of the whole design team, the entrance sequence, spatial experience, materiality and architectural language of this house will be sublime. I can also report that the house has been selected as a LETI Pioneer Project.

Figure 2.109
Map of potential 'From the Thames to Eternity' sites.

Figure 2.110
Granite blocks being removed near Somerset House, London.

While I was writing this case study, Wilton and Howland were trying to raise awareness of their 'From the Thames to Eternity' project, another collaboration with CSK Architects. The Thames River wall at Victoria Embankment was built as part of Joseph Bazalgette's famous sewer system, which is currently being modernised in the form of Tideway's new £4bn SuperSewer project. The work has included the removal of about 500 tonnes of rough-sided granite blocks from the river wall near Charing Cross Station, which are currently being stored on a farm near Basildon. The City of Westminster and Tideway were keen to find public reuse projects for this material, which is obviously of huge cultural significance and could contribute to many building life cycles over the next thousand years and beyond. Wilton and Howland are working with the City of London on a series of temporary public space installations which will provoke discussion about reuse, circular economy and cultural heritage at a time when stone can make a significant contribution to a more sustainable built environment. Keeping the blocks 'in play' in such a visible form has also increased the likelihood of finding longer-term uses for the stones, with a possibility that they could be used as part of the landscaping for a significant new public space project either in the City of London or in Truro, from where much of the granite was originally quarried.

Figure 2.111
Granite blocks in storage, awaiting a new use.

Figure 2.112
Cork model workshop for design ideas to rework the salvaged granite.

OPINION

Oliver Wilton and Matthew Barnett Howland prove that if you have the energy and commitment, mixing research and teaching with live architectural practice can be fruitful, inspiring and impactful for the industry. They have an academic ability to communicate an idea well while continually questioning, observing and then questioning again. They then mix this with a healthy degree of romantic poetic licence, wit and even a bit of whimsy, in order to reuse and adapt, and ultimately learn from histories.

CASE STUDY No.10

22 Baker Street and Oasis Nature Garden by Marks Barfield Architects

THE STORY

Julia Barfield formed her practice Marks Barfield Architects (MBA) together with her husband David Marks in 1990, and over the last 30-plus years they have established themselves as multi-award-winning architects who are known particularly for eye-catching self-generated projects such as the London Eye (formerly the Millennium Wheel) from 2000, and more recently the i360 in Brighton. What is perhaps less known is that in more recent times the practice has had a big impact in the world of climate activism and what we might call a more climate-literate architecture. Barfield is an early member of the UK Architects Declare Steering Group, as well as being a regular participant in events run by Architects Climate Action Network. Marks Barfield's practice statement states:

> For us design is a powerful tool for good, both social and environmental. At its best it improves the quality of people's lives and lifts their spirit, while drawing on a minimum of the Earth's limited resources.[11]

Barfield's enthusiasm for understanding and practising an authentic, low-impact architecture has seen a rapid transformation in the way her practice functions. How does a practice working on large iconic projects that come along sometimes, plus more 'normal' commercial office, bridges, larger infrastructure projects and community buildings, change its working methodology? Collectively, the practice has curated and workshopped a Strategy for Change moving towards regenerative practice, with the in-house Climate Action Team meeting weekly to implement this.

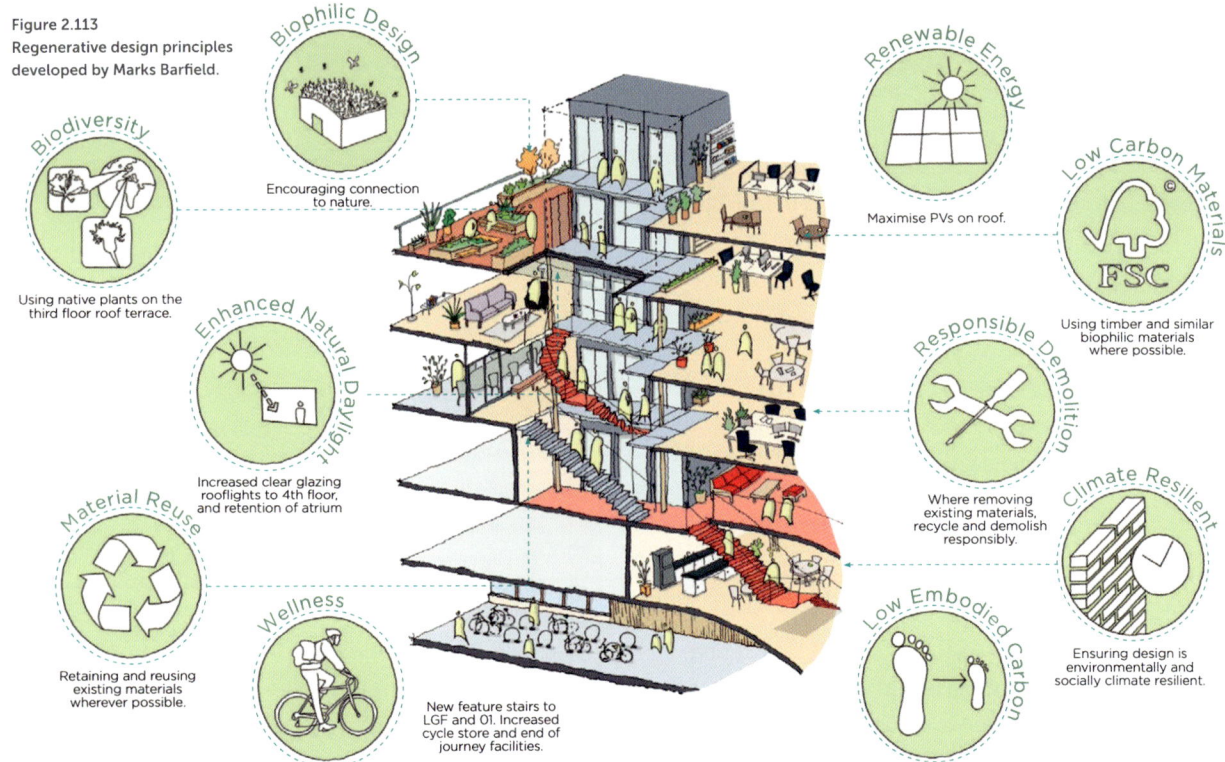

Figure 2.113
Regenerative design principles developed by Marks Barfield.

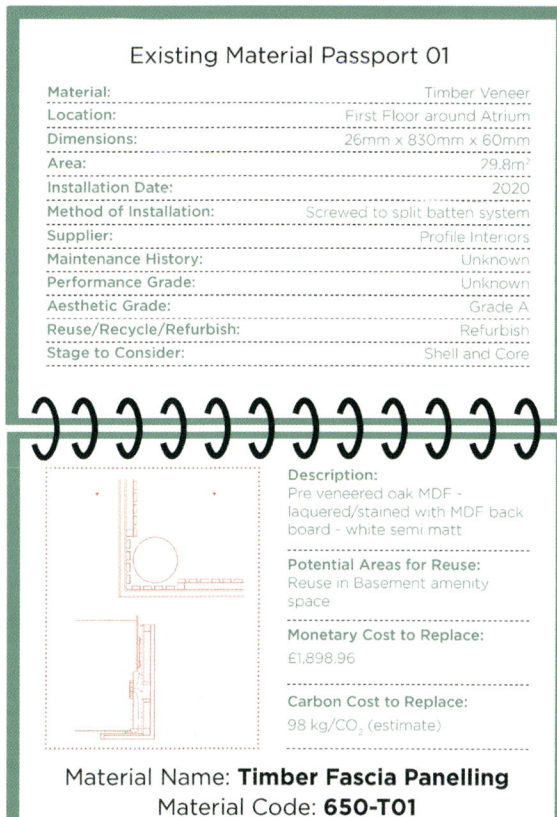
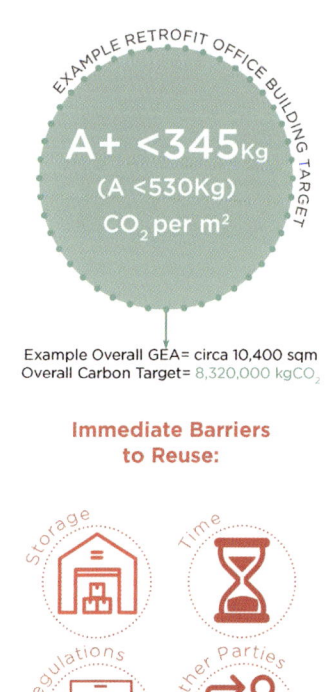

Figure 2.114
Marks Barfield's in-house material passport.

Marks Barfield have taken one of their own office refurbishment projects, 22 Baker Street in London, and convinced their client, Lazari Investments, to use it as a vehicle to test out emerging circular economy practices. First, the Marks Barfield team, including Ian Rudolph and Darcy Arnold-Jones, presented clear infographics to the client explaining the many benefits of regenerative design and moving from a linear economy to a circular economy. Clear carbon-saving performance targets were agreed, together with a working methodology that allowed time to question and rationalise the original brief. Three main routes for reuse were curated, with the ideal scenario to reuse materials in situ, failing this to relocate within the building or donate to a recipient building – a nearby charity project in Stockwell (the UK is currently lacking in infrastructure to facilitate the redistribution of materials). This was with a view to avoiding downcycling and enabling upcycling wherever possible. From their experience, often the term 'recycling' in demolition refers to a process of devaluing the existing materials with carbon-intensive repurposing processes. MBA conducted extensive site investigations and auditing at 22 Baker Street, creating a material

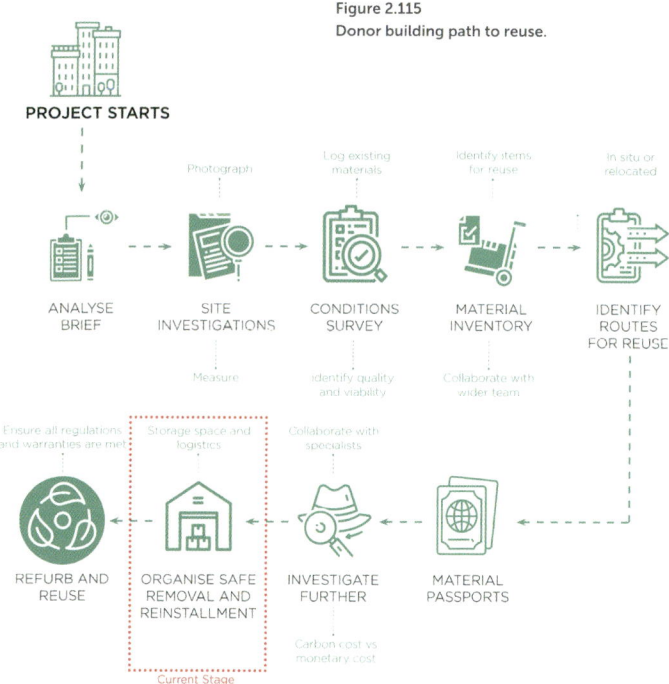

Figure 2.115
Donor building path to reuse.

OPINION

Marks Barfield are clear that reuse makes sense for all parties involved, but unfortunately these are still early days in the UK as far as extensive reuse is concerned. Until we get the infrastructure we need to facilitate the systems change a circular economy demands, disruptive architects and engineers such as Julia Barfield, plus their informed and similarly motivated clients, will have to try to do it themselves. MBA are currently organising workshops with insurers and specifiers (NBS), along with all players in the construction industry, to pinpoint the key barriers and push for real change. In addition to applauding Barfield's insight, energy and inspiration, I thought I would end this case study with the short list of the lessons Marks Barfield learnt from their first foray into the world of the circular economy, and reuse in particular:

1. Reuse in situ, with the materials in their existing form, is usually the best primary route in terms of cost, logistics and carbon.
2. Collaboration is key: in early design stages, get all relevant parties involved, including a deconstruction contractor to find a clear path for reuse.
3. Clearly plan out risks and address them as early as possible (surveys of existing doors for fire certification, for example).
4. A key practicality is storage and standardisation of the reuse inventory and logging system.
5. Ensure good records of manufacture, supplier and certification are kept, particularly with respect to fire-rated items.
6. Reuse items will need a demand – otherwise they will sit in a warehouse. (Good reuse hosts are usually small community/charity projects, but ideally this will soon become more mainstream.)
7. Building contracts and specifications need to be tailored to facilitate a circular economy, putting duties and responsibilities on the relevant parties.

Figure 2.116
Baker Street project – deconstructed materials.

Figure 2.117
Baker Street deconstructed materials in temporary storage.

inventory of the building, then identifying the routes for reuse, and in the process developing a system for material passports. Steered by Orms, they are currently working with an industry working group who are looking to standardise in this area. Currently at RIBA Stage 5, MBA are now focused on gathering existing material passports for the operation and maintenance (O&M) manuals to aid in the future reuse of these materials. As well as a detailed description of the element, there are details of its installation date, maintenance history, as well as the monetary (date sensitive) and carbon costs to replace said item.

While certainly a success regarding both monetary and carbon savings, the process also indicated clear barriers to reuse within the industry, in particular storage, time, warranties and certification and the changing of mindsets needed. At the time of writing, the interior spaces of 22 Baker Street were being carefully stripped out, with the components being carefully wrapped and protected for temporary storage. The issue of how best to disassemble and store material removed from a building is being discussed a lot in the UK at the moment, with numerous local authorities, private landlords and developers undertaking feasibility studies considering ideas for providing digital material exchange platforms (such as the Excess Materials Exchange and Material Index) or physical circular economy construction hubs (like Rotor in Brussels). Due to the lack of formal reuse/redistribution infrastructure in the UK, the design team are left with working it out for themselves, and in this case Marks Barfield's clients happened to have an empty building nearby which is currently being used to store materials for the recipient building, Oasis Nature Garden. This is a newbuild charity project initiated as a test case for a project built entirely out of reused materials. As with a number of architects incorporating reuse into new buildings, Marks Barfield have produced a beautifully rendered axonometric drawing explaining the origins of all elements that constitute the building.

CASE STUDY No.11

Resource Rows and Svanen Kindergarten by the Lendager Group

THE STORY

Anders Lendager is perhaps one of the architects making the most visual impact with his determinedly low-resource-consuming architecture projects, and with this point in mind, it's worth dwelling on Lendager's route into sustainable design. He first studied at the Aarhus School of Architecture, where, not unusually, sustainable architecture was not on the curriculum. As Lendager put it when I interviewed him for this book, 'There was a pragmatic approach to architecture', pointing students in the direction of OMA and MVRDV. However, Lendager was more interested in what he calls an 'American Approach of complex geometries', a digital approach to fabrication inspired by Greg Lynn and Neil Denari – an approach that considered how we could manufacture buildings in a more intelligent way'. It was only when Lendager went to SCI-Arc (Southern California Institute of Architecture) that he found another working methodology that immediately inspired him, and from which we can see a direct link to the way the Lendager Group operates today. Lendager worked with American architect and educator Michael Rotondi who, as Lendager puts it, 'was building with materials that were already there!'. In particular, Lendager cites a swimming pool made from an articulated lorry trailer. This was a pivotal moment in Lendager's life; not necessarily an overtly sustainable way of designing, but different from the normal ways of doing, creating a completely new narrative that was satisfying clients' requirements while offering a different material pallet.

By the early 2000s, Lendager was still fascinated by exploring alternative material sources. Like a number of people, he was

Figure 2.118
Detail view of the 'new' school buildings at Svanen Kindergarten.

From top:

Figure 2.119
One of the brick buildings used for source material for Resource Rows.

Figure 2.120
Angle grinding a second-hand brick panel.

Figure 2.121
Second-hand brick panels waiting to be installed.

looking into the viability of reusing shipping containers; there were just so many of them stacked up high along quaysides in coastal cities around the world. From Lendager's point of view, if one applied some design intelligence to these undervalued 'waste flows', then one would add lots of value to the situation, and this would enable a former waste product to be considered a valuable resource worth investing in. As with other consultants interested in challenging the idea of 'waste', Lendager is passionate about discovering waste from one sector and matching it as a resource for another to create beautiful architecture. He is also very interested in aesthetics – more of this later.

At the same time as being preoccupied with resource flows, Lendager found himself completing his master's in architecture while working with Hopkins Architects on the competition of the UK Antarctic Halley Research Station. What astounded Lendager was the fact that, like him, the scientists understood the consequences of excessive CO_2 emissions causing global warming that was affecting the massive ice shelf, but unlike him they were not so aware of the problems associated with the mass consumption of raw materials. It was at this point that Lendager realised that things could only change if humans changed the way we behave, and architects could affect such a change by becoming responsible 'resource managers'.

To avoid simply being the guy that 'puts stuff together' and with over seven years of frustrating experiences where 'I couldn't make an argument for sustainable architecture that would be understood', Lendager broke away and set up his own eponymous practice. With a promise to focus only on authentic sustainable design, to create a new systemic approach to architecture to allow himself to break free of existing systems, the Lendager Group was formed in 2011. One early decision was that to create a team of people with the diverse skills required to practise architecture in a different way, Lendager did not hire only architects. Old ways of architecture that provide drawings and written specifications without questioning the ways buildings are assembled and what they are made of would not do. In addition, Lendager realised that as well as the design team needing to skill up, clients often needed to be made aware of the many opportunities and challenges sustainable, closed-loop systems present. So, right from the outset, Lendager Group offered clients what we might call 'climate literacy' workshops, which gave them the opportunity to make clear what their ambitions were, while setting them within the context of sustainable, regenerative outcomes.

For the last decade, the Lendager Group has been one of the leading practices asking questions of our high-consuming, carbon-intensive buildings. Whether curating beautiful, thoughtful and powerful exhibitions such as 'Wasteland' in 2017 at the Danish Architecture Centre, or publishing books such as 2018's *A Change-Maker's Guide to the Future*, Anders Lendager has brought his energies and intellect to the international architecture stage. Projects such as Copenhagen's Resource Rows caught the attention of the international architectural press, perhaps because it is one of the first commercial architectural designs, rolled out at a larger scale, that appears to actively engage with the aesthetic potentials this new reuse sensibility presents to us all. It is interesting that the reused brick cladding for these 92 residential townhouses and apartments was gleaned from four redundant buildings due for demolition. Lendager convinced his clients to invest in carefully cutting up four quite different 1960s buildings due for demolition, instead of smashing them up into rubble as normal. It would prove to save money and reduce resources consumed.

The external brick cladding was cut into identical squares with a diamond-headed angle grinder. Interestingly, as the brick panels varied from red, to buff, to yellow, Lendager left it to the contractors on site to select the order in which the different brick panels would sit together to create the eye-catching chequerboard façade. Although the existing mortar binding the bricks together was strong, Lendager had to reinforce the panels by pouring a layer of concrete on the backside of the

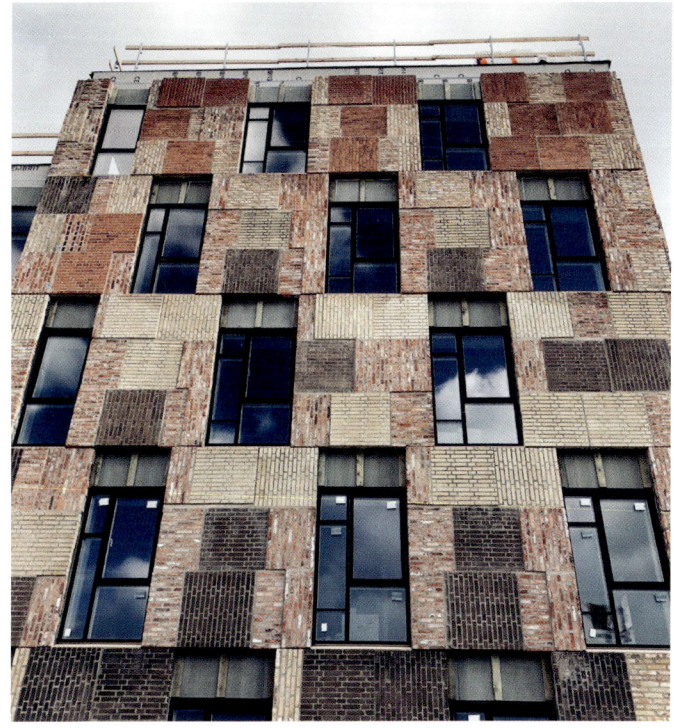

From top:

Figure 2.122
Second-hand brick panels installed at Resource Rows.

Figure 2.123
Detail of second-hand brick panels installed.

Figure 2.124
Resource Rows, almost complete.

Figure 2.125
Site strategy for the deconstruction and reconstruction of existing building material at Svanen Kindergarten.

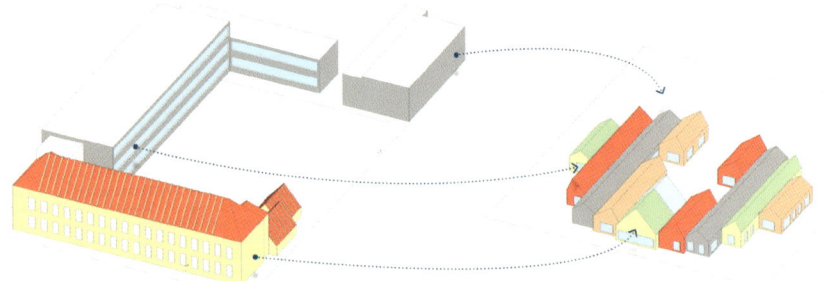

Figure 2.126
Exploded axonometric of the reconstruction of the 'new' school building using material from the old school.

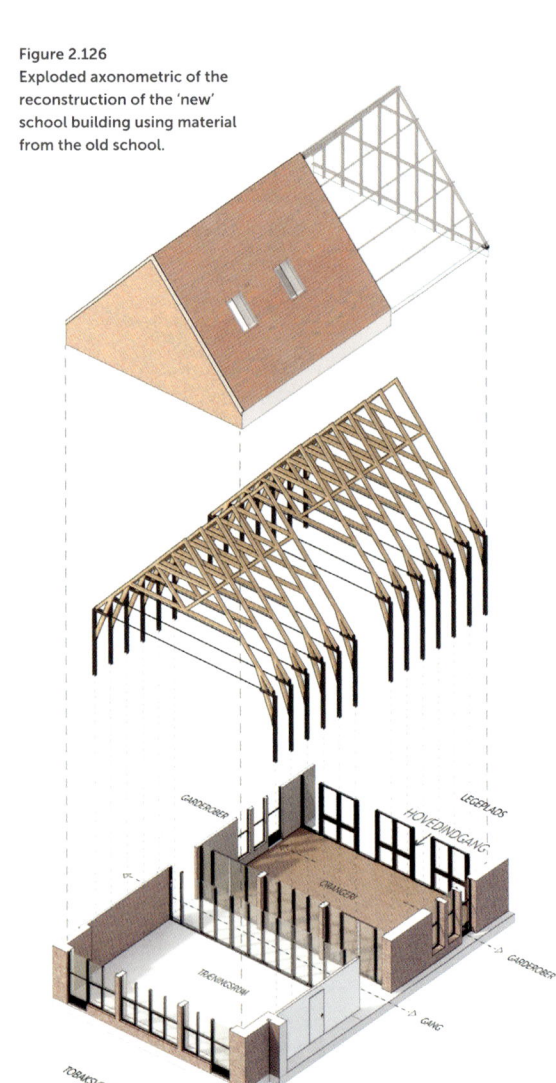

Figure 2.127
Detail drawing describing the reinforcement required to reuse existing timber trusses.

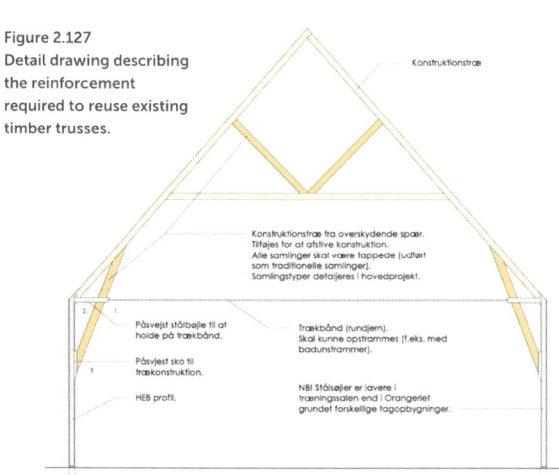

panels. Although 'low carbon' concrete, this detail could be seen as an unfortunate but necessary compromise. We would hope for alternative detail in future projects. The result, of course, is stunning; a clear signal towards a future where reuse is normal practice, but like most inventive, new ideas, it now appears like an obvious thing to do – but Lendager was the first.

Resource Rows, completed in 2020, has rightly attracted international attention. Its bold reappropriation of ubiquitous brick and cement-based mortar walls is to be applauded. In addition, this project reused waste timber offcuts, from a nearby metro construction site, for external façades and internal walls and floors. Second-hand windows were used to create 29 rooftop 'greenhouse huts', for cultivating homegrown vegetables, and large second-hand concrete 'TT' beams form a dramatic high-level bridge between two of the housing blocks.

Lendager estimate that this approach to the design of this residential housing scheme has prevented 463 tonnes of waste material going to landfill or incineration.

As with all Lendager projects, reuse of materials and products is only one facet of the sustainable and regenerative approach. The greenhouses and allotment gardens are producing over a tonne of vegetables for the community each year, and shared communal spaces provide a venue for a community choir, 'common house' meetings and a 'sharing station' and 'bike repair station'. In addition, homes have low utility bills, and the built fabric is extremely robust, which should mean long life and low maintenance.

Lendager Group has recently completed another project, the Svanen Kindergarten in Gladsaxe, near Copenhagen. The reuse ambitions of this project appear even bigger than Resource Rows, with Lendager claiming that it has 'the largest percentage of reused/upcycled materials in Denmark'. This project uses deconstructed material from the old school buildings on the adjacent site to help create the new kindergarten buildings. Unfortunately, the existing buildings were in such a bad state of repair that refurbishment was deemed inappropriate. So, back in 2016, the Gladsaxe Municipality commissioned engineers Niras to undertake a detailed resource map of the existing school buildings with a view to determining the amount of material and componentry worth salvaging for the newbuild project. Lendager Group was commissioned as architect because of its expertise in closed-loop, circular construction systems. The client's ambition was to reuse as much material as possible from the old school. Intriguingly, one of the reasons for doing this was to keep hold of some of the social histories imbued within these materials.

Lendager's response was to create a new kindergarten building, completed in 2023, that reads as a collection of separate but linked buildings dressed in a series of different material finishes – brick, clay tile, timber and aluminium – much of which once resided on the old school. The process of deconstruction, material selection, cleaning, storing and reuse

From top:

Figure 2.128
Deconstruction of existing school buildings at Svanen Kindergarten.

Figure 2.129
The process of reusing timber trusses.

Figure 2.130
Roof and wall materials were salvaged from the existing school.

Figure 2.131
Salvaged trusses were installed in the 'new' school buildings.

Figure 2.132
An aerial view of the 'new' school buildings.

was managed efficiently on the site, which had the space to deal with these unusual processes. One element of the old school building that is very apparent in the new kindergarten is the new orangery foyer, formed by six salvaged timber trusses that have been slightly altered to fit their new 21st-century role, and strengthened with some steel brackets and ties. In total, 27 trusses were removed in their whole state, with the others cut down. Due to fire regulations (60 minutes rating required) only six trusses were reused as trusses. However, the rest of the timber was either used within the new buildings or stored on site for the school to use in future shed and playground projects. Other surplus materials were collected by the deconstruction company, Tscherning, for use in its new headquarters building, which is currently under construction.

Lendager will soon be publishing thorough data on the amount of material reused, the carbon saved and problems encountered. But it's safe to say that this project happened because the client, the municipality and all the design team were committed to making it a success – and they had the space on site to deal with the unconventional processes required to turn a derelict 19th-century school into a new low-carbon, 21st-century kindergarten.

OPINION

Like many of the people we interviewed for this book, Anders Lendager was frustrated with the normal way things are done in the construction sector, and he decided to do something about it. What separates him from most is that he decided to tackle the behaviour and systems changes that need to happen while setting up his own idea of a practice. From the complete reimagining of what an architectural practice might do, who might be employed and what services he might provide, Lendager set about on an ambitious campaign of communication via books and exhibitions, before constructing any significant buildings. This appears to have got clients and collaborators up to speed with the energy and knowledge required to commence on a journey creating closed-loop architecture, one that begins to value the histories of the people, materials and even whole buildings/places that have been adapted in the name of reuse. This ambitious and holistic approach has also spawned companies (see the case study on a:gain in Step 1) which develop the products and materials that practices such as Lendager require. We will be keeping an eye on further developments and wish Lendager and his colleagues the best of luck for the future as he starts to collaborate with larger, more established practices.

STEP 3

Reducing Waste

DEFINITION

THIS CHAPTER COVERS projects that demonstrate an ability to reduce the amount of material used during the whole life cycle. These products could still use materials that are not 'circular' and in effect merely stall the inevitable problem (unless someone solves the problem) of how to dispose of synthetic and toxic material. These projects require strategic thinkers from the outset of the design process, people who have a deep understanding of existing design and manufacture processes and, crucially, material flows. Once the existing systems are understood, these innovators unpack them and look at ingenious ways of providing the same 'stuff' but in a less resource-hungry way.

WHAT IS RETROFIT: A REUSE/REDUCE OPPORTUNITY

If there is one subject that occupies the thoughts of many people in the construction sector more than most, it is retrofit. What is retrofit? How to do it? Who can do it? How can we afford to do it? Do we have the skill base and knowledge to support a national retrofit programme in the UK? Should our government subsidise low-carbon retrofit? Is it not a huge opportunity for green jobs? And if we are trying the sell the idea to a mass audience, can we not come up with a better word than retrofit? My colleague Graeme Brooker has even published a book (*50|50 Words for Reuse – A Minifesto*[1]) dedicated to considering alternative words for reuse, anything other than retrofit (see also Brooker's Foreword to this book).

Current discussions around retrofit come after one of the most disruptive times in modern human history. The rise of direct-action protests by numerous groups – including climate activist and school striker Greta Thunberg, Extinction Rebellion and others – have accelerated the understanding of the existential problems that the climate and ecological emergency present humankind. In 2019, over 90% of UK local authorities declared a climate and ecological emergency and committed to being net-zero carbon by 2030![2] Since then, COVID-19 has changed the world to such an extent that we in the Global North now occupy our built environment in ways never imagined pre-pandemic. Add to that an ongoing cost-of-living crisis accompanied by an energy crisis, and it's not surprising that there is a lot of interest in how to create buildings that are affordable and comfortable to occupy.

Perhaps most unexpectedly of all, groups of people have been exercising their right to peaceful protest by blocking traffic on busy roads across the UK, all in the name of insulating our homes![3] It is debatable how successful or not their actions have been in raising awareness of the need to retrofit the UK's infamously poorly insulated building stock. However, there is no getting away from the fact that issues more normally discussed by low-carbon-minded people in the construction industry are now part of everyday political discourse.

Back in 2005, there was no award category for reuse or retrofitting properties, and more precisely there was virtually no interest in it as an architectural pursuit. As a consequence, my award-winning retrofit project (Dyke Road Avenue, Hove) was described as an award-winning 'new house', rather than what it really was. Contrast that with today, where the *Architects' Journal* has been handing out awards for retrofit projects for over 10 years, and the RIBA introduced its Reinvention Award in 2023 that 'recognises buildings that have been creatively reused to improve their environmental, social or economic sustainability – increasing the longevity and energy efficiency of existing buildings and reducing the need for demolition and new construction'.[4] The *Architects' Journal* even has its own Retrofirst campaign that is asking the UK government to reduce value added tax (VAT) on domestic retrofit projects. VAT is currently running at a whopping 20% and is applied to all labour and material costs, whereas if you demolish an existing building and rebuild it new, there is no VAT.

How times have changed for our industry. There is now a Retrofit Academy, which has been set up to address the skills gap in the retrofit sector while raising awareness in government, industry and academia. Its mission is to train 200,000 competent retrofitters by 2030. In addition, there is the National Retrofit Hub, which aims to bring together all parties involved in retrofit to deliver a National Retrofit Strategy for the UK's more than 27 million homes. Since 2019, there have been numerous cross-sector publications on low-carbon design. All of them highlight the need to reduce our sector's massive whole-life carbon footprint. What has been encouraging since the publication of the *Climate Emergency Design Guide*[5] from LETI (the Low Energy Transformation Initiative) in 2019 is the cross-sector input and cooperation in the publication of these guidelines. With all major parties supporting LETI and subsequent publications by the RIBA (including the 2030 Climate Challenge), IStructE, RICS, etc., there appears to be an emerging consensus of what we might call a Whole-Life Carbon Decent Plan, in other words, what good practice looks like. IStuctE's 'Part Z'[6] campaign for building regulations to limit

From top:

Figure 2.133
The original Docks de Paris warehouse building, dating from 1907.

Figure 2.134
Night-time image of the completed Cité de la Mode et du Design.

Figure 2.135
The external steel-and-glass skin added a new layer of fabric and activity.

levels of embodied carbon has gained more traction of late. This has encouraged the presentation of three separate draft Bills to the UK Parliament over the last two years, and I feel that it is only a matter of time before the embodied carbon footprint of any development will need to be calculated, declared and, crucially, kept below pre-agreed benchmarks. As soon as limiting of whole-life carbon is adopted by Building Control then the reuse of buildings instead of demolition will be the default position for most developments. I would argue that this new *sensibility*, or way of doing, will naturally trickle down and incentivise deconstruction over demolition, as well as the reuse of second-hand components instead of supplying new. Retrofit will be the natural choice, albeit one that needs to be supported with the appropriate physical infrastructure, digital platforms and favourable legislation. As I write, the UK Net Zero Carbon Buildings Standard[7] is being developed. As with other recent initiatives, this one has the support of most institutions representing all key components of the UK construction industry, including client-representing groups. It is hoped that it will provide the set of rules our industry can apply to every building typology to meet our whole-life carbon targets over the next five, ten, twenty, etc. years, up to 2050 when we are committed to being net-zero carbon.

In addition to providing the guidelines that we all hope inform legislation, recent times have presented a change in architectural sensibility. For example, one of the most esteemed awards for a body of architectural work is the Pritzker Prize, which is awarded every year. In 2021, Lacaton & Vassal won the award, stating that one should 'never demolish, never replace'.[8] In 2023, the same prize was awarded to David Chipperfield, who was even more direct when he stated, 'Retrofit is not only the right thing to do, it's the more interesting thing to do.'[9]

Is it finally becoming cool to retrofit? There are certainly many more designers, architects and engineers presenting ideas for reuse and retrofit schemes, some of which are being realised. However, as the Grenfell Tower[10] disaster has shown us all, wrapping an existing building in external wall insulation is not a straightforward

Figure 2.136
No. 5 Dyke Road Avenue, Hove, before its retrofit.

Figure 2.137
No. 5 Dyke Road Avenue, after its retrofit: The Sunday Times Eco House of the Year 2005.

exercise. All our built environment, not just our homes, has to be adapted to become a low-carbon version of itself. In addition, it needs to be *climate resilient*: brand new or not, our built environment is hardly ever designed with current weather patterns in mind. The other consideration is a consequence of the way we occupy our buildings post-COVID-19. With many people now working much of every week at home, our office space is underoccupied, while our homes are over-occupied.

For all of the above reasons, the responsibility for retrofitting/renewing/upgrading our built environment needs joined-up thinking as well as a diversity of approaches, depending on the vintage of the building, its typology, use and programme, site conditions, etc. This is a challenging job, but one that, as David Chipperfield points out, is more interesting than newbuild. It is also a huge opportunity, but to take best advantage of this we need our best designers, architects and engineers involved, using the best available data, in order to create a new layer of built environment that works with the existing situation, responds to our new and emerging behaviours, while creating authentic, low-carbon, healthy and climate-resilient environments that support regenerative natural ecosystems. You won't get that simply by wrapping building stock with external wall insulation and solar panels. Upgrading our complex and delightful built environment needs to allow for many approaches towards a simple end.

One of my favourite retrofit projects is still Jakob + MacFarlane's transformation of the Docks de Paris building from 1907 into the Cité de la Mode et du Design (City of Fashion and Design), which opened in 2010. Although never conceived as a retrofit project, it accidentally presented a model for many future low-carbon upgrades. The massive in situ cast-concrete frame and floor plates from the original shipping depot were kept, with the architects designing what they call a 'plug-over', which is actually an external steel-and-glass skin complemented with timber and grassed decks. The new façade is pulled away from the old frame to allow for a new circulation zone. The roof is topped off with an array of solar photovoltaic panels.

The reason I like this building is simple: the architects have seen the value in this simple piece of concrete infrastructure from over a century ago. With the minimum of effort, Jakob + MacFarlane have transformed it into a centre for high culture, and they have done this in a visually expressive and exuberant manner that begs the viewer to ask questions of this clever retrofit project. They have also done this with the minimum of new material, as the lightweight steel-and-glass façade makes the most of the potential of the old, strong and thermally massive concrete frame to work hard for the new design.

The Cité de la Mode et du Design is an ingenious solution to a design challenge. However, the large size of the site and the single occupant make the project perhaps an easier nut to crack than the biggest retrofit challenge we have: how to convert multi-occupancy, unloved and poorly maintained housing estates. It is this challenge that we will consider now.

The UK, which has more than 27 million homes, has some of the most energy-inefficient dwellings in Europe. As a result, they are also the most expensive in Europe to heat. Some 50% of these homes were built before 1960, with only 10% built since 1990.[11] One of the consequences of this situation is that fuel poverty[12] is also at a higher level in the UK than in any other comparable EU country. Over 10 million families live in fuel poverty in properties with a leaking roof, damp walls and rotting windows. Despite this, UK CO_2 emissions have fallen by 35% when compared to 1990 levels.[13] However, the UK needs to reduce its CO_2 emissions by a total of 80% when compared to 1990 levels, and this needs to happen by 2050. Another issue is that many experts estimate that 80 to 90% of the houses currently standing will be the structures trying to meet these ambitious targets in 2050.[14] For numerous reasons, the UK doesn't build much housing or demolish it.

The lack of demolition is a good thing for the environment. However, the high-energy consumption associated with these leaky old structures is not. So, with this in mind I wanted to dwell briefly on the big challenge of how to adapt existing UK housing, new and old, so that it is climate-change resilient. This challenge should not be underestimated. The temptation to demolish large housing estates from the 1950 to 1970s is great, but as the UK learnt with the wholesale destruction of its so-called slums to make way for these large estates, along with the clearing of the Victorian terraces, the bulldozers destroyed whole communities. A well-informed retrofit project has the potential to greatly enhance the performance of a place without destroying the community it supports.

Retrofit is complex. This is plain to see for anybody having a go at it. The UK government's innovation agency, Innovate UK, undertook extensive research into this subject, supporting more than 80 retrofit case studies via its Retrofit the Future initiative. This programme gave architects and social landlords the challenge of retrofitting examples of UK social housing from the 1870s to the 1970s. All 84 case studies had a (large) budget of £150,000 to spend on often very modest buildings, together with an ambition to reduce CO_2 emissions to meet the UK government's 2050 targets. Only eight of the case studies met this target.[15]

Unfortunately, since the first edition of this book was published in 2017, it still feels like early days for retrofit. Despite the efforts of the Retrofit Academy, the National Retrofit Hub, etc., there are still few designers, contractors or clients who understand the actual complexities and challenges involved in delivering a successful retrofit project. Many retrofit projects deal with only some of the problems that a building might have. Some buildings have been overclad with external wall insulation that dramatically reduces heat loss through the building fabric. However, this fabric-focused approach often comes at a cost for the tenants, resulting in poor internal air quality due to a virtually airtight fabric and poor background ventilation. The knock-on effect, especially in winter, is mould on internal walls due to a build-up of moisture in the air. Another problem many people are anticipating is a new type of 'fuel poverty', i.e. the inability of some tenants to afford the bolt-on air-cooling devices to deal with overheating in the summer months. Retrofitting needs to be delivered in a holistic manner, where the design team and contractors have a deep understanding of building physics and a sensitivity towards the tenants they have to work around.

The good news is that there is an increasing number of architects and engineers providing excellent retrofit schemes, and a number of these are discussed at some length further on in this chapter. The wholesale retrofitting of our cities and towns to achieve an authentic, low-carbon lifestyle is one of society's biggest challenges and will require an innovative and visionary approach that, above all, is well informed with the knowledge and skills to deliver better places for everybody to live, work and play. External wall insulation and solar panels are only two of the tools at a designer's disposal: they will not create sustainable, circular cities on their own. These 'new' retrofitted, upgraded and adapted places have to function with hugely reduced carbon footprints, and this cannot be achieved without local, regional and central government's buy-in and support. Retrofitting our leaky homes cannot achieve a low-carbon lifestyle in isolation; it requires joined-up thinking and education.

CASE STUDY No.1

Rotor

THE STORY

Since writing this case study back in 2016, Rotor, based in Brussels, have decided to focus their services on advising design teams on the reuse potential of construction projects. In addition, they undertake deconstruction projects themselves, providing facilities to process, store and redistribute second-hand building components for new construction projects. They also run impactful research programmes, such as the €4.5 million Interreg FCRBE project, which 'aims to increase by +50%, the amount of reclaimed building elements being circulated on its territory by 2032'.[16]

I have interviewed more than 100 people for this book. All of them are fully engaged with different aspects of designing systems and products that, to a greater or lesser degree, can be described as being on the way towards a circular economy. However, I have found that Rotor, perhaps more than anybody else, are happy to try to unpack and critically evaluate the real challenges, intellectual and otherwise, presenting 21st-century human settlements that endeavour to exist in harmony with the planet. However tedious the research or dismantling/making processes are, Rotor will take the project on if they believe it will further their understanding of the potentials for a reuse economy.

I first came across Rotor when a colleague of mine, architect Anthony Roberts, reported back to me from the 2010 Venice Architecture Biennale. He had just stumbled across their 'Wear' exhibition for the Belgian Pavilion. It looked more like a 1960s installation by a minimalist artist, and Roberts was struck by the precision of the curating, the beauty of the artefacts displayed, as well as the sheer amount of white space on the walls. Entitled 'usus/usures', which literally means 'make/wear down', this exhibition was interested in considering the traces of use and wear on everyday building. Once you get past their beauty, these familiar objects reveal the effects of years of contact with human hands or feet. By being cleverly placed in the rarefied environment of a gallery, these objects were reappraised

Figure 2.138
Stair treads, Belgian Pavilion,
Venice Biennale, 2010.

Clockwise from top left:

Figure 2.139
Salvaged marble tiles waiting to be sold.

Figure 2.140
Commercial office downlighting carefully removed for reuse.

Figure 2.141
Marble tiles for resale.

Figure 2.142
Removing marble wall tiles for reuse.

Figure 2.143
Lifting ceramic floor tiles for reuse.

Figure 2.144
Dismantling a raised office floor for reuse.

Figure 2.145
A selection of worn artefacts, Belgian Pavilion, Venice Biennale, 2010.

OPINION

Rotor have adapted their design practice so that it now provides a one-stop shop for deconstructing, redesigning and rebuilding projects, promising a complete circular process. Rotor are able to supply this service because of the different skills within their practice. They have experienced architects, but also people such as Lionel Billiet, who have been prepared to work on in-depth research projects considering the real commercial potential within the construction industry of reused materials and fittings. For example, when Rotor had the opportunity to work on a government report testing the legal frameworks required to support a national reuse industry, Billiet, together with other members of Rotor and legal experts, grabbed the opportunity. The resultant document, entitled *Vade-Mecum for Off-Site Reuse*, is a manual with comprehensive guidelines for public works projects considering the reuse of building materials in the Brussels Capital Region. The guidelines are, of course, easy to adapt for other provinces in Belgium, elsewhere in Europe and beyond. The *Vade-Mecum* provides a step-by-step methodology helping clients to understand the processes of identification, reclamation and transfer of reusable materials, so that it is done in accordance with public procurement legislation. This work has gained Rotor the 'Publica Award', which is given to the most innovative tendering strategy promoting sustainable design. Their work makes it possible for people to salvage construction material for reuse that was previously designated as waste and, in effect, untouchable.

It is this sort of rigorous approach that sets Rotor's works ahead of most of their contemporaries. The fact that they can turn their hands to writing interesting books, curating thought-provoking and beautiful exhibitions, while writing legal handbooks and designing award-winning architectural projects, makes Rotor one of the true 'pathfinders' in the emergent circular economy.

by visitors as abstract artefacts. Once their true 'self' became apparent again, one could re-evaluate them and consider the narratives behind, for example, a red carpet from a social housing apartment in Antwerp that clearly demonstrates the position of a pivot chair and a table. Although Rotor are keen to point out that this was not an exhibition about reuse, it is clearly linked to their focus on reappraising the value in discarded artefacts. In their own words, the exhibition and accompanying publication is 'the result of an intensive investigation carried out in Belgium, analysing wear as a material phenomenon and as an agent capable of influencing actions. Wear is approached not as a problem in itself, the result of an error of conception that must be avoided at all costs, but as an inevitable and potentially creative process.' On reading this statement, one can clearly see the link to their current focus on material reuse – or 'deconstruction', as they call it.

Rotor's Deconstruction programme is the most pertinent part of their practice for this book. Filed under 'research' on their website, 'Rotor Deconstruction' is a hands-on business that has been informed after almost a decade of research on the flows of materials in numerous industries, including construction. The programme is now a separate cooperative company with its own website that has the skills and knowledge to focus on the careful dismantling of parts or the whole of a building and then selling on the reusable materials.

CASE STUDY No.2

Lacaton & Vassal

THE STORY

For over 30 years, Anne Lacaton and Jean Philippe Vassal have been practising together from their studio in Paris. Since I interviewed Lacaton in 2016 for the first edition of this book, they have been awarded the prestigious Pritzker Architecture Prize, with the award panel noting, 'There is a humility in the approach that respects the aims of the original designers and the aspirations of the current occupants.'[17] Lacaton & Vassal have said that architects should 'never demolish, never replace'.[18] 'Nuff said.

Lacaton & Vassal have a very clear position about the potential of design to benefit the day-to-day lives of individuals and communities. Their practice is characterised by a desire to work with the existing qualities of a site, seeing these as an opportunity and strength. They have a pragmatic approach towards issues of climate change and sustainability as a whole: never relying on expensive technological solutions, rather considering challenges in a genuinely holistic manner. Famously, when the partnership won a commission to overhaul and master plan a town square in France, after exhaustive research, they went back to their clients and confirmed that the current square was working perfectly fine except for a couple of park benches that were valued by the community and needed repairing. In effect, this lost them a large commission, although it gained the practice huge credibility among its peers, and as a direct result saved a huge amount of material resources as the client accepted their proposal.

They are, however, perhaps best known for having an acute awareness of how to make generous, beautiful spaces affordable: they make clients' money go further than most. One of their first projects that demonstrated this ability was the commission to retrofit the Palais de Tokyo in Paris. Originally opened in 1937, it had suffered from many decades of neglect, especially after the opening of the Pompidou Centre in the late 1970s. In the late 1990s, Lacaton & Vassal received a rather unusual enquiry from the Palais de Tokyo team. Since the mid-1990s, there had been plans to update the extensive Neo-Classical buildings: they were in a poor state of repair and not suitable for curating late 20th-century contemporary art. However, by the time Lacaton & Vassal were contacted, the Palais de Tokyo had just stopped renovation works on site: the construction and design team had spent three-quarters of the construction budget on one-quarter of the works. Lacaton & Vassal's challenge was to complete three-quarters of the works with one-quarter of the original budget. This they famously did.

The approach to this project was simple. They looked at the fabric of the building, which comprised an in situ cast-concrete frame that the previous design team were spending substantial sums of money covering over, and pretty much left the interior spaces in a state of partial refurbishment. They spent money in an informed, frugal way (where occupants touched materials) and delivered this successful project at build rates that were one-third of those originally anticipated.

Lacaton & Vassal have an extensive knowledge of construction materials and systems new and old, and they understand where to apply additional fabric and when to leave it alone. Their point of view is that by keeping everything 'raw' there is an honesty of materiality. When they were commissioned in 2010 to expand the Palais de Tokyo facilities into underutilised areas, they 'distanced themselves from the idea of seeking a form of aesthetic perfection and spectacular architecture'; they 'reactivated' the original qualities of a building which had been unloved for a long time.

The second project discussed here is in many ways even more successful at demonstrating an informed, cost-effective, resource-saving alternative solution. Lacaton & Vassal's approach to the challenge of creating a new 16-storey high-rise tower to replace the ageing 1960s Tour Bois-le-Prêtre, in Paris, saved a whole lot of materials from going to landfill, reduced the energy consumption on site by over 50% and, most importantly to the architects, provided hugely improved apartments for the tenants. The first smart move was not to demolish the building, but to partner with the original architect, Raymond Lopez, who had an intimate knowledge of

Clockwise from top left:

Figure 2.146
An extremely 'light touch' retrofit of existing buildings, Palais de Tokyo, Paris.

Figure 2.147
The complete transformation of the Tour Bois-le-Prêtre, Paris, undertaken without demolition.

Figure 2.148
The interior of a typical apartment in the Tour Bois-le-Prêtre before retrofitting works began.

Figure 2.149
A typical apartment in the tower after the addition of a new 'winter garden' and balcony.

Figure 2.150
La Tour Bois-le-Prêtre after a previous refurbishment in 1990.

Figure 2.151
A later project applying a similar strategy at Grand Parc in Bordeaux, before retrofit.

Figure 2.152
Grand Parc in Bordeaux, after retrofit in 2016.

the building. The team then proposed a radical solution to the idea of renovation. They decided to keep the interiors of the existing 96 'sheltered' apartments untouched but remove the ugly precast concrete cladding system that had been applied in the 1970s and replace it with fully glazed 'winter gardens' that rather amazingly extended all the apartments by about 2m. The concrete panels were removed, and each winter garden was applied while the tenants still occupied the apartments.

The new layer literally wraps the old building and in doing so provides greatly increased levels of natural light, increased natural ventilation, better quality of air, a reduced likelihood of overheating, which is a big problem with south-facing tower blocks (these unheated 'environmental buffer zones' keep the original apartments cooler in the summer and warmer in the winter). Crucially, all of these 'passive' low-tech devices are controlled by the tenants occupying the apartments: different tenants can have different setups.

Since the completion of the Tour Bois-le-Prêtre in 2011, Lacaton & Vassal have applied the exact same strategies to a larger project known as Grand Parc, in Bordeaux. Again, this was a collaboration with the original architects who designed this collection of three large residential blocks, and again the tenants did not have to leave while this radical transformation of their homes (completed in 2016) took place.

When I spoke to Anne Lacaton, she was keen to stress that they are not 'green' or 'eco' architects. Their primary ambition 'is always to create amazing environments for all people. Intelligent design should always address all environments.'

OPINION

These projects are inspiring, thought-provoking and, as with almost all good design, a simple, straightforward solution to a problem. Just think of how much waste material would have been created if the Tour Bois-le-Prêtre had been demolished and then simply replaced by another tower of a similar size, constructed in nearly identical materials. It is only the façades and services of contemporary high-rise buildings that are radically different to those constructed from the middle of the 20th century.

The projects identify the true value and potential of existing buildings, materials, systems and communities. By undertaking research at an almost forensic level, Lacaton & Vassal unearth unrealised potential, such as working with the original architect on the Tour Bois-le-Prêtre. The projects test the potential for our existing buildings to be material stores for the future: even the so-called difficult ones made of monolithic materials such as concrete and cement.

As they stated in their 2013 publication *Druot, Lacaton & Vassal Tour Bois-le-Prêtre*, 'Somebody who demolishes a building just to re-erect it on the same site but in a "contemporary look" has, in principle, gained absolutely nothing.'

Lacaton & Vassal have been true innovators. They question normal practice and use their skills as designers to create inspirational places for everybody that as a matter of course happen to be authentic, low-carbon solutions to everyday problems – and they do this with the minimum of fuss.

CASE STUDY No.3

Rented House Life by Sadaharu Komai

THE STORY

Japanese architects have a well-deserved reputation for being resourceful, often developing ingenious buildings on the smallest of plots, and with the minimum of resources. This is exemplified by the work of Tokyo's Atelier Bow-wow.

While teaching architecture, Sadaharu Komai, Associate Professor at Nagoya University of Arts, has also been building his own home in Kyoto for the past 25 years. Komai calls this project 'Rented House Life'. Over this time, he has built and then rebuilt his home, on four separate occasions and on four separate sites. Komai finds a site and leases the land or, in the first two cases, a building. He moves home when needs dictate: normally when his family expands. What is unusual is that when he leaves his old home, he dismantles it and takes it along to the new site. As each site to date has been bigger than the previous, he also brings new material in as well. So, the home expands each time.

It should be noted that even the latest Rented House 4 is by no means a large dwelling, with its floor area of just over 90m^2 – and that includes 24m^2 of carport and office. However, the first iteration, Rented House 1, was actually a 20m^2 extension wrapping around and on top of an existing dwelling. Komai moved in when he was still a student. This minute building was his home and workplace until he got married and his wife was expecting their first child.

The timber structure from the first project was dismantled and then reassembled in the new property. Komai's attention to detail ensured that the timber frame was originally assembled like flat-pack furniture. His building extensions were more akin to joinery.

In 1998, Komai, wife and new baby moved to Rented House 2. Komai states that this site 'was blessed with a beautiful surrounding environment and the rented house was also good quality, although old'. However, it was not large enough for his family, so Komai unpacked the two decks and the office structure from Rented House 1 and reassembled them at Rented House 2 to create a much-needed outdoor bathroom with adjacent living room/deck.

Rented House 3 was a small warehouse previously used by a picture framer. The original timber frame from Rented House 1

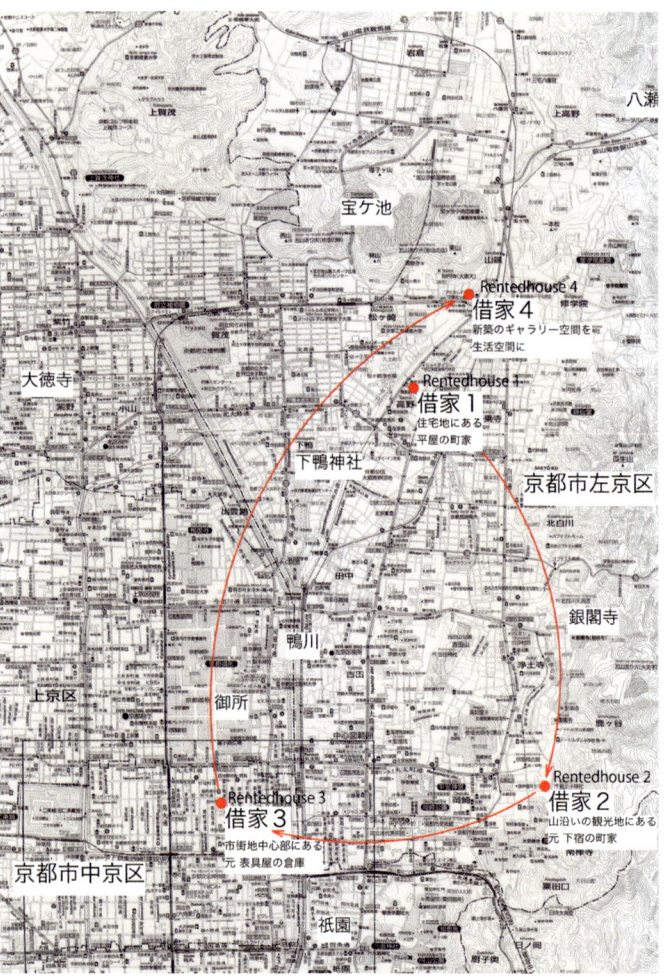

Figure 2.153
A map of Kyoto, showing the sites used for the four 'rented houses'.

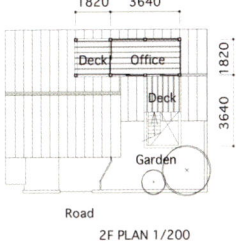
Rented house 1

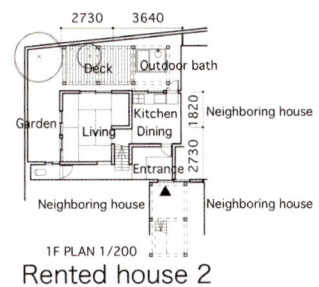
Rented house 2

Rented house 3

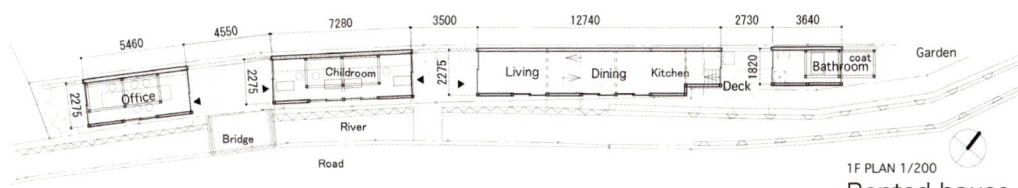
Rented house 4

Left and below:

Figure 2.154
Plans of the four iterations of Rented House 1–4.

Figure 2.155
Model of an addition to Rented House 1.

Figure 2.156
Model of Rented House 3, room within a room.

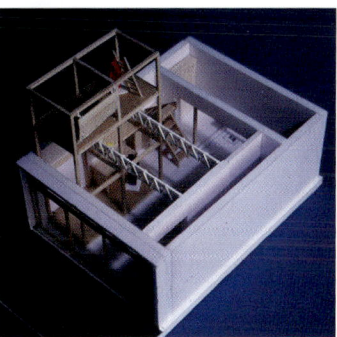

Left:

Figure 2.157
A room within a room in Rented House 3, being used by Professor Komai.

was reassembled here inside the existing building but turned on its head and added to it to create a three-storey intervention running through the vertical section of the building. It provided a home, office and now a gallery for this imaginative architect. The overall expansion of floor area was only 8m^2, but the existing warehouse was substantially bigger than previous rented buildings, and it needed to be – by this time Komai and his wife had four children.

The final iteration of this project presented quite a different challenge: there was no existing building, or conventional site. Komai's latest project, Rented House 4, sits on a former grass verge separated from a quiet residential road by a narrow river and backing onto a row of residential properties. At just over 2m wide, this site is more door threshold than a site to build one's new home. Again, the timber-frame structures were dismantled from the previous home, and, working with the original 1,820 x 3,640mm module, Komai repeated this module by a factor of three to allow this new dwelling to materialise as a narrow (1.8m) two-storey modular structure running along for about 40m. This is a modest yet beautiful home that also provides an office and gallery accessed via a bridge over a small river lined with trees. It is an ingenious and delightful outcome from a talented architect working on a very challenging site.

From top:

Figure 2.158
Timber from Rented House 1, creating washing and social space in Rented House 2.

Figure 2.159
A room within a room created in Rented House 3 using material from Rented House 1 and 2.

From top:

Figure 2.160
Model of Rented House 4.

Figure 2.161
The site for Rented House 4.

Figure 2.162
Rented House 4, completed.

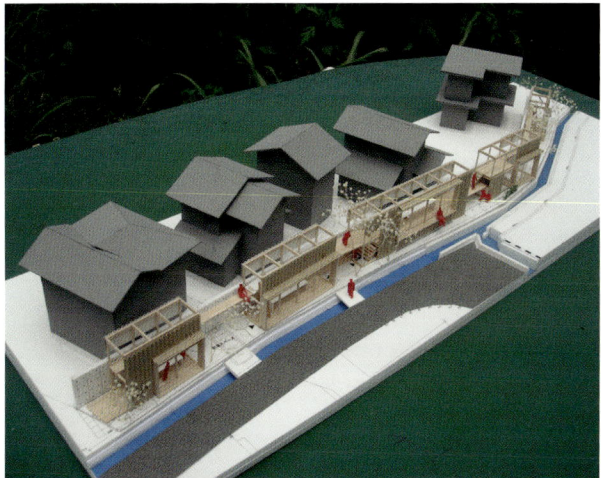

OPINION

It was unclear at the outset which 'step' Rented House should sit in. The timber frame from Rented House 1 resides in Rented House 4, along with additional material from the other two dwellings. The timber frame is reused again and again. This results in a reduction of material required for each new dwelling, and it appears that as the 'rented houses' have developed, a greater percentage of their building fabric has been reused for the next project, until we see the last iteration is a completely 'new' build project waiting for the next rebuild. In other words, Rented House 4 could be described as almost completely 'designed for remanufacture' and as a material store for a future project. As the project ran from its first to fourth iteration, it dealt with both the 'Reuse' and 'Reduce' steps, with Rented House 4 poised to demonstrate that it is a closed-loop system.

This project may appear modest and simple. However, it completely depends on a designer to detail it for deconstruction in the first place. Komai stuck rigorously to the 1,820mm x 3,640mm module used in all four projects. From the first dwelling to the last, the same timber frame has been reused but with quite different outcomes. By adding more of the same material, this construction system has been able to expand into ever bigger spaces, but in quite different ways. The timber-frame module goes from flat-pack furniture to becoming two mini towers and a bridge, a three-storey house within a house, and finally a 40m-long series of linked timber-framed boxes. This project demonstrates that with enough design ingenuity and foresight, closed-loop, humanmade systems are achievable.

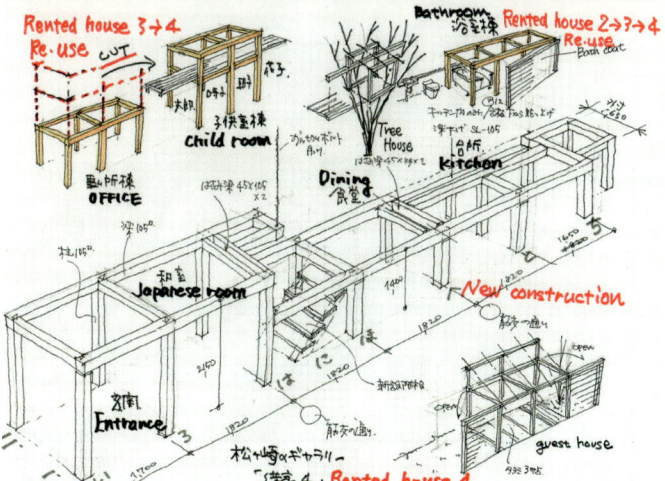

Figure 2.163
3D sketches describing the reused elements from Rented House 2, 3 and 4.

CASE STUDY No.4

Harry Paticas and RAFT

THE STORY

This case study is quite unlike any other in this book. Instead of focusing on the built manifestation of an idea, when discussing the work of RAFT (Retrofit Action for Tomorrow) and, in particular, their founder, the architect Harry Paticas, we will be examining the particular inclusive working methods used to enable the engagement of whole school communities in the low-carbon, cost-effective retrofitting of often neglected English state schools.

While Harry Paticas was studying for a degree in Astronomy ('I got a first for Relativity!'), he developed a fascination with the mathematics of art, which led him to study Art and Architecture in 15th-century Italy with the Open University. Once immersed in the history of perspective and the work of Alberti, Brunelleschi *et al.*, Paticas was hooked. He completed his undergraduate architecture studies at Kingston University and then had a particularly impactful experience studying his master's in architecture at the Architectural Association School of Architecture (AA) in London, where he spent a month in Peru studying the 'excreta practice' (a phrase that came from a World Bank report) of people living in rapidly expanding shanty towns. This deep-dive research involved Paticas working with epidemiologists and sanitation engineers to learn how and why cholera streams had spread so quickly across Peru. Focusing on human systems gave an insight into this community's impact on the planet and themselves.

Paticas's master's thesis project proposed a 'minor civilisation' of adaptable, desiccating toilets that responded to local climate, culture, available materials and the need to enrich low-grade soil. His passion to realise a prototype led to Paticas installing a temporary 20-tonne earth latrine in Exhibition Road near the Science Museum in London as part of the London Festival of Architecture. This installation highlighted the potential of human excrement to be processed into compost, as well as shining a light on a process that normally goes on out of sight, below our feet, an approach that would inform the latest work with RAFT. He says, 'I've always been interested in visualising invisible things, or things that are not seen, but we depend upon, such as Bazalgette's extensive network of sewers just below London's streets.'

Paticas says he was always aware of environmental issues. Being of both Greek and English descent, he spent many summer holidays as a child snorkelling in the clear Mediterranean Sea. Acutely aware of humans' often destructive presence, Paticas realised from a young age that the natural world is in fact not fragile, 'It's only fragile for the way we want to use it.'

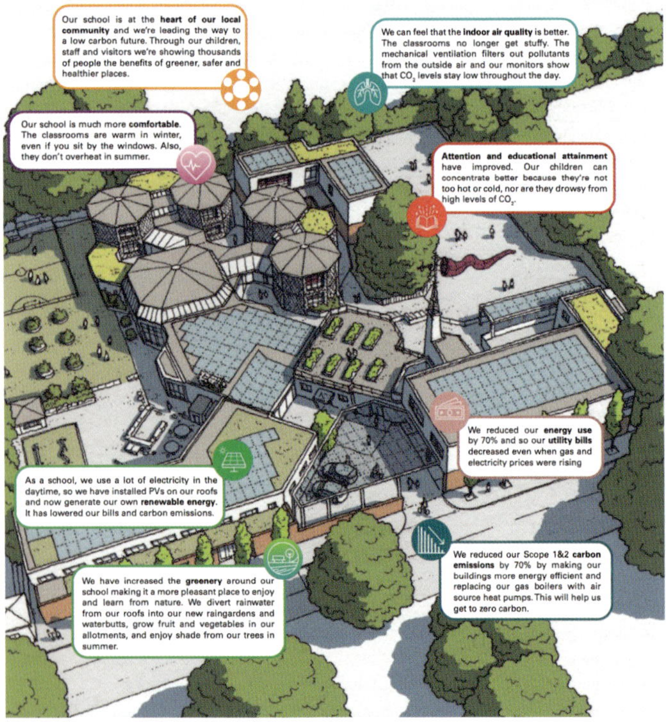

Figure 2.164
The five-year Phased Retrofit Plan for St Winifred's School, in the London Borough of Lewisham.

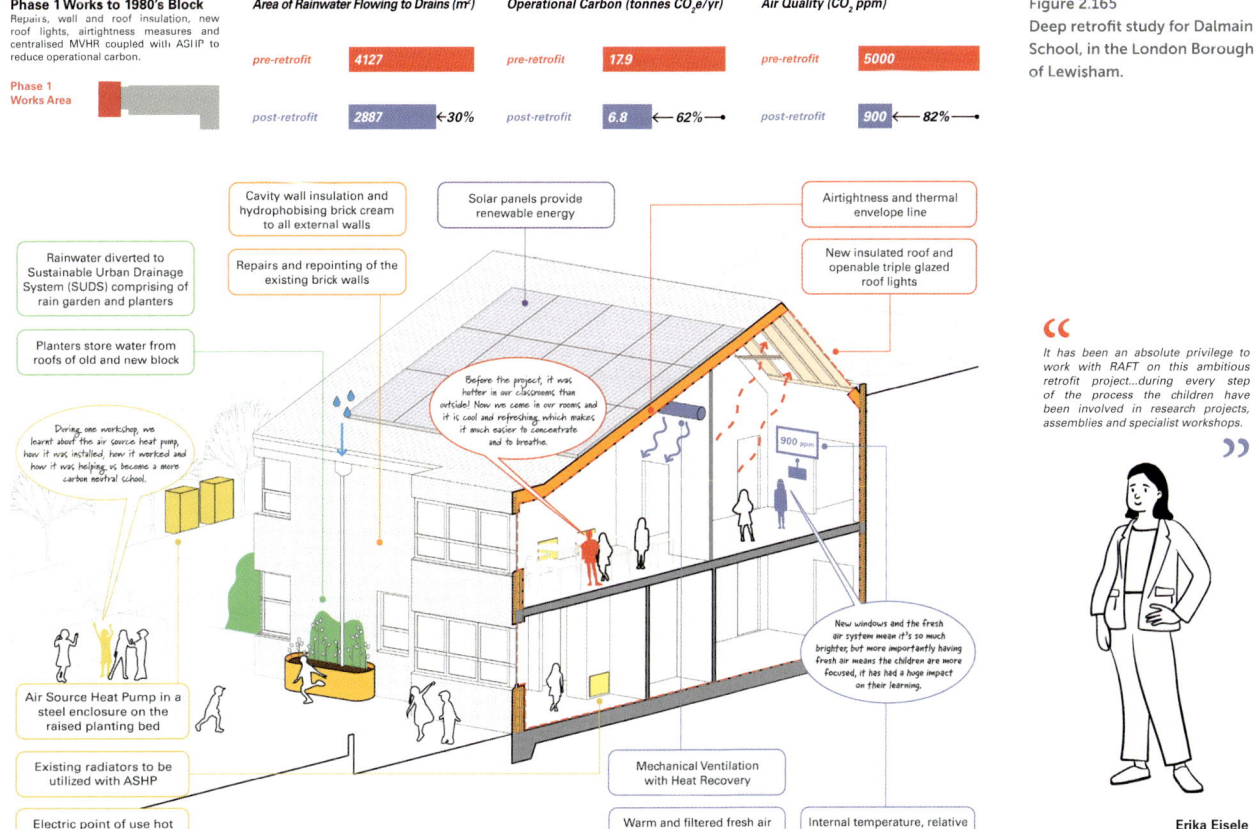

Figure 2.165
Deep retrofit study for Dalmain School, in the London Borough of Lewisham.

"It has been an absolute privilege to work with RAFT on this ambitious retrofit project...during every step of the process the children have been involved in research projects, assemblies and specialist workshops."

Erika Eisele
Head Teacher
Dalmain Primary School

Once qualified as an architect, Paticas spent some time working with the practice van Heyningen and Haward on 'robustly detailed and thoughtfully designed' buildings such as hospitals for children and young people, often working closely with engineers. During the period that he set up his first practice, Arboreal Architecture, he invested in training as a certified Passivhaus Designer, a process he found easier than most of his colleagues because of the scientific and mathematical training during his degrees. Paticas says he is grateful for the discipline, methodology and thinking that Passivhaus training gave him, 'because it opened my eyes to how I could be in control of a building's performance. It had never occurred to me before that architects could take control and didn't have to always rely on engineers. Control is very liberating.' Paticas then spent several years in private practice delivering bespoke one-off residential deep-green retrofit projects, applying Passivhaus methodologies to existing buildings, including a Grade II listed building that is featured as a case study on Historic England's website.

However, Paticas began to wish he could be more impactful with his planet-friendly way of practising architecture. He had just completed the first key stage of retrofitting on his own home, a process that, to his surprise, had fascinated his eight-year-old son to such an extent that he got involved with product research, including the selection of cork insulation. Another by-product of this home retrofit project was that his son started to make A3 posters in response to the different issues the project was addressing. For example, posters dedicated to air tests, thermographic surveys and even the detailed workings of the MVHR installation were all topics that Dimitri presented to his classmates, with the teacher allowing him to set up a permanent exhibition in a corner of the classroom. It was this process of working with his young son, and the level of excitement and wider engagement, that got Paticas thinking that perhaps they were onto something.

Paticas calls his son 'the true founder of RAFT'. RAFT was formed with the ambition of turning poorly performing schools into

Clockwise from top left:

Figure 2.166
RAFT founder Harry Paticas and school pupils.

Figure 2.167
Baked potato insulation test to demonstrate issues of heat loss to school pupils.

Figure 2.168
Pupils at Myatt Garden School, in the London Borough of Lewisham, pointing to an air-source heat pump.

Figure 2.169
Thermal imaging of Dalmain School pupils.

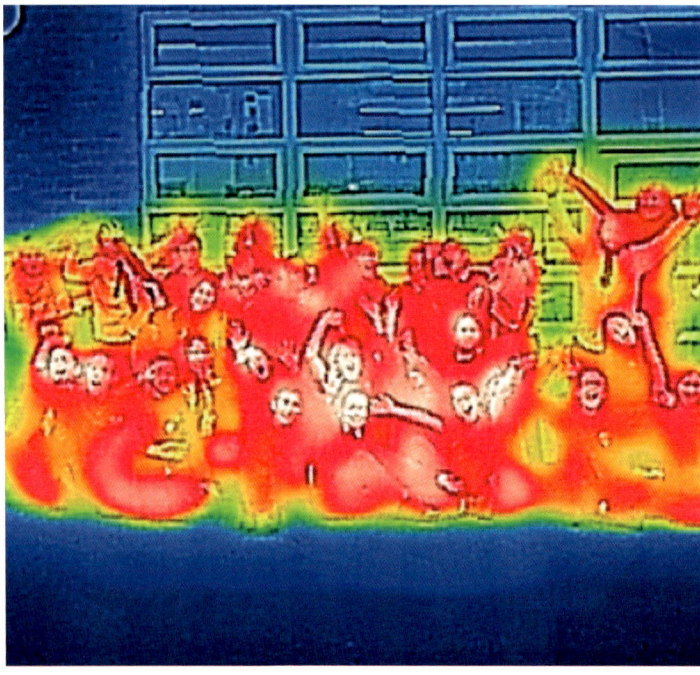

zero-carbon, climate-resilient and healthy places for learning. Its mission was clear from the beginning: 'to respond to the climate emergency by providing education and retrofit advice to schools and surrounding local communities, resulting in energy and emissions reductions, resource efficiency and climate resilience.' A not-for-profit Community Interest Company (CIC), RAFT was set up to be fully aligned with local authorities, schools and communities in their collective desires to meet 2030 to 2050 net-zero carbon commitments. RAFT hoped that by setting up as a CIC, schools would have confidence in their planned outcomes and as such overcome some of the current barriers to positive action.

RAFT is engaged in deep retrofit, engagement and zero carbon. Paticas believes in delivering a proper package of engagement work and professional services. Many school buildings in the UK have been neglected over the last 20 years and it can be hard simply to keep them warm and dry, let alone develop plans and deliver zero-carbon retrofit. One of the first workshops RAFT delivers to staff in schools is aimed at sharing the multiple benefits of retrofit in terms of carbon reduction, lower energy bills, improved classroom air quality and climate resilience. This workshop sets the scene for ongoing engagement with the children and development of a plan for decarbonisation.

Like most start-ups, RAFT's first project was modest in size. RAFT applied for a £15,000 Community Energy Fund Grant from the London Borough of Lewisham. RAFT delivered what Paticas described as '£45,000 worth of professional services' that included surveys, air tests of classrooms, building fabric audits and user feedback. In addition, four climate crisis and retrofit workshops were given to pupils and staff. The result of what turned out to be six months of work was RAFT's first Enhanced Heat and Decarbonisation Plan, which included details of how to improve the fabric performance of the school buildings; in addition to this, the school had a core group of pupils and staff who could champion the reasoning behind why time and money should be spent to enable the retrofitting works.

RAFT was set up just as COVID-19 kicked in and schools closed. So its initial development included a rapid and short period of online delivery to schools during lockdown. Fast-forward to the present day, and RAFT has worked in detail with more than 20 schools, providing them with Zero Carbon Action Plans that normally include a phased retrofit plan, allowing them to raise the money they need to implement the works over a short-, medium- and long-term period. The process of engagement is tailored to the requirements of each particular school.

> ## OPINION
>
> Harry Paticas and RAFT are trying to change the world of architecture, this much is clear. The fact that schoolteachers, governors, pupils, parents and even building managers are also appreciating their work is extremely encouraging. RAFT is also expanding its staff numbers exponentially, with an impressive collection of school retrofit projects emerging from this fully inclusive way of working. I was struck by how Paticas was really trying to shake up our industry, to get it to engage with the massive challenges and opportunities that well-informed retrofit presents our built environment. Most impressively, RAFT is getting on with the task in hand, with many new clients who are appreciating the added benefits of appointing architects who can solve the problems of leaking, cold classrooms while inputting into their curriculum and teaching the school community about the benefits of low-carbon retrofit.
>
> This is impactful practice at its best. I speculated that some of Paticas's colleagues at RAFT might soon be working with central government and the Department for Education – in particular to influence policy that supports retrofit and increases understanding of its benefits to the school environment. Paticas considered this for a moment:
>
>
>
> We have learnt a huge amount about the UK building stock and the many opportunities and challenges to retrofit, including a soon-to-be-published report on the whole-life carbon of step-by-step retrofit and strategic decarbonisation plans for whole school estates. It's really lovely to work with building officers at an estate scale but also children, dedicated headteachers and committed staff, teaching assistants and premises managers in schools.
>
> Well said.

CASE STUDY No.5

Sala Beckett by Flores & Prats Arquitectes

THE STORY

Eva Prats and Ricardo Flores formed their research-led practice in 1998 after working for Enric Miralles. Based in Barcelona, they have gained an international reputation for delivering well-considered, sensitive and thought-provoking buildings. Often gaining commissions by winning open competitions, Flores & Prats Arquitectes describe their studio as one investigating 'fields such as rehabilitations and reuse of abandoned or ruined constructions, social housing and its capacity to build communities … with neighbourhood participation'. However, for many people it is the way they work as much as what they work on that has gained them many fans and admirers, with their engaging films and stop-frame animations gaining plaudits from both the international art and architecture communities.

Unusually for contemporary practices, Prats and Flores spend a lot of time drawing by hand, and they see their role as that of making time to think, reflect and evolve schemes via the very act of drawing, a process they see as 'a two-way exchange of ideas: a dialogue with our clients and collaborators'. They also see drawing as a more accessible way of developing ideas. As Prats states, 'The process is more public than CAD, which is often presented on a single small screen with one person in control.' Initially, the practice was based in Barcelona during one of its many construction booms. As a result, they were able to have some sort of control over the type of practice they wanted to run. Prats states, 'The decision on how you allocate your time is reflected in the size of the studio you have. We realise that if we want to keep drawing by hand, our practice has to remain quite small.'

Prats and Flores are supported by collaborators who draw with CAD. However, they have their own 'drawing table' that can move around the studio to sit next to whoever they need to work with. They also work with paper and card models, although it's mainly collaborators who deliver these and, as Prats points out, 'Models always follow drawings.' Flores adds,

'We draw as the main way of evolving our thoughts, using models as tests to visualise some specific moments in the project.' Models provide a register of different steps in the evolution of design ideas. They also present moments that could possibly inform future projects. They are therefore slightly reluctant to throw models out, and as such the studio often gets overcrowded, to such an extent that a client's warehouse has had to be used as temporary storage, or the 'archive of ideas and conversations', as Flores calls it.

Prats and Flores are especially keen on working with communities and neighbourhoods to enliven existing derelict buildings; what they describe as 'the architecture of reuse'. Perhaps one of their most successful projects is Sala Beckett theatre, Barcelona, won in competition in 2011 and delivered in 2016 after 15 months on site. The story behind the construction of the original building is fascinating. Built in the 1920s to serve as a neighbourhood social club, it finally closed its doors in the late 1970s and remained closed for 40 years. Prats and Flores noted that the neighbourhood has 'all the memories of the place and activities that occurred within the building despite its derelict condition'. This point is reinforced further when they tell me that the original building was constructed by the workers who used it. They felt it was important for them to understand the physical condition of the building, but of equal importance was the social and emotional heritage.

The internal finishes of this partially derelict building were beautiful: the tiles and mosaics, together with all the windows, doors, stairs and other joinery items. However, they were also commonplace in Barcelona, produced to supply the rapid expansion of the city's 'grid plan' at the end of the 19th century and the beginning of the 20th century. These materials can often be seen thrown into skips, even today. Flores & Prats Arquitectes had other ideas for them in this building.

Although the floor levels and some of the internal walls would have to be moved to allow for new elements of the Sala Beckett

From top:

Figure 2.170
Street view of the theatre building before the work took place.

Figure 2.171
The former theatre stage.

Figure 2.172
The former social club café.

Figure 2.173
Axonometric of the final scheme.

Figure 2.174
Colour section through the vestibule.

programme, as well as to satisfy contemporary standards for structural engineering, fire and acoustics, Prats and Flores were very keen to reuse as much of the fabric as possible. It is the way they mapped and quantified the 'material resource' that is particular to this most idiosyncratic of practices.

All case studies in this chapter are presented with the challenge of quantifying the structural stability, types of materials, components, etc. that are salvageable in an existing building. Methods for doing this efficiently are rapidly improving and are almost entirely undertaken utilising digital technologies and even big data. This case study is an exception to that rule, and as such deserves dwelling upon in some detail. The ways in which Flores & Prats Arquitectes survey the buildings they are charged with renovating, to create what they call 'a vast inventory of materials', is labour intensive and requires skills many architects have neglected for decades. Initially, the practice spent three months on site surveying the existing structures in plan, drawing by hand. Two additional architects were then brought in to document the internal walls in elevation. This was done using pen and watercolours. Noting everything they could see, measuring the positions and types of wall and floor tiles, their various patterns and colours, as well as interior joinery, plaster ceiling roses, the extent and type of plaster and floor finishes, the architects documented the historic layers of other finishes applied up until the late 1970s.

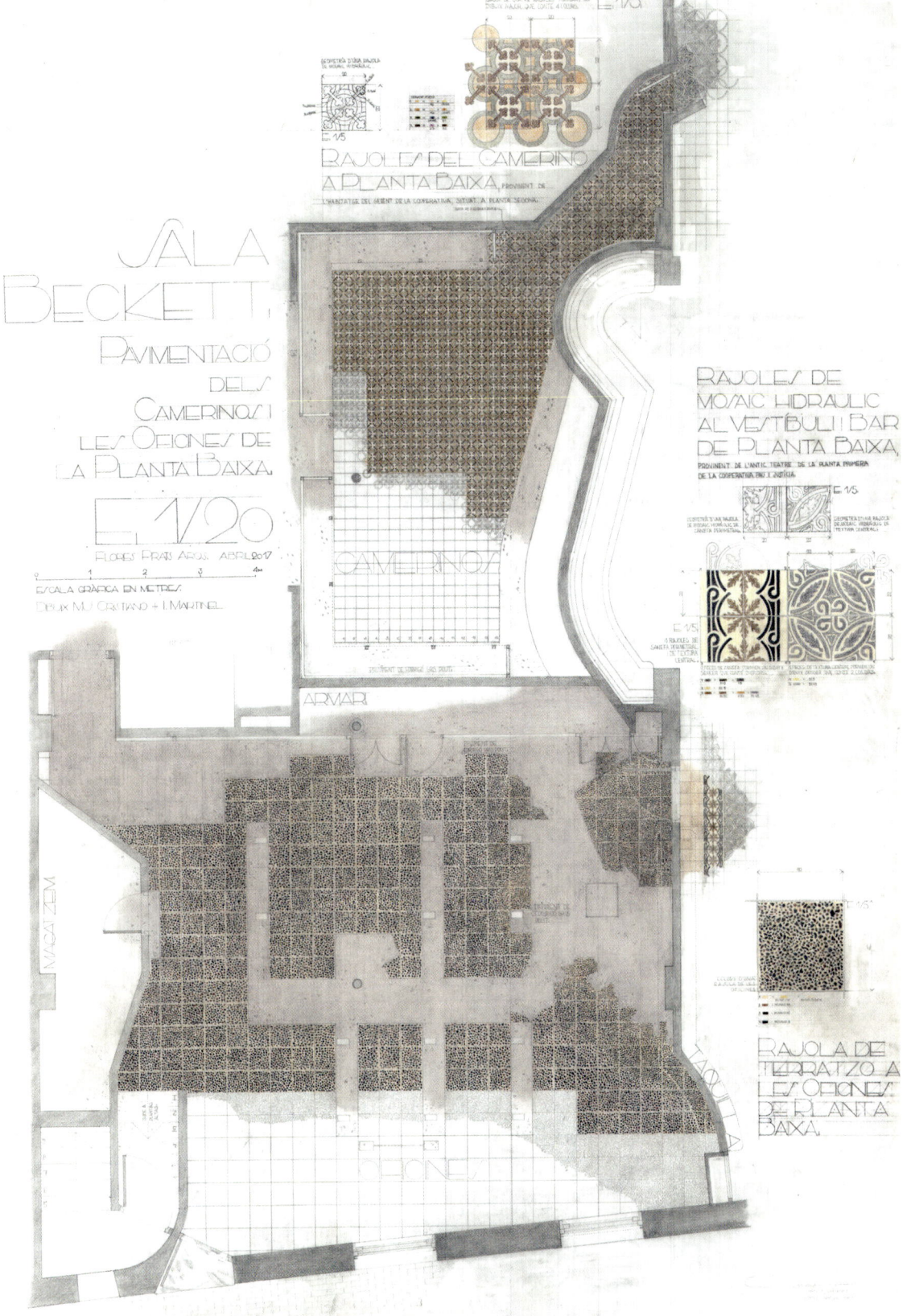

Figure 2.174
Floor finishes of the offices and changing rooms.

Clockwise from top left:

Figure 2.176
The main entrance off Pere IV Street.

Figure 2.177
The first-floor lightwell. .

Figure 2.178
Bar Beckett.

Figure 2.179
The rehearsal room in the former bar.

All items were numbered. This exercise created a 100-page hand-drawn inventory that was presented to the contractor who delivered the renovation project.

Although much of the building's fabric was kept in situ, including flexible and acoustically sensitive lime plaster ceilings reinforced with straw, known as 'scagliola', other elements were carefully removed, cleaned up and put into temporary storage until they were needed. Flores and Prats were pragmatic about original fixtures and fittings: they were reused whenever possible on site, but not necessarily where originally installed. The original building was constructed with load-bearing brick walls that were only 150mm thick and structurally fragile. However, with roof trusses providing an uninterrupted 11m span, and a 30m-long plan with a 6m clear head height, Flores and Prats realised that the original building was constructed in a very similar way to the numerous industrial buildings in the district; buildings within which local people spent most of their working lives.

Contractors with specific experience of adapting existing buildings were appointed, and Flores considers the project's 15 months on site as 'very quick for a reuse project'. However, it was not without its challenges. On more than one occasion they had to salvage an item meant for reuse out of the skip. As with most renovation projects, and despite deep intrusive surveys, the building presented many surprises to the team. They were also concerned that the heavy equipment needed to install underpinning to load-bearing walls would undermine the very structures they were brought on site to support. It was at this point I asked Flores if the Sala Beckett clients had ever suggested that it might be cheaper if the building be demolished. In fact, the client was completely on board with the value of the social history imbued within the existing building. The iniquitous situation in the UK where VAT at 20% is applied to retrofit projects is not the case in Spain. Therefore, put quite simply, if you are reusing the structural and other material on site, then you are not paying for new material, and therefore reuse is almost always the more cost-effective option.

OPINION

The budget for Sala Beckett was not big: at only €800/m², 'less than for a parking lot!' as Flores put it. I'm not quite sure how the project was realised, but realised it was. Obviously, there are numerous reasons for including this project in this book, not least the sheer humanity of it. There is currently a massive amount of debate about the many benefits of retrofit and reuse, with much of it quite understandably focused on issues relating to the cost-of-living crisis, the climate emergency and the need for climate resilience in architecture. However, not demolishing has many added benefits, not least that in the case of a public building such as Sala Beckett, the community asset and its cultural, social and historical heritages can be preserved, even enhanced.

The other reason for including this project is to highlight this way of working: some might call it old fashioned, out of date even, but for certain types of projects and client groups it provides many benefits. By spending so much time with the building, Flores & Prats Arquitectes get to know it almost as well as the original community that built it. This knowledge and 'slow' way of working gives the architects an opportunity to reflect on what they are looking at, something that many of us working with digital 3D surveys may not have the opportunity to do. As Flores says, 'Hand drawing gets you slowly into the minds of the previous people who drew and constructed the building. 3D scanners cannot reflect any of this.'

Perhaps more than anybody else I interviewed for this book, Flores and Prats really articulated beautifully and concisely what they were thinking. So, I will leave you with a couple more quotations from my conversation with them.

> For us, the architecture of reuse is a dialogue, a conversation with past generations and things that have been done before. This creates a discussion like a collaboration with time.
>
> Each person has a kind of reflection: reflecting on your childhood, your past, and this creates a personal engagement with the building. When visitors see the building, it feels familiar, and this is important as the building becomes part of the actual use.

CASE STUDY No.6

No. 1 Triton Square by Arup etc.

THE STORY

As discussed elsewhere, commercial buildings in financial districts of cities create a disproportionately high amount of waste. This is due to several reasons, not least fashion and taste. Buildings owned by clients in charge of successful multinational corporations do a lot more than provide a workplace for employees: they are more often than not the public face of a corporation, and as such, when they go out of fashion, there is a perception that they need to be updated. Interiors are refitted on a cycle of only five to seven years, and buildings are often demolished when they are only 25 to 30 years old. However, times are changing, with many clients appreciating that they need to do a lot more for the environment than simply update their ESG (Environmental, social and corporate governance) statements every year.

No. 1 Triton Square, in London, was designed for British Land by Arup over 20 years ago. In many ways it is a building typical of its time, and as such was a serious contender for being demolished and rebuilt, as is the norm. However, British Land appointed its previous design team, Arup, and set them the task of trying to adapt and extend the existing building with the ambition of 'challenging the status quo' and salvaging as much of the existing building as possible. This included the external façade, which of course is normally high on the priority list of items needing updating. So, it is this approach to the reuse of the external façade that is perhaps the most interesting element of the project, and most challenging for clients used to rebranding their companies. This decision to reuse the façade means that at first glance the building looks unchanged, rooted in the mid-1990s, with its late Post-Modern multi-toned limestone cladding.

Soon after receiving the commission in 2018, Arup put together a complete design team of architects and engineers, including their in-house Life Cycle Assessment (LCA) team, who benchmarked embodied-carbon emissions against current best practice data for newbuild developments from Real Estate Environmental Benchmark (REEB). At this point, I could write another 1,500 words on the merits or not of one retrofit strategy calculating whole-life carbon footprints over another. What I will say is that it is an important and ongoing discussion that our industry is only just getting to grips with.

Much of the original building was either kept on site, or dismantled, upgraded and reinstalled. Arup state that they 'chipped away at every aspect to save carbon, cut waste and deliver the best working environment possible'. They describe this approach as one of 'marginal gains … like Olympic athletes seeking major performance gains through small incremental improvements across every possible area'.[19]

Arup reconnected with many of the original suppliers. This included Scheldebouw, who supplied the glazed façade system. Although it was 19 years later, they were very happy to carefully remove over 3,500m^2 of the curtain wall system, comprising over 25,000 separate parts, and take it to a temporary workshop about 30 miles away from the site. Here it was cleaned up, reconditioned and reinstalled on the original building. Crucially, the façade suppliers gave their refurbished product the same warranty that a new system would have: by doing this, they have proved that reuse is viable in the competitive world of commercial office building.

Arup claim that the reuse of the glass façade alone saved 2,400tCO^2 compared to using a new façade. In addition, reusing the existing structure (it was also added to and upgraded in parts) and fabric – which included 3,300m^2 of limestone, 35,000 tonnes of concrete and 1,877 tonnes of steel – accounted for 45% of the total carbon saving for the project.

Figure 2.180
No. 1 Triton Square, completed in 2022, with reused existing and second-hand imported stone cladding.

Figure 2.181
The reused curtain walling system arriving at the temporary 're-manufactory'.

Figure 2.182
Cleaning the refurbished second-hand curtain walling.

OPINION

As well-informed discussions continue as to the merits of one low-carbon retrofit/adaptation scheme over, say, another Passivhaus newbuild project, the construction sector is beginning to understand that it will play a massive part in humankind's struggle to meet its own self-imposed net-zero targets. Obviously, many engineers and architects, as well as clients, are becoming 'climate literate', gaining an understanding of the challenges the climate and ecological emergency presents, as well as understanding strategies to reduce our collective burden on the planet. As a consequence, individuals, as well as companies small and large, NGOs and governments are beginning to enable an environment that is far more favourable for circular systems to thrive. Obviously, we are not there yet, but with the expertise and drive of Arup's design team, together with the support of their client, the decision to salvage No.1 Triton Square and not demolish it is hugely significant. In time, perhaps, it will be seen as a game-changer project: the time when our industry realised that reducing the consumption of our planet's valuable resources was a worthwhile and significant thing to do.

Figure 2.183
Existing concrete columns, strengthened with carbon-fibre fabric reinforcement.

CASE STUDY No.7

Paddenbroek Education Centre by Jo Taillieu

THE STORY

Jo Taillieu is the son of a carpenter joiner. As a young boy, he spent hours watching his father work on timber, transforming it into the most beautiful furniture. Unfortunately, his father died when he was only 16, but the love of making, especially with timber, is still very much part of Taillieu's life. For a long time, he wanted to combine drawing and mathematics, wavering between wanting to study product design or architecture. He chose architecture, which he feels is 'so much more open than product design'. Taillieu is currently Professor at EPFL (Swiss Federal Institute of Technology Lausanne) as well as managing his own practice, 'jo taillieu architecten' in Ghent.

After qualifying, Taillieu found himself in 1995 working for MAX1 in Rotterdam, an office set up by Rients Dijkstra (who worked for eight years as a project architect at OMA) and Rianne Makkink. Taillieu then won a design competition to transform a former fruit farm with farmstead buildings (gifted to the Belgian village of Gooik) into a centre highlighting farm culture, biodiversity and the identity of the Pajottenland region it sits within. Ideas of developing a sense of play and recreation, while enhancing the surrounding ecological systems and encouraging tourism, were also to be considered. As is often the case, the clients who set the competition brief assumed that architects would be proposing ideas to demolish the existing farmstead buildings.

After visiting the site, Taillieu was convinced that plenty of the buildings were worth saving, despite the fact that some others were full of asbestos and had no foundations. The clients, however, were convinced they needed a new building to

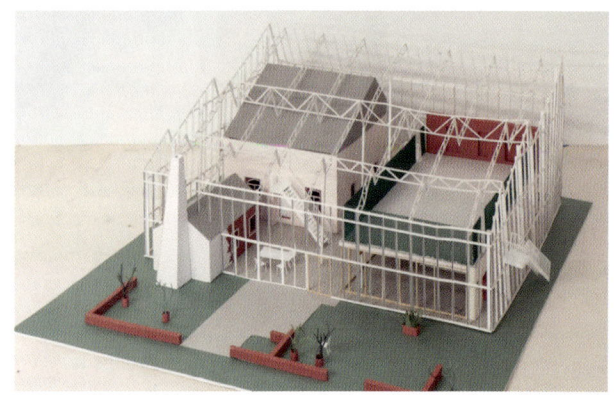

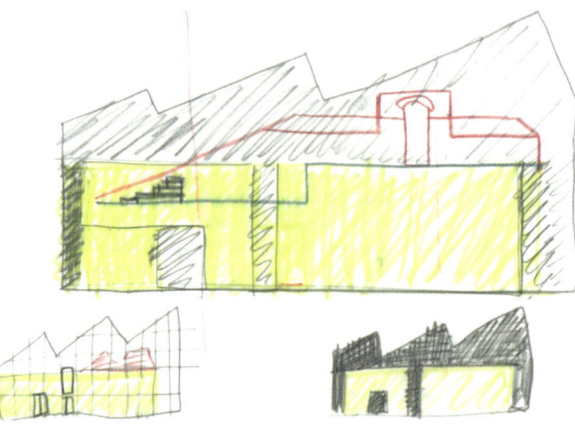

Figure 2.184 (top left)
Original buildings at the former fruit farm.

Figure 2.185 (left)
The original design concept sketch.

Figure 2.186 (above)
The original architectural model of proposals.

satisfy their emerging brief. In addition to the clients' need for a small café, a teaching space, office and WCs, the rest of the programme was being developed by Taillieu as a response to the site, the existing heritage and surrounding landscape. After some time, Taillieu expanded the programme to incorporate 'functions we don't know' (i.e. functions that allow for flexibility). It was at this time that he realised that these unknown functions were perhaps best housed in spaces that didn't have high thermal comfort: places that kept you out of the wind and rain, but where you kept your coat on.

Taillieu also had an ambition to make the very fabric of the building have the responsibility of moderating internal climatic considerations, rather than applying a layer of MEP (mechanical, electrical and plumbing) services. To do this, he had to convince his clients to invest in an environmental engineer at the beginning of the design process, arguing that this approach to front loading the design would save money (and resources) in the construction and occupation of the resultant buildings. Armed with his environmental engineer, Taillieu was able to propose placing a new megastructure over the whole of the existing farmstead to create a series of new 'in-between conditions' – an unheated 'thermal buffer' that allowed the once-open spaces between the farm buildings to be occupied with a new flexible programme and activities. The resultant 'sawtooth' big roof provided renewable energy via south-facing PV panels atop a sloped solid roof deck, with north-facing glazed clerestory lights that open to ventilate the space below. In addition, a single-glazed façade dropped from the roof to the ground, enclosing the farmstead. With opening windows and bright-red doors providing access, and cross ventilation via black-framed windows with fixed fly mesh, this completes the new envelope, providing the aforementioned 'third condition': an environmental buffer zone. This strategy also reveals additional spaces such as the first-floor event space, which is open to the big roof and overlooks the main entrance foyer.

Figure 2.187
Roofs removed, leaving masonry for reuse.

Figure 2.188
Existing masonry capped, plus new steel frame.

As well as providing additional usable accommodation, this low-tech yet high-impact and cost-effective design solution creates a semi-sheltered environment, not just for humans, but also for the original farmstead buildings. Taillieu exploits this situation in several ways. Firstly, the finishes to the existing walls are detailed in ways that would not be practical were they fully exposed to the elements. Windows to the old bakery are single glazed and planted onto the external brick walls rather than being treble glazed and within the structural opening.

Clockwise from top left:

Figure 2.189
Completed scheme, 2018.

Figure 2.190
The new usable spaces between.

Figure 2.191
External wall insulation applied only where needed.

Figure 2.192
The existing bakehouse, plus new spaces.

Slate tiles for the roof are left uncut and pointy without the need for gutters. Insulation (timber fibre board and lime render) is only applied to buildings, or parts thereof, where users are seated/relatively stationary (the office and the education spaces) and liable to get cold in the winter months. Again, this understanding of the potential for different types of spaces keeps costs down. This single-glazed environmental buffer zone between the former farm buildings may only be 5–10 degrees warmer than freezing external conditions, but it is dry and wind-free, protecting the fully insulated internal environments from the extremes, while allowing visitors to complete activities that might have had to be cancelled due to inclement weather. In the summer, excess heat is released by opening the high-level clerestory lights. Solar gain in winter pre-warms air before it enters the sealed and insulated accommodation.

At one level, the resultant project, completed in 2018, is very clear and straightforward, as well as being cost-effective and, more importantly for this book, resource efficient. However, there are layers of complexities and ways of reading this building that this essay does not have the space to expand upon. Jo Taillieu has clearly had a lot of fun with this building. It is full of visible pointers and clues, not only to what is new and what is old – his approach is much like Carlo Scarpa, though deliberately (choosing my words carefully here) more accessible. Colour is used to allow visitors to read the building without relying on signage.

New elements such as the main staircase and balustrading are brightly coloured, while existing materials are left almost as found. Taillieu also pushes the idea of 'inside' and 'outside' by specifying streetlight fittings for all 'in-between conditions'. Finally, the application of external wall insulation is transformed into a 21st-century version of decorative pargeting (a traditional waterproofing plaster creating a relief or pattern, applied to walls), and I haven't even mentioned the fireplaces transformed into windows, and the slipped relationship between existing and new façades. And there is more.

OPINION

This project presents an alternative way to retrofit the built environment, one that sees the value of histories, cultures and previous ways of doing, while proposing an architectural language capitalising on the idea that buildings are a series of layers, some of which don't have to line up. It also presents a careful and precise model based on reliable data informing thorough design testing, which is only feasible if the whole design team are employed at the beginning of the project. In this case, new elements not only provide additional accommodation but work hard, creating environmental buffer zones (compensating for virtually no MEP) for existing and new accommodation constructed in ways that add a sense of delight and playfulness to the building, while providing a low-cost option to the normal retrofit approach of external insulated wrap plus renewables.

Jo Taillieu has a reputation for transforming existing buildings with the most meagre of budgets, whether it's the gorgeous and thought-provoking Verzameld Werk Gallery in Ghent, where he literally just cut away the bottom half of a wall and door, leaving the top halves suspended and new space revealed, or the delightful Critas Psychiatric Institute in Melle (with De Vylder Vinck Taillieu), where new domestic greenhouses are installed within the existing building. Taillieu is constantly questioning the need for creating a built environment using new stuff, and would much rather find values in the existing.

CASE STUDY No.8

De Ceuvel by Space & Matter

THE STORY

Space & Matter was founded by Sascha Glasi, Tjeerd Haccou and Marthijn Pool in 2009. Based in Amsterdam, the three partners were 'united by a desire to improve the world for their children and all future generations'. Their first project was a competition-winning scheme for the province of Noord-Holland, an area being transformed from intensive farmland to accommodate 200,000 new homes. As with most projects in the Netherlands, water is a big issue, and in this case the storage of excess surface water, which had previously been dealt with by local farmers. Space & Matter came up with an ingenious solution where the new homes worked with the watery landscape and where farmers were rewarded for storing water by being given rights to develop carbon-neutral floating homes.

Space & Matter's ability to think in an unconventional way has served them very well since. Always focused on turning linear systems into circular ones, the practice started to attract projects like the collection of charming floating homes known as Schoonschip, a community-led vision that took over 10 years to complete. Schoonschip consists of 30 water plots for floating homes housing over 100 people. Half the floating homes are

Figure 2.193
Schoonschip renewable systems.

SOLAR ENERGY & SMART GRID
- heat exchange
- electricity
- sharing and storing energy

WATER SYSTEM SEWAGE
- tap water
- grey water
- black water
- water purification
- nutrients and phosphate
- biodiversity

SHARING COMMUNITY
- circular & smart
- food production
- health & well being
- shared site and technology
- financially feasible
- low-impact & circular materials

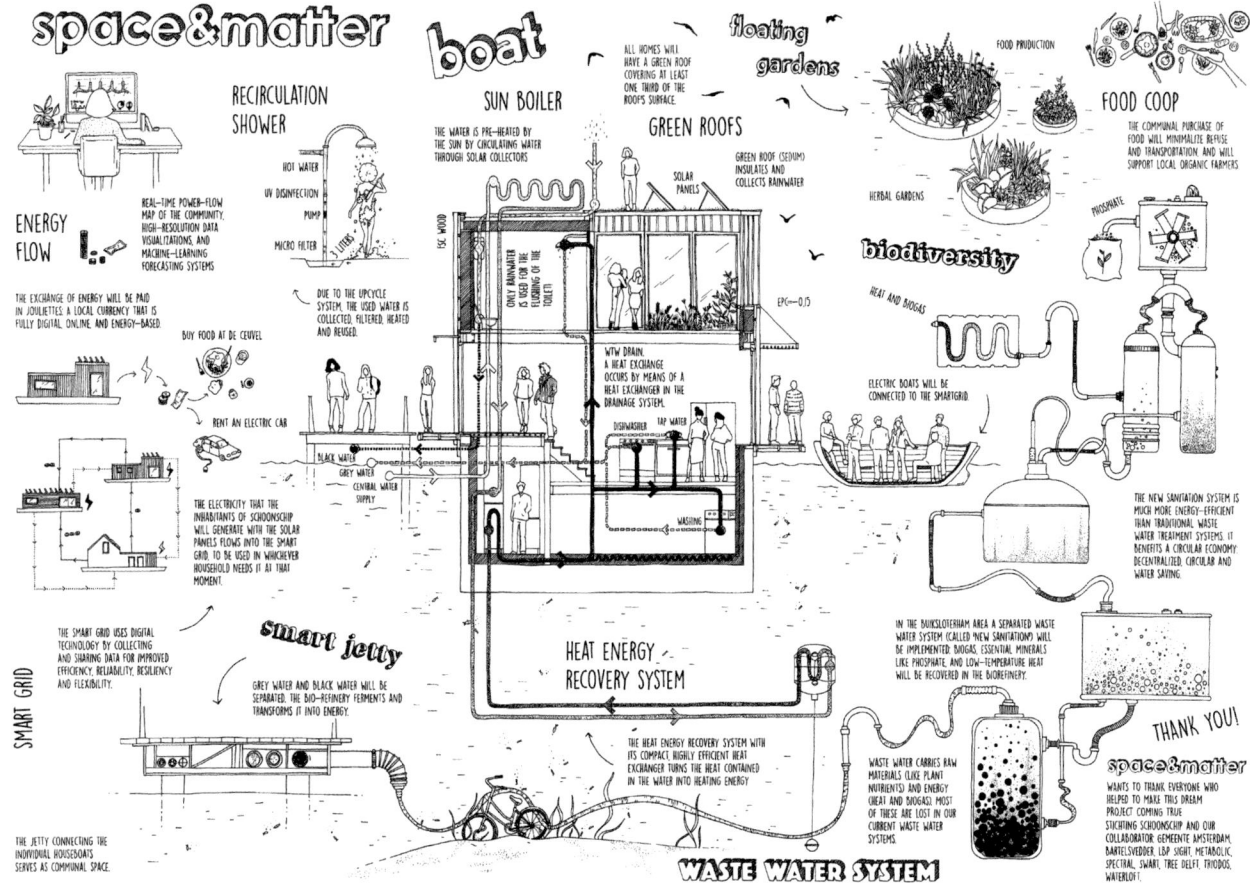

Figure 2.194
Circular systems at Schoonschip.

shared between two families and all 46 homes are unique as each one was designed in collaboration with the occupants. Every floating home is topped off with a large array of solar PV panels connected to a smart grid where residents trade energy using blockchain technology. The scheme, completed in 2012, also contains decentralised and renewable solutions to water, energy and waste systems, as well as submersed heat exchangers for heating and cooling.

Over the last 15 years or so, the practice's work has been characterised by the continued questioning of established linear systems and the promotion of circular alternatives. In addition, Space & Matter have always considered the positive social and environmental impact that architecture can have on communities. Perhaps their most impactful community-led project to date, and one that also embraces closed-loop systems, social enterprise and sustainability, is the delightful De Ceuvel. The temporary community is carefully placed on timber stilts so that it sits just above wasteland that is polluted by decades of heavy industry, including shipbuilding. Working in partnership with the University of Ghent, the polluted soil is currently being cleaned over the next decade. This is done by introducing a selection of plants that break down and absorb pollutants such as mercury and heavy metals, while also producing biomass annually for the site. This technique of natural soil cleaning is known as phytoremediation. It is envisaged that after 10 years the site will be clean, and the land can be returned to the municipality of Amsterdam, much healthier than when the project began.

In the meantime, De Ceuvel, situated in the Noord area of central Amsterdam, is a community of 15 studio spaces created from retrofitting old house boats. In addition to the studios, there is a delightful café, bar and restaurant selling food and drinks made on site: one of the former houseboats has been converted into a biodynamic brewery

From top:

Figure 2.195
An aerial view of Schoonschip.

Figure 2.196
Installing a houseboat.

Figure 2.197
The Schoonschip neighbourhood.

Figure 2.198
Installing a reused houseboat at De Ceuvel.

From top:

Figure 2.199
A reused houseboat at De Ceuvel, plus a structure for an elevated walkway.

Figure 2.200
An aerial view of De Ceuvel.

Figure 2.201
An elevated walkway, plus converted houseboats.

Figure 2.202
An evening event at De Ceuval.

and greenhouse. By retrofitting old houseboats and installing renewable energy production, Space & Matter estimate that over 200,000 tonnes of CO_2 emissions will be saved during the decade De Ceuvel stays on site. All buildings are linked by a winding raised timber boardwalk that feels like it is hovering over the lush soil-cleansing greenery below. Closed-loop systems are everywhere in this project, which might be modest in size but has huge ambitions to effect change. Space & Matter call it 'a cleantech playground for the exploration and testing of new green technologies as they become available', and since it opened in 2014, tens of thousands of people have visited. A centre for art and culture as well as one of the Netherlands' most famous circular economy demonstration sites, it also functions as a place locals can come to work or have some down time.

OPINION

A relatively small project with big ambitions to raise awareness of the many benefits that closed-loop systems present to humans, De Ceuvel is a huge success. In its current form it might not be around for much longer, but the once heavily polluted site will be handed back to the city nice and clean. In addition, numerous projects in Amsterdam, the Netherlands and beyond can thank Space & Matter (and everybody else responsible for this exemplary project) for showing us a vision of what closed-loop systems might look like. Many people have visited the site and, like me, marched off to try to match its ambition. For example, the clients for the ABN AMRO Bank's CIRCL Pavilion in Amsterdam's financial district (see the CIRCL Pavilion case study, in Step 4), not five miles away, cite De Ceuvel as their inspiration. De Ceuvel presents an optimistic view of the future, one where humans get their collective heads around the problems of our throwaway way of living and start to really implement authentic, closed-loop systems. And that starts with clearing up the mess we have made.

CASE STUDY No.9

Bath Schools of Art and Design

Grimshaw, Arup, Mann Williams, Montressor, Structura, Willmott Dixon

THE STORY

It's not often that architects get to revisit buildings they designed nearly 50 years previously. The original brief for the Herman Miller furniture factory dates from 1975, when Terry Farrell and Nick Grimshaw were working in partnership. The building they designed was constructed in 1978 and, incredibly, remained functioning as a furniture factory for 37 years. In the meantime, the building was Grade II listed. Considered by many as one of the high points of early UK High Tech, the resultant innovative design was as much about the client's original brief as it was about the energetic and intelligent response of the original design team.

The original brief, dating from 1975, asked the architects to create an environment that 'Welcomes all, is kind to the user, is subservient to human activity, forgives mistakes in planning, is open to surprise, is comfortable with conflict', and, crucially, 'has flexibility, is non-precious and non-monumental'. Today Grimshaw are clear that the success and longevity of the original building was in part because the architect's design made sure that the resultant building could adapt to the changing needs of the business without impacting on day-to-day operations. This was achieved by designing a building as a kit-of-parts. This idea was, of course, a key preoccupation of many High Tech architects in

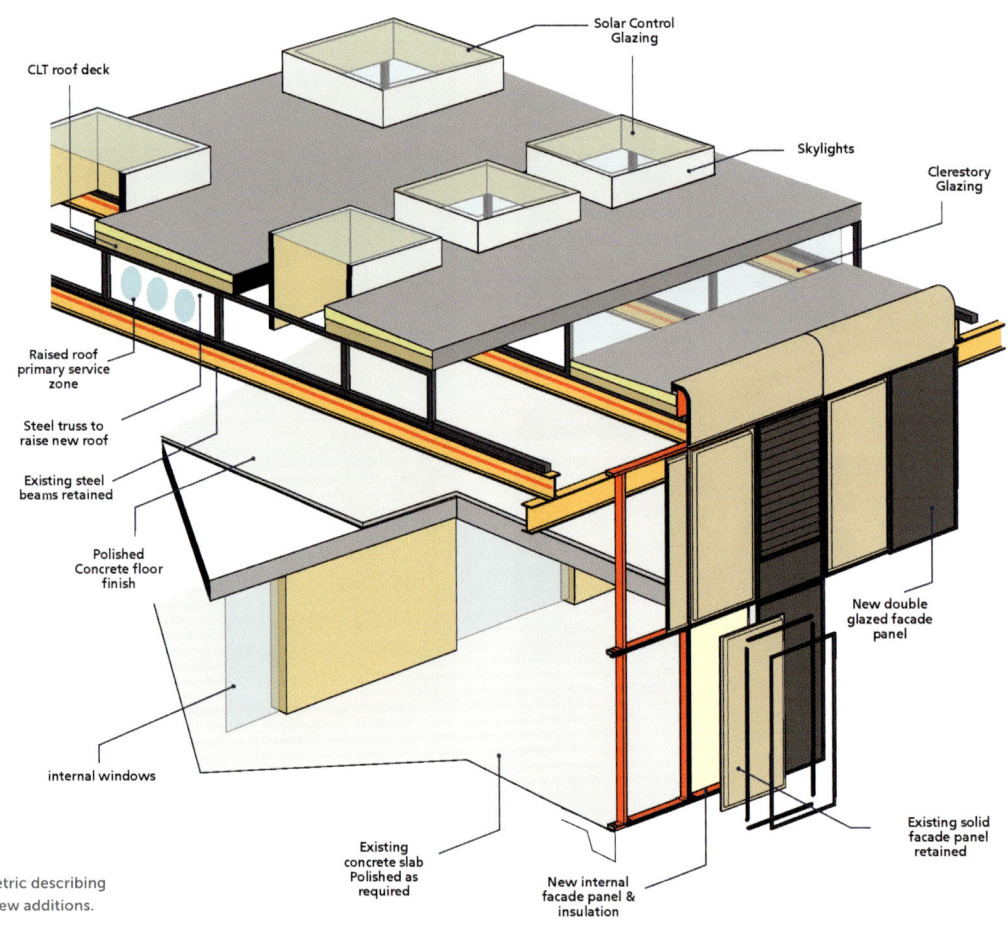

Figure 2.203
Detailed axonometric describing refurbished and new additions.

the 1970s, and it has served the Herman Miller factory very well. Adaptive reuse is also a key theme for contemporary designers focused on achieving a regenerative built environment through the application of circular economy principles.

The adaption of the existing factory building into a new home for the Bath Schools of Art and Design was a fantastic opportunity to test the original design thesis, as well as the robustness of the built artefact that Grimshaw state had 'flexibility codified into the building's fabric to maximise the positive environmental, social and economic impacts of the school, its students and the local community'. The original brief from 1975 had asked that 'the buildings must be capable of adapting to changing needs without impacting day-to-day operation'. The new brief for 2021 would test this last statement. Was the original building really an adaptable kit-of-parts with elements capable of being kept in situ or deconstructed for reuse on site? Could it be adapted from a factory into a teaching facility with contemporary levels of performance not considered in the mid-1970s brief (i.e. high levels of thermal insulation, natural light and ventilation, proper acoustics and low operational energy consumption)?

From top:

Figure 2.204
Upgrading existing modular panels.

Figure 2.205
Refurbished modular wall panels waiting to be reinstalled on the existing building.

Figure 2.206
The entrance to the completed building.

Figure 2.207
The completed building at dusk.

Grimshaw's approach was to keep two key elements of the building almost completely untouched. The original ground-floor concrete slab was left alone, as was the signature primary steel structure, painted a distinctive yellow. The original modular steel façade system was designed to have interchangeable solid or glazed units, but with little insulation value. This element of the building would need to be either replaced or adapted.

The original solid GRP (glass reinforced plastic) panels were carefully removed, assessed for their ability to be reused, then repaired as necessary and refurbished. Even the panels with duct holes drilled through them were repurposed. In addition, Grimshaw added a new layer of insulation to the inside of the modular façade without compromising the future interchangeability of the panels. Finished internally with timber, these panels now offer crucial acoustic absorption for the interior environments. All windows were replaced with high-performing double-glazed units that were still compatible with the retained fixing systems. This ensured that the thermal performance of the façade was improved substantially without undermining the future adaptability. Nearly all the steel façade frame was retained and refurbished, except for two portions of the frame that were removed to allow for two new entrances. The removed modular elements of frame were then reused to replace parts that had corroded.

The new brief and accompanying programme demanded that the original building be extended, while still allowing for future flexibility and cost-effective adaptations. New interventions follow the ethos of sustainability, adaptability and designing the building as a material store for future buildings. This is achieved by introducing a new roof raised 1m above the existing roofline, constructed of cross-laminated timber planks, sitting on new Vierendeel steel trusses, in turn bolted onto the existing steel structure. This detail allows for the original structural frame to stay structurally independent, facilitating the future disassembly of the new structure, which is straightforward to reuse, while the original stays intact.

The raised roof allows for several performance improvements critical for the success of this retrofit project, namely its environmental performance in-use as well as its future adaptability. A network of 'plug and play' services runs through the Vierendeel structure and allows the spaces below to be reorganised as required. New roof lights (over 100!) and clerestory glazing, both with an integral diffusing capillary interlayer to control glare and solar gain, provide increased levels of natural lighting, and the improved structural capacity allows for the introduction of a large array of photovoltaic solar panels on the roof. The project was completed in 2023.

OPINION

The constraints of this book mean that I am primarily focusing on ways construction projects have reduced the consumption of resources during construction, as well as ways they facilitate future adaptation and reuse. This focus sometimes means that other important issues are not discussed – issues such as the level of operational energy reduction, the ability of a project to encourage the regeneration of natural environments and systems, and, most importantly, the social and societal benefits that architecture can enable. These are all issues this project (and others in this book) have a go at addressing. Grimshaw's low-carbon retrofit transformation of the former Herman Miller furniture factory into Bath Schools of Art and Design must be applauded for its ambition of intent as well as the quality of the project as delivered. To be able to revisit one of your projects and to get to test its original design intent is an incredible opportunity. Was the original building *really* constructed so that it could be adapted and upgraded? Could it accommodate a completely different programme from the original brief? The fact that the original building is Grade II listed only adds to this challenge, one that Grimshaw appear to have met. The fact that so much of the original structure and the modular façade were suitable for adaptation and not removed from site is testament to the ambition of the original design team and the investment of Herman Miller in a top-quality building as constructed. As Sir Nick Grimshaw said at the time of the original construction project in the 1970s, 'Architects in the future must design their buildings so that they can easily be changed, either by themselves or by others. Buildings in the future should be valued as a resource.'

STEP 4
The Circular Economy

DEFINITION

THIS CHAPTER CONSIDERS projects that create zero waste during their life, from design, through to manufacture, use and reuse. They are designed with an end-of-life strategy for perpetual reuse without undermining their initial sophistication; in fact, they never generate any waste at all and function as part of a healthy circular economy. Within a healthy circular economy, parts from, say, old cars are the source material for new cars, and recycling is the last and least-desired option.

CASE STUDY No.1

Circular Economy Pedagogic Methods by Prof Dirk Hebel

Prof Dirk Hebel has been pushing the boundaries of architectural teaching for over 15 years. His work considers ways to 'activate' unusual building materials, which over the years have included air, water, bamboo and, most recently, locating sources of waste material. Hebel has worked around the world, including at the National Research Foundation in Singapore and the Ethiopian Institute of Architecture, Building Construction and City Development in Addis Ababa, where he was Director. This has afforded him the opportunity to experience the development of architecture in hugely contrasting environments from the perspective of resource consumption. Hebel states that his current research 'concentrates on a metabolic understanding of resources and investigates alternative building materials and construction techniques and their applications in developed as well as developing territories'.[1]

This case study is unusual because it partners the pedagogic practice of Hebel, who is Assistant Professor of Architecture and Construction at ETH Zurich, with a large residential development in the heart of District 4 in Zurich. The project, in partnership with housing cooperative GBMZ, is the design and construction of 140 new apartments plus a kindergarten, common areas for residents and a shared laundry. All elements will follow the principles of building for disassembly. The development aims to test the idea that buildings can be developed so they are a material store for the future: all materials used in this development will be genuinely reusable. This concept is beginning to be well understood. However, there are not many examples of contemporary buildings delivering upon these ideals, let alone large residential developments designed, as this is, by students.

This project highlights that many natural resources are becoming increasingly scarce, even aggregates such as sand and gravel for concrete production. It also focuses on the potential of other material sources or 'flows' that have piled up over centuries, the materials that constitute our towns and cities that can now be conceived as our future mines. Cities that of late are purely consuming entities can now become providers of valuable material resources to repair and rebuild new and existing cities. This takes the pressure off the natural world to provide this material, which in turn could allow it to begin to flourish again.

Figure 2.208
Front cover of the brief issued to Prof Dirk Hebel's students, who are creating apartments 'designed for disassembly'.

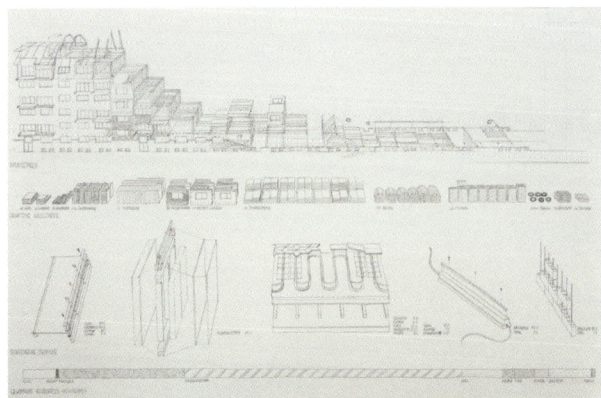

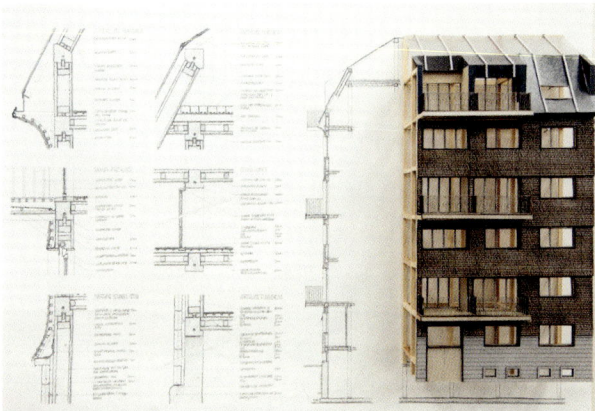

Figure 2.209
Student drawing describing the construction and disassembly processes for the residential development in District 4, Zurich.

Figure 2.210
Student drawing and model of the Zurich apartments 'designed for disassembly'.

In practice, this urban mining can be time consuming and it could therefore be seen as expensive to dismantle or unpack a building instead of simply blowing it up. However, you will see from other case studies in this book (Rotor and Superuse, among others) that this preconception is now being challenged, although it is still the case that buildings from the 19th century or earlier are far more straightforward to dismantle. This is mainly because of the way buildings were assembled: bricks used soft lime mortars; timber and steel frames were bolted. Many 20th-century buildings are stuck together with mortar, glues, welds, etc. that make disassembly impractical.

Hebel is keen that his students consider the challenges of designing architecture for disassembly by looking at a wide range of issues, from urban systems through to the design of jointing techniques at full scale. It is hoped that by designing in this holistic manner, a genuine circularity can be achieved whereby this new development will address 'the social and resource-related situation of our generation'. Once the students have developed and tested the design brief with their tutors and client, GBMZ, the resultant design will be implemented over the forthcoming years.

OPINION

Buildings are rarely considered a material or product resource for the future. However, urban mining clearly demonstrates how waste can be reused at the end of its conventional life span and used and reused on numerous occasions thereafter. Designers need to facilitate this by considering the 'waste state' of a product at the beginning of its life. This point is made very clearly by Sophie Thomas of the RSA's 'The Great Recovery', who points out that '80% of decisions made at the beginning of the design process either lock or unlock the potential for a product or building to be reused'.[2] So, to enable more straightforward disassembling of buildings, designers must, to a certain extent, relearn how to design.

In their text *Mine the City*, Ilka and Andreas Ruby describe how contemporary culture is beginning to realise that many everyday raw materials that are becoming rather scarce in the 'natural realm' are more common within the 'cultural domain' of our buildings. They state, 'The material resources of construction are becoming increasingly exhausted at the place of their natural origins, while inversely accumulating within buildings. For example, today there is more copper to be found in buildings than in earth. As mines become increasingly empty, our buildings become mines in themselves.'[3] In other words, our cities are containers of buildings, and these can be considered as mines supplying resources for future development.

This concept is pursued further by Thomas E Graedel from the Yale School of Forestry and Environmental Science. He considers the question of how much energy is saved by the reusing or even recycling of material normally destined for landfill or incineration. He suggests that buildings do not only store material for future generations to reuse, but that often they help reduce the future carbon footprint of buildings. Aluminium, for example, is a material commonly used in contemporary buildings. As a number of our case studies demonstrate, aluminium is relatively straightforward to recycle. This process consumes energy. However, it requires only 5% of the energy originally used in its production to recycle it into a 'new' product such as a window frame. Graedel therefore argues, 'It is not inaccurate to regard this aluminium as "urban ore" and cities as "urban mines".'

CASE STUDY No.2

School Buildings by Francis Kéré

THE STORY

It is almost impossible to write about the work of Kéré Architecture without reference to the story of how its founder, Francis Kéré, became an architect. He was born in the village of Gando in Burkina Faso and was lucky enough to be the first child from his village to be sent to school. This education led to Kéré becoming a carpenter, which in turn led to him gaining a scholarship to complete an apprenticeship in development aid from the Carl Duisberg Society in Germany. Afterwards, he went on to study architecture at the Technical University of Berlin, where today he bases his practice. Kéré was determined to give something back to those who had helped him achieve academic success. In 1998, he set up Schulbausteine für Gando or Building Blocks for Gando, to fund the construction of a primary school in his home village of Gando, which was completed as his diploma project in 2004.

Figure 2.211
School pupils stand outside the completed Gando School extension, Burkina Faso.

Clockwise from top left:

Figure 2.212
Villagers constructing part of the Opera Village, with sun-baked, hand-thrown clay bricks, Laongo, Burkina Faso.

Figure 2.213
Villagers utilise old clay pots to create roof lights for the Gando School Library.

Figure 2.214
Women making a rammed-earth floor for the Gando School extension.

Figure 2.215
Interior image of the stunning natural light in the Gando School Library.

Figure 2.216
Young women carry rocks for the foundations of the Gando School extension.

OPINION

Why are these projects interesting to us as far as the circular economy is concerned? The buildings designed by Francis Kéré are constructed primarily out of organic material (stone, earth and timber) that one day will compost or return to the ground beneath the villagers' feet. The steel roof structures and finishes are easy to disassemble for reuse. These two separate outcomes are the two 'circular systems' that describe the circular economy that will be fed by either organic or inorganic 'nutrients'. Remember, waste is 'food' for the circular economy.

Kéré has identified the potential of his people to relearn skills that were lost or undervalued due to more than 100 years of colonialism and the forced dependency upon outside funding and resources that resulted. Kéré has also allowed his fellow countrymen and women to reacquaint themselves with material resources that their forefathers knew well. This has given this community a sense of confidence to investigate new and emerging design techniques to create genuinely comfortable and beautiful buildings. They also feel confident enough in their newly acquired skills to experiment with the materials they formerly took for granted as second-rate. Gando is now the site of many architectural and construction experiments that involve the whole community in their development. The carbon footprint of these substantial new buildings is almost non-existent, and the material sources are completely circular.

Kéré Architects have plans for even bigger buildings, such as a new people's parliament building in Burkina Faso. Let's wait and see how their European, Chinese and North American commissions compare as circular systems.

Figure 2.217
School pupils enjoy the shade under the roof of the Gando School extension.

This was a hugely ambitious project involving most members of the village as there was little or no money. For example, children from the village collected stones for over a year to form the foundations of the building. Women prepared the beautiful, compacted-earth floors while men made bricks. Perhaps the biggest challenge Kéré faced was convincing his fellow villagers that large buildings, such as the new primary school for 700 pupils, could be made of mud and timber, as these materials were considered substandard and only for poor people who couldn't afford 'proper' materials. They were also concerned that adobe walls would be washed away after a storm or two. Kéré overcame this issue by designing a gently curving roof that oversailed the walls to protect them. He also remembered how hot the tin roofs made the classroom that he had learnt to write in. So he lifted the roof up to allow the natural cross-ventilation of air, as well as to provide rain protection. The result is that the school is still standing: now it is one of a cluster of buildings, including a library, teachers' houses, an extension to the original school and a new secondary school. All these buildings were constructed by the villagers themselves.

The resultant ensemble of large buildings has not only empowered the citizens of Gando, but many other people throughout Burkino Faso. Kéré deliberately developed a contemporary architectural language for his new buildings in Gando to overcome local prejudices against local materials. At the same time, by developing designs for these buildings with the villagers themselves, Kéré has empowered people to believe again that they can be responsible for the significant infrastructure projects more often outsourced to European or Chinese mega-companies.

CASE STUDY No. 3

Hy-Fi Organic Compostable Tower by The Living

THE STORY

To achieve a true state of circularity, many people have identified a need to divide resources into 'technical' and 'organic' nutrients or flows. The organic cycles or ecosystems already exist in nature, and the technical ones will hopefully exist when things large and small are designed for disassembly, incorporating new intelligent synthetic materials. The idea of constructing products and buildings with materials that are organic and capable of composting is not a new one. Historically, many buildings and artefacts have done just this. However, contemporary designers have tended to avoid organic materials, although there are a number of interesting practices and scientists who are considering ways of literally growing their buildings. One of these is Brooklyn-based architects/artists/researchers The Living, who were formed in 2006 with a mission of 'creating the architecture of the future' through the exploration of 'how new technologies come to life in the built environment'. Their projects blur the boundaries of avant-garde art, design and horticulture.

They are perhaps best known for their Hy-Fi installation for MoMA PS1, in New York, completed in 2014. These temporary towers were constructed out of over 10,000 bricks that were grown rather than manufactured, using a combination of agricultural by-products (chopped-up corn stalks) and mushroom mycelium that acts as a natural, digestive glue. Working in partnership with Ecovative, a company that

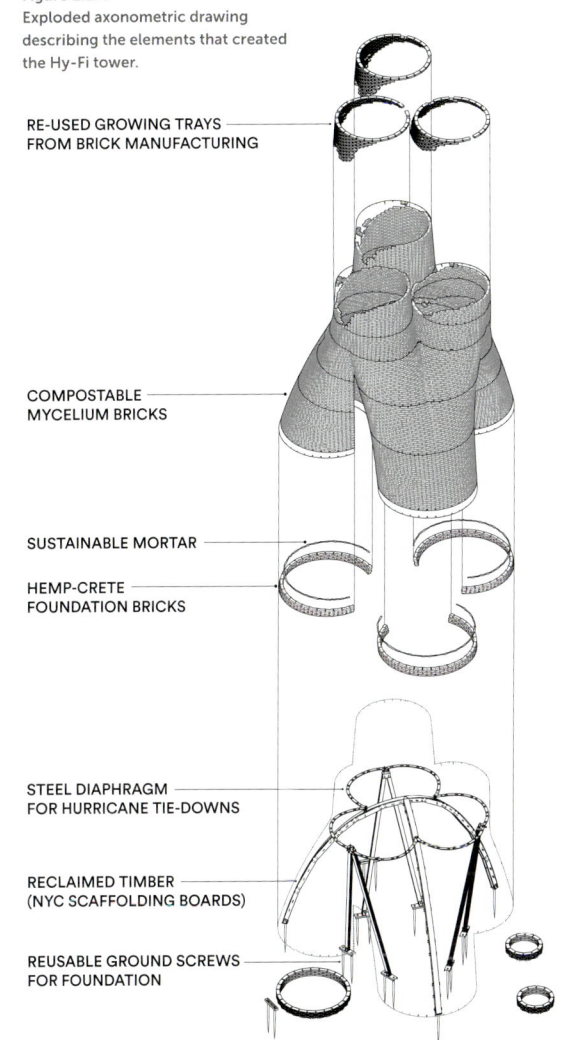

Figure 2.219
Exploded axonometric drawing describing the elements that created the Hy-Fi tower.

Figure 2.218
How to grow a mycelium brick.

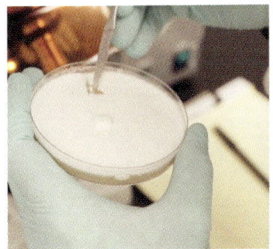    

From top:

Figure 2.220
Mycelium bricks, incubating for three days.

Figure 2.221
Mycelium bricks in their moulds.

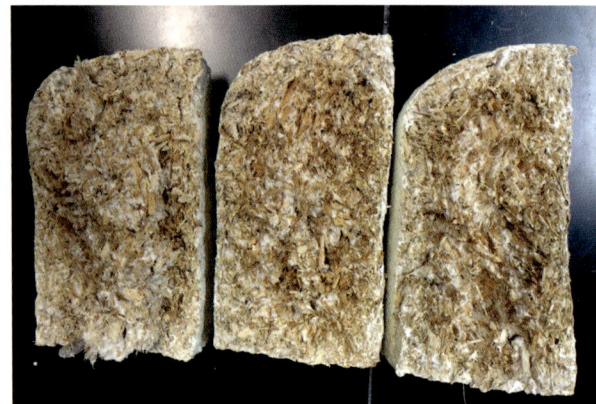

Figure 2.222
Sample mycelium bricks broken in two to reveal corn-husk aggregate.

Figure 2.223
Testing the compressive strength of mycelium bricks.

specialises in developing organic grown materials and whose own mission is to 'rid the world of toxic, unsustainable materials', The Living created brick-shaped moulds that Ecovative used to grow its mycelium-based material in. Through a process of iterative design, growing and physical testing, The Living and their collaborators (including Ecovative, Arup for structural engineering, and a material testing lab at Columbia University) developed bricks that were strong, load-bearing and tolerant of bad weather – they were tuned to last outdoors for three months without any change in mechanical properties. So, it is now possible to build with bricks that one day, if they cannot be reused, can be composted. It should also be noted that the growing of these bricks (they can be any form you want) does not have to consume fossil fuels: the chemical process does not require heat. This is one of the big issues associated with conventional clay bricks: the huge carbon footprint. Ironically for a project with the ability to compost organically, Hy-Fi was eventually acquired for MoMA's permanent collection.

Figure 2.224
Constructing the Hy-Fi tower.

Figure 2.225
The Hy-Fi tower installed.

Figure 2.226
Looking up from inside the Hy-Fi tower.

OPINION

The Living could be classified as avant-garde architects: more thought than built. This may be so. However, their ideas are rooted in very tangible concerns to observe and learn from nature. In this case, they turn senseless linear processes into circular ones. Designing contemporary structures that introduce these systems into the everyday is to be commended and many people believe that in future many new buildings will be grown. The Living's Amphibious Envelope project is perhaps more a thought-provoker than a strategy to be rolled out again and again. It wraps part of an existing building with timber-framed glass tanks housing snails and frogs! However, their Bionic Partition (in partnership with Autodesk) for Airbus tries a different tack. It creates a new type of partition wall separating the plane's galley from the passenger seating area. In an industry trying to reduce energy consumption by making aircraft lighter, The Living designed the Bionic Partition with a 40% saving in weight. They did this by utilising 3D printing using new algorithms based upon slime mould concepts and bone growth. So, on this occasion they learned from natural systems rather than emulating them and with a saving in weight over the current partition of 40%, they more than met the client's brief to reduce the weight by 30%.

Despite appearing to be on the fringes of the design world, The Living's projects are increasingly influential, attracting numerous awards from around the world. Fast Company ranked them third after Bjarke Ingels Group (BIG) in its list of the World's Most Innovative Companies in Architecture. The Living are onto something.

CASE STUDY No.4

The Enterprise Centre, UEA, by Architype

THE STORY

The University of East Anglia (UEA) was established in 1963. It has a long-standing tradition of commissioning innovative buildings from leading UK architects, starting with its famous 'ziggurats' designed by Sir Denys Lasdun (1968), followed by the Sainsbury Centre by Sir Norman Foster (1978) and Europe's largest low-energy building project, student accommodation by Rick Mather Architects (1992). In 2012, together with Morgan Sindall and the Adapt Low Carbon Group, UEA continued this worthy tradition by appointing Architype to design a new building dedicated to nurturing the growth of small and start-up businesses, as well as providing educational and conference facilities. Architype have a long-established record of delivering buildings with deep-green credentials and are perhaps the UK's most successful exponents of authentic sustainable design solutions.

The team behind the project took advantage of this unusual commission to test the viability of constructing a large (3,425m^2) university office building using locally sourced materials, whether that meant organic and grown, second-hand or material from local waste streams. Not exactly self-consciously designed for remanufacture, the focus here is to reduce the carbon footprint of the project, from the inception of the design, through the construction process and then while occupied. Architype predicts that the complete CO_2 footprint for this building will be 500kgCO_2e/m^2 over a 100-year life cycle. This might not mean too much until you put the figure into the context of a similar university building built to 'best practice' standards, which can expect to have emitted 800 to 900kgCO_2e/m^2 by the first day of occupation.

This has been achieved by focusing on specifying locally sourced materials to reduce road, air and sea miles to the minimum, and to use as much grown material as possible because it locks CO_2 until it is burnt or composted. The team also specified the reuse of local second-hand materials and complemented this with a policy of using local tradespeople and suppliers. These strategies have created a series of closed-loop systems, as well as at least 27 new permanent jobs for local people. The team, working with Forestry Commission local suppliers and various key players in the East Anglian timber industry, endeavoured to collect local timber, which is normally overlooked as substandard, to provide the timber frame for the building. The external timber columns are formed of glue-laminated larch sourced from Thetford Forest, within 30 miles of the site.

However, this project, completed in 2015, has achieved its fame because of the unusual material it is wrapped in. The Enterprise Centre has a vast and spectacular thatch roof and, unique to this building, similar thatch cladding. This material combines the robust carbon-locking rain screen with organic cellulose insulation made from either wastepaper or waste wood fibre. Architype provided me with the following statistics:

- 47% of external walls (by mass) are locally grown thatch
- 11% of roofs by mass are locally grown reed
- 70% of studwork-forming walls is local Thetford Corsican pine; 30% is Irish Sitka spruce
- 40% by volume of all material is locally sourced, which in this case means sourced within 100 miles of the site; this includes the thatch, the local studwork timber, the glulam columns to the canopy, aggregates and the oak cladding
- 50% by volume of all material used can be composted one day.

Soon after receiving the commission to design the building, members of the design team contacted local farmers and bought up future crops of wheat to provide material for the thatch wall cladding and reed from the Norfolk Broads for the roofs. They thought of specifying heather thatch for the roof, but abandoned the idea as it would have had to be sourced from Northumberland. The resultant thatch cladding comprises prefabricated timber cassettes in-filled with 'Yeoman' wheat straw that has a slightly shorter stem than that used for roofs. This innovation could only happen because the suppliers and

Clockwise from top left:

Figure 2.227
Thatch panels in construction near the site.

Figure 2.228
Creating the thatch panels.

Figure 2.229
Trimming thatch panels once installed.

Figure 2.230
Thatchers installing the roof finish.

Figure 2.231
Detail of the thatch panels and timber cladding.

Figure 2.232
The main elevation.

Figure 2.233
Façade and columns, utilising African iroko wood from salvaged chemistry worktops.

Figure 2.234
Most of the material shown in this image locks CO2 and will compost one day.

installers, specifically the Thatching Straw Growers Association, worked closely with the design team to create a closed-loop cladding system. Stephen Letch was the thatcher who facilitated much of the procurement and implementation for this project. Letch saw the potential benefits for the project, as well as for the construction industry as a whole. He also located smaller closed-loop systems as a by-product of the thatch. The wheat's offcuts were turned into flour and wheat beer.

In addition to producing a building that can genuinely claim to have been grown from the surrounding landscape, Architype located other local material sources for the project. Flints from Holt were used in the lecture theatre, the SUDs pool and around the building perimeter, as well as on the roof of the lecture theatre. Above the main entrance are panels of planed African iroko (a rare and protected hardwood normally off-limits to eco-friendly projects) that was salvaged from old lab desks recovered from the university's chemistry building, designed by Sir Denys Lasdun. The timber species was confirmed by the building's original project architect, Gordon Forbes. The remainder of the cladding is 20-year-old seasoned oak from a local timber yard that cited the oak's origins from a local estate. Even the new reception desk is actually an old reception designed by Norman Foster for the nearby Sainsbury Centre.

OPINION

When completed, the Enterprise Centre was recognised as the greenest building in the UK. Architype and their team have ensured that the building is certified to Passivhaus standards. It is carbon neutral in terms of energy consumed by the building in use, extremely airtight and has achieved BREEAM Outstanding – i.e. it achieves all the 'normal' sustainable best-practice benchmarks. If that had been it, then the project wouldn't be in our book. What is significant about this project is Architype's rigour and tenacity when considering genuinely low-carbon, closed-loop material sources and construction systems. About 40% of this high-spec building comes from the surrounding landscape, where it was grown. Over 50% of the building is compostable. Its very existence has created at least 27 new permanent jobs and acts as an advertisement for the potential of wealth-creating closed-loop systems.

The cost of constructing this building, at about £2,800+VAT/m2, is competitive when compared to a normal build rate for a building of this type and quality. The Enterprise Centre at UEA will, over its 100-year life, treat the planet with more kindness than most buildings occupied in the UK and beyond. In many ways there are parallels here with the work of Francis Kéré. Just like Kéré, Architype have highlighted the true value of local organic materials that have been neglected by the construction industry. By rediscovering the potential of these materials to do a 'proper' job, perhaps the Enterprise Centre and other projects of its type – large, commercial architectural projects – can provide a clear way forward for humankind to develop in a circular way. One day this building may return the favour and feed the landscape that has recently nourished it, or perhaps it will be dismantled and reused for other future buildings, just like timber-frame and thatch buildings from previous centuries.

CASE STUDY No.5

Brummen Town Hall and New HQ for Alliander by RAU Architects and Turntoo

THE STORY

Rau Architects were formed in the early 1990s with a remit to deliver buildings creating the smallest possible ecological footprint. Issues of energy consumption and material sources have particularly interested the practice. By the mid-2000s, their founder, Thomas Rau, had developed a high profile as both a successful architect and a future thinker, considering ways in which humankind's development could be less dependent on raw materials and by consequence less damaging to the environment.

Not content to stick with designing buildings, in 2010 Rau formed Turntoo together with Sabine Oberhuber, a company dedicated to working on new, circular business models. The company now develops closed-loop systems, products and services for private and public organisations that they hope will 'facilitate the continuity of life on Earth'. The ambition is to develop an open network of companies that act as closed-loop suppliers for their architectural projects.

Once constructed, the buildings can be considered as material depots for future projects. Turntoo have also developed the concept of material passports for second-hand material flows and components. By researching a particular waste source, Turntoo add value to it: 'Information turns waste into valuable material.' A material passport is a fascinating concept that will document all the materials used in a building, categorised as far as their exact specification, including level of toxicity, location in the building (structure, skin, etc.), function, as well as their ability to be dismantled for reuse or recycling. The project is still in development.

Perhaps the most famous partnership Turntoo have developed is their Circular Lighting concept with Philips Lighting. The idea is simple, but quite possibly brilliant. Instead of buying light fittings, customers lease light – or to be more precise, they lease the appropriate lux level for the function required. Leasing lux for 10 or 15 years instead of buying light fittings puts the responsibility for the maintenance, performance and disposal of said fittings firmly with the manufacturer. The idea is that this will encourage far greater levels of corporate responsibility. So, for example, as manufacturers will have to deal with the light fittings at the end of their functioning life, perhaps they will be more inclined to design their fittings for remanufacture: perhaps they will consider their products as a material resource to reuse in the future?

Inspired by this, the founder of MUD Jeans set up a lease-a-jeans company. In partnership, Turntoo helped MUD Jeans develop the concept. Mud Jeans state that 'on average 30% of all garments in our cupboards have not been worn for almost a year'. A year or so after you have leased your MUD Jeans, they will accept the worn-out garment and recycle it into 'new' garments to lease. This is a particularly big deal when one considers that the cotton industry currently has the nickname of a 'dirty crop' because although only 2.4% of the world's cultivated land is dedicated to the growing of cotton, it accounts for about 24% of the world's toxic insecticide market! So, considering material sources before you design a pair of jeans, or a building, can really make a difference.

Two recent RAU Architects building projects that are worth considering are both situated in the Netherlands: the new HQ for Alliander, in Duiven, which involved the reworking and extension of existing buildings, and a newbuild extension to the town hall in Brummen. Both projects were extensions to existing buildings, although Brummen Town Hall had the added challenge of conservation of a designated monument.

The original town hall in Brummen was designed as a standalone villa, dating from 1890. As with many municipal buildings, the original fabric had been altered and extended to such an extent as to almost obliterate the original valuable architectural heritage. RAU Architects' approach was to restore the original fabric of the villa using materials that matched the original 19th-century specifications. It should be noted that materials from the original extensions were mostly 'remanufactured' – stone was crushed, and the blockwork was used for the façade of the basement.

Clockwise from top left:

Figure 2.235
Work in progress on the Brummen Town Hall site.

Figure 2.236
Aggregates from buildings demolished on site, being reused for new buildings on site.

Figure 2.237
Low-grade timber salvaged from pallets and used to overclad existing and new buildings.

Figure 2.238
Detail of existing building, overclad with insulation and reclaimed timber.

The new extension is designed to use as little material as possible, incorporating a prefabricated and modular supporting structure, and timber floors and façade. This all helps reduce the initial ecological footprint of the development and allows for simple dismantling at the end of the building's life. This approach also reduced the construction time significantly. However, what is more unusual, and more ambitious, is the design of the new timber columns and beams. They have been designed to be popular sections and lengths to ensure the broadest options for reuse at the end of their current life. They are not designed for the specific situation on site. Many other components and materials used on site are Cradle to Cradle certified, which means that during their whole life cycle they have minimal environmental impact. The lighting and flooring are on the Turntoo-type lease agreements previously mentioned.

The New Town Hall at Brummen was constructed by BAM Utilitetisbouw and completed in 2013. RAU Architects suggest that the biggest challenge for these contractors was what they describe as 'the montage – re-montage' guidelines they put into the construction contract – in other words, the particular way the building was assembled to allow for 'dry' processes to replace normal 'wet trades' such as in situ cast concrete, plaster and mortar joints, as well as bolting steel elements together instead of welding. 'Re-montage' is the concept of disassembly and for understandable reasons it is the strategy that proved the most challenging for BAM when constructing this building: many 'normal' practices had to be unlearned.

The second RAU Architects project to discuss here is the headquarters building for energy network Alliander in Duiven. At first glance this looks like a brand-new building. However, it is actually another retrofit and extension of an existing structure, an overcrowded 30-year-old office building. It was originally designed to accommodate 600 people, but the new brief asked for facilities to be expanded to allow for 1,500 people.

Clockwise from top left:

Figure 2.239
Photovoltaic solar panels were installed on the Alliander HQ at the beginning of the construction process to power construction equipment, as well as the building in-use.

Figure 2.240
Interior environment of the Alliander HQ, highlighting reuse of reclaimed timber.

Figure 2.241
The Alliander HQ, completed in 2015.

Figure 2.242
The ultra-lightweight steel roof of the Alliander HQ, designed by a roller-coaster manufacturer, is bolted together for easy reuse.

On this occasion the original buildings are not immediately apparent as their original façades, including the windows, have had an additional layer or 'skin' of second-hand low-grade timber overlay. This provides additional insulation, which in turn reduces both heat loss and heat gain. The timber has been heated up in a controlled environment, which adds to the material's ability to be weatherproof. In addition to this, the insulation used with this new layer of cladding was made from shredded clothing, including old work clothing from the client Alliander.

A new roof oversails both the original and new enclosed accommodation, allowing for well-lit communal social spaces and environmental buffer zones. Large windows open onto the new central atrium that helps create better levels of natural ventilation and air quality, and increased levels of natural light, and therefore greater levels of wellbeing.

RAU state that despite what appears to be a wholesale rebuild, the following statistics make the Alliander HQ an unusual construction project:

- 90% of the materials that comprised the original buildings were reused for the new project.
- 50% of all materials used are reused from the old buildings.
- 42% of the remaining 50% 'new' materials are tagged 'recyclable' by the NIBE (Dutch Institute for Building Ecology).
- Therefore, a total of 92% of all materials used can be labelled circular in use.

Second-hand salvaged timber was specified for the newbuild elements as well as the retrofit elements. Concrete stripped out of some of the existing buildings was reused on site, as was steelwork. Asphalt from existing roofs was reused on site, as well as existing toilets and ceiling plates. Even existing doors were turned into furniture. The steel structure for the new mega-roof was designed with the help of a roller-coaster construction company, which has experience in designing with the minimum amount of material. The resultant structure was 30% lighter than normal, using 35% less material and allowing for disassembly at the end of the building's life. Raw material passports are applied to all materials supplied to this development. RAU insist this will ensure that the building can be a material depot for future developments.

This building is (almost inevitably) 'carbon neutral' as far as in-use energy consumption is concerned (the building generates a surplus of energy, which is distributed via a local energy grid). Renewable energy is generated by photovoltaic panels installed on the roof of the parking deck. These same cells now produce energy for the completed building. The construction site was also the cleanest construction site in the Netherlands. All surplus materials were sorted and prepared for reuse and recycling.

By creating the infrastructure, structures, systems and knowledge to support an authentic circular system, RAU Architects appear to have ensured that this building will in time become a valuable material resource for future generations who may not have access to the raw materials we tend to take for granted today.

OPINION

Many 'pathfinder' designers have had to invent systems – products even – that enable their visions to be realised. Architects Michael and Patty Hopkins developed hi-tech, prefabricated steel and neoprene cladding systems for their early buildings because the established supply chain couldn't deliver on their futuristic designs. Craig White of White Design did the same in 2006, when he created a separate company that developed ModCell prefabricated timber, straw and 'hempcrete' panels. RAU Architects have an established reputation as imaginative architects testing ideas of sustainable development. However, it is with Turntoo that they have the potential to create the mechanisms (the specifications and contractual agreements) and, crucially, the new concepts (leasing products, material passports, buildings as material stores) that the design and manufacturing industries need if we are to start changing well-established and unintelligent linear processes into genuine circular closed-loop systems.

CASE STUDY No.6

No. 6 Orsman Road by Waugh Thistleton

THE STORY

Andrew Waugh was born in Milton Keynes, envisaged as the largest of the New Towns to be developed in the south of England and which expanded fast during Waugh's formative years in the 1970s and 1980s.

During his mid-20s, while completing his Diploma in Architecture, Waugh realised that he wanted a career that 'gave something to society', an attitude he attributes to his parents, who were 'small L liberals, Labour Party members, who marched a bit' – a habit that Waugh has passed down to his daughters.

When I interviewed Waugh, he was keen to communicate that he considered the way he practised architecture as 'a social function'. Expanding further, he stated, 'Even when I was designing houses for people, it was always for *them*, not for me.' As he completed his Diploma, Waugh got his first commission (with Sarah Featherstone) to design a nightclub, The Blue Note in London's Hoxton Square. This became one of many nightclub, shop and restaurant commissions that established Waugh and his partner Anthony Thistleton as one of London's most successful architecture practices in this sector. However, Waugh was not content, and in 2006/2007 he had what he now calls his 'black urinal moment', where he found himself at 2am in the morning searching for a black urinal supplier in the USA. It was at this point that he thought, 'What are we doing? I've had enough of this!' Waugh and Thistleton immediately agreed that they should transform themselves from 'a nightclub practice' to one that focused on sustainability and social housing. This decision was transformative for the practice, which very quickly reduced from 30 to 10 people – this was not a short-term business proposition, but a change in practice ethos and sensibility. As Waugh says, 'We took a big hit.'

Waugh has always found the 'chaos of construction really dissatisfying'. This quickly led to further realisations about the massive environmental devastation associated with 'mining, quarrying, waste, single-use stuff' and a commitment to 'no mining/extraction/taking'. This led to an interest in low-waste, off-site, prefabricated construction systems, which was inspired by his own practice creating a small cross-laminated timber (CLT) building in 2003. By 2007, Waugh Thistleton had delivered the world's first high-rise prefabricated CLT scheme, Murray Grove, a housing scheme for a Registered Social Landlord (RSL) in London.

In 2016, Waugh Thistleton took their practice to Austria for a week to visit the forests and sawmills that supply Europe and the UK with the majority of the CLT panels used in construction projects. Waugh Thistleton are leading the cry for mass timber

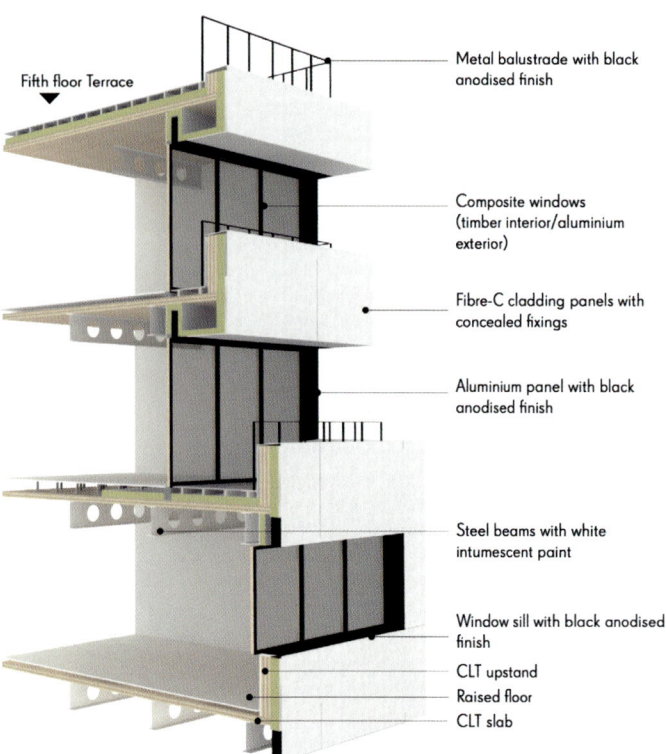

Figure 2.243
Construction detail of wall and floors at No. 6 Orsman Road.

Clockwise from top:

Figure 2.244
Frame installed, view from Orsman Road.

Figure 2.245
View of the steel frame and CLT deck from the upper floor.

Figure 2.246
Stairs made from waste CLT.

construction in the UK, delivering a range of building typologies with carbon-sequestering timber at their core. However, the practice is still in the habit of expanding and contracting in size. You might ask why I would want to dwell on this, as this happens to most architecture practices. As a regulatory response to the disastrous fire at Grenfell Tower, the Mayor of London banned timber from all new high-rise residential buildings in 2022. Because of this, all of Waugh Thistleton's UK-based residential projects were put on indefinite hold, leaving only their non-residential projects to be further developed. And so, it is one of these projects that I want to focus on for the rest of this case study. (On a positive note, it should be noted that Waugh Thistleton still have high-rise residential projects being constructed across Europe.)

From one point of view, No. 6 Orsman Road, in Haggerston, north London, represents a straightforward response to a client's (in this case British Land) brief to design private commercial workspace that provides flexible office size, layout

THE CIRCULAR ECONOMY STEP 4 149

Opposite, clockwise from top left:

Figure 2.247
The view from Orsman Road.

Figure 2.248
View of No. 6 Orsman Road from Regent's Canal.

Figure 2.249
The upper-floor interior, with exposed services.

and length of lease. However, flexibility is not often achieved in architecture. It often manifests itself as the longer-term adaptation of interior spaces involving extensive stripping out of redundant 'temporary' walls, fixtures and fittings. In this case, Waugh Thistleton appear to have delivered a building (completed in 2020) that is more straightforward than normal to adapt. This is achieved by designing a six-storey building with a CLT mass timber core and floor plate combined with cellular steel beams and 'only two columns per space, with no internal support walls'. A hybrid construction system was proposed because, although the site was also very tight in plan, the overall height restrictions meant that cellular steel beams were needed to accommodate non-intrusive mechanical ventilation and heat recovery ductwork. Waugh Thistleton wanted 'to treat the building as a reusable product', designed as a material bank for future buildings, and therefore easy to dismantle in the future. Carbon-sequestering CLT is the perfect medium to achieve this ambition. In addition to the whole structure being bolted together, external cladding panels, steel balustrades, windows, doors and modular partitions are all easily removed for future reuse. This sensibility informed the specification of most components comprising this innovative building.

CLT is left exposed to core walls and all ceilings. While providing a beautiful interior finish, the CLT used in this building feels quite everyday; not precious, but serviceable. And it is this last point that was tested during the construction of the project. Sometime into the construction programme, the clients changed hands. This resulted in a change of brief, which in turn meant that an additional staircase needed to be inserted into the centre of the floor plan after the CLT floor plates had been installed. The resultant additional stairwell had to be cut into the newly installed floor plate. The fact that this was possible was because cross-laminated timber, with its inherent structural integrity, can accommodate this type of post-installation alteration, whereas it would have been a huge challenge for the more often installed in situ cast concrete. An additional benefit of specifying CLT floor plate was that the material removed to form the stairwell was able to be reused on site to form the new staircase installed within.

Nearly all components comprising this building were manufactured off-site, which reduced the impact of deliveries and noise associated with 'normal' construction processes, as well as reducing waste flows on site to nearly zero. Concrete was limited to the pile foundations – after all, this building sits next to Regent's Canal. Other 'wet trades' were virtually eliminated on site, and consequently waste flows were all but eliminated. Operational CO_2 emissions are predicted to be very low, at 14.6kgCO_2e/m^2, with embodied/whole-life carbon at a very respectable 582kgCO_2e/m^2.

OPINION

Of course, the embodied/whole-life carbon figures quoted above don't represent the whole life story that Andrew Waugh told me when he showed me around No. 6 Orsman Road. Designing the building so that it can be disassembled and reassembled for reuse asks questions of our industry and the way it quantifies our consumption of resources. The construction sector is only just getting its head around embodied carbon calculations, which currently assume timber is burnt at the end of its first 'life'. By suggesting that existing buildings can provide the resources required for future buildings, Waugh Thistleton and others in this book are asking profound questions of the way our industry consumes vast amounts of natural resources, often for just moments in time. The challenge we all face is summarised by Prof Walter Stahel as (quoting from his own website) 'the shift from a linear industrial economy managing flows to a circular economy managing stocks'[5] – or put another way, a complete system change.

CASE STUDY No.7

Amsterdam Temporary Courthouse, Building Part D(demountable) and The Green House by cepezed

THE STORY

Since 2000, Menno Rubbens has been a Director and Project Developer at cepezed, helping to set up an offshoot company cepezedprojects. He originally studied economics for two years at Erasmus University in Rotterdam, but gave that up to study architecture and engineering at Delft University of Technology. Studying under Prof Kas Oosterhuis, Rubbens was one of the first student architects to graduate by presenting a single 3D model of his architectural design rather than hand-drawn drawings. Heavily influenced by his mentor, Rubbens' designs were extremely fluid, and back when he was designing them in the mid-1990s, almost impossible to construct. This inability to construct frustrated Rubbens, who made a conscious decision to step back and re-evaluate what he wanted to achieve. After some time, he decided to consider a different approach: what about 'the intelligent cube'? It was at this point that he joined cepezed.

cepezed was formed in 1973 and has grown into a one-stop shop offering design and construction services, even developing and owning its own properties, quite unlike anything in the UK. cepezed has always been interested in the relationship between design and manufacturing processes, with an ambition to develop efficient production methods for all parts of the procurement of a building. This has meant dealing with specialist subcontractors, as well as the supply chain, to make the path from design concept through to the delivery of a completed building as smooth as possible. Being responsible for the whole design and construction process has its challenges and responsibilities. However, if you get it right, it also has its efficiencies, be they time saving, cost saving, material/resource saving or the continuity in the communication of a radical idea.

This particular approach that cepezed brings to its projects is perhaps why it has been able to deliver so many projects that ask questions of the normal way of doing things. And cepezed is currently one of the companies at the forefront of delivering authentic closed-loop projects demonstrating circular economy principles, such as constructing 'buildings as material banks' for future buildings. It is also involved in the Netherlands' ever-expanding deconstruction and reuse industry; what we are calling the network of 'urban miners'.

Rubbens leads on cepezed's circular economy projects. Since he first considered the idea of an 'intelligent cube', he has been passionate about understanding as much as possible about the processes involved in making a building's components. This naturally led to him being interested in resource efficiency – understanding that materials have multiple uses. Rubbens also began to compare buildings to other products, such as cars and smartphones, where the manufacture process was often much more resource efficient. Rubbens and his colleagues realised that by considering buildings as products, or a flexible kit-of-parts, and by applying rational design and production values to an architectural project, aesthetics were not undermined: in fact, the exact opposite was often achieved.

What cepezed is particularly interested in is understanding that every building one designs does not have to be a one-off prototype – once certain details are optimised for a particular function, perhaps it is better to refine them for the next job, rather than reinvent them. And so, cepezed has spent many years looking into how to optimise the design of all sorts of building types. This focus led cepezed towards issues of resource efficiency, designing out waste and applying closed-loop, circular principles to the buildings.

When cepezed got the opportunity to bid for a new temporary courthouse in Amsterdam, Rubbens was keen to be involved. The brief responded to Amsterdam's ambitious zero-waste targets, and so it insisted on a project that served the complex needs of the city's biggest courthouse, while virtually eliminating waste during the construction and deconstruction process. The brief also asked teams to consider what the next use of the building might be. Rubbens states that other teams bidding for this commission

Clockwise from top left:

Figure 2.250
Exterior view of the completed Amsterdam Temporary Courthouse, 2016.

Figure 2.251
Interior view of courthouse's staircase.

Figure 2.252
The bridge structure and glazing being removed during the disassembly of the courthouse, in 2022.

Figure 2.253
Cleaning off expanded foam from the steel frame of the courthouse.

Figure 2.254
Collecting concrete floor deck and windows from the disassembled courthouse.

Figure 2.255
Parts from the courthouse in storage, before being moved to their new site in Enschede.

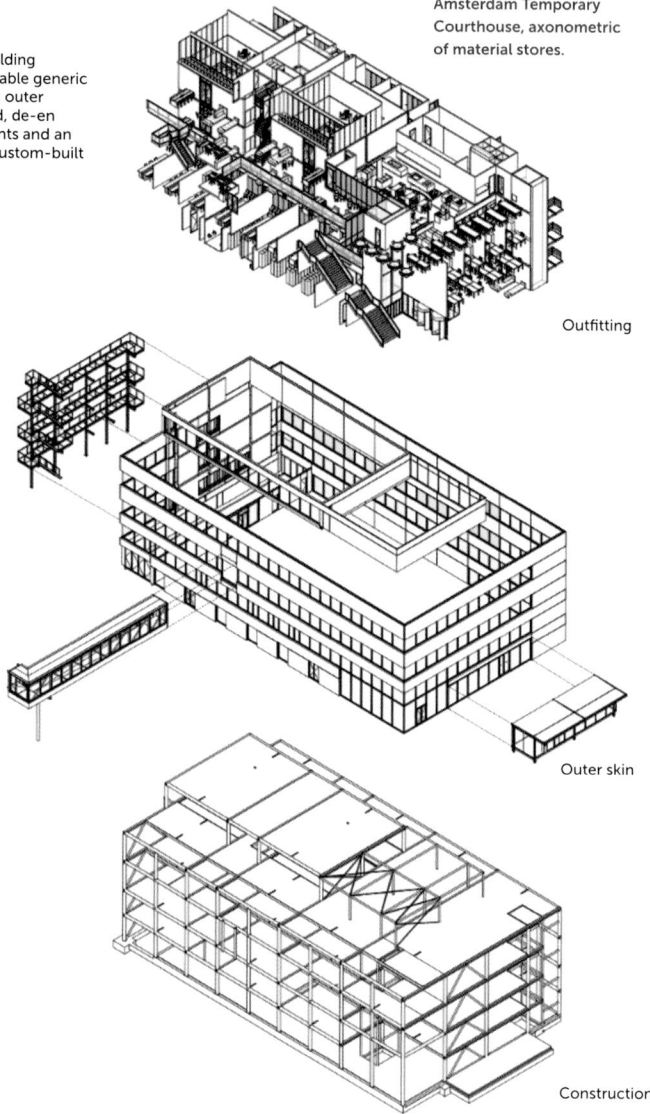

Figure 2.256
Amsterdam Temporary Courthouse, axonometric of material stores.

The setup of the building consists of an adaptable generic construction and an outer skin of prefabricated, de-en remountable elements and an outfitting which is custom-built and replaceable.

focused on the building being a temporary structure. cepezed had a different approach, designing a permanent building that would be a temporary courthouse, albeit one that was designed for disassembly after five years. cepezed also realised that it was impossible to determine the second use of the courthouse building, and therefore focused on developing a design that could be adapted for many uses; one that embraced uncertainty. Although the underdogs in the competition, cepezed's rational approach to the project gave it the edge over its larger competitors, and it secured the commission.

cepezed produced a set of assembly and disassembly drawings of the courthouse, which was constructed in 2016. The building served its first purpose for six years instead of the predicted five. In 2022, it was carefully disassembled, not by the original cepezed team but by a company called Lagemaat, one of the Dutch companies now focusing on deconstruction. Lagemaat was also responsible for moving the parts that were recently the courthouse and reassembling on another site in Enschede, where this time the building will serve as a multi-tenanted business hub.

cepezed recently delivered several new buildings by applying its rational, low-resource-consuming approach to closed-loop design. Of particular interest is the Building Part D(demountable) circular office in Delft, completed in 2019. When one considers the minimal range of prefabricated built elements – lift and stair core, steel frame, structural timber deck, curtain wall system plus first- and second-fix mechanical and electrical installations – this building is really stripped to its circular core. Particularly impressive is the fact that only three people worked on the construction site, assembling these prefabricated elements with apparent ease, and with a construction period of only 16 weeks plus 10 weeks in factory production. Rubbens' vision of an 'intelligent cube' appears to have been realised. This project is deceptively simple, and to me quite beautiful.

One other cepezed project of note is another elegant 'intelligent cube'. The Green House project embraces addition sustainable issues close to cepezed's heart: namely, the production of local, low-carbon, sustainable food, as the Green House is a restaurant that grows the vegetables its customers eat, within the fabric of the building itself. These plants also assist in tempering the internal environment of the building, by improving air quality and providing shading from excessive solar gain in the summer.

cepezed is also deconstructing the temporary Zuiderstrandtheater in Scheveningen, the Netherlands. The theatre is no longer used and will soon be the site of a housing project. Cepezedprojects, in partnership with Lagemaat, is working with the current owners to broker a deal to deconstruct the building and ship it to Oss, also in the Netherlands, where the De Lievekamp Theatre needs additional facilities.

1. Cut slots in two cores of the hollow core slab
2. Apply DEMU anchors
3. Pour concrete onto slots and fix hollow core slab to SFB beam using (adjustable) bolts

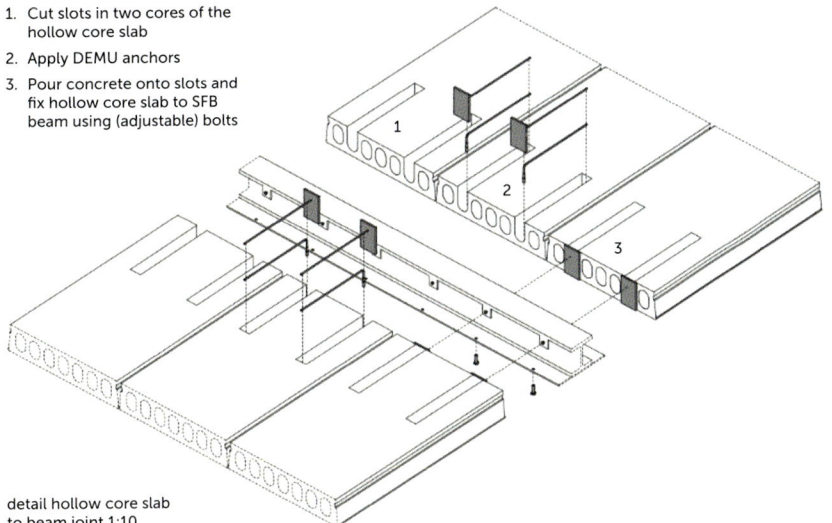

detail hollow core slab to beam joint 1:10

1. Adjustable bolt for fixation of hollow core slab
2. Nut welded on mounted tab
3. DEMU sleeve anchor
4. Bolt for fixation of hollow core slab

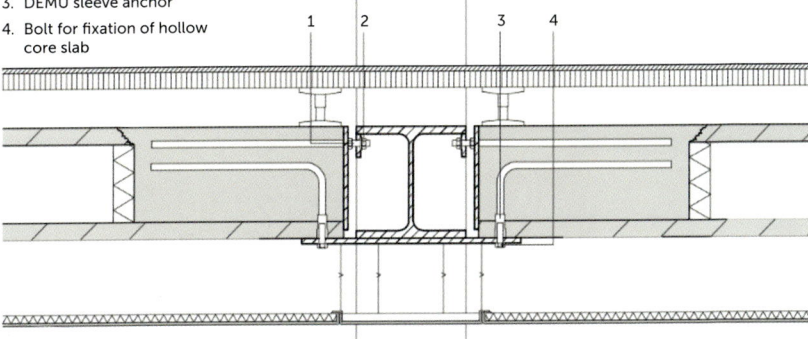

Figure 2.257 Frame-to-deck disassembly drawing for the courthouse.

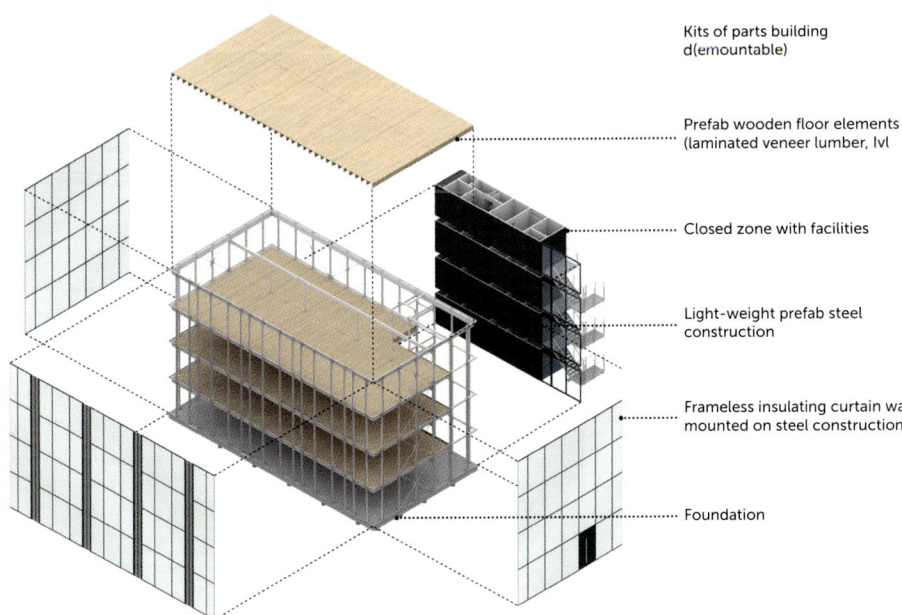

Kits of parts building d(emountable)

Prefab wooden floor elements (laminated veneer lumber, lvl)

Closed zone with facilities

Light-weight prefab steel construction

Frameless insulating curtain wall mounted on steel construction

Foundation

Figure 2.258 Building Part D(demountable), exploded kit-of-parts.

Figure 2.259
A crane installing the steel frame of Building Part D(demountable).

Figure 2.262
Removable soundproofing and floor finish.

Below top to bottom:

Figure 2.260
The timber cassette is installed into the steel frame of Building Part D(demountable).

Figure 2.261
Building Part D(demountable)'s steel frame, with the timber cassettes installed.

Figure 2.263
Night-time image of the exterior of Building Part D(demountable).

OPINION

cepezed has provided clients with a complete design and build service since its inception in 1973. Over the decades it has been able to refine its ideas, test them and deliver projects that meet its own, as well as its clients', aspirations. Perhaps the reason that it appears to be able to adopt the systems change required to integrate circular economy principles into architectural projects is because it is in complete control of the whole building procurement process, from inception to handover. This approach ensures that all parts of the design and construction team have been involved with and understand the reasons why a particular building is designed in a certain way. This is a refreshing approach, albeit one that is virtually unknown in the UK. In addition, cepezed is taking positive action in response to cities and municipalities such as Amsterdam and The Hague that have forward-thinking legislation demanding near-zero levels of waste. The Netherlands has an ambition to be completely circular by 2050, with the consumption of primary raw materials halved by 2030. To enable systems change in our industry, we need to be transparent; to share knowledge and break down the silos wherever they exist. Perhaps being as ambitious as cepezed is too big a challenge for many, but we can still learn from the pioneers who happen to have the skills and resources to effect change.

CASE STUDY No. 8

Circular Economy Routemap by Brighton and Hove City Council

THE STORY

Brighton and Hove sit on the south coast of the UK and have, for many reasons, a reputation for leading on discussions about sustainability and many other so-called 'green' issues. They have had the UK's only Green MP, the splendid Caroline Lucas, as well as my genius colleague Cat Fletcher (see Part 1, Chapter 2) who, among other things, is still working for Brighton and Hove City Council as one of the UK's only 'resource managers'. The council was one of the first to sign up to and adopt a 'One Planet Living Action Plan', and, of course, declared it wanted to be net-zero carbon by 2030(!). Signing up to declarations, employing Heads of Sustainability, etc. is great, but creating an environment where these things actively impact in a positive way on the stuff of running a metropolitan district with more than 290,000 citizens, including more than 35,000 students, plus more than 9 million tourists each year, is always going to be challenging.

I do have to declare an interest here. I have been involved in the following projects in a relatively minor way, but I feel that the story of how Brighton and Hove City Council adopted its very own Circular Economy Routemap for the construction sector, and then used it to positively impact on its own projects, is well worth sharing.

One of the unsung heroes of the UK's circular economy movement is Dr David Greenfield (author of Chapter 3 of this book) who, among many things, runs the London Chapter of the worldwide Circular Economy Club (CEC). Based near Brighton, David also hosts CEC events in the city with his colleague Peter Desmond. Greenfield has a background working in waste management with local authorities and has been collaborating closely with the City Council since 2017 in the development of a circular vision. This approach ensured that key officers in the council were supporting the idea that circular economy principles should inform their ambitions to be net-zero carbon by 2030. This led to a Circular Economy Routemap being formally integrated into the Brighton and Hove City Council Economic Strategy for 2018 to 2023 and the development of the wider circular economy programme. (The Routemap has been developed alongside the Circular Economy Action Plan discussed in Chapter 3 of this book.)

Over a period of about 18 months, only being interrupted by COVID-19 lockdowns, Greenfield and Desmond hosted a series of circular economy 'accelerator' workshops to more than 120 council employees from departments as diverse as Housing, Major Projects, Transport and Procurement. Participants had

Figure 2.264
Front cover of Brighton and Hove City Council's Circular Economy Routemap.

From top:

Figure 2.265
Aerial view of the construction site of the 42 flats, in Victoria Road, Portslade.

Figure 2.266
The installation of metal decking.

Figure 2.267
Installing the metal frame.

a morning of presentations explaining circular principles, including one from me that evidenced precedents from the construction sector. The afternoon sessions were dedicated to breakout groups where participants brought along real projects they were working on, and it's at these sessions where I believe we all learnt the most, seeing the potential and challenges involved in applying closed-loop systems.

To their credit, several council officers attended more than one workshop. One of these was Nick Fishlock, one of the council's Regeneration Project Managers. Fishlock worked on a number of housing projects for the council, which builds its own affordable housing. And it's one of these projects that I want to consider for this case study.

Working for the University of Brighton has afforded me the opportunity to watch numerous high-rise buildings being constructed over the last three to four years. From the beach to the South Downs, these buildings have different forms, heights, cladding and functions, but to my dismay they have one thing in common: their frames, floors and, in many cases, their external walls are formed by pouring concrete on site, reinforced by steel. It's one high-carbon structural solution for all these different buildings.

So, when I heard about a project for new affordable housing commissioned by Brighton and Hove City Council that was being constructed using a bolted-together light-gauge steel frame system built off-site in load-bearing modular panels,

I was very interested. I soon found out that the clients were represented by Nick Fishlock, and that his team had folded circular economy principles into the design brief for the project. At the time, Fishlock was so immersed in the circular economy that he was being invited by ACAN (Architects Climate Action Network) and others to speak about his work.

The project was designed by the council's in-house architecture team, with Morgan Sindall responsible for the build, which comprises 42 flats, in Victoria Road, Portslade. Sounds all very normal. However, due to the creation of the Circular Economy Routemap and attendance at accelerator sessions, the designs were reviewed to consider circular principles. Because the brief referenced the RIBA Climate Challenge and circular principles such as designing buildings as material banks, etc., this five-storey building did not use concrete above the ground. Following on from discussions with the client group at RIBA Work Stage 3, the project employed a light-gauge steel frame bolted together and infilled with steel-framed modular panels manufactured off-site and also secured with bolts.

A preconstruction carbon assessment was undertaken by Morgan Sindall, piloting their Carbonica WLCA tool, which helped inform the decision to work with the steel frame. The team proved that by choosing a steel frame instead of the ubiquitous in situ cast concrete, there would be a saving of 177 tonnes of embodied carbon at practical completion, with 290 tonnes saving over the life cycle of the building. And that was just the saving for the frame of the building. The lighter-weight frame also reduced the amount of poured concrete needed for the foundations. Overall, the project, completed in 2023, achieved a figure of 926.15kgCO$_2$e/m^2 for embodied carbon, which is a 23% reduction against the RIBA's 2030 Climate Challenge 'business as usual' metric, and 76kWh/m^2/year regulated and unregulated operational energy.

In addition, the frame and modular elements of this building can one day be deconstructed and reused, depending on future circumstances. Since 2022, Brighton and Hove City Council's Regeneration team have required project briefs for tall housing to include a circular economy opportunity assessment, meeting the RIBA 2030 Climate Challenge targets. This will measure the amount of reused and recycled content for all construction materials used on site, aiming for this content to be at least 20% by weight. In addition, contractors will be required to measure the amount of reusable and recyclable content at end of life for all construction materials used on site, aiming for reusable content to be at least 50% by weight, with an ambition for 50% of new material to hold certified EPD (Environmental Product Declaration).

OPINION

This case study is all about the impact of a few inspired individuals who have a passion to effect change. By understanding how to pass on knowledge to others in key roles within Brighton and Hove City Council, David Greenfield and his colleagues were able to force change from within. At one level, this is only one relatively modest affordable housing scheme. However, it proves that well-intentioned guidelines, such as the Circular Economy Routemap, don't have to stay up on the shelf. Despite no laws (yet – they will come) insisting on circular economy principles being applied to construction projects in the UK, a well-written brief supported by an informed client and a willing delivery team will effect change. This case study proves that the frame and fabric of this housing project did not have to be made from the construction system with perhaps the largest embodied carbon footprint, one without the ability to ever be adapted, deconstructed and reused. It is also interesting that construction waste on site while the frame and fabric were being installed was only 18% of 'normal' amounts: in other words, this case study is not the complete closed-loop circular deal. It is a couple of steps in the right direction; a useful precedent to build upon. It should be noted that a single piled ground-source heat pump (not an air-source heat pump) supplies heat to all flats. Moving forward, Brighton and Hove City Council is commissioning new affordable housing schemes with even more ambitious whole-life carbon targets. I wish them luck.

CASE STUDY No.9

People's Pavilion by bureau SLA and Overtreders W with Arup

THE STORY

When I agreed to write the second edition of this book, I made a promise to my (very patient) editor that I would focus on examples of larger, commercial projects that would demonstrate how circular economy principles were becoming more attractive for everyday projects, not one-off pavilions. Well, I'm ignoring those guidelines here because there is one issue that is often difficult to quantify, but even more difficult to ignore, and that is – beauty. In addition, I am interested in projects that deliberately tackle the question of how the aesthetic and architectural language of a building responds to the demands of the circular economy – and I believe the People's Pavilion begins to do these things.

Designed as a temporary venue hosting talks as part of the 2017 Dutch Design Week in Eindhoven, the People's Pavilion was developed as a collaboration between architects bureau SLA and Overtreders W, who specialise in the design of temporary pavilions and have a passion for reuse and recycling (see the Overtreders W and Pretty Plastic case study in Step 1). Multidisciplinary engineers Arup dealt with the particular structural challenges this project presented, and Arup also know a thing or two about the circular economy.

The team claim that 100% of the materials used to make the pavilion were borrowed, and apparently not just from building suppliers, but from Eindhoven residents as well. Borrowing 100% of the materials for only a few months means that 100%

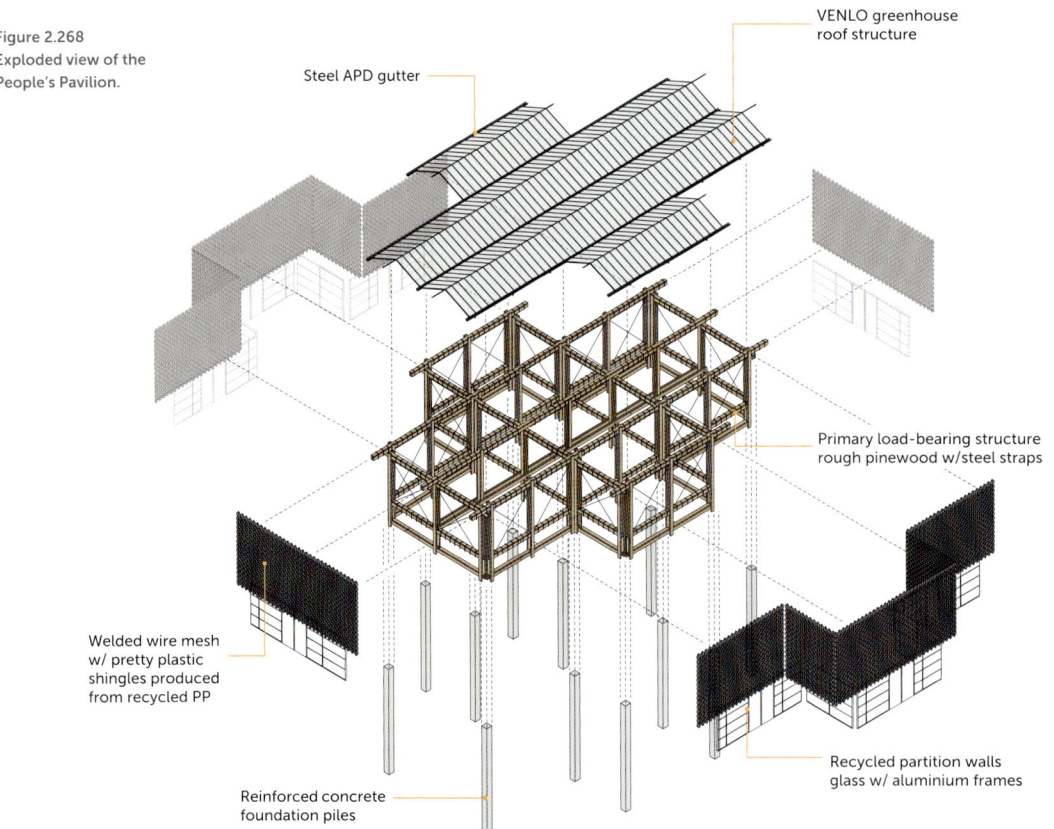

Figure 2.268
Exploded view of the People's Pavilion.

From top:

Figure 2.269
People's Pavilion unpacked (1).

Figure 2.270
People's Pavilion unpacked (2).

Figure 2.271
People's Pavilion, interior structure.

Figure 2.272
People's Pavilion, internal detail.

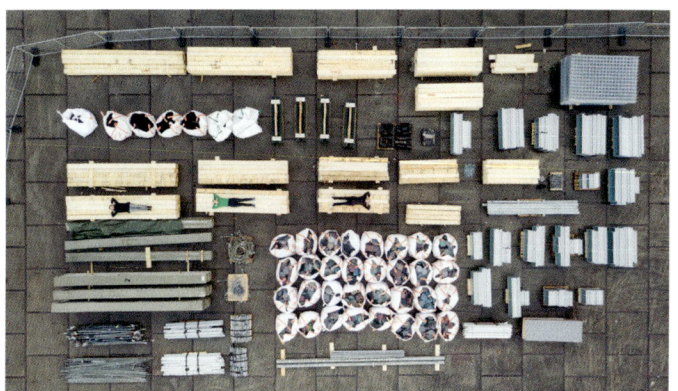

of the materials need to be returned in good shape. This negates the option to glue or cut bits together, and in this case the team also banned screws and drills from the site. The frame of the pavilion was formed by 7m-tall prefabricated concrete columns normally used for piling. It should be noted that there are no foundations required for this pavilion. These concrete columns sit directly on the ground.

Steel rods from a demolished office building were reused to provide cross-bracing. Solid timber beams (locally sourced from Stiho, a Dutch wholesaler of building materials) were strapped to the concrete piles to extend the height of the building and, in turn, support matching cross beams supporting the glazed roof structure, borrowed from a local greenhouse supplier. All of this was strapped together with high-capacity ratchet straps that not only had to hold the building together but also withhold a large wind loading. Arup's engineers had the responsibility of ratifying the structural calculations to prove that these straps were up to the job. This was undertaken by doing numerous practical tests and experiments in partnership with the Technical University of Eindhoven. This was first-hand research as nobody had ever proposed to construct a building of this size with all major structural elements simply tied together.

The lower glass façade and entrance doors were surplus material from an office development in Utrecht. Along with all other parts of the pavilion, these were reused in another project when the pavilion was deconstructed. Lighting and heating systems were also borrowed, as was the bar.

One of the most strikingly beautiful elements of the pavilion are the multicoloured tiles supplied by Pretty Plastic (see the case study in Step 1). The colour range of the tiles came from the original colour of the source plastic. The waste plastic for the tiles was collected from households near to the pavilion site.

Figure 2.273
External view of the People's Pavilion during the day.

OPINION

Yes, this is a small (250m2) temporary pavilion with walls presenting no thermal performance. The building didn't have to meet the stringent levels of performance that permanent buildings need to adhere to, and it is often these regulations (especially airtightness) that present the big challenge to designing buildings as future material banks. However, I really appreciate the rigour, clarity and care that went into the assembly of each of the components that comprise this building. The structural frame dominated internally, with the very visual strapping making it clear that this is no ordinary building. And externally, the beautiful tiles do the job of demanding your attention, with a muted version of their colourful presence apparent from the inside, as well. This is a simple but elegant building that asks questions of what an architecture might look like if it is designed for many different lives. The photographs of the disassembled building spread out carefully on the ground are particularly enticing.

Figure 2.274
External view of the People's Pavilion at night.

162 PART 2 CIRCULAR INSPIRATIONS

CASE STUDY No.10

Durley Chine Environmental Innovation Hub by Footprint Architects

THE STORY

Footprint Architects are one of a growing number of practices around the planet who are very clear about their position on the climate and ecological emergency – they take a holistic approach, embracing environmental and social issues with equal vigour. They are also discovering that more and more clients are equally passionate and well informed. Despite these advances, how best to effect the behaviour changes required to meet ambitious low-carbon targets is still the big challenge. However, sometimes a project comes along with an enlightened brief and a well-informed client.

Every year 2,000 tonnes of waste are removed from Bournemouth, Christchurch and Poole's (BCP) popular beaches every year. It is such a big problem that BCP Council is investing a lot of time and resources into coming up with ways to stop people from dropping litter on their beaches. As well as encouraging behaviour change, BCP Council wants to improve its environmental waste management systems, with an ambition of becoming a Green Economy Leader by enabling a step change in the reduction of single-use plastics while increasing recycling along this part of the UK's coastline. This will be achieved by partnering with local seafront businesses, major public and private sector organisations, together with academic institutions and volunteering sectors. All good, but why mention it here? It's because BCP Council decided that these aspirations and ambitions should be exemplified in built form, and so they developed a brief for a new building, namely the Environmental Innovation Hub located at Durley Chine, which is one of Bournemouth's internationally recognised Blue Flag beaches suffering from huge amounts of litter.

From the outset of the commission, Footprint Architects were focused on reducing the whole-life environmental impact of the

Figure 2.275
View from the beach of the Durley Chine Environmental Innovation Hub, which opened in 2023.

development. The schedule of accommodation was interrogated to make sure that all parts of the building were working hard for the project brief. In addition to designing out surplus spaces, the design was simplified as much as possible, with the pallet of materials drawn from either locally sourced and second-hand or new locally sourced, nontoxic, organic (carbon-locking) and sustainably managed sources. Plastics were reduced to a bare minimum. Some 52 tonnes of salvaged groyne members were reclaimed from the Bournemouth beachfront, to be repurposed for the cladding and the grass-canopy roof that sails over the whole complex, which consists of a kiosk, public WCs, plus a two-storey teaching block with welfare facilities for the beach staff. Salvaged groynes also created balustrading for the building. Primary structural columns were formed of new FSC-certified hardwood, which, claim the architects, has a tenth of the carbon footprint of the equivalent in steel and enabled the successful reuse of the salvaged materials. Hardwood timber is more durable than its softwood equivalent, sequestering more CO_2, with a smaller embodied carbon footprint (no kiln drying required); and, of course, being more durable, hardwood is more likely to be repurposed one day.

Walls for the kiosk were constructed by mixing local sand and other aggregates, bound with low-carbon GGBS (ground granulated blast-furnace slag) cement replacement, to form a beautiful, solid load-bearing wall, looking at first glance like super-durable rammed earth. Almost all structural rebar was designed out of these walls, reducing the carbon footprint and increasing the walls' life span (thanks to the reduced chance of rebar exposure). The two-storey teaching block façade takes its cue from nearby beach huts, which incorporate upturned decks. The cladding was orientated to mimic these beach huts and creates a delightful rhythm of verticals and horizontals. The cladding was created by reusing offcuts from the structural groynes salvaged from the beach nearby. The salvaged groyne timber was not suitable for reusing for the various timber decks that are in and around the building as there is a requirement for people to be able to walk barefoot. So, the team sourced salvaged timber decking which had previously been used in a German submarine base. This timber, with FSC chain-of-custody certification, enabled the reuse of a now-redundant product which was durable and therefore fit for purpose.

Weathertight accommodation is well sealed and well insulated to Passivhaus standards with Warmcell cellulose insulation sourced from recycled newspaper. Other areas providing space for public exhibitions are not insulated, but they are sheltered by the oversailing roof and some external walls. This strategy ensures that the expensive construction elements are kept to a minimum, while providing other sheltered places at a much-reduced cost/m^2, or, as the architects themselves put it, 'We separated independent functions of the brief into independent buildings, enabling efficient buildings with a bespoke thermal envelope aligned to the intended use … all oversailed by the uniting roof structure.'

The education and welfare building, designed to Passivhaus standards, was by default designed to the highest levels of insulation and airtightness, supported by MVHR (mechanical ventilation with heat recovery), creating a stable and comfortable internal environment. This part of the building was constructed as an off-site, timber-framed modular system, reducing beachside and highways disruption on site, and thus reducing waste and the associated carbon footprint of this high-performing element. In contrast, the public WC part of the project is left unheated and uninsulated, with trickle vents providing background ventilation. Even here though, the IPS (integrated plumbing system) panels are manufacturer from recycled plastic bottles supplied by the wonderful Smile Plastics (see Adam Fairweather and Smile Plastics case study, in Step 1).

The kiosk is a transient space with low levels of insulation and minimal heating demands, leading to the Visitor Centre Experience hosted under the oversailing roof, but otherwise open to the elements. Some 90m^2 of photovoltaic panels are installed to ensure that the building runs as an operational zero-carbon development.

From top:

Figure 2.276
Close-up external view.

Figure 2.277
Close-up of reclaimed timber.

Figure 2.278
The reclaimed timber structure.

OPINION

Footprint Architects visited the Brighton Waste House (see Part 3 of this book) in 2017. Inspired, they managed to find a project brief, a site and clients who were as switched on to the benefits of a circular economy as they were. Together with a brilliant design and delivery team, Footprint Architects have produced a building made from predominately salvaged and recycled material, performing to extremely ambitious whole-life carbon figures. In addition, the building actively encourages people to reuse and recycle material. These issues are implicit in the building itself as well as in the programme of events and activities that are ongoing within and next to the Durley Chine Environmental Innovation Hub. Let's hope it impacts upon the people who have the good fortune to visit this building.

CASE STUDY No.11

Pikku-Finlandia by Jaakko Torvinen

THE STORY

As an active academic who runs an architecture practice, my idea of 'living the dream' is when these two elements combine to create what are often called 'live research projects'. As many of you will be aware, these are few and far between. I believe wholeheartedly that they should be encouraged and celebrated, and there are several brilliant 'live projects offices' in schools of architecture around the world.

Pikku-Finlandia (Little Finlandia in English) is the product of a master's student's thesis design project, produced in 2019. The design brief was set across both the Building Design and Wood Programmes to architecture students studying at the Aalto University Department of Architecture. Over one semester, 18 students were asked to develop designs for a temporary event building that would open for three years while Alvar Aalto's world-famous Finlandia Hall, in Helsinki, was being renovated. The idea was that the building had to be made of as many carbon-locking timber products as possible, and that it should be designed for deconstruction, as its first life was only for three years. Four student schemes were chosen for further development, where students worked together with professional structural and MEP (mechanical, electrical and plumbing) engineers. This process also included value engineering to ensure that proposals were financially viable. At the end of the semester, tutors selected one of the student designs to be constructed.

The lucky student was Jaakko Torvinen. He originally called his winning project 'Finlandia Forest' because it was inspired by Finland's own boreal forest. The building was designed using locally sourced pine trees that were barely processed, thus dramatically reducing the embodied carbon footprint of the construction process. This approach was pursued to such an extent that trunks were left with branches still intact. The tree trunks were installed to create views through an internal 'forest' of load-bearing columns. It should be noted that Torvinen's other preoccupation is with the relationship of buildings with urban spaces/the public realm via what might be called 'colonnades'. 'Finlandia Forest' gave Torvinen an opportunity to test a number of theoretical ideas at the same time.

During design development, Torvinen was supported in his endeavours by three of his student colleagues, namely Havu Järvelä, Elli Wendelin and Stine Skott-Pedersen. In addition, they

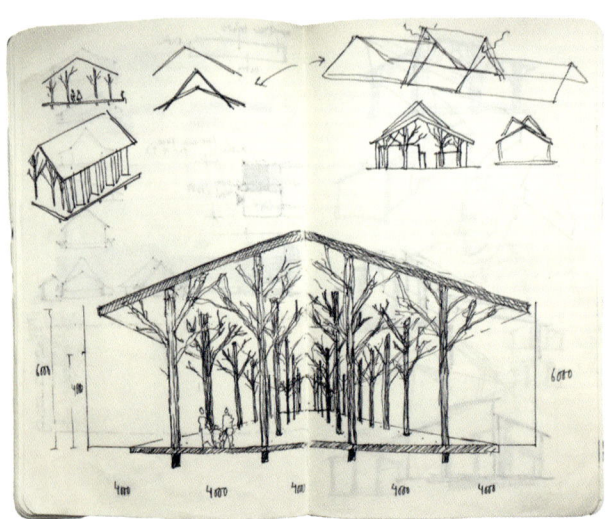

Figure 2.279
A concept sketch for the Pikku-Finlandia temporary event building.

Figure 2.280
An early 3D view.

PIKKU-FINLANDIA
DESIGN FOR A TRANSPORTABLE WOODEN BUILDING

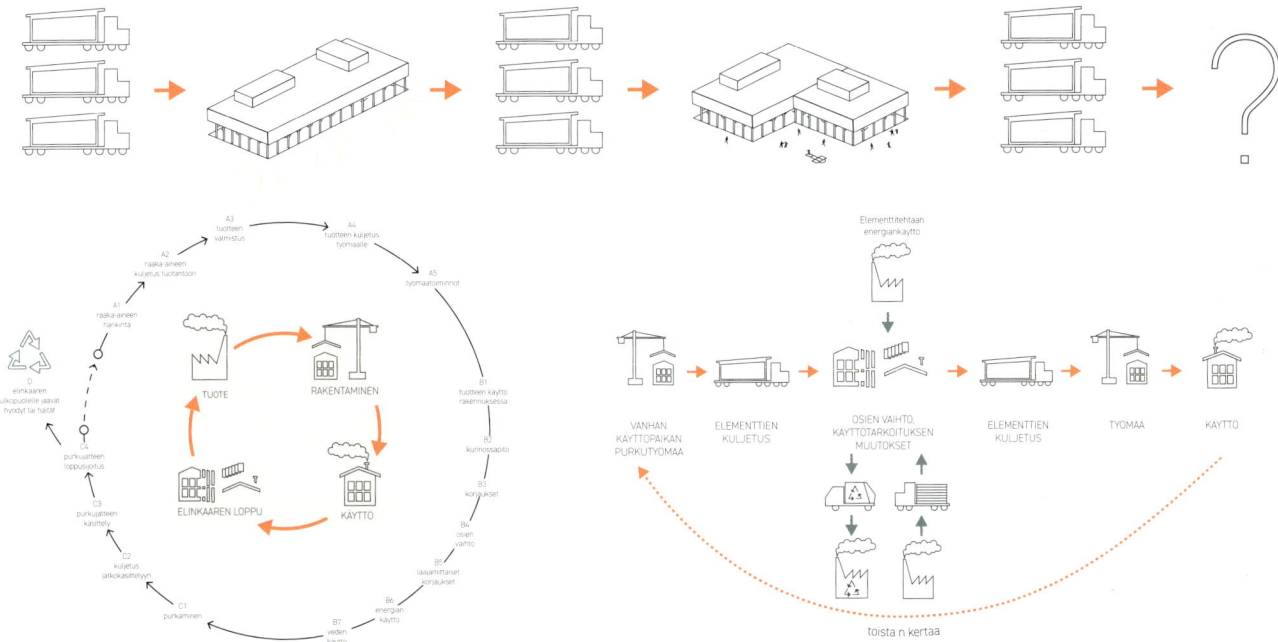

Clockwise from top:

Figure 2.281
Design for Pikku-Finlandia, a deconstructable timber building.

Figure 2.282
Assembling the roof structure on site.

Figure 2.283
Choosing the trees.

Figure 2.284
An aerial view of the completed Pikku-Finlandia.

Figure 2.285
Pressure washing the bark off the trees.

From top:

Figure 2.286
The external terrace.

Figure 2.287
The external terrace, overlooking the lake.

Figure 2.288
The new building, adjacent to existing trees.

were assisted by Prof Pekka Heikkinen with Architects NR and structural engineer Asko Keronen. This newly assembled design team (plus students from the Wood Programme) initially went to work on a mini pavilion prototype they called the Katve Pavilion, which was constructed using just two pine tree columns.

Torvinen and Wendelin then collaborated on a written dissertation that further investigated principles informing Reversable Building Design (RBD). Potential for disassembly was analysed this way, with 'dismountability' challenges identified in advance of detail design. Interestingly, these ideas were explored through a series of axonometric disassembly drawings. Because of this rigorous research, Torvinen came up with three design principles: visible solutions, separate systems and 'dismountability'. Applying these to the project results in what Torvinen calls 'Rewindable Building Design'.

With the testing completed, the team set about selecting 95 Scots pine 'top logs' from forests in southern Finland. Top logs are usually processed into paper pulp or burnt for energy. Wading through waste-high snow, the architects set out to find the perfect trees they needed. Pines were felled without damaging branches. Felled trees were then stripped of their bark by washing them with a powerful jet wash to leave the tough timber surface revealed. This process was inspired by a conversation Torvinen had with a master carpenter who was an expert in traditional Japanese timber construction.

Not surprisingly, the main contractor for the build, FM-Haus Oy, is a construction company specialising in manufacturing off-site prefabricated timber construction systems. In addition to virtually unprocessed load-bearing timber columns, Torvinen and his team designed prefabricated timber CLT panels for the walls, together with LVL hollow-core roof components and glulam beams – all bolted together. The new multipurpose building currently provides 2,700m^2 of event space plus ancillary accommodation (café, four halls and meeting rooms) for up to 1,000 people visiting the gorgeous Töölönlahti Bay.

Figure 2.289
Pikku-Finlandia in the snow.

Figure 2.290
The sheltered terrace at dusk.

OPINION

This project presents us with a truly exemplar case study demonstrating that, if enough parties collaborate, academic theoretical investigation can produce beautiful, constructed architecture asking testing questions of our industry. Jaakko Torvinen, his tutors and student colleagues had to work very hard to turn a master's dissertation into a real building, satisfying a real brief, while pushing the ideas around closed-loop systems, sustainable and regenerative design and the circular economy. In addition, unnamed people from the main contractors FM-Haus Oy, the City of Helsinki and Finlandia Hall, together with the structural engineers and the rest of the team, must all be applauded for enabling this most brilliant of 'live research projects'.

It should be noted that Torvinen now spends 50% of his time teaching on the Wood Programme at the Aalto University. He is also embarking on his PhD, researching whole wood technology, especially looking at ways to utilise more of the timber felled annually from Finnish forests. The Pikku-Finlandia team has already developed plans for deconstructing and rebuilding Pikku-Finlandia in a different location, but this time as a kindergarten. Torvinen also has plans to enter more architectural competitions in the future. Good luck to him.

CASE STUDY No.12

The Modular Campus at Canada Water by Hawkins\Brown Architects

THE STORY

Many of the case studies discussed in this book have come about because of the vision, ambition and sheer drive of one or two people from either the client group or design team. This case study is no exception. When I interviewed Andrew Tindale of Hawkins\Brown he told me that he had 'always been interested in MMC'. MMC, or more precisely, Modern Methods of Construction, is a term that was first used after World War II, when there was a huge need to build lots of new homes very quickly. MMC focuses on off-site construction techniques, normally involving prefabrication. Such processes can dramatically reduce waste generated on site, as well as during the manufacture process of the modular systems, which are also quick to assemble on site. For 20 years or so, MMC has been reappraised as it offers the potential for delivering on several low-carbon challenges for the industry: not least those presented by the circular economy.

Tindale helped set up strategies and systems for using MMC on forthcoming newbuild housing projects at the housing association L&Q. At the same time, he was working on a large retrofit project with British Land called The Printworks, which had formerly been home to the printing presses of newspapers including the *Daily Mail* and *Evening Standard*, until closing down in 2012. The Printworks was initially utilised by British Land for several meanwhile uses, which included TEDI-London occupying the former canteen on a temporary basis. TEDI-London approached British Land with the idea of establishing its academic campus as part of British Land's Canada Water Masterplan. The initial priority for TEDI-London was to get it established on site as soon as possible, while continuing to work with British Land looking for a more permanent site. However, this was proving hard for a brand-new university without the buying power of a more established academic institution. The good news was that British Land had a vacant site in Canada Water, London, and Tindale had lots of experience designing buildings made of prefabricated modular systems, buildings that were quick to assemble and, crucially, easy to adapt: to expand as necessary, as well as being quick to disassemble.

And so, the idea for a temporary, cost-effective Modular Campus was proposed, with TEDI-London forming the first phase. The chosen site had previously been a car park, which was perfect as it meant that temporary buildings could sit directly on the existing hard standing without the need for deep foundations – although trenches were dug for drainage and incoming services. The site is also about 500mm lower than its surroundings, which was also convenient as the prefabricated modules, supplied by Premier Modular, required about 300mm of space below them. This allowed the ground-floor level of the TEDI-London buildings to be well connected to surrounding sites.

I'll declare my position on TEDI-London – it's a good-looking academic building. However, it is one that comprises just 41 prefabricated, lightweight, steel-framed modules, although they are clad with beautiful larch timber that is meticulously fixed to each of the shelf modules. As Tindale said when I interviewed him, 'It's actually a very modest building made from everyday off-the-shelf components, normally used as site accommodation.' However, with this ingenious design solution, 'the ordinary' has created something quite beautiful, and as Tindale states, 'We've managed to squeeze a lot of quality out of an ordinary thing.' This included double-height spaces and beautiful external courtyards. Tindale's colleague at Hawkins\Brown, Louisa Bowles, suggests that this project presents, 'the nub of the circular economy, which is often thought of as "other" or "different" or "hard" – and it can be all of these things, but TEDI-London demonstrates that it can be possible'.

TEDI-London was handed over to its users only nine months after the lease was signed on the land – which is incredibly quick for a 1,400m^2 academic building. It opened to students in September 2021. It has planning approval for 10 years, with options at the end of its first life to be

Clockwise from top:

Figure 2.291
An aerial view of the Modular Campus.

Figure 2.292
Assembling the preloved modular units on site.

Figure 2.293
The modular units assembled.

Figure 2.294
An external view of the completed TEDI-London.

Figure 2.295
Detail of the timber cladding.

dismantled and returned to Premier Modular, who now have a platform selling 'preloved' versions of their modular systems and components, which include the structural modules (including floors), windows and doors, internal fixtures and fittings and all interior ceilings windows, doors and even the MEP systems.

Tindale points out that he has proved the concept of reuse of these modular systems on another project that Hawkins\Brown inherited: the relocation of the Southwark Construction Skills Centre from Elephant Park to an adjacent site in Canada Water in 2022. This was a completed modular building that needed deconstructing as it had come to the end of its first life. Originally designed by other architects, Hawkins\Brown were asked to creatively rearrange the building to fit on a new site. Planning approval was attained for 'lifting and shifting' the modules from one site to another. Some of the modules were 'specials' (classroom modules that are two standard modules bolted together, losing the central wall panels). This project proved that these 'special' modules can be unbolted and reused. Tindale notes that although the building was rebuilt with the same plan as before, they were able to improve the external central courtyard, which improved the building environment for the 'new' skills centre.

As I write, the second phase of the Modular Campus is on site. It is a lot larger than TEDI-London, and this time Hawkins\Brown have prioritised the use of 'preloved' modular products that include floor and ceiling panels, the four corner posts and wall panels, as well as the modular steel frame. It is envisaged that 96% of Phase Two, which numbers 104 modules, will be 'preloved'. In addition, Tindale reworked the original scheme as designed to incorporate Premier Modular's standard details, including standard window openings, to increase the likelihood of finding second-hand components. Because of this commitment to reuse, the buildings at TEDI are consuming a lot less new material than normal; as Tindale suggests, these constraints have allowed architects to 'step outside these tight boundaries and sprinkle a bit of delight over the design'.

OPINION

The idea for a temporary Modular Campus is not revolutionary as such. There have been many temporary schools and university buildings established while the permanent accommodation is being constructed elsewhere. However, there are several exciting details about this development that make it worthy of being a case study. The fact that the modular buildings will be occupied for a least 10 years is impressive and, better still, that the suppliers will accept 'preloved' returns, and that the current phase of the Modular Campus is being developed using said 'preloved' modules, is a great example of a company establishing an authentic closed-loop circular system for us all to take advantage of. In addition, an architect with a passion and knowledge of MMC has been able to apply a rigorous approach to these projects to ensure that successive projects learn from the previous one. And finally, the design team has delivered on the most important of ambitions, that of creating a delightful low-carbon built environment in a cost-effective manner; one that will provide future buildings with some or all of the material they need when TEDI-London (and other occupiers) decide to move on.

CASE STUDY No.13

Triodos Bank Building by Thomas Rau and Sabine Oberhuber

THE STORY

When Thomas Rau was only 10 years old, he was severely burned from the waist down after an accident during a family barbecue. Rau spent a year receiving treatment in hospital, but from this early age he realised that 'we are temporary guests on Planet Earth'.

Initially, Rau studied architecture at the Technical University of Aachen in Germany. However, this only lasted a couple of years because of the focus on the technical understanding of architecture, rather than what Rau describes as 'architecture as a service to humanity'. He explains, 'We didn't learn anything about the brand human.' Rau then went to the University of Bonn School of Art Design and Architecture, where he had the opportunity to learn about dance, sculpture, painting and theatre, as well as architecture.

Rau set up practice in 1992 in Amsterdam. His childhood experiences still informed his philosophical position, which in early 1990s terminology would be described as 'sustainability'. On setting up his practice, Rau announced to his colleagues, 'I have a big problem guys – I only want to design in a sustainable way.' And so, over the next 20 years or so, Rau worked intensively on pilot projects demonstrating different ways to meet various sustainable goals and creating an international reputation at the same time.

A brush with scarlet fever at the age of 50 induced what Rau calls 'an immediate reset'. He agreed with his wife, Sabine Oberhuber, to set up a new studio in parallel to Rau's architecture studio. The new studio, Turntoo (see the RAU Architects and Turntoo case study earlier in this chapter), gave the couple an opportunity to focus on whole system change, because, as Rau said when we met, 'If we don't change the architecture of the system, then nothing will change.' This new approach quickly led to working with the Ellen MacArthur Foundation, where Rau's ground-breaking ideas, such as 'leasing lux' with Philips – see p 144, would be presented to the world.

Since Rau launched Turntoo in the 2010s, he has also focused on presenting lectures promoting principles of the circular economy. These issues were not taken seriously initially, a talk at the World Economic Forum at Davos being a case in point. However, Rau did get the opportunity to present to the Pope in the Vatican, which raised his profile and his credibility.
Today, Rau has no problem being heard, being invited across Europe to present between 50 and 60 lectures a year. Rau also helped to form the Madaster Foundation, which has helped create a database of thousands of products and materials.

Figure 2.296
A CLT panel arriving at the Triodos Bank Building site.

Figure 2.297
Installing CLT panels.

Clockwise from top:

Figure 2.298
CLT floor deck and structure.

Figure 2.299
Unprocessed timber log column.

Figure 2.300
Aerial view of the CLT structure, installed.

Figure 2.301
External view of the completed building.

Figure 2.302
Aerial view of the green roof.

Figure 2.303
Night-time view of the completed building.

Clockwise from top left:

Figure 2.304
Interior view of the glulam structure.

Figure 2.305
Interior view of the unprocessed tree trunk column.

Figure 2.306
The spiral staircase.

In 2021, Rau completed a new 12,500m² office building for the Triodos Bank. Situated in a beautiful site surrounded by trees in Landgoed De Reehorst, Driebergen-Rijsenburg, in the Netherlands, this is Rau's latest attempt to instil circular principles into what is for many the rather ruthless old-school, single-bottom-line world of commercial office space. Not so here, where Rau presents us with a building testing the notion that 'standardisation results in free form', a point exemplified in the free-flowing amoeba-like plan and the ambition to construct the building out of five standard elements, namely the timber lift core, the glue-laminated timber beams, CLT floorplates, the window and door sections, and the bio-composite buoy boards.

The building is certainly an essay in the potential of simple, yet beautiful load-bearing mass CLT timber elements repeated many times to form beautiful working environments. Rau has designed this building to be 'fully reconstructable' (a material bank for the future) and so it is fixed together with 165,312 screws. Visible materials are new and mainly CLT, with the external envelope comprising floor-to-ceiling glazing on all sides, sheltered by the existing woodland, topped off with a growing roof and a photovoltaic array. Impressively, Rau states that 'mostly non-visible materials are second-hand'. These included the 'drywall' system, which was reused from local office buildings, together with miscellaneous elements such as second-hand timber beams and floors for the restaurant. In addition, timber from local woodlands is used for some of the flooring and furniture. Rau has also ensured that all materials and components are closely monitored by the Madaster platform, the materials passport online repository. This will allow not only for the building's owners to understand exactly what they have as a material bank, but also for an understanding of its value should they wish to sell it, whole or in part.

OPINION

There is no doubt that in Thomas Rau and Sabine Oberhuber we have the definitive circular-economy power couple setting the academic agenda and testing it with real architecture projects and system-changing concepts, such as 'leasing lux' and material passports. It's inspiring to me that Rau has stuck with the construction sector, and in particular the practice of architecture, to test their theories, and, crucially, to be honest about the failures and well as the successes. In short, as Rau said when I interviewed him, 'Humans need to learn to think in a different way.' We have to constantly share knowledge and ideas; to help each other to implement the complete change in 'the architecture of the system' that Rau and Oberhuber's closed-loop practice demands.

CASE STUDY No.14

CIRCL Pavilion by Hans Hammink

THE STORY

Success came to Hans Hammink at a relatively young age when he was one of 20 student winners of a design competition to be given an opportunity to build their temporary home designs. Hammink had a site, but little or no budget. However, he got the 3 x 8m 'weekend house' built on its 20 x 20m plot of land with the help of other students, as well as by sourcing second-hand and surplus material nobody else wanted. In addition, he was able to install lots more insulation than was the norm back then (this was 1987!) and he used organic (nontoxic) linseed-oil-based paint to the interior and external timber boards. In addition, Hammink believes that the timber-framed house would be quite straightforward to disassemble. So, circular principles were always informing Hammink's work, and it is testament to the quality of the original build quality that when I interviewed him for this book some 36-plus years later, he was sitting in the very same weekend house.

After a brief spell in London, Hammink spent the next 25 years or so working with his own small practice. However, he got increasingly frustrated at the lack of opportunity to develop more sustainable and ultimately more impactful architecture, and so about 10 years ago Hammink made the decision to leave his practice to work for one of the Netherlands' largest and most commercial practices, namely de Architekten Cie (see also Cycle Station case study in Step 2). Hammink's rationale was straightforward – a large practice with many different clients and projects should have many more opportunities to introduce innovation, one small step at a time.

One of the clients Hammink got to work with over a number of years at de Architekten Cie was the ABN AMRO Bank, which had a small plot of vacant land next to its headquarters in Amsterdam. There had been several unrealised projects for pavilion buildings on this site, but nothing serious had been developed until ABN AMRO urgently needed some additional

Figure 2.307
The CIRCL Pavilion, completed in 2017.

From top:

Figure 2.308
External view at dusk.

Figure 2.309
Detail of the external green wall.

Figure 2.310
Restaurant interior, with second-hand timber.

Figure 2.311
Steps up to the roof garden.

meeting space. Hammink designed a pavilion, and it was only at the point when the basement was already formed, the piles already sunk, that the clients approached him with a radical change of brief: they wanted the pavilion to be an exemplar of sustainable design, an issue the bank was now taking a lot more seriously. BAM, the contractors delivering the project, were also building an underground bicycle store next door, so they were able to pause works on site while Hammink worked up a more sustainable scheme, which initially meant triple glazing instead of double glazing, plus some additional solar panels. The client wanted more radical ideas, such as wall panels filled with energy-creating green algae. Hammink and his team were concerned that they could not integrate these last-minute design changes into the project. However, the client persisted. And so, Hammink stopped the project.

This project is interesting for several reasons, but I don't think I've come across another instance where the client has been so insistent that the team raise their game from a sustainability point of view. Hammink had to stop the design process as his team weren't hitting the mark. When I asked him about the motives of the client, he suggests that it was a case of needing to reinvent the company brand: ABN AMRO had only recently been released from central government dependency after the government rescued the bank when it almost went bankrupt.

During this period of uncertainty, Hammink and his colleagues at de Architekten Cie decided to pursue a new design for the pavilion, one that responded to their client's higher green aspirations, and one that, in Hammink's words, 'was as sustainable as possible'. At the same time, he had just been made aware by a new employee of the ideas behind the circular economy, and so he decided to employ this new concept in the new design of what was to become the CIRCL Pavilion.

Hammink and his team then reported back to their client that they had ideas for the pavilion to demonstrate circular principles. The client instructed Hammink to develop a new design along these innovative and almost entirely untested

Figure 2.312
The roof garden.

OPINION

With hindsight, Hans Hammink can reflect on how unusual this project was in its development. It started out as a straightforward pavilion sited next to the corporate HQ of the ABN AMRO Bank, but a radical change in brief while the project was already on site led to it becoming the first building in a European financial district to so evidently demonstrate sustainability, and in particular circularity and closed-loop systems. ABN AMRO Bank needed to project a new positive and forward-thinking image, and it very quickly realised that the circular economy could be just the image it needed. In addition to underwriting the costs of the CIRCL Pavilion, ABN AMRO became committed to circular economy principles, to such an extent that it now offers circular economy consultancy to clients. Petran van Heel, the client representative for the project and a corporate banker himself, explained to my students and I when we visited the CIRCL Pavilion, 'ABN AMRO has a portfolio of property investments of over €600 billion. We are a financial bank, but now we are a "materials bank" as well.' Normal business models in relation to the built environment assume that the building will be a financial deficit at the end of its life. By applying circular principles to this model, the building remains a financial asset at the end of its 'first' life, with the materials and components assembled in such a manner as to be easily disassembled.

One last thought. If you ever get to visit the CIRCL Pavilion, I believe you will be impressed with how much Hans Hammink and his team learned about circular economy principles during the protracted construction process and then applied them very visibly to the project. However, look more closely and you will notice that this building has a split personality. The first phase of works (the basement) is cast in steel-reinforced concrete piles and retaining walls, none of which exemplify anything near to the circular principles shown off above. This point was not missed by my students when they visited. On the positive side, this duality forces a discussion, and in this case perhaps I could argue that the story behind this building marks the point at which corporate banking went from thinking linear to thinking circular.

At the point of writing, there were embryonic plans for the CIRCL Pavilion to be deconstructed and reassembled on a new site, as yet not selected.

principles. As Hammink says, it was 'incredibly brave for a client'. Hammink also adds, and I feel this is crucial, 'We had been working for them for many years, so I think it helped them to trust us.' And so, the design for what has become known as the CIRCL Pavilion was developed and ultimately realised in October 2017. Hammink got up to speed with circular principles, declaring at the time, 'Our design strategy has been to avoid waste wherever possible. Our first consideration was to use materials that have already had a previous life. During the construction phase, we aimed to make as many elements as possible reusable should they ever need to be removed or replaced. Several parts, like elevators and light fixtures, have been acquired via a leased construction agreement and remain the property of the suppliers.' In addition, old jeans were collected from bank employees and recycled into acoustic insulation panels. Floors are made from second-hand timber, with internal partitions made from old window frames. The beautiful timber structure is detailed in such a way as to limit the number of holes made for securing it together with bolts. This ensures that the timber will be easier to reuse one day.

Circular economy principles inspire the in-house café, which serves locally grown food from, among others, the De Ceuvel site also featured in this book (see Step 3). It should be noted that this elegant and, in the best sense of the word, 'corporate' attempt at circularity quite clearly takes its inspiration from De Ceuvel, its less formal cousin across the water in the Amsterdam Noord.

PART 3

The Ongoing Waste House Story

(A STEP 2 PROJECT)

In June 2014, a design team, of which I was coordinator, completed the construction of the Brighton Waste House, Europe's first permanent building made of approximately 90% materials that others had discarded. It is also a low-energy building with an EPC (Energy Performance Certificate) rating of A, as well as being classified as a 'carbon negative' building, because it creates 25% more energy than it consumes. It was originally commissioned by the University of Brighton as a vehicle to test the idea that collaborative 'live' construction projects were excellent pedagogic tools for young designers and makers (and older ones) to learn about the challenges of delivering on the ideals of sustainable design. The Waste House also aimed to prove that undervalued so-called waste material has potential to become a valuable resource and therefore prove 'that there is no such thing as waste, just stuff in the wrong place'. It also aimed to prove that a contemporary, innovative, low-energy building could be constructed almost entirely by young people studying construction trades, architecture and design. To this end, more than 360 students from the University of Brighton and City College, supported by apprentices and an experienced site agent from The Mears Group, worked together on the project, which was initially fabricated in the workshops of City College, and then assembled and completed on site by students and apprentices.

More of a provocation than a future way to construct buildings, the Waste House is a 'live' research project that provokes enquiry and gets people thinking about where materials come from and where they end up.

Materials that have gone into the house include old vinyl banners that you might see tied to streetlamps during festivals, which tend to be date sensitive and are therefore used only once. These are used as internal vapour control layers. Construction waste such as bricks, ply sheets, timber offcuts and plasterboard are supplemented with everyday domestic 'rubbish', including 19,800 toothbrushes, 2 tonnes of denim, 4,000 DVDs and 4,000 video cassettes, which were slotted into wall cavities, creating low-grade insulation for the house. These unusual walls are currently being monitored by a PhD student from the Faculty of Science and Engineering, to see how efficient their insulation qualities are. Old floppy discs are also used in the wall cavities, and 10 tonnes of chalk, destined for landfill, creates a rammed chalk wall, with help from a compressor and pneumatic rammer. Heavy material such as rammed earth can contribute to the overall energy efficiency of buildings by literally storing heat until it is needed.

The Brighton Waste House was initially going to be a completely different project. It was originally conceived as the rebuild of 'The House that Kevin Built' (THTKB)[1] from 2008 (see Part 1, Chapter 1).

Frustrated with the lack of knowledge, and indeed interest, around issues of sustainable design within the UK construction industry, I was keen to create a 'live' teaching project that included young learners, practitioners, educators, contractors and suppliers in the process of design and construction. The premise was that if the challenge was to deliver a truly innovative building and address some of the many issues under the umbrella title of 'Sustainable Design', then a greater understanding of said issues across practices within the design and construction industry would hopefully be attained.

Themes influencing the research

1 The UK generated 200 million tonnes of waste in 2021; over 62% of this was generated by construction. Commercial and industrial activities generated 19%, with households responsible for a further 12%.[2]

2 Approximately 15–20% of all material arriving on building sites ends up incinerated or going to landfill: 30% of this is new material never used. Finding ways to reduce or eliminate waste from the construction process could help reduce environmental destruction from mining etc., as well as add value to material resources currently defined as waste.[3]

3   Many large corporations, such as Apple, Caterpillar Inc., Kingfisher plc and others, are very concerned about resource security and high levels of taxation associated with corporate responsibility (including dealing with waste/end-of-life products). They are taking issues of reuse and, by association, principles laid out in Cradle to Cradle[4] very seriously. The circular economy has the potential to galvanise industries that are looking to make money providing services and goods while working in harmony with the planet.

4   Proving that material currently discarded as waste can make a contemporary public building that performs to very high standards will draw attention to its potential as a valuable resource. This could reduce the amount of waste created in the future and encourage a change in construction techniques to promote low-waste alternatives, such as off-site fabrication and designing for demolition/remanufacture, while creating new jobs within this sector.

5   Learning about designing and constructing buildings is often undertaken in academic and vocational 'silos'. The need to share research data, whether academic or 'at the coalface' from a 'live' construction site, is particularly important in the UK as many so-called 'low-energy' projects do not perform as well as expected when occupied. It is currently very difficult to understand and then to meet the challenges of designing and constructing in a 'circular' or sustainable manner. Getting the whole design team (designers, makers, suppliers and constructors) to work together in a completely inclusive manner in order that they might learn together and from each other, and to document the outcomes, is perhaps the main objective of this ongoing project.

Methodology

Developing the design thesis and design team

The UK construction industry is very wasteful. In the spring of 2012, I became convinced that we could create a new construction project tackling broader issues than those embraced by THTKB, a project that would eventually deliver the UK's first permanent building made from material discarded by the construction industry.

To prove it was possible to construct a building using waste material, it was crucial that this project would not be another temporary shed or bus shelter. We had to create a permanent building, with very high levels of energy efficiency that attained full planning and contemporary building regulations approval. This ambition would ensure that all students and other partners involved would learn how to construct a genuinely low-energy building, something myself and others were convinced was lacking within the design and construction industry, and that this process would be properly recorded for others to learn from.

In August 2012, I called a mini 'waste summit', where I met Cat Fletcher (see Part 1, Chapter 2), who helped form Freegle UK – an exchange for unwanted stuff – with more than 2.2 million subscribers. Together, we met with Dr Ryan Woodard, a Research Fellow at the University of Brighton who has been working in waste-management research for over 15 years, together with product designer and academic Nick Gant and Diana Lock, from Re-Made Southeast. The team contrived a plan for redesigning the build so that it was constructed of waste and surplus material from the construction industry. Following Cat's suggestion, we also considered collecting items of waste material currently flooding domestic waste sites – material such as VHS videotapes and CDs. The idea developed from focusing only on waste from the construction industry to a project that would raise awareness of how wasteful we all are going about our everyday domestic lives. This would open up the project to a bigger audience, as well as change it from an exemplar construction project that could directly inform the construction of many other buildings, to a project more akin to a polemic, a thought provoker. As the judges for the RIBA's Stephen Lawrence Prize noted when the Brighton Waste House was shortlisted in 2015:

> The Brighton Waste House has sufficient scientific integrity to be taken seriously by the construction industry and just enough political clout to influence recycling policy. It is clear this interesting project will continue to question important issues of recycling that affect everyone.[5]

The design team comprised architects (BBM Sustainable Design), Structural Engineers (BBP Consulting Engineers) and Environmental Engineers (Robinson Associates). My role was brief definer, coordinator and academic.

Developing the detail design

It was agreed that the building should be designed to be as energy efficient as possible. Due to the unusual constraint of being built with waste, the design team didn't try to deliver a project that met Code for Sustainable Homes or BREEAM requirements. It was decided to run an IES (Integrated Environmental Solutions) digital model to set energy-efficient benchmarks relating to the site, the programme, the form and orientation, levels of U-values required through the external fabric, as well as ideas for the cost-effective primary energy source (conventional and renewable). It was decided that the building would be electric as far as heat and power were concerned, due to services constraints on site. Also, the mechanical, electrical and plumbing (MEP) installations would be designed to be as efficient as possible: the building would not show an array of 'green technologies' as many demonstration eco-houses do, as these buildings are often overly complicated and too expensive to install. The team wanted to prove that this low-energy building made of waste would be cost effective, fuel efficient and that it could be built on time and on budget.

The first challenge was to decide on the design of the load-bearing walls or frame for the building. The team had previously been successful at sourcing second-hand timber from skips and ply sheeting from large top-tier construction contractors for temporary pavilions exhibiting student work. It was decided to take advantage of this by designing a timber and ply frame comprising 400 x 400mm section beams and 400 x 400mm section columns at approximately 2.5m centres. In between the columns, we designed 400mm-deep, 900mm-wide and 2,400mm-high ply boxes (like cupboards). We called these boxes 'cassettes', which would later prove a bit confusing. However, it was these cassettes that provided the opportunity for collecting and, in effect, storing waste material from sources other than the construction industry.

The vaulted roof structure over the top-floor studio was initially designed as a glue-laminated timber truss. Enquiries into sourcing a glue-lamination press led to one of the best partners for the project, discussed later on in this chapter.

A 4kW array of photovoltaic solar panels sits on the largest south-facing facet of the roof. It provides approximately 25% more electricity than the building requires over a year.

Current building regulations U-value levels for the roof, external walls and ground floor were achieved by applying 'returned' and/or damaged polyurethane insulation (normally used in the construction of buildings), secured to the outer face of the 400 x 400mm timber box frame and 'cassettes'. This 400mm external 'wall zone' was used for 'storing' waste material, either heavyweight material providing internal air-temperature-stabilising 'thermal mass' or lightweight material providing, to various degrees of success, additional insulation. All walls were to be monitored for condensation, temperature and off-gassing.

It was decided that external windows and doors would be supplied as new high-performance units. Second-hand units are not easy to source, and their thermal effectiveness could not be relied upon. The team felt that waiting for second-hand high-performance units would delay the project for a year or so, as the whole design revolved around the size of external openings.

The design of the foundations and over-site was agreed as low-carbon concrete – concrete with a 40% reduced cement content (replaced with pulverised fuel ash) plus aggregates from demolished concrete buildings. It was not possible on this project to avoid the specification of cement. The ground conditions were quite unstable as they were (rather ironically) made-up ground with a high degree of spoil (including composting rubbish) from a former car park.

This, and the specification of below-ground drainage and generic performance specifications for other key elements, was the extent of the design that initially went to Building Control for a conditional building regulations approval. Building Control was hugely supportive of this project, allowing us to develop the rest of the design during the construction of the building. The Building Control Officer even attended design development meetings on site.

The construction team

The Mears Group, a national contractor charged with servicing and maintaining a large percentage of the UK's social housing stock, including Brighton and Hove's, were keen to help build the project as they had a healthy apprenticeship scheme in Brighton and wanted an opportunity for their apprentices. In the spring of 2011, the Mears Team stabilised the ground on site, constructed the foundations, installed the drainage and cast the ground-floor slab for the Waste House. Mears also agreed to provide an experienced site agent to run the construction site, together with their apprentices. We planned to start the next phase of works on site in the autumn of 2012.

It was during this period that I had a fortuitous meeting with tutors delivering construction courses at City College Brighton and Hove, as they wanted to see if they could construct a glue-laminated timber beam for the roof of the building. City College couldn't make a glue-lam beam, but they did want to build the Waste House: every year they build the equivalent of a new two-storey house in their three-storey workshops. In addition to this, the team employed Cat Fletcher of Freegle UK to source waste material for the project. The team was finalised.

Results

The construction and learning process

Mears took control of the construction site and were responsible for security, coordination and all aspects of health and safety. In addition, Mears supplied up to four apprentices every day. However, they were on standby to do 'normal' Mears work on nearby housing estates, so they would often have to leave site. Mears were the main contractors. In addition to this, the project had City College student carpenters, electricians, plumbers, bricklayers, decorators and so on, supervised by qualified tutors. They were the subcontractors. City College students were on site two or three times a week; however, the site agent wouldn't know from day to day whether he had two students to work with or 30. Managing a construction site with an unknown number of relatively untrained subcontractors was one of the biggest challenges for this project. Despite this, the building frame was constructed within three months by students in City College workshops and then assembled and completed by 360 students, apprentices and volunteers on site in only 12 months. In addition, we had specialist suppliers who would often install their products or systems in partnership with our young constructors and their tutors.

During the on-site construction period, there was a Volunteer Summer School Camp in 2013. More than 50 students completed the most challenging part of the construction process during this period – the vaulted roof structure. Around 25 of the volunteers were City College students, and another 25 were architecture students, with many of these from the University of Brighton's Interior Architecture School. This was perhaps the most profitable time for skills and learning exchange among students, apprentices and the professional tradespeople we had on site. It was the one period where design students could spend three, four, maybe six weeks in a row working on site. Some of these committed design students became so adept at their new trade that they ran small teams of volunteer carpenters on site; teams that included City College carpentry students. It was during this time that Mears promoted five City College students to apprentices because of their work on our project. Several of our students received Achievement Awards from Mears.

We also worked with deaf students, as well as several students with learning and behavioural difficulties. Construction sites have always been a social and intellectual leveller, and so it proved with the Waste House. We recorded 25 short films during the construction period that included interviews with students from all institutions taking part. We also welcomed more than 750 pupils from local primary and secondary schools, as well as other technical colleges from around the Southeast. This unusual learning environment was completely facilitated by our immensely patient site agent, David Pendegrass, who had to do a Health and Safety Induction for every person who arrived on site, whether they wanted to work or simply visit; and remember, he also had to get the Waste Hose built on budget and on time. This he did.

Locating appropriate waste material

I would meet the construction team on site every week to check progress and identify materials and products that needed to be sourced. Often the conversation would involve the site agent and Cat Fletcher.

There were basically two strategies put in place to find material. The first strategy was the conventional one. Mears, BBM and City College Brighton and Hove employed their contacts and networks within the construction industry to source second-hand, surplus and waste construction material.

The second strategy was less conventional. Cat Fletcher used her Freegle UK social media networks to locate waste material. Individuals, local authorities, building contractors and suppliers, schools and businesses from all over the UK supplied the project with materials such as 25,000 toothbrushes from Gatwick Airport, 2 tonnes of waste denim, 4,000 VHS video cassettes and 4,000 DVDs.

In addition, I sourced waste material from demolition sites that BBM were working on. UK VAT rules dictate that retrofit and extension works to residential properties attract VAT at 20%, but newbuild residential projects are 'zero rated' and attract no VAT. BBM were working on a project where, to avoid VAT in excess of £360,000, the client instructed that his home be completely demolished. BBM collected timber from the demolition and reused it to form the vaulted roof structure of the Waste House. As an aside, back in 2014 I was campaigning with the Green Party to alter VAT to favour retrofit projects over newbuild projects.

Utilising waste from the Waste House

It is estimated that over 40 tonnes of waste was diverted from landfill or incineration by constructing the Waste House. However, the process of constructing the Waste House itself created waste material. Whenever possible, we set up projects using this material. Architecture students created designs and built them after locating and using waste from the Waste House. In addition, a local zero-waste restaurant called Silo constructed tables and shelving from surplus material from the Waste House. A local community group used waste material to create chairs, and an allotment shed nearby used surplus carpet tiles, vinyl banners and timber from the Waste House.

Specifying new material and products

There are several products and systems that contemporary buildings require where it is not possible to install as second-hand. Electrical circuits comprising wire stripped out of buildings will require too many joints or junction boxes to be reliable.

Second-hand above- and below-ground drainage and waste pipes are technically a health hazard and not appropriate to reinstall without a professional cleaning operation. We sourced second-hand light fittings: five of them from a scrapped 60-year-old container ship. However, light bulbs had to be new.

In short, it is difficult to reinstall what the construction industry calls 'first fix' services: piping work and wiring. However, fittings such as sinks, WC pans, IT equipment, the mechanical ventilation with heat recovery (MVHR) system, and even flat screens for presentations, were second-hand and straightforward to source.

Achieving building regulations approval

Brighton and Hove City Council Building Control were very supportive of the Waste House and were an integral part of the design team, attending design and progress meetings. Installing DVDs, videos and denim into external wall cavities does not, in fact, test building regulations as they are separated from the internal environment by the internal wall linings. The Waste House is constructed primarily of timber and ply sheets with various second-hand plastics acting to a greater or lesser extent as low-grade insulation. Most homes built in the UK in the 21st century are timber framed with plastic insulation infilling wall cavities and plastic vapour-control membranes sitting behind internal plaster or timber wall linings: pretty similar to the Waste House, in fact.

The most challenging aspects for the Building Control Officer were proving the fire and flame resistance of the 2,000 second-hand carpet tiles used for external wall cladding, and the ply wall linings used in the main first-floor studio. To satisfy these queries, we set up a test rig of 15 carpet tiles fixed on a brick wall, as they would be installed on the Waste House. In the presence of the Building Control Officer, our site agent directed a hand-held blowtorch onto the tiles for 5 seconds and then for 10 seconds. On both occasions, the tiles started to smoke quite heavily. However, as soon as the blowtorch was taken away, the tiles immediately extinguished.

The first-floor wall linings were more straightforward. They were constructed of third-hand ply sheet that had previously been used by the team to create a 9m-high Waste Totem at the EcoBuild 2013 exhibition in London. Material for the totem had to be flame-proofed before it was decorated with second-hand paint and installed in the exhibition hall. This flame retardant ensured that we could reuse this material as the internal wall finish of the first-floor studio space without any fear of Building Control not approving it fit for purpose.

The academic legacy

The Waste House is an ongoing research project, involving new generations of students being set projects that test, improve and update the Waste House, whose performance is being constantly monitored by the University of Brighton's School of Science and Engineering. The university hosts a webpage focusing on the development of the Waste House as an idea through to completion. It is regularly updated and serves as an archive and learning resource.[6]

The themes and challenges embraced by the Waste House have influenced the core curriculum of the undergraduate architecture and interior architecture courses at the university, as well as at partner institution City College Brighton and Hove. I coordinate architecture technology and practices modules at the university, which use the process of designing and then constructing the Waste House as an inspiration, awareness raiser and vehicle to deliver RIBA-approved learning outcomes.

Architecture students considered design projects that value waste as a resource, as well as broader issues relating to the circular economy. One undergraduate architecture student designed a timber construction system that inspired the 'cassettes' used in the Waste House. Construction students from City College completed learning modules of their carpentry, electrics, plumbing, bricklaying, plastering, decorating and maintenance by working initially in the workshop, but then crucially on the 'live' construction site. Cat Fletcher and I

Clockwise from top left:

Figure 3.1
Launching the construction of the Brighton Waste House on site, in August 2012.

Figure 3.2
Installing the timber frame, made from surplus ply and timber from skips.

Figure 3.3
Schoolchildren, visiting the site, drop off their old toothbrushes.

Figure 3.4
Some 2 tonnes of denim, formerly the legs of jeans cut off to make shorts, was used as insulation.

Figure 3.5
Some of the 50 summer camp volunteers who built the vaulted roof.

Figure 3.6
Some of the 4,000 VHS video cassettes used as low-grade insulation.

Figure 3.7 (left)
Street elevation of the Waste House.

Figure 3.8 (below)
Detail of the rammed-chalk wall.

delivered lectures to both City College construction students and University of Brighton architecture students as part of their core curriculum. The students gave presentations about waste and designing for a circular economy aimed at children as young as six years old. As part of the university's ongoing Widening Participation Programme, more than 750 young people were shown around the construction site during the construction period.

The Waste House has served as an inspiration for many visiting students from regional tertiary colleges, as well as for students from the University of Brighton's School of Science and Engineering. Indeed, while on site, a Jordanian PhD student approached the university asking if he could be involved in the digital monitoring of the external wall fabric. He moved to the UK to do just this. The Waste House also hosts regular school visits on Wednesdays, where open design workshops are held.

In March 2013, Nick Gant (my University of Brighton colleague) and I curated a three-day seminar entitled 'The WasteZone',[7] where 12 guest speakers discussed the idea of waste as a valuable resource from many different perspectives. The Waste

Figure 3.9 (above right)
Part of the open studio, lined with third-hand decorated ply that had previously been the 9m-high Waste Totem.

Figure 3.10 (right)
Some of the team, celebrating the opening of the Brighton Waste House in 2014.

House team also designed and erected the 9m-tall Waste Totem, drawing the attention of the 65,000 visitors towards issues of reuse. Since that event, UBM, who then owned EcoBuild, started up a new reuse-themed zone of their own called Resource, situated within the larger exhibition.

The Waste House also hosts the University of Brighton's Sustainable Design MA, with students working in the first-floor studio two days a week. Prof Jonathan Chapman and Nick Gant have their office on the ground floor. Community groups, local schools and other educational establishments, as well as local and international businesses and local authority groups, use the Waste House. The building hosts meetings, lectures and symposia with large construction contractors, as well as commercial enterprises such as The Body Shop and Marks & Spencer.

However, perhaps the biggest legacy the Waste House project leaves is that of raising awareness of the negative issues associated with society's linear, throwaway, consumer-led lifestyle. The building has many stories associated with the materials collected and residing within it. For example, an airline cabin service company at Gatwick Airport collected 25,000 plastic toothbrushes for the project in only four days. These statistics get you thinking about where 'stuff' comes from and where it currently ends up. Perhaps they will also get more people realising the potential for reuse and, more particularly, the potential for designers to play a huge part in our future circular economy, and of course, to understand 'that there is no such thing as waste, just stuff in the wrong place'.[8]

Lessons learnt

Lesson 1

Designing structural beams and columns using second-hand, waste and surplus material raises unusual challenges for a structural engineer. If you don't know where the timber materials originate from, you won't know the stress grade and therefore the actual strength of the product. Our structural engineer had to assume it was the weakest material on the market. This initially manifested itself in a draft design from the engineer that suggested larger structural beams and columns than normal and thus far more material than normal. It was only when the design was refined over a number of weeks, so that it became more specific to the actual loads on each structural member, that it became more material efficient.

During the manufacture of these elements, the structural engineer had to oversee and approve every structural element in the workshop: they were constructed by young people with as little as two months' time spent on a carpentry course.

Lesson 2

The team designed a timber-framed building assuming we could source over 400 sheets of waste ply and approximately 2km of timber studwork: we had, after all, done this before when constructing temporary graduation pavilions. However, in 2012 we were not able to do this as there was a period of particularly heavy rain. Initially we were receiving water-saturated and delaminated ply that was not appropriate to use. It took the team two months to find ply suitable to use, and this delayed the project. We learned to find material first and then think about how it might be useful or not, instead of designing while assuming materials would be available: a completely different process to normal.

Lesson 3

Materials would often be offered weeks or even months before they were needed. We learnt that it was crucial to the success of this project that we could store material, keeping it safe and dry. Brighton and Hove City Council let us borrow a building nearby to use as a temporary resource store.

Lesson 4
If properly briefed and supported, young people with limited skills and experience within the construction industry can construct a building using unusual materials that performs at very high levels of energy efficiency.

Lesson 5
A 'live' construction site can run effectively while shutting down for an hour a week to allow visiting tours from over 750 schoolchildren interested in the project.

Lesson 6
Young people from different backgrounds, and with different skill sets, can learn successfully from each other and work together to deliver a complex constructed project.

Conclusion

Reflections on the 2014 build
The Brighton Waste House started out as a design and build project, as well as an inclusive learning process to prove that construction waste and surplus material was worth salvaging and not throwing away. Via further research and a policy of inclusive design, the project evolved into more of a polemic rather than an exemplar for the UK housing industry to copy. The Waste House is a vessel containing hundreds of stories associated with the salvaged materials it contains. These stories resonate through the building and ensure that students, consultants, academics, and whoever asks questions when they use the building, will know more about where stuff comes from and where it normally ends up, and then perhaps they might ponder upon how things might be done differently: how our unintelligent linear economy that finds material, then processes it into things that we then throw away, could be changed into a circular economy where materials and goods are in a state of perpetual reuse.

The Waste House acquired more than 40 partners during its development. Many of these partners are able to use the building. Schools visit the Waste House and take part in sustainable design workshops with designers, poets, writers, artists and constructors. The University of Brighton's MA in Sustainable Design is based in the building, and many community groups use it as well.

The unusual external fabric of the building is being monitored to see how it performs compared with more straightforward materials. This information will be published in due course.

More than 450 articles have been published around the world via newspapers, web-based magazines, TV and radio. This project has got people speaking about waste as a valuable resource. To date it has won 10 awards. It appears to have struck a chord.

The ongoing research at the Waste House, 2017 onwards
Since it was completed in 2014, the Waste House has continued to provide an inspiring teaching space for the University of Brighton, as new generations are encouraged to add their design ideas to the original building. It has attracted more than 10,000 visitors from the UK and Europe, as well as further afield. However, one of the big successes has been the Waste House's ability to attract the interest of other academic institutions, companies, etc., keen to collaborate on 'live' research projects. And so it was that a couple of years after the Waste House first opened, we received an enquiry from a Paris-based consultancy called Normandeis. They had been successful in receiving support for an EU-funded Interreg (VA FCE) project that required four partner institutions (two from France, two from the UK) to consider the same research question, and to do this while partnering SMEs close to said institutions.

Our academic partners on this project were UniLaSalle in Rouen, ESITC Caen and the University of Bath. In addition to these, we were partnered with international waste management company Veolia, together with the UK's Alliance for Sustainable Building Products (ASBP), the French construction industry digital platform Construction 21 and the University of Brighton's own in-house 'community of practice', Community21. This team was charged with developing three separate prototype panels of insulation made from waste material that would be suitable for supplying the social housing sector. In other words, to turn waste into useful products. The project required each prototype's carbon footprint to be at least 25% lower than that of standard insulants on the market, such as glass wool and rock wool. The project proposed new solutions which, by exploiting waste and agricultural co-products from the area, allow both a reduction in CO_2 emissions and the preservation of natural resources.

The waste material for each of the prototype panels was sourced from waste flows located near to the pilot test sites in Rouen, the Brighton Waste House and Bath. The project was called the Interreg SB&WRC (Sustainable Bio and Waste Resources for Construction) project[9] and aimed to design and develop three prototypes of thermal insulation for buildings, made from biobased and waste-based raw materials. Two out of the three prototypes were produced from agricultural co-products: Prototype 1, developed by UniLaSalle in Rouen, utilised (or valorised, to use the technical terminology) waste rapeseed and corn stems with elements from pith. Prototype 3, developed by the University of Bath, continued the university's long-established research into the potential of wheat straw to be used as insulation. Our focus at the University of Brighton, Prototype 2, considered the idea of recycling textile waste. Our team had expected to reprocess (recycle) waste clothing into insulation batts. However, when we asked our partners at Veolia what their biggest problematic textile waste stream was, almost without hesitating, they said, 'bulky bedding'. It's a strange state of affairs, but in most parts of the UK, it is cheaper to buy a new duvet than it is to get one washed. In Brighton and Hove we have two universities and lots of hotels (it is a tourist destination), resulting in hundreds of duvets being thrown away every month. And so, with the help of Veolia, we collected 100 waste duvets in just one week. Around 75% of them were made of polyester, with 25% filled with duck, goose or chicken feathers. Significantly, by sourcing duvets we had found insulation – duvets keep us warm while we are in bed and come with a tog value which describes their ability to insulate – and so we didn't need to recycle (reprocess) our waste stream, we could simply wash it and reuse, which represented a significant saving in carbon footprint.

After sourcing the duvets, the next task was to consider what, if anything, needed to be changed to make this material suitable to install as insulation in timber-framed house construction. In 2018, and at the recommendation of my co-investigator Nick Gant, we appointed Ben Bosence of Local Works Studio (see Local Works Studio case study in Part 2, Step 1) to make the prototype insulation panels that would be sent to our partners in Rouen, Caen and Bath to be tested. In addition, we were committed to using some of the external walls of the Waste House to test all three insulation prototypes.

Partly because the University of Brighton team didn't have to reprocess waste textiles into insulation – we had found a waste material that was already insulation – Ben Bosence was able to experiment a bit more with the feather and polyester material inside the duvets, as well as consider another waste flow or two. As a result of this opportunity, Bosence had time to source another waste stream. He found a well-known restaurant only half a mile away from the Waste House. English's of Brighton is well known for its oysters, and must be doing quite well as it throws away more than 55,000 oyster shells every year. Bosence, who is an expert in traditional UK construction techniques and a big fan of lime technologies, realised that there was an opportunity to recycle some of these oyster shells into quick

Clockwise from top left:

Figure 3.11
English's restaurant in Brighton, which supplied the oyster shells that were made into tiles.

Figure 3.12
Waste oyster shells from English's restaurant.

Figure 3.13
Collecting waste duvets, to be made into insulation batts.

Figure 3.14
Material experiments with waste duvets, chalk, clay, oyster shells and masonry.

Figure 3.15
Waste duvets being monitored in the Waste House external wall.

Figure 3.16
Oyster shell tiles installed on the Waste House.

Figure 3.17
Recycled duvet insulation by Thermafleece.

Figure 3.18
Installing waste duvets into the Waste House external wall.

lime. Simply by putting them in a furnace and firing at 900°C, he and his life/business partner Loretta Bosence were able to create their own quick lime. They then added a bit of water to create a paste, and to that they added crushed oyster shells, mixing this together and then spreading it into a tile-shape silicon mould. Two weeks later, they had the most beautiful cream-white 'concrete' tile – made from 100% waste oyster shells! The process of creating this material was pretty much as the Romans would have done over 2,000 years earlier. About 20 of these tiles were made, mixing in other waste streams such as brick debris from local building sites. Once they were cured enough, after about three weeks, the tiles were used to protect the 900mm-wide x 1,800mm-high duvet insulation panel (the University of Brighton's Prototype 2) that had been inserted into the external walls of the Waste House for monitoring.

By end of the SB&WRC project in 2019, the team had installed both Prototype 2 (duvets) and Prototype 3 (wheat straw from the University of Bath) in the external walls of the Waste House, where our colleague Dr Ryan Woodard was able to monitor the performance. However, perhaps one of the most exciting aspects of this research was creating a working relationship with Ben Bosence. His deep understanding of how humans in Northern Europe were able to manufacture building materials for construction before the first Industrial Revolution enabled our project team to turn waste oyster shells into beautiful and robust external wall tiles. This work has since raised awareness of the value of traditional, or vernacular, construction techniques from a time when resources were never plentiful. As you will see from a number of case studies in this book, Bosence's passion for traditional building techniques has transferred quite easily into the contemporary construction industry.

In 2018, samples of these oyster shell 'concrete' tiles were exhibited in Adelaide, Australia, in an exhibition associated with the Unmaking Waste 2018 conference[10] organised by the University of South Australia in partnership with the China-Australia Centre for Sustainable Urban Development.

The work of our team at the University of Brighton on the duvet insulation panel inspired our SB&WRC project partners ASBP to find commercial partners to develop an insulation batt for the construction sector, and crucially to take it to market. As a consequence of this study, since November 2021, waste duvets are now being reprocessed (recycled) into SupaSoft[11] insulation batts by supplied by Thermafleece.

The Brighton Waste House, with its ability to continually test ideas and question how we behave, still has the capacity to inspire the construction industry, whether that is in the UK, Europe or as far afield as Australia.

PART 4

Looking Forward

CHAPTER 4

Product Moments, Material Eternities

Prof Jonathan Chapman, Professor of Sustainable Design and Director of Design Research at the University of Brighton

At its best, design is a powerful tool for cracking problems and leveraging opportunities for new products, services and systems that drive a more resource-efficient economy and create value for policymakers, businesses and consumers. However, despite being an incredibly dynamic and vibrant cultural phenomenon, design is an extremely wasteful and destructive one, too. This is largely due to its ephemeral nature, fuelled by the ceaseless consumer hunt for change, novelty and innovation. This chapter shows how sustainable design recalibrates the parameters of good design in an unsustainable age. It advances and broadens the agenda of the design system – with its established emphasis on economic sustainability and development, at all costs – so that it is fit for purpose in unravelling the Gordian knots of sustainability, through the design of more sustainable goods and services.

Better, not more

Simply having more stuff stopped making people in Britain, the USA and other wealthy countries happier decades ago; we need an economy of *better*, not *more*; one in which things last longer, age gracefully and can be repaired many times before being recycled. The UK government is one of several proposing an economy where resources are used sustainably through design for longer life, upgrading, reuse or repair. Product life extension strategies – like *emotionally durable* design[1] – have a vital role to play here: combatting rising levels of e-waste and obsolescence; tackling the challenge of weaning people off their desire for the new; and helping shape new sustainable business models; supporting users in keeping products, components and materials at their highest utility and value throughout their lifetime. Indeed, the success of a resource-efficient, and circular, economy depends on new business models that are able to truly capitalise on longer product life spans over time.[2] Simply put, it helps us design products that are built to last longer, and provide a longer-term experience. The term *emotionally* is used here because wasteful patterns of consumption and waste are driven, in large part, by emotional and experiential factors – we tire of things, novelty wears off all too quickly and we fall out of love with them, so to speak.

By questioning the very primacy of design production itself, of acts of *designing* in favour of acts of *use*, it is then a careful attentiveness to modes, experiences and patterns of consumption that needs to be fostered. Why are people drawn to certain objects, only to then rapidly discard them while they are still able to perform their practical tasks perfectly? Deluges of manufactured objects flow through our lives, providing mere glimpses of meaning along the way. From paperclips, cutlery and footwear, to armchairs, kettles and cars, we engage with this stuff in the hope that it will fulfil some kind of need, or lack, yet it seldom does. Sociologist Robert Bocock tells us that 'consumption is founded on a lack – a desire always for something not there. Modern/postmodern consumers, therefore, will never be satisfied. The more they consume, the more they will desire to consume.'[3] Bocock claims that consumer motivation, or the awakening of human need, is catalysed by a sense of imbalance or lack that steadily cultivates a restless state of being. Compulsory material overconsumption is therefore motivated when discrepancies are continuously experienced between *actual* and *desired* conditions.

From linear to circular

Conventionally, industrial activity involves a linear production–consumption system with inbuilt environmental destruction at either end; sustainable product design activity over the past 45 years has made these wasteful and inefficient ends of the scale marginally less wasteful and inefficient. The Earth is finite, balanced, synergistic and reactive, and yet we design the world as though it were separable, mechanical and lasting, leading to what G Bateson refers to as a fundamental epistemological error[4] that shapes practically all that we do, and one that can be found at the very root of unsustainability. Indeed, human destruction of the natural world is a crisis of behaviour, and not one simply of energy and material alone, as is often assumed in design; the decisions we make as an industry, the values we share as a society and the dreams we pursue as individuals collectively drive all that we accomplish, while shaping the ecological impact of our development as a species.

We need to move away from linearity in our design thinking, to reconnect with design on a more circular and systemic level, if we are to achieve the degree of transformation our current situation demands. These new approaches require designers and manufacturers to take greater control over material flows; closing the loop through clear and systematised processes of product design, production, delivery and takeback. A circular economy is one in which resources are kept in use for as long as possible. The maximum value is extracted from them, while materials and energy are recovered or recycled as much as possible at the end of any product's life. In the circular economy, materials and resources *flow through* products and into new ones, as opposed to being designed into products, then locked into landfill.

Global businesses, supported by governments, are also beginning to look at product life extension as a viable route to waste reduction, and value creation. Electronic waste (e-waste), in particular, is growing at three times the speed of any other form of waste in the EU. Today, practically everything is disposable – it is culturally permissible to throw away anything from a barely used smartphone, television or vacuum cleaner, to an entire three-piece suite or fitted bathroom.[5] Given the huge quantities of precious resources (including gold and other rare metals) that find their way into our gadgets, it would surely be worth us taking more care of them, repairing them when broken, and keeping them for longer.

In fact, the opposite is happening: product life spans are shortening as material culture becomes increasingly disposable.[6] Hence, we live in a world drowning in objects:[7] households with a television in each room; kitchen cupboards stuffed with waffle makers, blenders and cappuccino whisks; drawers filled to bursting with pocket-sized devices powered by batteries – batteries which themselves take a thousand times more energy to make than they will ever provide. A child's remote-control tank, for example, contains a thumbnail-sized microchip containing over 65% of the elements in the periodic table. There is more gold in a tonne of phones than in a tonne of rock from a gold mine. Yet rock-bound gold is more economically viable to extract than its phone-bound counterpart.

In the circular economy, materials flow purposefully through products, adopting diverse forms throughout their lifetime, in continuous flux. Change is part of the basic nature of some, if not all, things. Whether we are talking about major changes in state – such as the demolition of a 40-storey block (one minute it is there, the next it is not) – or something more discreet – such as the barely noticeable growth of our fingernails – change is all around us. Of course, our experience of the everyday tends to happen through a series of fleeting glimpses, which provide a fragmented, artificial portrayal of reality. These passing snapshots capture isolated moments in a far longer and more complex timeline of an object, material or building, for example. Only through sustained and attentive engagement with a given thing – be it a house, armchair, car or pen – can we begin to understand it in the lengthier context of *flow* and change over time. As if to disprove this, we fabricate the made world as though it can be fixed, set in place and frozen. Through this, we form expectations of permanence, of things that last for centuries, unchanged. This is, of course, folly.

This idea of *flow* draws from the famed Greek remark *panta rhei*, in English literally 'everything flows', originally attributed to pre-Socratic philosopher Heraclitus and later reported in the writings of Plato and Simplicius, in particular. The Heraclitean concept of *panta rhei* uses the image of the river to evoke the eternal flow of time and change – a continually moving, shifting thing in constant flux. This remark serves to remind us that, in our pursuit of permanence, we are fundamentally at odds with the most essential underlying principle of the natural world – change. Indeed, Heraclitus's river itself could be described as a different river from moment to moment, since what composes it – the water flowing – is different from moment to moment. This concept is essentially meant to stress the uniqueness of each discrete experience of the world. On an atomic level, this principle is true of all physical things, no matter how solid and stationary they may seem. For example, a child constantly changes, and we are predisposed to accept and expect this. Importantly – like the changing Heraclitean river – the child doesn't become a different child with each change. Rather, the child has changed and adapted in some way, hence becoming a slightly 'evolved' version of what he or she was before. As users, we are in a permanent state of becoming, whereas the objects we attempt to engage with have already become. In this scenario, obsolescence is a somewhat inevitable outcome – the story, effectively, has nowhere to go as it has already been fully told.

Reflecting on this unfolding process, Cameron Tonkinwise asks the compelling question of 'whether designers are capable of designing things that are not finished'.[8] Whether directly, or by proximity, a concern with the finished, complete nature of products has been a steady presence in design practice and theory, particularly post turn of the century. Several conceptualisations of this issue have attempted to grapple with its implications for both acts of designing and acts of using. 'Continuous design and redesign',[9] 'tactical formlessness',[10] 'design after design'[11] or 'metadesign'[12]: these are some of the better-known labels adopted to discuss the topic. What these perspectives seem to share is their intentions to question designers' absolute authorial claims, to instead promote user agency precisely by blurring the threshold between acts of design and acts of use. Amplifying the 'voice' and agency of users through the object's open-endedness is certainly a step in the right direction in that it widens the user's sphere of action. This holds true at least until objects will be provided with the ability to *respond* in their own terms, rather than being programmed to do so or forced to oblige in any possible way. To be clear, such brief is by no means meant to encourage a dystopian 'nightmare in which tyrannical things command our daily lives'.[13] Rather, it speaks of things emerging in their eventfulness and asserting their own voices throughout person-thing encounters. That is, it speaks of the capacity for objects to *really* have an inherent process of their own, as Tonkinwise puts it.

The imperative significance of *change* has been a central concern across a number of fields. In evolutionary biology, for instance, 'it is not the most intellectual of the species that survives; it is not the strongest that survives; but the species that survives is the one that is able to best adapt and adjust to the changing environments in which it finds itself'.[14] Similarly, in 'resilience thinking', the capacity to absorb disturbance and accept change – rather than defensively resist and block it – is considered key to success. Adaptive resilience, says M Robinson, is 'the capacity to remain productive and true to core purpose and identity whilst absorbing disturbance and adapting with integrity in response to changing circumstances'.[15]

There is a growing sense that the consumer electronics industry must transition from a linear to a circular economy; one in which resources are kept in use for as long as possible – the maximum value is extracted from them, while materials and energy are recovered or recycled as much as possible at the end of any product's life. This is a seismic shift in thinking, affecting everything from the design and delivery of short-life throwaway products, to that of longer-lasting material experiences. Of course, the notion of a 'throwaway society' is nothing new. American economist Bernard London first introduced the term 'planned obsolescence' in 1932 as a means to stimulate spending among the few consumers who had disposable income during the Great Depression. The concept was popularised by Vance Packard in his seminal book *The Waste Makers* (1964).[16] Though informed by the work of both Bernard London (1932)[17] and Earnest Elmo Calkins (1932)[18] on consumer engineering, Packard's dualistic theories of *functional obsolescence* and *psychological obsolescence* assert that the deliberate shortening of product life spans was unethical, both in its profit-focused manipulating of consumer spending, and its devastating ecological impact through the nurturing of wasteful purchasing behaviours. In fact, the concept of disposability was a necessary condition for America's cultural rejection of tradition and acceptance of change.[19]

Over the past decade, issues of sustainability have become well established within Design – strategies like design for recycling, disassembly, service and energy efficiency, for example, have become commonplace in today's process. Designing for *emotionally durable* products and user experiences helps reduce the consumption and waste of resources by building lasting relationship between users and the products they buy. A deeper understanding of acts of use can be helpful in extending both the physical and emotional durability of products, enabling designers to encourage longer-lasting interactions with products and services, consequently minimising the consumption of resources.

Can sustainable design drive change?

Promoting sustainability by production can be a response to the ecological impact of relentlessly wasteful manufacturing practices. The constant flood of products, interventions, experimental and conceptual work adopting strategies such as recycling or upcycling is clear testament to a predominant focus on production-related concerns within design discourses. It could be argued that the dominance of such methodologies that don't risk 'offending' existing commercial and capitalist conventions is, on some level, a compliant approach to sustainable transition.[20] This conservative modus operandi, as it were, then liberates consumers' consciences and, in doing so, generates even more waste. By refusing to understand and engage with the problem of sustainability at a level of foundational causality, designers thus fail again and again to grasp the deeper roots of what Tony Fry defined as 'structural unsustainability'.[21] Until these roots are firmly grasped, sustainable design will always teeter around the edges of impact, but never drive the transformational changes it so passionately advocates. In this way, a truly sustainable design discipline has to undergo a radical cultural shift that would hinge upon a concern for *immaterial* issues, prior to and as a precondition for *material* ones.

In design terms, we can support greater levels of emotional longevity when we specify materials that age gracefully, and that develop quality over time. We can design products that are easier to repair, upgrade and maintain throughout their life span. These are effective product life extension strategies, and while they can come at an increased cost at point of purchase, they generate revenue downstream, through the introduction of service and upgrade packages. Extending the life of a product has significant ecological benefits. For example, take a toaster that lasts about 12 months. Even if the toaster's life is extended to just 18 months through more durable design, the extra longevity would lead to a 50% reduction in the waste consumption associated with manufacturing and distributing it. Scale this up to a national or international population of toaster-buyers, and it's clear how significant an impact this could be. Designing products that can be kept for longer also nurtures a deeper relationship with both the product and the brand, which increases the likelihood of brand loyalty maturing. Therefore, such *emotionally durable* design doesn't just make sense from an environmental and resources perspective, but can be seen as a commercially viable business strategy in an increasingly competitive globalised world.

CHAPTER 5

The Wiki Waste Workshop

Nick Gant, Founder of Community21/Social and Sustainable Design Research Group, and Ryan Woodard, Independent Researcher and Consultant

Waste[d] opportunities

Globally, 2.1 billion tonnes of municipal solid waste[1] are generated annually, with levels projected to increase by 56% to 3.8 billion tonnes by 2050 if urgent action is not taken. Currently, 38% of this waste is managed in an uncontrolled way where no systems are in place to mitigate the impact of waste on the environment and public health, and 2.7 billion people still do not have access to waste collection.[2] It is estimated that only 19% of waste is recycled and composted globally and in the European Union alone, 60% of the total waste generated is not reused, composted or recycled.[3] The linear system dominates – there are many waste(d) opportunities. In many countries, waste is disposed of in poorer neighbourhoods, manifesting as a form of social repression. Waste is therefore a development issue as well as an environmental problem. Here, we explore how *working with waste* can empower communities and offer practical solutions to local environmental issues, while providing new social and cultural opportunities – these 'spin out' from circular design methods when *thinking in the round*. Our case study project aimed to develop a local, off-grid making resource (workshop) that uses low-cost, accessible technology and processes to manufacture products, utilising local resources as feedstock. Products are co-designed in a collaboration between the community and designers and makers in the UK, taking into account the needs and values of the community. Blueprints and material recipes are shared, adapted and reused to benefit other communities (wiki). The Wiki Waste Workshop seeks to engage with many of the UN's Sustainable Development Goals, including addressing poverty, empowering women, promoting economic development and responsible production and consumption. It takes inspiration from the work of Baillie *et al.* (2011),[4] David Hakkens[5] and organisations such as Waste Aid[6] and the Living Earth Foundation,[7] who have worked to develop products and technologies to empower communities to address waste problems and to support local economic development. In this context, the aim is to flip the waste narrative to re-forming waste as a material opportunity, using circular methods to enact change through collaboration. New cultures of practices have emerged for contemporary creative networks to openly share and distribute insights into making methods using waste in differing localities and, moreover, for these transformations to be celebrated through the material language and vernacular of objects. Technology provides context, content and catalyst and offers opportunities for makers to experiment and contribute to new models for making, some of which can be transformative socially, economically and environmentally.

The Wiki Waste Workshop (WWW) project started in 2015 and has continually sought to shift and reverse the negative environmental and social impacts of poorly managed waste, reimagining the accumulation of rejected materials as an opportunity to be exploited, not just as a problem to be solved. Methods of 'meaning making' and 'value adding' (valorisation) are co-defined between a community of makers, which form part of a sustained, collaborative and mutually beneficial process of research, development and co-learning.

Our case study community and site for the WWW project is the community of Melkhoutfontein in the Western Cape, South Africa. At the time of the project, no formal recycling system was in place, with the municipality collecting and disposing of all waste at a landfill site.

Locally, the Dreamcatcher Foundation has been working for three decades to address and remove barriers to economic and skills empowerment, with a focus on women and children. It aims to develop models for sustainable socioeconomic and environmental development. The NGO is based in Melkhoutfontein and is embedded in the community. The founder of Dreamcatcher, Anthea Rossouw, provided important information on the community, including its background, socio-demographics, cultural heritage and value chains. She facilitated communication between the UK researchers and the community throughout the project. The UK participant researchers included members of the Community21 design research group (based at the University of Brighton), with specialists in making with waste including us (Nick Gant and Ryan Woodard), Tanya Dean and Stefano Santilli. Students from the 3D Design and Craft undergraduate programme used the project as the basis for their accredited practice-based academic work, building on a long history and culture of working creatively with waste materials.

Methods and approach

A system design model was initially co-devised (Figure 4.1) that sought to form a transferable 'virtuous circular economy', which the project used as a basis for engagement, critique and co-learning. Both the community and university partners benefited from learning together about the value of working with waste in terms of material techniques but also for local social, economic and environmental improvement.

This model involved learning together and gathering local intelligence about the needs and values of the 'place', the all-important waste/resources, what products could be created to respond to the needs and values, and the processes and

Figure 4.1 (left)
Skype video Wiki Waste Workshop between the UK and South Africa, using mobile devices and television, 2016.

Figure 4.2 (above)
System design model for the initial Wiki Waste Workshop approach by Nick Gant and Ryan Woodard, 2015.

machines that would be required as part of the workshop. In the initial stages of the project, the UK researchers used digital means to interact with the community, facilitated by the NGO. Skype video calls enabled co-design workshops and creative critiques, and we created a blog and digital map page (community21.org) to support knowledge exchange regarding the different skills and materials available.

The team engaged the system model and discussions and made prototypes, which were then iteratively presented back and forth between the communities, mediated through the technology platforms. As the programme and workshop developed, members of the UK team were invited to visit Melkhoutfontein to help ensure relevant support for safe and productive working practices and to further develop working relations and knowledge transfer between participants. Throughout the process, all parties were engaged in establishing and assessing how they would elevate the status of the waste materials being used and create value for the community and how to develop new skills and augment established skills locally. Process and product 'how to' videos were created and archived for use in training.

Place

Melkhoutfontein was proclaimed a township for 'coloured and black' South Africans only in 1971, during the apartheid regime. The population has increased from 800 in 1985[8] to 4,111 in 2020;[9] however, with many residents living in informal shacks, anecdotal evidence suggests the population is far higher. The area is famous for its heritage and beautiful surroundings. Melkhoutfontein is located within the Cape Floral Kingdom, which has 4,500 botanical species, many of which are rare.

Estimated unemployment levels in Melkhoutfontein are 40%, with particularly high rates among the youth. There was a lack creative or design-and-making education provided – thus it was considered that harnessing the waste stream as an opportunity for production, while embracing the circular economy, could foster community development and job creation. Historically, waste from the surrounding area was delivered to a site in Melkhoutfontein and burnt in the open air, having detrimental health impacts on the local population. Household and business waste is now collected and disposed of at a site 45km away. At the time of the project, apart from deposits paid on glass bottles and metal taken to the local scrap dealer, no formal recycling services were offered – valuable resources were being lost. The Dreamcatcher office itself is located on the site of the former waste dump, which now hosts a botanical garden.

What was apparent to the whole team was the rich historical context of the place and how this offered opportunities for creative reference and cultural engagement.

Needs and values

The primary needs of the community ranged from improvements to their homes to practical resources to support children carrying books to school and identified opportunities to support tourism and visitors. The need for job creation and economic development was clear. Tourism is important to the area. The community is situated within a recognised area of significant flora and fauna but is blighted by the poor waste management and nonindigenous, invasive plants species (in particular Acacia cyclops). While there was no creative design skills being taught to young people, skills in sewing and needlework were sustained by some elders, and fed into the scope for products. Among the community, there was a low understanding of the rich history of the area and the important heritage of their ancestors. There was the opportunity to celebrate this, thereby increasing awareness among the community and tourists. This collaborative reflection and scoping provided a focus for collaborative design ideas. This included products made from materials sourced by the removal of invasive, nonindigenous plants and the rejuvenation of the landscape into a botanical garden. It also involved products

Figure 4.3
Reworking invasive Acacia cyclops in the new maker space.

Figure 4.4
School bag made from abundant carrier bags, fruit nets and food packaging.

for retail and tourism markets that encompassed heritage references, all derived from waste materials formerly burnt or buried in landfill.

Co-learning and developing more aspirational identities for community members featured high on the values mapped by community participants – positive environmental change and improvement to the wellbeing of the community could be provided through better management of waste and understanding of the implications of such systems. The actual physical environment could be improved from a botanical and biodiversity point of view, as well as improvements to air quality and litter – this all feeds into the design thinking and model for a holistic system and a more virtuous circular economy.

Materials

To understand the resources available, community members were supported to analyse waste, identifying high levels of organic material. This was being addressed in a parallel composting project and therefore the focus was on other dry recyclable materials, such as plastics from food packaging, which could provide opportunities for makers. The nonindigenous Acacia cyclops was identified as a potential resource – declared an invasive species, it has had a devastating impact on the biodiversity locally, in what is considered to be a naturally rich environment. It is abundant within the community, providing design opportunities to help reinstate local flora and fauna in this area of significant natural interest.

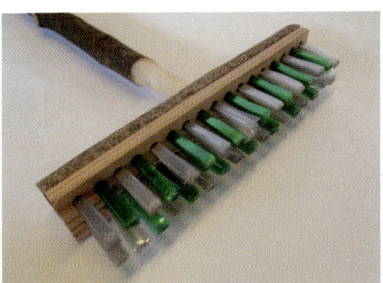

Figure 4.5
Proposed broom, made from the wood of the invasive Acacia cyclops and from drinks bottles.

Products

Several initial prototypes were formed that responded to the system design model and integrated methods that add value in different ways. Over time, the UK and South African teams shared knowledge of making methods that they each could use in the development of new opportunities. Different approaches focused on identified needs, having engaged with the values

Figure 4.6
'Cook with Kamamma' spoons,[10] made from wood from the invasive Acacia cyclops and from food packing plastics, proposed by UK student Zoe Rae.

Figure 4.7
Community member Elmordine using local natural heritage for visual references; the products are made from recycled plastic bags using a simple t-shirt heat press.

Figure 4.8
Beautiful bowls referencing local natural heritage, made by community member Elmordine.

in a variety of ways. The designs adopted visual typologies that were often defined by the function and sometimes determined by the material, while others sought to reference defining features of the landscape, nature or cultural history through more expressive, visual or material techniques. Through ongoing periodic conversations via internet platforms, the community understandings were forming as to what would work and what would not. Emerging products included tools for the botanical garden, such as trowels, self-seeding plant tags and containers. Some products met needs such as rain protection clothing, school supplies and bags, which could also double-up as souvenirs for tourists. Other products were more broadly retail items, such as furniture, cooking utensils and lighting accessories. Each proposal integrated some material strategy for adding value to what was the all-too-prevalent waste, and researchers mapped these to add to developing knowledge in the form of a Valorisation Framework.

The workshop (and processes)

As designer-makers, the consideration of product, material and process are intertwined. The UK and South African team identified machines and processes that are as accessible and as inclusive as possible to use, while maximising the opportunity to create value and support personal creative interpretation. The workshop is where open, collaborative community making takes place, but some educational and theatrical aspects of making are also facilitated, which provide interest to tourists and attract further community engagement. This supports community cohesion between different and often disconnected members of the community and between different age groups.

The machines and processes used can be transformative in terms of what they can help the community to make, but there must be a level of appropriateness. This raised interesting questions as to 'what is appropriate for the community?' Are we to aim to maximise the explicit handmade nature of a product and to develop skills of making that manifest in overtly 'crafted

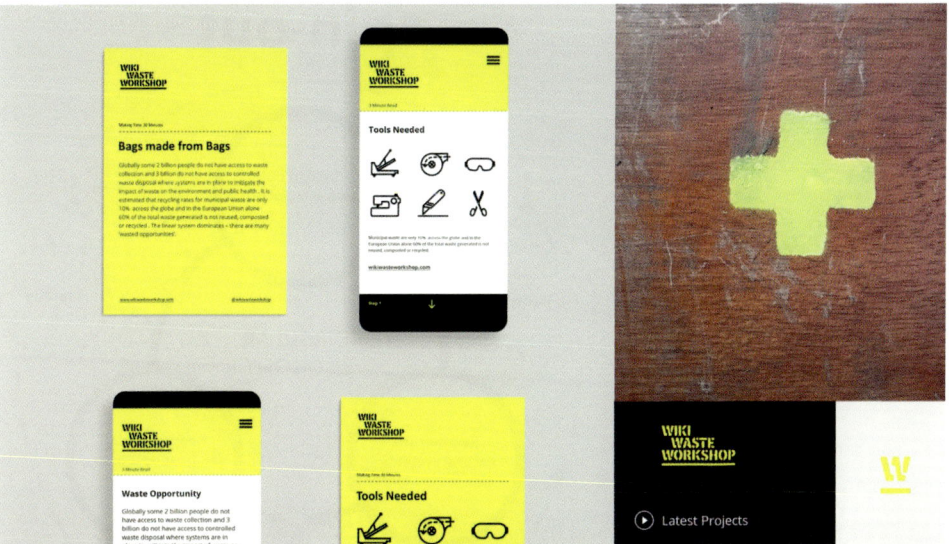

Clockwise from top:

Figure 4.9
Digital shareable resources and processes – Nick Gant and Colin Jenkinson.

Figure 4.10
Community members sharing processes and techniques using a simple t-shirt heat press.

Figure 4.11
A house number made from recycled plastic.

objects'? Or do we aim to utilise technologies that have helped revolutionise DIY, start-up and community production, such as those often specified in Fab-labs,[11] which perhaps result in more homogenised and/or consistent products? In this case, the team and community opted to consider both as potential opportunities for the workshop in this experimental stage – arguably these are contemporary concerns for many makers.

The workshop is considered an open set of methods and processes that are shared and made available online as much as in a physical space – participants were actively encouraged to build communal knowledge and opportunity throughout the project, to result in a range of resources. Ultimately, consideration of the financial cost of investment in the different machines and processes versus the various values that result from their use will require long-term study and in-depth evaluation in relation to the community's changing situation.

Reflections, frameworks and 'spin-out' benefits

Certain (waste) materials may lend themselves to being recycled (more than once) and so the workshop will consider these as part of the development of more circular economy opportunities. However, of equal consideration in this context is the social empowerment afforded through the transformation of waste as a collaborative venture.

By reflecting on the design proposals, we identify, categorise and frame the active, value-adding elements: for example, the use of plastics that contain ephemeral and/or branded graphics that can be identified within the new products that add character and local provenance or which change their meaning when recycled; or the fusing of fruit nets together with carrier bags for extra strength and durability.

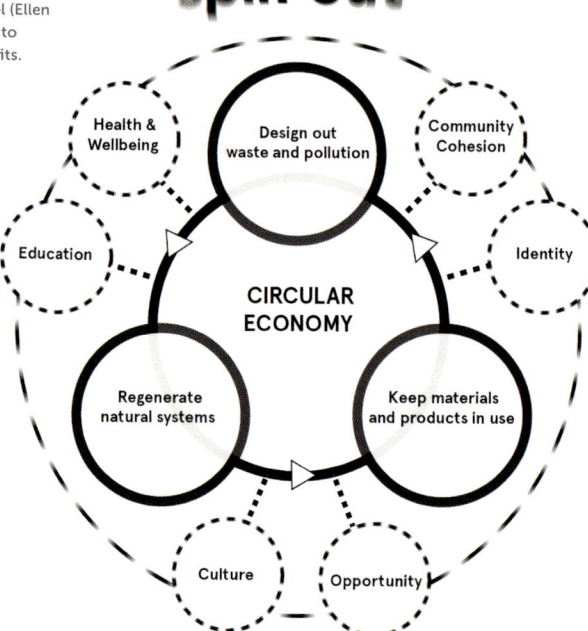

Figure 4.13
Redrawn version of the circular economy model (Ellen MacArthur Foundation) to include 'spin-out' benefits.

Through tactical making, the processes and products provide agency as tools and means of cultural communication, adding value to would-be waste but also helping to construct some local cultural identity and meaning and embodying these social and material values. The 'emerging beauty' inherent in the designed use of waste or rejected materials has a communicative power but *material literacy* often remains a tacit art that needs more explicit and definitive methods that support better knowledge exchange and prolific use. The underlying nuance of creative-work-with-waste is no longer well conveyed by limited, general terms such as *recycling*, *upcycling* and *reuse*. Moreover, there is a need for further analysis of the virtues of different creative approaches to adding value to waste within circular economies. The research imperative is to continue to develop a better, more descriptive vocabulary and understanding of how we develop value and construct meaning through our use of materials. This will help designers to learn the significance and resonance of circular design methods. We argue that a greater capacity to articulate and apply understanding of diverse and locally significant 'material values' in the context of waste evidently leads to greater awareness, promotion and adoption of more sustainable models for material use and life cycles.

We aim to add to the material vocabulary related to making with waste, developing greater material literacy. Within the culture of reuse, we hope this helps inform understanding and improves learning, while materially expressing the value of different remaking strategies.

Virtuous circular economies

This project and others like it have led to the development of new enterprises and social, cultural and environmental spaces – the workshop in Melkhoutfontein has received additional investment, allowing the creation of a totally off-grid community maker space. Post-pandemic enterprises are still collecting recycling and making products for sale, branded under 'Made in Melkhoutfontein'. In 2024, they will be moving into a new workshop integrated into the Dreamcatcher Sustainability Futures Centre. Removal of invasive species has helped grow and promote a new botanical garden and improve the space for biodiversity in the area as a tourist attraction; waste is now a properly managed commodity rather than a toxic environmental and social problem.

Figure 4.12
Community members in 're-maker' (workshop) space.

Clockwise from left:

Figure 4.14
Colourful products made from recycled plastic bags using a simple t-shirt heat press.

Figure 4.15
The 'Made in Melkhoutfontein' logo, inspired by the ochre drawings and colour palette of the Blombos Cave.

Figure 4.16
Members of the Melkhoutfontein community.

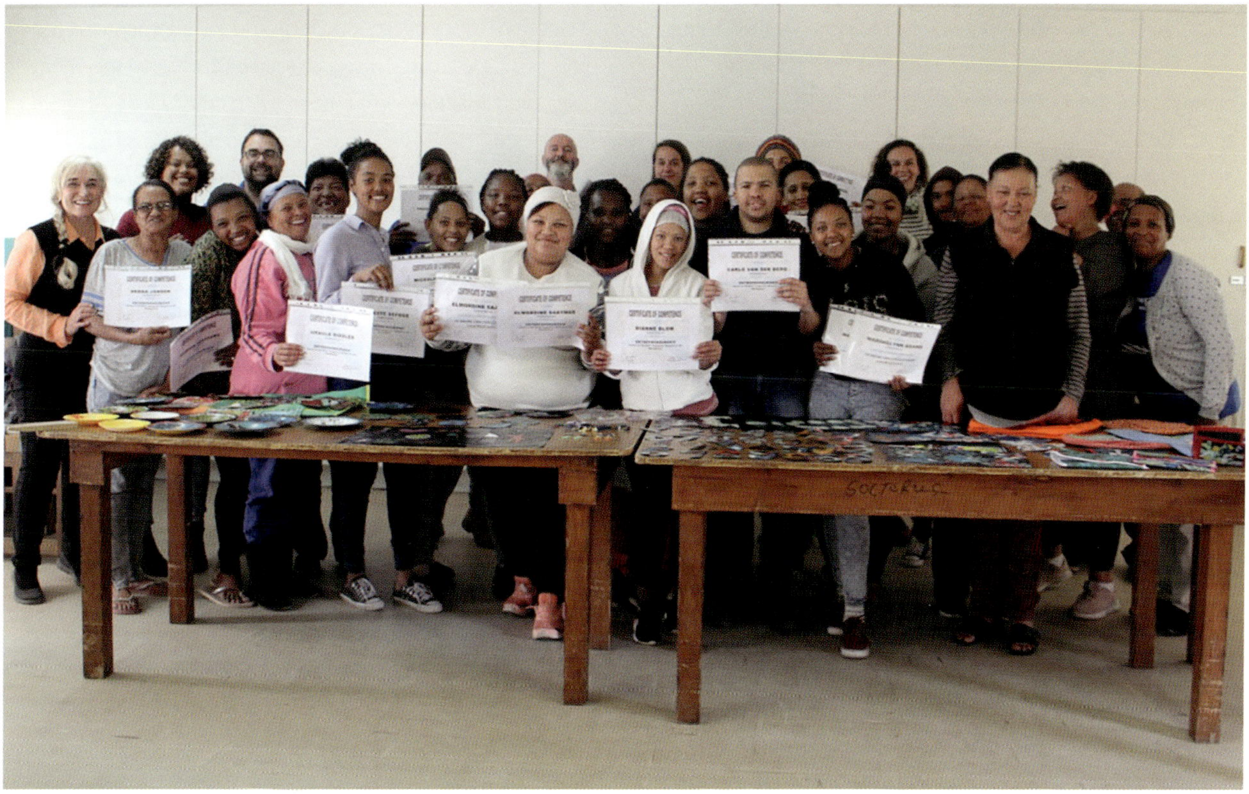

The project has helped identify the value of locally authenticated, communally derived and openly shared knowledge, enthused by a collective ambition to turn the negative impacts of waste into more *meaningful stuff*. This shift and change in perspective can be transformative in catalysing new opportunities for community education, social interaction and engagement with local natural and cultural history and identity, and can encourage healthy interpersonal exchange. These 'spin-out' benefits add further value to the function of circular thinking and action when working with waste.

Acknowledgements

The authors would like to thank Dreamcatcher South Africa, with special mention to founder Anthea Rossouw for commissioning the project, and the Utopia Foundation and Dreamcatcher Foundation Netherlands and British Council DICE fund for funding support. They would also like to thank the community of Melkhoutfontein and all University of Brighton staff and students who worked on the project, with special mention to co-contributors Tanya Dean, Stefano Santilli, Jim Wilson, Dani Lane, Matilda Grover and Colin Jenkinson.

CHAPTER 6

It's all change now ... isn't it?

Duncan Baker-Brown

December 2023 – Written just after returning from COP28 in Dubai, UAE

I wrote the first edition of this book over the spring and summer of 2016. What a lifetime ago that was. Since then, practically all of humankind has woken up to the fact that our very existence has, so far, had an utterly disastrous impact on the natural systems sustaining our host planet. Climate-change deniers can still be found; some in very powerful positions. However, whatever way they dress it up, whether it's 'unpatriotic to invest in renewables' or humans simply re-enacting the latest version of some kind of destruction-redemption myth, it seems as though most people are now experiencing the side effects or the direct impacts of severe climate change. Climate change is not a hard sell, well not as a concept, anyway. As we enter the middle part of the third decade of the 21st century, it feels like the time when big systems-change-type decisions need to be made. Things are getting a bit scary out there. At just the point when we need massive collective decisions for the good of us all, humans are doing what humans have always done – waging war to gain land, power and ever more scarce natural resources.

One thing is for sure, since the last edition of this book was published there are many more people realising that resource security is a thing of the past, and perhaps, by default, they realise that our precious planet and its valuable resources are finite. It should also be noted that we (the construction sector) appear to have got our collective heads around the concepts of 'embodied carbon' and 'whole-life carbon', with energetic discussions around the best way to calculate these important figures running as I write. Again, there was little understanding of these (beyond our colleagues at the RICS, et al.) in 2016, let alone arguments about where the best source information was to be found for embodied carbon, or whether carbon off-setting was just another way to delay authentic low-carbon commitments.

Yet it still might appear to many of you that, after much consideration (and nearly 30 COPs!), we must admit it, we would prefer to reap the benefits of burning fossil fuels now, rather than handing over a healthy planet to sustain future generations of humans. Implementing a complete system change often feels like too big a risk to take as it will upset the current status quo as far as who owns what and therefore who has the power.

Our current economic, geopolitical and environmental pressures have created resource scarcity (including the energy crisis), high inflation and a cost-of-living crisis, with ever-higher subsidies still being sent in the direction of the fossil fuel procurers. As a result, our built environment is too expensive to heat and power (let alone build or retrofit), ever more prone to being uninhabitable in the summer and winter, and, post-COVID-19, either underoccupied in the case of commercial, education, public and leisure buildings, or over-occupied in the case of our homes. In short, our built environment is not only ecologically illiterate, it is not in any way fit for purpose.

Reasons to be cheerful

Well, that was pretty bleak, but you must admit, there is no quick-fix vaccine for the climate and ecological emergency. However, I would counter this by saying that, at the same time, there are many positive things happening which I believe act as a kind of antidote to the apparent intransigence of many of our world leaders and those superrich petrol states. For example, back in 2019 the UK government paused its ongoing debate on Brexit and dedicated some time to voting through a bill declaring that there was indeed a Climate and Ecological Emergency. Since then, over 90% of UK local authorities have pledged to be net-zero carbon by 2030, and around the world, over 814,000,000 people now live in regions that have declared a Climate and Ecological Emergency.[1] The 2023 'Global Climate Litigation Report'[2] confirms that in 2022, 2,180 climate-related cases were filed in 65 jurisdictions, including regional courts, tribunals and Special Procedures at the United Nations. That's up from 1,550 cases in 2020 and 884 in 2017. The years leading up to and after the COVID-19 pandemic have seen a marked increase in impactful protests, raising awareness about the climate and ecological disaster. Good work – you know who you are.

Perhaps most incredibly, this has directly impacted our own built environment sector. We now live in a time where peaceful protestors have served prison sentences in the UK because they campaigned for improved insulation levels for our homes, and this at a time when over 40% of our households were in fuel poverty,[3] suffering from a national cost-of-living crisis! We even had the situation in November 2019 where a fully qualified architect risked being struck off the UK Architects Registration Board because he was arrested by police for obstruction at an Extinction Rebellion rally on Waterloo Bridge in London. However, out of this climate of increased civil resistance have emerged numerous climate-literate groups focused on reducing the negative environmental impact of the construction sector. One of these is UK Architects Declare which was formed in 2019. It currently has more than 7,900 signatories globally, including 43 groupings across 28 different countries. In addition, we have the fantastic Architects Climate Action Network (ACAN), also formed in 2019. Both groups host thought-provoking events and publish very helpful guides for all parts of the design and delivery team. In addition, the RIBA, IStructE, RICS, UK Green Building Council, CIBSE and others have produced many guides to low-carbon, whole-life carbon and circular design. Being a climate-literate designer/architect/engineer/activist is now an established way of being for many – and that was definitely not the case in 2016 when the first *Reuse Atlas* was written.

I find it interesting that many of the most impactful declarations and supporting guides were published during the periods of lockdown imposed by our national governments during the COVID-19 pandemic. One such guide appeared (for me) from apparently nowhere. In January 2020, LETI (Low Energy Transformation Initiative) published its *Climate Emergency Design Guide*,[4] which presented in a very clear and direct manner (in other words, brilliantly clear infographics) what appeared to be a pan-industry consensus for a whole-life carbon descent plan for the construction sector. What was equally impressive is that LETI had involved more than 1,000 people in the development of the document, and these people were drawn from all parts of the construction industry. As a result of this impressive collaboration, the document was cited via all the leading institutions and then in subsequent guides and initiatives, such as the RIBA's ambitious 2030 Climate Challenge. Those so-called impenetrable silos had been breached, and that is exactly what needs to happen if we are to implement systems change – we need to share our knowledge and help each other.

From January to May 2021, right in the middle of lockdown, ACAN hosted nine online lunchtime events focusing on the huge opportunities that a circular economy presents the construction sector. I was lucky enough to help curate these events. However, it was the ACAN team who came up with the idea of using the RIBA Plan of Work Stages as a way of breaking up the nine sessions. In other words, the first being RIBA 00 Strategic Definition, then RIBA 01 Preparation and Briefing, all the way to the last session, RIBA 08 Deconstruction, which was an ACAN invention as it currently doesn't exist in the 'real' RIBA Plan of Work. However, what we hadn't appreciated was how popular these online sessions would be. Perhaps it was because everybody was working from home due to the COIVD-19 lockdown, but the first session had more than 650 participants, with the second and third broadcasts attracting around 900 people each. They were Zoom calls like no other that I had ever attended.

If one considers where our sector is right now, as far as all things low carbon, net zero and circular, I honestly feel very positive about the near future. And please forgive me for presenting an opinion from the UK perspective, but that's where I am based. Yes, there have been many guides published over the last few years, with some of them being impactful. However, a guide is just that, and what we need in order to effect big systems change is new legislation and government subsidies to enable a reuse, retrofit and circular economy industry. So, with this in mind, I can confirm that I draw optimism from the fact that IStructE's Part Z campaign for the regulation of embodied carbon has influenced the presentation of the Carbon Emissions (Buildings) Bill to the UK Parliament on three separate occasions in the last 18 months. When adopted (I believe it will only be a matter of time), this bill will ensure that all building owners must calculate and declare their building's embodied carbon footprint, which will be benchmarked to pre-agreed low-carbon commitments. Part Z will then be adopted into the building regulations and once that happens, embodied carbon benchmarks must be adhered to in law. Because of this, the business of reuse, retrofit, deconstruction and the designing of new buildings as future materials stores will all make the best economic sense as well as being best for the natural world. In addition to this, as I write this chapter there are more than 350 very talented people working on defining the criteria and rules to enable the construction industry to work out how best to spend its rather restricted carbon budget in order to meet our 2050 net-zero targets, with those 2035 intermediary targets already not so far away. The UK Net Zero Carbon Buildings Standard, as it has been called, will be published in 2024, and it is hoped that it will be another device to help the UK government buy into whole-life carbon measurement and appropriate restrictions thereof. And it isn't just the UK getting busy. The European Union appears to be taking the circular economy seriously by publishing its new Circular Economy Action Plan (CEAP)[5] in March 2020, as one of the key building blocks of the European Green Deal. In addition, we have the imminent publication of the EU's Whole Life Carbon Roadmap for the Built Environment, which will demand large reductions in whole-life carbon to meet the demands of its own Energy Performance of Buildings Directive (EPBP).

It's clear to me our industry is well set up to embrace this low-carbon approach to construction. We know what to do. We simply must share the information we have and, crucially, we must all be prepared to learn from our peers and other colleagues. There are still many new initiatives emerging from within our sector, not least the RIBA introducing mandatory Climate Literacy tests for all its members in the near future, through to the United Nations Buildings Breakthrough initiative that hopes to get a consensus from all nations of 'what good looks like' as far as near-zero carbon construction is concerned.[6] I also note that recent Pritzker Prize winners have stated that one should 'never demolish, never replace'[7] (Lacaton & Vassal in 2021) and 'Retrofit is not only the right thing to do, it's the more interesting thing to do'[8] (David Chipperfield in 2023). Bringing our best designers to the low-carbon circular-economy table is a big deal. In addition, there appears to be no end to the numerous outraged news headlines generated whenever a property developer proposes to demolish a perfectly adaptable building. This never used to happen unless the building in question was valued for its perceived 'heritage' rather than now, where issues of embodied energy and the amount of waste generated are becoming a big deal to many people. Our students are also demanding to be taught a climate-literate curriculum, one that arms them with the skills required to develop new low-carbon, resource-considerate, regenerative and healthy places by adapting the existing built environment in creative, just and inclusive ways, without throwing the old places 'away'. If you haven't already, check out the amazing work of Anthropocene Architecture School in this exciting area.[9]

Compared to 2015 and 2016 when I did the research for the first *Reuse Atlas*, the biggest challenge I have had with this second edition is simply keeping up with the amount of circular economy innovation embraced by the construction sector. I felt like everybody I interviewed knew of two, three or four other projects in addition to their own. As a result, this edition has taken me a lot longer to put together than its predecessor. It has been quite a challenge to stop the process of researching, interviewing and writing up the 39 case studies that comprise this book. There could have been many more. So, apologies if you have a fantastic project that I didn't include within these pages. However, the

Clockwise from below left:

Figure 4.17
Mine the Anthropocene.

Figure 4.18
Swiss Sound Box, by Peter Zumthor, Hanover Expo, 2000.

Figure 4.19
Buildings as material banks.

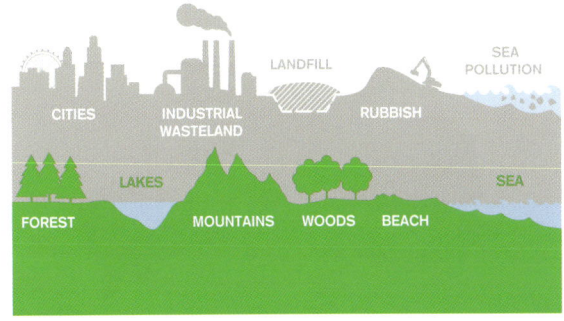

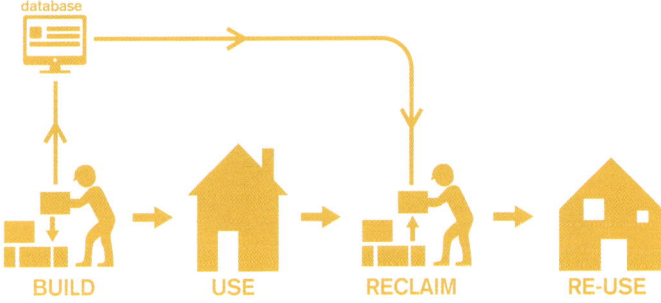

longer-than-anticipated time spent on this book has allowed me to develop my ideas further, and with this in mind, I'd like to refer you to Figure 4.21, which I have been developing with my colleagues at BakerBrown Studio (thank you Johana Krejčí). It describes the material sources one should utilise when aiming for a successful, resource-efficient, low-carbon and, crucially, regenerative building project. As a priority, we should work with and adapt existing buildings and other structures. Additional materials should be gleaned from the site itself, before looking around the immediate locale for second-hand and so-called waste streams, before doing the same for further afield – we tend to look at 5km, 10km, 25km, 50km and 75km radii from the development site. That's what we call 'mining the Anthropocene' or, as recently corrected, 'mining the Anthroposphere'. Additional new materials should be gleaned from the 'Biosphere', i.e. locally managed sustainable, organic and regenerative timber, straw, hemp, reeds, etc. Once you have exhausted those options, and only then, you will need to utilise your 'normal' sources. I hope that the infographic begins to do the job of describing this emerging practice, and I wish you all the best of luck with your own retrofit, reuse and closed-loop, circular projects.

One last piece of good news. Since the first edition was published, there are now a very healthy collection of consultancies and companies providing the services required to, for example, undertake a deconstruction audit (Reusefully,

Orms, Rotor, Local Works Studio, BakerBrown Studio, Material Index and many others), supported by a growing network of digital platforms offering second-hand material, together with numerous plug-ins for Autodesk's Revit enabling not only whole-life carbon calculations but also material passports. As discussed in my introduction to Step 2, in Part 2 of this book, there are also emerging networks of the types of physical infrastructure we require to enable a circular economy where

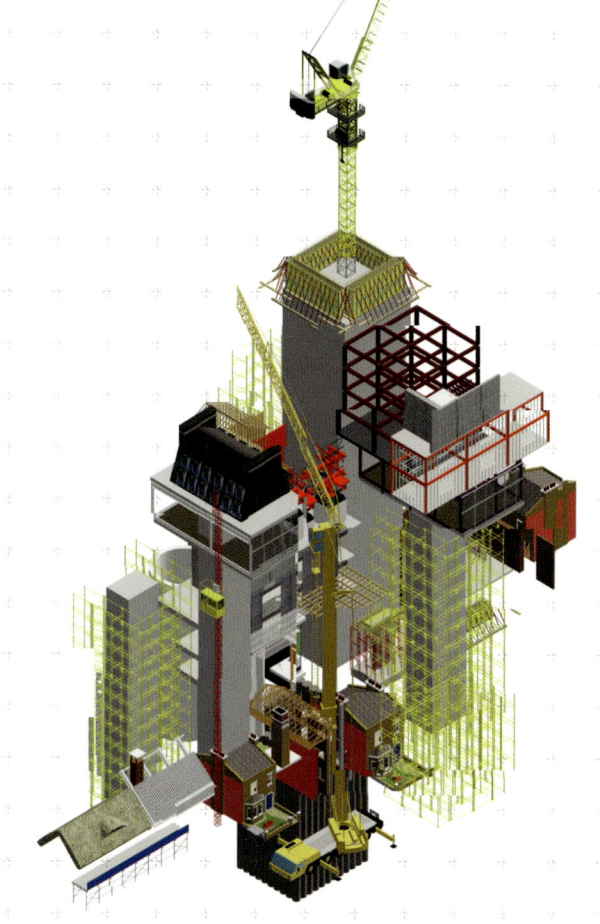

Figure 4.20
The Eternal Building School, master's project by Bongani Muchemw, University of Westminster, 2016.

almost nothing is thrown away. Whether they are called 're-manufactories' (my favourite) or circular economy construction hubs, they are already out there in the Netherlands, Denmark, France and Belgium, with numerous UK local authorities considering the viability of investing in similar facilities, while the more ambitious of clients are doing it themselves anyway. Times have certainly changed and continue to change (for the good – honest!) at an ever-increasing pace.

One last point. Please remember that collectively we know what to do. So, I ask you all to consider (if you are not already), what is stopping you from doing the right thing and implementing systems change today?

Finally, I would like to take this opportunity to thank the many people who have allowed me to interview them – there were more than 60 interviews. And most importantly, I want to thank my colleagues at BakerBrown Studio, my editor Liz Webster and Helen Castle at the RIBA for their collective patience and ongoing support while they waited for this book to be completed.

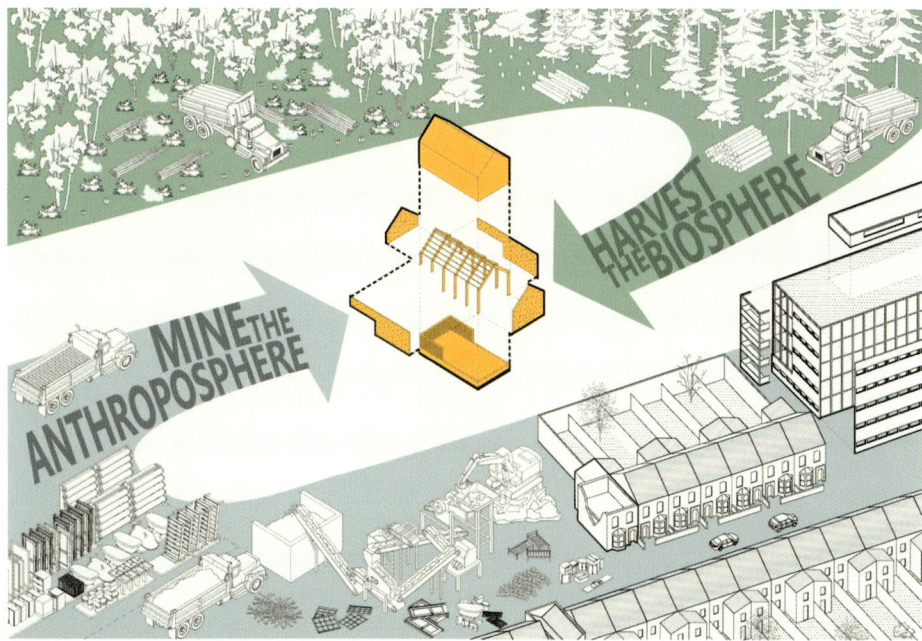

Figure 4.21
Diagram explaining circular material sourcing.

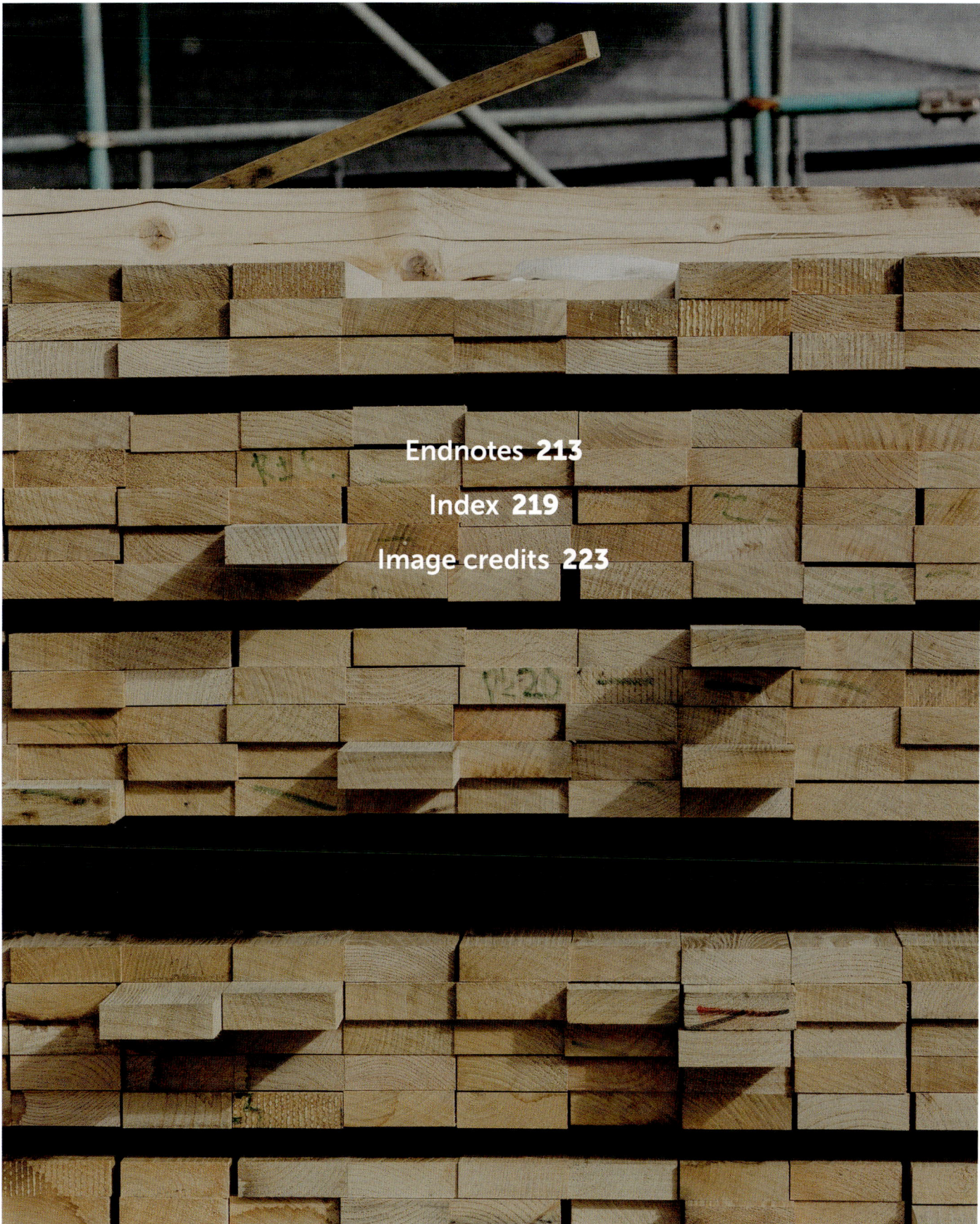

Endnotes **213**

Index **219**

Image credits **223**

ENDNOTES

FOREWORD
1. Brooker G and Stone S, *Rereadings: Interior Architecture and Design Principles of Remodelling Existing Buildings*, RIBA, 2004.
2. See https://2023.rca.ac.uk/programmes/interior-design-superreuse-2yr (accessed 19 February 2024).

PREFACE
1. The Bailey bridge is a type of portable, prefabricated truss bridge normally made of steel. It was developed by the British Army and saw extensive use during World War II. Some Bailey bridges are still in use today, for instance in remote areas in France.
2. Maslow A, 'A theory of human motivation', *Psychological Review*, 1943.
3. Franconi E *et al.*, 'Circular business opportunities for the built environment', in *A New Dynamic 2: Effective Systems in a Circular Economy*, Ellen MacArthur Foundation, 2016.
4. Altogether, the new tunnel system consists of 152km of tunnels and produced 28 million tonnes of evacuated rock. Source: 'Aus dem Berg in den See und Anderswohin', *Neue Zürcher Zeitung*, 24 May 2016, p 7.
5. http://www.clubofrome.org/a-new-club-of-romestudy-on-the-circular-economy-and-benefits-forsociety/#more-1300
6. http://www.idsa.org/sites/default/files/Nemerson.pdf (accessed 1 March 2024).

INTRODUCTION
1. Braungart M and McDonough W, *Cradle to Cradle: Remaking the Way We Make Things*, North Point Press, 2002.
2. Talk by Prof Dr Michael Braungart, 'Being Human', at the SCIN Gallery, London, 18 May 2015.

PART 1, CHAPTER 1
1. Girardet H, *The Gaia Atlas of Cities: New Directions for Sustainable Living*, Gaia Books, 1992.
2. Associated Press in Rio de Janeiro, 'Brazil: Amazon deforestation drops 34% in first six month under Lula', *The Guardian*, 6 July 2023, https://www.theguardian.com/world/2023/jul/06/brazil-amazon-deforestation-lula (accessed 28 February 2024).
3. Braungart M and McDonough W, *Cradle to Cradle: Remaking the Way We Make Things*, North Point Press, 2002.
4. Royal Society for the Encouragement of Arts, Manufactures and Commerce, founded in 1754.
5. RSA, *The Great Recovery: Rearranging the Furniture*, 2015, https://www.thersa.org/discover/publications-and-articles/reports/the-great-recovery-rearranging-the-furniture (accessed 19 February 2024).
6. Girling R, *Rubbish! Dirt on our Hands and Crisis Ahead*, Transworld, 2011.
7. WRAP, 'WRAP's vision for the UK circular economy', https://wrap.org.uk/taking-action/climate-change/circular-economy/wraps-vision-uk-circular-economy (accessed 28 February 2024).
8. European Commission, 'Circular Economy Action Plan', 2020, http://ec.europa.eu/environment/circular-economy/index_en.htm (accessed 19 February 2024).
9. WRAP, 'Circular Economy Study', 2015, http://www.wrap.org.uk/content/circular-economy-study-identifies-3-million-jobs-across-europe
10. Stahel W, *The Potential for Substituting Manpower for Energy*, Vantage Press, 1981.
11. Stahel W, 'Product-Life Factor', 1981, http://www.product-life.org/en/major-publications/the-product-life-factor (accessed 24 February 2024). The paper won the 1982 Mitchell Prize.
12. http://www.product-life.org (accessed 20 February 2024).
13. http://epea-hamburg.org (accessed 20 February 2024).
14. https://www.ellenmacarthurfoundation.org (accessed 20 February 2024).
15. https://www.theguardian.com/sustainable-business/2016/aug/11/worlds-first-circular-economy-mba-student-graduates
16. https://online-learning.tudelft.nl/courses/circular-economy-design-and-technology (accessed 20 February 2024).
17. http://bbm-architects.co.uk/portfolio/built-ecologies
18. https://bakerbrown.studio/news/the-house-that-kevin-built#:~:text=%27The%20House%20that%20Kevin%20Built,interesting%20building%20systems%20and%20materials (accessed 20 February 2024).
19. A former specialist consultancy offering waste auditing, support for environmental management system development and training.
20. Eurostat, 'Waste Statistics', January 2023, https://ec.europa.eu/eurostat/statistics-explained/index.php?title=Waste_statistics (accessed 28 February 2024).
21. Department for Environment, Food and Rural Affairs, 'UK Statistics on Waste', updated 28 June 2023, p 9, https://www.gov.uk/government/statistics/uk-waste-data (accessed 20 February 2024).
22. Eurostat, 'Waste Statistics', January 2023, https://ec.europa.eu/eurostat/statistics-explained/index.php?title=Waste_statistics (accessed 28 February 2024).
23. https://citychangers.org (accessed 28 February 2024).
24. Circular Economy Foundation, 'Circular Gap Report', 2022, https://www.circularity-gap.world/2022 (accessed 28 February 2024).
25. Department for Environment, Food and Rural Affairs, 'UK Statistics on Waste 2018–2022'.
26. https://www.brighton.ac.uk/research/research-news/feature/brighton-waste-house.aspx (accessed 20 February 2024).
27. Carrington D, 'The Anthropocene epoch: Scientists declare dawn of human-influenced age', *The Guardian*, 29 August 2016, https://www.theguardian.com/environment/2016/aug/29/declare-anthropocene-epoch-experts-urge-geological-congress-human-impact-earth (accessed 20 February 2024).

PART 1, CHAPTER 2

1. Lock S, '"It felt like a funeral": William Shatner reflects on voyage to space', *The Guardian*, 11 October 2022, https://www.theguardian.com/culture/2022/oct/11/it-felt-like-a-funeral-william-shatner-reflects-on-voyage-to-space (accessed 20 February 2024), quoting Shatner's book *Boldly Go: Reflections on a Life of Awe and Wonder*.
2. Abbott K, '"Just don't waste": David Attenborough's heartfelt message to next generation', *The Guardian*, 19 October 2019, https://www.theguardian.com/tv-and-radio/2019/oct/19/just-dont-waste-david-attenborough-advice-bbc-seven-worlds-one-planet (accessed 20 February 2024).

PART 1, CHAPTER 3

1. On 30 November 2022, the European Commission published the Circular Economy Package II. The main objectives of the proposal are to ensure that consumers have reusable packaging options, to get rid of unnecessary packaging and to provide clear labels to support correct recycling.
2. Theodore Roosevelt, 'Seventh State of the Union', 3 December 1907, https://archive.org/details/stateoftheunionaddresses uspresidents19011908_2010_librivox.
3. http://europa.eu/rapid/press-release_IP-15-6203_en.htm (accessed 20 February 2024).
4. Ibid.
5. WRAP, 'WRAP's vision for the UK circular economy', https://wrap.org.uk/taking-action/climate-change/circular-economy/wraps-vision-uk-circular-economy (accessed 28 February 2024).
6. http://www.wired.co.uk/news/archive/2015-03/10/ekocycle
7. Bidgoli H, *The Handbook of Technology Management, Supply Chain Management, Marketing and Advertising, and Global Management*, Wiley, 2010, p 296.
8. http://hubpages.com/money/How-to-stay-ahead-of-planned-obsolescence
9. Ibid.
10. http://www.greatrecovery.org.uk/resources/designing-for-a-circular-economy (accessed 20 February 2024).
11. http://www.theguardian.com/sustainable-business/10-things-need-to-know-circular-economy
12. http://www.ellenmacarthurfoundation.org/circular-economy/schools-of-thought/cradle2cradle.
13. House of Commons Environmental Audit Committee, 'Growing a Circular Economy: Ending the Throwaway Society', Third Report of Session, July 2014, p 3, https://publications.parliament.uk/pa/cm201415/cmselect/cmenvaud/214/214.pdf (accessed 20 February 2024).
14. http://www.mrw.co.uk/opinion/merging-the-circular-economy-and-waste-hierarchy/8654179.article (accessed 21 February 2024).
15. https://www.scu.edu/environmental-ethics/environmental-activists-heroes-and-martyrs/ansel-adams.html (accessed 4 March 2024).
16. HM Government, 'Prevention is Better than Cure: The Role of Waste Prevention in Moving to a More Resource Efficient Economy', December 2013, p 9, https://assets.publishing.service.gov.uk/media/5a7c087640f0b645ba3c6479/pb14091-waste-prevention-20131211.pdf (accessed 21 February 2024).
17. Ellen MacArthur Foundation, 'Towards a Circular Economy: Business Rationale for an Accelerated Transition', 2015, https://archive.ellenmacarthurfoundation.org/assets/downloads/publications/TCE_Ellen-MacArthur-Foundation_26-Nov-2015.pdf (accessed 4 March 2024).
18. Institution of Civil Engineers (ICE), *Proceedings of the Institution of Civil Engineers – Waste and Resource Management*, Vol 168, Issue 1, February 2015, pp 3–13, 'The circular economy: From waste to resource stewardship', Part I, Julie Elizabeth Hill.
19. HM Government, 'A Green Future: Our 25-Year Plan to Improve the Environment', 2018, https://assets.publishing.service.gov.uk/government/uploads/system/uploads/attachment_data/file/693158/25-year-environment-plan.pdf (accessed 21 February 2024).
20. Department for Environment, Food and Rural Affairs, 'Resources and Waste Strategy for England', 18 December 2018, https://www.gov.uk/government/publications/resources-and-waste-strategy-for-england (accessed 21 February 2024).
21. European Union, 'Circular Economy Action Plan', 2020, https://environment.ec.europa.eu/strategy/circular-economy-action-plan_en (accessed 21 February 2024).
22. HM Government, 'Prevention is Better than Cure'.
23. Mayor of London, 'London Infrastructure Plan 2050', 2014, https://www.london.gov.uk/programmes-strategies/better-infrastructure/infrastructure-policy/london-infrastructure-plan-2050?ac-31637=31634 (accessed 21 February 2024).
24. As updated by the 'Further Alterations to the London Plan' (FALP) in March 2015.
25. RSA, *The Great Recovery: Rearranging the Furniture*, 2015, https://www.thersa.org/discover/publications-and-articles/reports/the-great-recovery-rearranging-the-furniture (accessed 19 February 2024).
26. HM Government, 'Digital Built Britain, Level 3 Building Information Modelling – Strategic Plan', February 2015, https://assets.publishing.service.gov.uk/media/5a807e6ee5274a2e87dba20a/bis-15-155-digital-built-britain-level-3-strategy.pdf (accessed 21 February 2021).
27. https://en.wikipedia.org/wiki/Building_information_modeling (accessed 21 February 2024).
28. http://igniteyourthinking.beca.com/the-three-worlds-of-bim
29. Mayor of London, 'Design for a Circular Economy Primer', 2020, https://www.london.gov.uk/sites/default/files/design_for_a_circular_economy_primer_ggbd_web2.pdf
30. Ibid, p 10.
31. Ibid, p 30.
32. Mayor of London, 'Circular Economy Statement: Guidance', March 2020, p 12, https://www.london.gov.uk/sites/default/files/ggbd_circular_economy_statement_guidance_2020_web.pdf (accessed 21 February 2024).

33 https://www.towerhamlets.gov.uk/Documents/Planning-and-building-control/Supplementary-guidance/SPD/RRW-Adoption-statement.pdf (accessed 21 February 2024).

34 West Midlands Combined Authority, 'West Midlands' Circular Economy Routemap', 2021, https://www.wmca.org.uk/media/wxrfkpfq/wmca-circular-economy-routemap.pdf (accessed 21 February 2024).

PART 2, STEP 1

1 https://www.oceansplasticcleanup.com/Cleaning_Up_Operations/Parley_AIR_Avoid_Intercept_Redesign_Ocean_Plastic_TV.htm#:~:text=PARLEY%20AIR%20OCEAN%20PLASTIC%20AVOID%20INTERCEPT%20REDESIGN&text=PARLEY%20%2D%20Organise%20beach%20cleaning%20parties,threat%20of%20marine%20plastic%20pollution (accessed 28 February 2024).

2 Prof Braungart was speaking at 'The Waste Zone', an event curated and hosted by the author.

3 https://wrap.org.uk/resources/guide/waste-prevention-activities/real-nappies/overview (accessed 28 February 2024).

4 A discussion between van Soest and the author in 2018.

5 Belfield M, 'Chewing gum campaign hits Oxford Street', 26 October 2015, https://resource.co/article/chewing-gum-campaign-hits-oxford-street-10581 (accessed 28 February 2024).

6 https://www.overtreders-w.nl/en/wie:~:text=For%20Overtreders%20W%2C%20the%20fact,when%20strolling%20through%20unknown%20terrain (accessed 22 February 2024).

PART 2, STEP 2

1 https://www.worldbank.org/en/topic/urbandevelopment/overview#:~:text=Globally %2C%20over%2050%25%20of%20the,1.5%20times%20to%206%20billion (accessed 29 February 2024).

2 https://data.worldbank.org/indicator/SP.URB.TOTL.IN.ZS?locations=GB (accessed 29 February 2024).

3 Circular Economy Foundation, 'Circular Gap Report', 2022, https://www.circularity-gap.world/2022 (accessed 28 February 2024). https://citychangers.org (accessed 28 February 2024).

4 Girling R, Rubbish! Dirt On Our Hands and Crisis Ahead, Transworld, 2011.

5 Lynch K, Wasting Away – An Exploration of Waste: What it is, how it happens, why we fear it, how to do it well, Sierra Club Books, 1991.

6 Rotor, Interreg research project known as FCRBE (Facilitating the Circulation of Reclaimed Building Elements in Northwestern Europe), https://rotordb.org/en/projects/interreg-nwe-fcrbe (accessed 29 February 2024).

7 Kay T, 'The carbon benefit of reusing reclaimed building material', 2016, https://www.researchgate.net/publication/332878600_The_carbon_benefit_of_reusing_reclaimed_building_material (accessed 29 February 2024).

8 Project Summary, Overview on Interreg FCRBE website, https://vb.nweurope.eu/projects/project-search/fcrbe-facilitating-the-circulation-of-reclaimed-building-elements-in-northwestern-europe (accessed 29 February 2024).

9 A 'doughnut city' is one that aims to adhere to the constraints of planetary and human wellbeing when applying economic planning. These constraints are defined in the book Doughnut Economics: Seven Ways to Think Like a 21st-Century Economist, by economist Kate Raworth (2017).

10 WRAP, 'WRAP's vision for the UK circular economy', https://wrap.org.uk/taking-action/climate-change/circular-economy/wraps-vision-uk-circular-economy (accessed 28 February 2024).

11 https://marksbarfield.com/practice (accessed 22 February 2024).

PART 2, STEP 3

1 Brooker G, 50|50 Words for Reuse – A Minifesto, Canalside Press, 2018.

2 https://climateemergencydeclaration.org/climate-emergency-declarations-cover-15-million-citizens/#:~:text=In%20Britain%20around%2095%20per,have%20declared%20a%20climate%20emergency (accessed 29 February 2024).

3 https://insulatebritain.com (accessed 22 February 2024).

4 https://www.architecture.com/awards-and-competitions-landing-page/awards/RIBA-Reinvention-Award#:~:text=The%20award%20recognises%20buildings%20that,for%20demolition%20and%20new%20construction (accessed 22 February 2024).

5 https://www.leti.uk/cedg (accessed 22 February 2024).

6 https://part-z.uk (accessed 22 February 2024).

7 https://www.nzcbuildings.co.uk (accessed 22 February 2024).

8 Wainwright O, '"Sometimes the answer is to do nothing": Unflashy French duo take architecture's top prize', The Guardian, 16 March 2021, https://www.theguardian.com/artanddesign/2021/mar/16/lacaton-vassal-unflashy-french-architectures-pritzker-prize (accessed 22 February 2024).

9 Waite R, 'Interview with Pritzker winner David Chipperfield', Architects' Journal, 8 March 2023, https://www.architectsjournal.co.uk/news/interview-with-pritzker-winner-david-chipperfield-its-a-very-interesting-moment-to-be-an-architect (accessed 22 February 2024).

10 BBC, 'Grenfell Tower: What happened?', 29 October 2019, https://www.bbc.co.uk/news/uk-40301289 (accessed 22 February 2024).

11 BRE Trust, 'The Housing Stock of the United Kingdom', 2020.

12 Fuel poverty is defined in the Warm Homes and Energy Conservation Act, 2000.

13 www.gov.uk/government/statistics/final-uk-emissions-estimates (accessed 22 February 2024).

14 UK Parliament, 'Building to Net Zero: Costing Carbon in Construction', House of Commons Committee Report for First Session 2022–23, https://publications.parliament.uk/pa/cm5803/cmselect/cmenvaud/103/report.html (accessed 29 February 2024).

15 https://ukgbc.org/resources/retrofit-for-the-future-innovate-uk (accessed 29 February 2024).

16. Interreg FCRBE Project, https://vb.nweurope.eu/projects/project-search/fcrbe-facilitating-the-circulation-of-reclaimed-building-elements-in-northwestern-europe (accessed 29 February 2024).
17. https://www.pritzkerprize.com/laureates/anne-lacaton-and-jean-philippe-vassal#laureate-page-2291 (accessed 22 February 2024).
18. Wainwright O, 'Sometimes the answer is to do nothing'.
19. https://www.arup.com/projects/1-triton-square (accessed 1 March 2024).

PART 2, STEP 4

1. https://fcl.ethz.ch/people/Module-Lead/DirkHebel.html (accessed 23 February 2024).
2. https://www.thersa.org/reports/the-great-recovery-rearranging-the-furniture (accessed 1 March 2024).
3. Ruby I and Ruby A, *Mine the City: Re-Inventing Construction*, Ruby Press, 2010, pp 243–247.
4. Graedel T, *Urban Mining: Recycling Embodied Energy*, http://greenbuilding.world-aluminium.org/facts/urban-mining (accessed 22 January 2014).
5. http://www.product-life.org (accessed 1 March 2024).

PART 3

1. https://bakerbrown.studio/news/the-house-that-kevin-built#:~:text=%27The%20House%20that%20Kevin%20Built,interesting%20building%20systems%20and%20materials (accessed 20 February 2024).
2. Department for Environment, Food and Rural Affairs, 'UK Statistics on Waste', 2021.
3. Waste and Resource Action Plan (WRAP), 2011.
4. Braungart M and McDonough W, *Cradle to Cradle: Remaking the Way We Make Things*, North Point Press, 2002.
5. Santos S, 'RIBA announces shortlist for 2015 Stephen Lawrence Prize', *ArchDaily*, 8 September 2015, https://www.archdaily.com/773226/riba-announces-shortlist-for-2015-stephen-lawrence-prize (accessed 26 February 2024).
6. https://www.brighton.ac.uk/research/research-news/feature/brighton-waste-house.aspx (accessed 20 February 2024).
7. 'The Waste Zone' was part of EcoBuild 2013, and presentations were made by designers, academics and waste professionals.
8. Source: treehugger.com 2011
9. https://www.channelmanche.com/en/projects/approved-projects/sustainable-bio-and-waste-resources-for-construction (accessed 26 February 2024).
10. https://wp.architecture.com.au/news-media/unmaking-waste-2018-transforming-design-production-consumption-circular-economy (accessed 26 February 2024).
11. https://asbp.org.uk/epd/supasoft-recycled-pet-microfibre-insulation (accessed 26 February 2024). (The stuffing that fills many duvets is polyester made from recycled plastic bottles, known as PET.)

PART 4, CHAPTER 4

1. Chapman J, *Emotionally Durable Design: Objects, Experiences and Empathy*, Earthscan, 2005.
2. Bakker C, Hollander M and van Hinte E, *Products that Last: Product Design for Circular Business Models*, TU Delft Library, 2014.
3. Bocock R, *Consumption*, Routledge, 1993, p 46.
4. Bateson G, *Steps to an Ecology of Mind*, University of Chicago, 1972.
5. Thackara J, *How to Thrive in the Next Economy: Designing Tomorrow's World Today*, Thames and Hudson, 2015.
6. Cooper T, 'Which way to turn? Product longevity and business dilemmas in the circular economy', in Chapman J (ed), *The Routledge Handbook of Sustainable Product Design*, Routledge, 2017.
7. Sudjic D, *The Language of Things*, Allen Lane, 2008.
8. Tonkinwise C, 'Is design finished? Dematerialisation and changing things', *Design Philosophy Papers*, 2, 2014, p 190.
9. Jones JC, 'Continuous design and redesign', *Design Studies*, 4, 1983, pp 53–60.
10. Hunt J, 'Just re-do it: Tactical formlessness and everyday consumption', in *Strangely Familiar: Design and Everyday Life*, Walker Art Center, 2003, pp 56–71.
11. Redström J, 'RE: Definitions of use', *Design Studies*, 29, 2008, pp 410–423.
12. Ehn P, 'Participation in design things', in *Proceedings of the Tenth Anniversary Conference on Participatory Design*, Indiana University, 2008, pp 92–101.
13. Taylor D, *Design Art Furniture and The Boundaries of Function: Communicative Objects, Performative Things* (PhD Thesis), University of the Arts London and Falmouth University, 2011, p 227.
14. Megginson LC, 'Lessons from Europe for American businesses', *The Southwestern Social Science Quarterly*, 44(1), 1963, p 4.
15. Robinson M, 'Making adaptive resilience real', Arts Council England, 2010, p 14.
16. Packard V, *The Waste Makers*, Penguin, 1964.
17. London B, *Ending the Depression Through Planned Obsolescence*, Pamphlet, US, 1932.
18. Calkins EE, 'What consumer engineering really is', in Sheldon R and Arens E, *Consumer Engineering: A New Technique for Prosperity*, Harper & Brothers, 1932, pp 1–14.
19. Slade G, *Made to Break: Technology and Obsolescence in America*, Harvard University Press, 2007.
20. Chapman J and Marmont G, 'The temporal fallacy: Design, emotion and obsolescence', in Egenhoefer RB (ed), *The Routledge Handbook of Sustainable Design*, Routledge, 2017.
21. Fry T, *Design as Politics*, Berg, 2011.

PART 4, CHAPTER 5

1. Municipal solid waste (MSW) includes all residential and commercial waste but excludes industrial waste.
2. United Nations Environment Programme, 'Beyond an Age of Waste: Turning Rubbish into a Resource', 2024, https://www.unep.org/resources/global-waste-management-outlook-2024 (accessed 8 March 2024).
3. Kaza S, Yao L, Bhada-Tata P and Van Woerden F, 'What a Waste 2.0: A Global Snapshot of Solid Waste Management to 2050', Urban Development Series,

World Bank, 2018, doi:10.1596/978-1-4648-1329-0. Note this data is for residential, commercial and institutional waste only. Ellen MacArthur Foundation, 'Towards the Circular Economy – Economic and Business Rationale for An Accelerated Transition', 2013.
4. Baillie C, Matovic D, Thamae T and Vaja S, 'Waste-based composites – Poverty-reducing solutions to environmental problems', *Resources, Conservation and Recycling*, Vol 55, 2011, pp 973–978.
5. David Hakkens, Precious Plastic, https://preciousplastic.com (accessed 26 February 2024). See also the mention in the Adam Fairweather and Smile Plastics case study in Part 2, Step 1.
6. Waste Aid, https://wasteaid.org (accessed 26 February 2024).
7. Living Earth Foundation, Waste to Wealth, http://www.livingearth.org.uk/projects/waste-to-wealth
8. Lundall P and Kriel A, 'A Socioeconomic Overview of the Riversdale District with Particular Reference to the Village of Melkhoutfontein', 1987, https://www.opensaldru.uct.ac.za/bitstream/handle/11090/573/1987_lundall_swp67.pdf?sequence=1
9. Hessequa Local Municipality, 'Amended Integrated Development Plan 2022–2027', https://www.hessequa.gov.za/document-library
10. 'Kamamma' is a term for matriarchs or family/community leaders.
11. Fab Foundation, https://fabfoundation.org (accessed 26 February 2024).

PART 4, CHAPTER 6

1. https://climateemergencydeclaration.org/climate-emergency-declarations-cover-15-million-citizens (accessed 1 March 2024).
2. UN Environment Programme, 'Global Climate Litigation Report: 2023 Status Review', 27 July 2023, https://www.unep.org/resources/report/global-climate-litigation-report-2023-status-review?gad_source=1&gclid=CjwKCAiAloavBhBOEiwAbtAJO9tU-SkXzzc9-NBRtgz6Wlx9GLa0dQODSxixAOy9E5jQZi90jxhbWxoCbf4QAvD_BwE (accessed 1 March 2024).
3. Friends of the Earth, 'Who's impacted by fuel poverty in 2023', March 2023, https://policy.friendsoftheearth.uk/insight/whos-impacted-fuel-poverty-2023 (accessed 1 March 2024).
4. https://www.leti.uk/cedg (accessed 26 February 2024).
5. https://environment.ec.europa.eu/strategy/circular-economy-action-plan_en#:~:text=The%20new%20action%20plan%20announces,for%20as%20long%20as%20possible (accessed 26 February 2024).
6. https://www.unep.org/news-and-stories/press-release/buildings-breakthrough-global-push-near-zero-emission-and-resilient (accessed 26 February 2024).
7. Wainwright O, '"Sometimes the answer is to do nothing": Unflashy French duo take architecture's top prize', *The Guardian*, 16 March 2021, https://www.theguardian.com/artanddesign/2021/mar/16/lacaton-vassal-unflashy-french-architectures-pritzker-prize (accessed 22 February 2024).
8. Waite R, 'Interview with Pritzker winner David Chipperfield', *Architects' Journal*, 8 March 2023, https://www.architectsjournal.co.uk/news/interview-with-pritzker-winner-david-chipperfield-its-a-very-interesting-moment-to-be-an-architect (accessed 22 February 2024).
9. McAulay S, 'A new education for climate change', *RIBA Journal*, https://www.ribaj.com/intelligence/anthropocene-architecture-schoolscott-mcaulay-climate-emergency (accessed 1 March 2024).

INDEX

Page numbers in *italics* refer to illustrations.

22 Baker Street by Marks Barfield Architects 84–6

A

Aalto, Alvar 166
ABN AMRO Bank 176–8
Adams, Ansel 17
a:gain 42–4
agro-fibres 31–2
'AIR' initiative (Avoid/Intercept/Redesign) 27
Alliander 144, 145, *146*, 147
Amazon rainforest 11
(A)mend project *viii*
Amsterdam Temporary Courthouse, Building Part D(demountable) 152, *153*, 154, *155*, 156
ANA Intercontinental Hotel xiv
Apple Inc 9
Architects Climate Action Network (ACAN) 207
Architype 70, 140, 143
Arnold-Jones, Darcy 85
Arup 118, 160–2
Atelier Bow-wow 104
Attenborough, Sir David 10, 13, 27, 28

B

Baars, Michael 52
Bakker, Reinder 38–9
Barcelona 112, *113*, 114, *115–16*, 117
Barfield, Julia 84
Barnes, Mat 35
Bartlett, The, UCL 79, *80*, 81–3
Bateson, G 194
Bath Schools of Art and Design 128–30
BBM 7–8, 184
BC Materials 30
BCP Council 163–4
BDP 70
Belgian Pavilion 98, 100
Bicknell, John R xv
BIM (Building Information Modelling) 18–19
Biohm *31*, 32
Bishop, Wendy 70
Bloomberg, Michael xiv
'Blue Planet' TV series 10, 28
Bocock, Robert 194
Boddington, Anne 8
Bolsonaro, Jair 11
Bosence, Ben 40–1, 190, 192
Bosence, Loretta 40–1
Braungart, Michael 1, 6–7, 29
brick x, xiii, 4, 30–1
Brighton and Hove 19, 30, 157–9
Brighton Waste House 180–5, *186*, 187–90, *191*, 192
British Land 170
British Rail xv
Brooker, Graeme 94
Brummen Town Hall 144–5, *146*, 147
'Built Ecologies: Translating Landscape into Architecture' exhibition 8
Bullus, Anna 37
bureau SLA 160–2
Burkino Faso 134, *135*, 136

C

Calkins, Earnest Elmo 196
Cambridge Institute for Sustainability Leadership (CISL) 70
cepezed 152, 154, 156
chestnut 8
chewing gum 36–7
Chipperfield, David 95, 96
CIRCL Pavilion 176–8
CIRCuIT (Circular Construction in Regenerative Cities) 20
circular economy x, xi, xii–xiii, xv, 1–2, 131, 195
    BIM 18–19
    definition 5–7
    EU 208
    origins 16
    pedagogic methods 132–3
    primer 20–1
    requirements 14–15
Circular Economy Routemap by Brighton and Hove City Council 157–9
Circular Steel 53
Cité de la Mode et du Design 95, 96
cities 46–53, 132–3
City College Brighton 181, 183–4, 185, 187
CITYFÖRSTER 63, 65
cladding 8, 32, 78, 89, 147, 164
    glass *63*, 65
    thatch 140, *141*, 143
Cleveland Steel 53, 73, 74–5
Climate Action Network 84–5
climate change xiv, 4–5, 94, 206–7
CLT (cross-laminated timber) 63, *64*, 148–9, 151, 175
CO_2 emissions xiii, xiv, 7, 10, 53, 97, 208
Compression Artefact *viii*
consumerism 12, 194
Cork House and Phoenix House by CSK Architects 79, *80*, 81–3
COVID-19 pandemic 10, 11, 94, 96, 206–7
Cradle to Cradle philosophy 1, 5, 6–7, 16, 26, 145, 181
CSK Architects 79, 83
Cycle Station by ProRail and de Architekten Cie 76–8

D

Dahy, Dr-Ing Hanaa 31–2
Dalmain School, London *109*–110
de Architekten Cie 77, 78, 176–8
De Ceuvel by Space & Matter 124–5, *126*, 127
Dean, Tanya 199
deconstruction and reuse 49–50, 152
Dellea, Arthur 15
Denari, Neil 87
Desmond, Peter 157–8
Dijkema, Eva 76
Dijkstra, Rients 120
dimension stone x, xiii
Dock de Paris warehouse 95, 96
Dreamcatcher Foundation 198–205
Durley Chine Environmental Innovation Hub 163–5
Durmisevic, Elma 50–1
duvets 30, 190
Dyke Road Avenue, Hove 94, *96*

E

EAC (Environmental Audit Committee) 16
Ecovative 31, 137–8
EkoCycle 15
Ellen MacArthur Foundation (EMF) 7, 16, 17, 173
emotionally durable design 194, 197
Empire State Building, New York xii
energy xiii–xiv, 4–5, 73, 94
Enfield, Jane 33, 34
Enterprise Centre, UEA 140, *141–2*, 143
Entopia Building for Cambridge Institute for Sustainability Leadership 70–1, *72*, 73
Environmental Protection Encouragement Agency (EPEA) 7
European Union (EU) 6, 16, 66, 208
 Innovation Deals 17
 Interreg research projects 10, 189–90
Extinction Rebellion 94, 207

F

Fairweather, Adam 33–5
Farrell, Terry 128
Fastnet Rock xv
FCRBE (Facilitating the Circulation of Reclaimed Building Elements in Northwestern Europe) 48–9
Fishlock, Nick 158, 159
Fishwick, Roy 53, 74
Fletcher, Cat 5, 157, 181, 183, 184
floating homes (Schoonschip) 124–5, *126*, 127
Flores & Prats Arquitectes 112, *113*, 114, *115–16*, 117
flow 195–6
Footprint Architects 163–5
Forbes, Gordon 143
Foster, Sir Norman 140, 143
Freear, Andrew 54, 56
Freegle UK 181, 183, 184
French, John 70
Future Initiative 97

G

Gant, Nick 29, 30, 40, 199
 Brighton Waste House 181, 187, 190
gas 4, 11
Ghent Design Museum 41
Gilchrist, Steve 53
Girardet, Herbert: *The Gaia Atlas of Cities* 4
Glasi, Sascha 124
Gotthard Base Tunnel, Switzerland xii
Govaplast 39
Graedel, Thomas E 133
'Grand Designs' TV programme 8
Grand Parc, Bordeaux 103
Green House by cepezed, The 152, *153*, 154, *155*, 156
Greenfield, David 157–8, 159
Grenfell Tower disaster 95, 149
Grimshaw, Nick 128–30
GS8 30–1
Gumtech 36–7
Guterres, António 4

H

Haccou, Tjeerd 124
Hakkens, Dave 29, 35
Hamilton, Paul A xv
Hammink, Hans 77, 78, 176–8
Harvest Mapping 58
HawkinsBrown Architects 170, *171*, 172
Hebel, Dirk 132, 133
Heem Wonen 66
Heikkinen, Pekka 168
Heraclitus 195–6
heritage buildings xiii, xiv
Herman Miller factory 128–9
Hill, Julie: *The Secret Life of Stuff* 17
Hoffman, LA: '1880 Northern Montana' 4
Hoolahan, Rachel 53
House of the Future 7
'House that Kevin Built, The' (THTKB) 8, 180
Howland, Matthew Barnett 79, 81, 82–3
Hub67 by LYN Atelier 60, *61*, 62
Hy-Fi Tower by The Living, New York *xi*, 137–9

I

IDSA Principles of Design for Environment xiv
Ikea 12
Insert 52, *53*
Institute of Building Structures and Structural Design, University of Stuttgart 31–2
insulation 28–9, 30, 31, 207
 Brighton Waste House 182, 190, 192
 retrofits 94, 95–6, 97
Internet of Things (IoT) xiv
IP Callison 56
ISG 73
IStructE 94–5, 208

J

Jakob + MacFarlane 96
Japan xiii, xiv
Järvelä, Havu 166, 168
John Lewis 12–13
Jongert, Jan 57
Junckers 43

K

Kamphuis school (Brienenoord) *57–8*, 59
Kay, Thornton 48, 53
Kéré, Francis 134, 136
Keronen, Asko 168
Komai, Sadaharu 104, 106

L

Lacaton, Anne 101, 103
Lacaton & Vassal 95, 101, *102*, 103
Lagemaat 51–2, 154
Lasdun, Sir Denys 140, 143
LED lighting 73
Lendager, Anders 42, 43, 87–92
LETI (Low Energy Transformation Initiative) 94, 207
Lightweight Tiles 30
Lions Park (AL) 56
Living, The 137–9

Local Works Studio 30, 40–1
Lock, Andrew 60, 62
Lock, Diana 8–9, 181
London, Bernard 196
Loop 13
Lopez, Raymond 101, 103
Lucas, Caroline 157
Lula da Silva, Luiz Inácio 5
LYN Atelier 60
Lynch, Kevin: *Wasting Away* 47
Lynn, Greg 87

M

MacArthur, Dame Ellen 7
McKay, Ian 7
McMillan, Rosalie 34–5
Madaster Foundation 53
Makkink, Rianne 120
Marks Barfield Architects 84–6
Marks, David 84
Maslow, Abraham x
materials xiii, 14–15, 201–2, 209
    mapping 20
    waste flows 28–32
Maurer United Architects 66, *67–8*, 69
Mears Group 183, 184
Melkhoutfontein, South Africa 198–205
Metabolic 51
Milne, Dido 79
Miralles, Enric 112
MMC (Modern Methods of Construction) 170
Mockbee, Samuel 54
Modular Campus at Canada Water 170, *171*, 172
modular system buildings xiii
Morgan Sindall 159
MUD Jeans 144
Myatt Garden School, London *110*
mycelium 31, 32, 137–8
Myco Board 31

N

nappies 29–30
National Retrofit Hub 94
natural resources x, 6, 26, 132
Nestlé xii
New Horizon 52
Newbern (AL) 54, *55*
No. 1 Triton Square by Arup etc. 118–19
No. 6 Orsman Road 148–9, *150*, 151
Nolting, Nils 63
Normandeis 189
nuclear power stations xiv

O

Oasis Nature Garden by Marks Barfield Architects 86
Oberhuber, Sabine 144, 173, 175
obsolescence 15–16, 196–7
oceans 26, 27
ODA (Olympic Delivery Authority) 60, 62
oil 4, 11
Orms 53
Overtreders W 38, 160–2
oyster shells 40, 190, 192

P

Packard, Vance. *The Waste Makers* 196–7
Paddenbroek Education Centre by Jo Taillieu 120–1, *122*, 123
Paddington Maintenance Depot (PMD) xv
Palais de Tokyo, Paris 101, *102*
Paris Agreement 11
Parker, Thomas 81
Parley for the Oceans 27
Passivhaus 109, 164
Paticas, Harry 108–9, *110*, 111
People's Pavilion 38, 39
People's Pavilion by bureau SLA 160–2
Philips Lighting 144
Phoneblocks 29
photovoltaic energy xiv, 96, 130, *146*, 147, 164, 182
Pikku-Finlandia 166, *167*, 168–9
plastic x, xiii, 1, 11, 26, 27

Precious Plastic 29
Pretty Plastic 38–9
    Smile 33–5
pollution 2, 11
Pool, Marthijn 124
Prats, Eva 112
Precious Plastic 29, 35
Pretty Plastic 38–9
Printworks, The 170
Pritzker Architecture Prize 95, 101, 208
product life 195, 196–7
Product-Life Institute, Geneva 7
ProRail 76–8

R

RAFT (Retrofit Action for Tomorrow) 109, 111
Rau, Thomas xiii, 173, 175
RAU Architects 144–5, 147
recycling 21–2, *23*, 27, 40
Recyclinghaus 65
Reday, Genevieve 6
refill 12, 13
'Remade Southeast' 8–9
Renew Hub, Manchester 13
Rented House by Sadaharu Komai 104, *105*, 106–7
repair viii, xiii, 12
Resource Rows by the Lendager Group 42, 89–92
retrofit 94–7
reuse x, xii, xiii, xv, 2
    definition 45
    Renew Hub 13
    Selfridges 12
 urban environments 21–2, *23*, 47–53
Rick Mather Architects 140
Roberts, Anthony 98
Romney Marsh Visitor Centre, Romney Warren, Kent *7*, 8
Roosevelt, Theodore 14
Rossouw, Anthea 198
Rotondi, Michael 87
Rotor 48–9, 57, 98, *99*, 100
RRW (Reuse, Recycling and Waste) 21–2, *23*
Rubbens, Menno 152

Rubber House and Recyclinghaus by CITYFÖRSTER 63, *64*, 65
Ruby, Ilka and Andreas: *Mine the City* 133
Rudolph, Ian 85
Ruø Rasmussen, Mathias 42, 43, 44
Rural Studio 54, *55*, 56

S

St Winifred's School, London *108*
Sala Beckett by Flores & Prats Arquitectes 112, *113*, 114, *115–16*, 117
Salvo 48–9
Santilli, Stefano 199
SB&WRC 30
School Buildings by Francis Kéré 134, *135*, 136
Selfridges 12
Shatner, William 13
sheep's wool 28
Skott-Pedersen, Stine 166, 168
Smile Plastics 33–5
Southwark Construction Skills Centre 172
Space & Matter 124–5, *126*, 127
Spencer, Ben 30–1
spoil 30–1
Stahel, Walter 6–7
stocks xii, xiii
stone 81–3
StoneCycling 30
straw 8, 31
students 183–4, 185, 187–8
sunflower stems 31
Superlocal by Maurer United Architects 66, *67–8*, 69
SuperSewer project 83
Superuse Studios 49–50, 57–9
sustainability 194–7
Svanen Kindergarten by the Lendager Group 91–2
Switzerland xii, xiii, xiv

T

Taillieu, Jo 120–1, 123
TEDI-London 170, 172
thatch 140, *141*, 143
Thistleton, Anthony 148
Thomas, Sophie 5, 16, 133
Thunberg, Greta 94
Tidridge, Gin 7
timber x, xiii, 7–8, 168
    Brighton Waste House 182, 188
    Enterprise Centre, UEA 140, 143
    Rented House 104, 106
    see also CLT
Timmermans, Frans 14
Tindale, Andrew 170, 172
Tonkinwise, Cameron 196
Torvinen, Jaakko 166, 168–9
Tour Bois-le-Prêtre, Paris 101, *102*, 103
Tower Hamlets, London 21–2, *23*
Triodos Bank Building 173, *174*, 175
Trump, Donald 11
TU Delft 7
Turntoo 144–5, 173

U

UK Architects Declare 207
UniLaSalle 31, 190
University of Brighton 33, 49, 180, 183–4, 185, 187–8, 190, 192, 198–9
University of East Anglia (UEA) 140, *141–2*, 143
urban mining xii, 46–53, 132–3

V

Van Assche, Peter 38
Van de Beek, Arend 51
Van Dijk, Hester 38–9
Van Soest, Tom 30
Vassal, Jean Philippe 101
Veolia 30, 190

W

waste x, xii, xiii, xiv–xv, 6, 9–10
    construction materials 28–32
    electronic 195, 196
    England 18, 21–2, *23*
    planned obsolescence 15–16
    reduction 93
    Wiki workshop 198–205
Waste House 10
Waugh Thistelton 148–9, 151
Wendelin, Elli 166, 168
West Midlands 23–4
Wiki Waste Workshop (WWW) 198–205
Will.i.am 15
Williamson, Colin 33, 34
Wilton, Oliver 79, 81–3
wind energy xiv, 59
windows xii, 63, 65, 59, 70, *72*
Woodward, Ryan 4, 30, 181, 199
WRAP (Waste and Resources Action Programme) 6, 15

IMAGE CREDITS

Fig 0.1 Jie Zheng;
Fig 0.2 Tianheng Zhao;
Fig 0.3 Sina Daryoushnezhad;
Fig 0.4, 2.225 Barkowphoto;
Fig 0.5 Walter Stahel;
Fig 0.6–0.7 Dr Ryan Woodard;
Fig 1.1 The RSA – The Great Recovery Project (2012-2016);
Fig 1.2–1.4, 3.2, 3.4, 3.6, 3.9 BBM Sustainable Design;
Fig 1.5 Leigh Simpson;
Fig 1.6 Cat Fletcher;
Fig 1.7 Rabobank;
Fig 1.8–1.10 David Greenfield;
Fig 1.11 Beca;
Fig 1.12 © Brighton & Hove City Council;
Fig 1.13–1.14 HSY / CIRCuIT Grant Agreement No. 821201 funded by the European Union's Horizon 2020 research and innovation programme;
Fig 1.15–1.16 GLA;
Fig 1.17–1.18 Tower Hamlets Council;
Fig 1.19–1.20 West Midland Combined Authority;
Fig 2.1 © Ivan Jones;
Fig 2.2–2.4 © Biohm;
Fig 2.5–2.7 © Smile Plastics;
Fig 2.8–2.11 By permission of CAN Architects;
Fig 2.12–2.15 © Gumdrop;
Fig 2.16, 2.268, 2.274 © Overtreders W;
Fig 2.17–2.18 © ST Oelbert;
Fig 2.19–2.20, 2.269–2.271 © Jeroen van der Wielen;
Fig 2.21, 2.24, 3.11–3.12, 3.14–3.15 © Local Works Studio;
Fig 2.22–2.23, 2.25–2.26, 2.33, 2.136–2.137, 3.16–3.18, 4.17, 4.19, 4.21 © BakerBrown Studio;
Fig 2.27–2.32 © a:gain;
Fig 2.34 © Salvo;
Fig 2.35 © Superuse;
Fig 2.36 © Metabolic;
Fig 2.37 © Elma Durmisevic;
Fig 2.38 © Lagemaat BV;
Fig 2.39 © INSERT;
Fig 2.40–2.45 Tim Hursley;
Fig 2.46–2.54 © Superuse;
Fig 2.55, 2.59–2.61 Jill Tate;
Fig 2.56–2.57 Lyn Atelier;
Fig 2.58 Adam Walker;
Fig 2.62–2.70 © CITYFÖRSTER;
Fig 2.71–2.77 © Maurer United Architects;
Fig 2.78–2.83 © Architype Ltd;
Fig 2.84–2.87 © Cleveland Steel;
Fig 2.88–2.93 © Hans Hammink;
Fig 2.94–2.112 © CSK Architects;
Fig. 2.113–2.117 © Marks Barfield;
Fig 2.118–2.132 © Lendager Group;
Fig 2.133–2.134 © Jacob & MacFarlane;
Fig 2.135 © Photographie Nicolas Borel;
Fig 2.138–2.145 Rotor;
Fig 2.146, 2.151–2.152 Philippe Ruault;
Fig 2.147–2.150 Druot, Lacaton & Vassal;
Fig 2.153–163 Sadaharu Komai;
Fig 2.164–2.168 © RAFT;
Fig 2.169 © Agness Sanvito;
Fig 2.170–2.179 © Flores I Prats;
Fig 2.180–2.183 © Arup;
Fig 2.184–2.192 © Jo Tailieu Architecten;
Fig 2.193–2.194, 2.200, 2.202 © Space & Matter;
Fig 2.195–2.197 © Isabel Nabours;
Fig 2.198 © Jean-Pierre Jans;
Fig 2.199, 2.201 © Martijn van Wijk;
Fig 2.203–2.205 © Grimshaw;
Fig 2.206 © Chris Wakefield;
Fig 2.207 © Paul Raftery;
Fig 2.208–2.210 Dirk Hebel;
Fig 2.211, 2.213–2.216 Kéré Architecture;
Fig 2.212, 2.217 Erik-Jan Ouwerkerk;
Fig 2.218, 2.220–2.224 The Living;
Fig 2.219 Justin Lui;
Fig 2.226 Iwan Baan;
Fig 2.227–2.228 Henrietta Williams Photography;
Fig 2.229–2.234 Darren Carter / Morgan Sindall;
Fig 2.235–2.236, 2.238 Thomas Heye;
Fig 2.237, 2.239–2.242 Thomas Rau;
Fig 2.243 © Waugh Thistleton;
Fig 2.244–2.246 © Tim Crocker;
Fig 2.247–2.249 © Ed Reeve;
Fig 2.250–2.251 © Jannes Linders;
Fig 2.256–2.258, 2.263 © cepedez;
Fig 2.252–2.255, 2.259–2.262 © Lucas van der Wee;
Fig 2.264 © Brighton & Hove City Council;
Fig 2.265–2.267 © Morgan Sindall;
Fig 2.272–2.273 © Filip Dujardin;
Fig 2.275–2.278 © Footprint Architects;
Fig 2.279–2.284, 2.287–2.290 © Jaakko Torvinen;
Fig 2.285 © Mikko Raskinen;
Fig 2.286 © Mikael Linden;
Fig 2.291–2.293 © Hawkins\Brown;
Fig 2.294–2.295 © Francesco Montaguti;
Fig 2.296–2.298, 2.300–2.306 © RAU;
Fig 2.299 © Marcel van den Burg;
Fig 2.307–2.311 © Ossip;
Fig 2.312 ©Ernst van Raaphorst;
Fig 3.1, 3.3, 3.5, 3.7–3.8, 3.10 The University of Brighton;
Fig 3.13, 4.1, 4.5–4.6, 4.9, 4.13 © Nick Gant;
Fig 4.2, 4.4 © Nick Gant and Tanya Dean;
Fig 4.3 Image Jim Wilson;
Fig 4.7–4.8, 4.10–4.12, 4.14 Matilda Grover;
Fig 4.15–4.16 Dreamcatcher Foundation;
Fig 4.18 © Peter Zumthor;
Fig 4.20 Bongani Muchemw.

Chapter openers
Part 1 opener © BakerBrown Studio;
Part 2 opener © Lucas van der Wee;
Part 3 opener © BakerBrown Studio;
Part 4 opener © Biohm.

Author's image
© Ivan Jones